Peers and Politics, c. 1650–1850:
Essays in Honour of Clyve Jones

Clyve Jones at Wentworth Woodhouse, 2017

Peers and Politics, c. 1650–1850: Essays in Honour of Clyve Jones

Edited by

Richard A. Gaunt

and

D.W. Hayton

WILLEY

for

THE PARLIAMENTARY HISTORY YEARBOOK TRUST

John Wiley & Sons

Registered Office
John Wiley & Sons Ltd, The Atrium, Southern Gate, Chichester, West Sussex, PO19 8SQ, UK

Editorial Offices
101 Station Landing, Medford, MA 02155, USA
9600 Garsington Road, Oxford, OX4 2DQ, UK
The Atrium, Southern Gate, Chichester, West Sussex, PO19 8SQ, UK

For details of our global editorial offices, for customer services, and for information about how to apply for permission to reuse the copyright material in this book please see our website at www.wiley.com/wiley-blackwell.

Library of Congress Cataloging-in-Publication Data

Library of Congress Cataloging-in-Publication data is available for this book

ISBN 9781119680611

A catalogue record for this title is available from the British Library
Set in 10/12pt Bembo
by Aptara Inc., India
Printed and bound in Singapore
by C.O.S. Printers Pte Ltd

1   2020

CONTENTS

LIST OF ILLUSTRATIONS

NOTES ON CONTRIBUTORS

John Beckett is professor of English regional history at the University of Nottingham. His doctoral thesis at Lancaster University was supervised by Professor Geoffrey Holmes. At that time Holmes and Clyve Jones were editing the London diaries of Bishop Nicolson of Carlisle, and John's thesis was on the Cumbrian landowners, 1680–1750. His books include *The Aristocracy in England 1660–1914* (1986), *The Rise and Fall of the Grenvilles, Dukes of Buckingham and Chandos, 1710–1921* (1994), and *Byron and Newstead: The Aristocrat and the Abbey* (2001).

Richard Connors is an associate professor in the department of history and in the faculty of law at the University of Ottawa. He has research interests in early modern, legal, and imperial British history.

Robin Eagles is editor of the House of Lords 1660–1832 section at the History of Parliament. He has written widely on parliament and politics in the 17th and 18th centuries with previous publications including *Francophilia in English Society 1748–1815* (2000) and an edition of the *Diaries of John Wilkes 1770–1797* (2014). He was one of the main contributors to the *History of Parliament: The House of Lords, 1660–1715*, ed. Ruth Paley (2016).

Richard A. Gaunt is associate professor in modern British history at the University of Nottingham. He has published widely on aspects of British politics, electioneering, and political culture between c.1780 and c.1850. Major works include *Sir Robert Peel: The Life and Legacy* (2010) and two volumes of selections from the diaries of the 4th duke of Newcastle: *Unhappy Reactionary: The Diaries of the Fourth Duke of Newcastle, 1822–1850* (2003), and *Unrepentant Tory: Political Selections from the Diaries of the Fourth Duke of Newcastle, 1827–1838* (2006). A further volume, covering the period 1839–50, is forthcoming. Dr Gaunt has been co-editor of *Parliamentary History* since 2013.

Ben Gilding is the Don King junior research fellow in history at New College, Oxford. His research currently focuses on domestic responses to imperial crises in the British Empire in the 'age of revolutions' (c.1765–95).

Stuart Handley is a senior research officer in the House of Lords 1660–1832 section of the History of Parliament. He studied for a PhD at Lancaster University under the supervision of Geoffrey Holmes and subsequently worked on the History of Parliament's volumes on *The House of Commons, 1690–1715* (2002) and *The House of Lords, 1660–1715* (2016), as well as writing hundreds of articles for the *Oxford Dictionary of National Biography*.

Frances Harris was formerly head of modern (i.e., post-1603) historical manuscripts at the British Library and is the author most recently of *The General in Winter: The Marlborough-Godolphin Friendship and the Reign of Queen Anne* (2017).

D.W. Hayton is emeritus professor of history at Queen's University, Belfast, a visiting professor at Ulster University and a member of the Royal Irish Academy. His publications focus on the political history of Britain and Ireland in the late 17th and early 18th centuries and he was co-editor of *Parliamentary History* from 2015 until 2019. His most recent book is *Conservative Revolutionary: The Lives of Lewis Namier* (2019).

Charles Littleton is a senior research officer in the House of Lords 1660–1832 section of the History of Parliament. He has published on the parliamentary reporting of Abel Boyer and on the estate bills of the earls of Derby 1662–92. His essay in this volume derives from work on the Barons Ossulston for the published volumes on the House of Lords 1660–1715. Another article on the family's relations with the earl of Arlington is forthcoming.

Jason Peacey is professor of early modern British history at University College London, and the author of *Politicians and Pamphleteers: Propaganda in the Civil Wars and Interregnum* (2004), and *Print and Public Politics in the English Revolution* (2013). He is currently working on Anglo-Dutch political culture in the 17th century, with a particular focus on the diplomacy of print and news, and overlapping and interlocking publics.

Daniel Szechi taught at St John's College, Oxford, Auburn University, and latterly at the University of Manchester. In February 2017, he retired and is now emeritus professor in early modern history at Manchester and honorary professor at the University of Aberdeen. He continues to write and research and also runs a historical consultancy business. He has published extensively on the history of jacobitism and his latest book, *The Jacobites: Britain and Europe 1688–1788* (2nd edn) appeared in 2019.

Graham Townend is a self-employed researcher and writer.

Clyve Jones and Parliamentary History

D. W. HAYTON

Clyve Jones did not begin his research career as a parliamentary historian. He served his apprenticeship with a scholarly edition of the correspondence of Henry Cromwell, son of the lord protector; letters dating from Henry's service in Ireland between 1655 and 1659. This was undertaken as an MLitt thesis at Lancaster University under the supervision of Professor Austin Woolrych, and already exhibited many of the qualities which would characterise Clyve's mature work: careful scholarship, a thorough grounding in primary sources, which were carefully sifted and analysed, and a prospector's eye for the telling piece of evidence, the gold nugget shining in the dross.[1] Clyve had come to Lancaster in 1964 from Castleford Grammar School, then best known for producing the sculptor, Henry Moore, and a succession of stars of the sports field, cricketers and rugby league players. He was one of the first generation of students at the university, domiciled in digs in the bracing air of Morecambe. After completing his thesis – which his supervisor confessed at graduation was substantial enough to have been entered instead for a PhD – he undertook an MA in librarianship at the University of Sheffield (his dissertation forming the basis for his first publication), and obtained a post as assistant librarian at London University's Institute of Historical Research.

The Institute was in many ways a perfect environment for him. At that time, members of the library staff were expected – indeed were encouraged through the provision of sabbatical leave – to undertake their own research, which for many of Clyve's colleagues was bibliographic. His own work returned him to the thickets of political history: not the England of the Protectorate, this time, but the decades following the Glorious Revolution, and in particular the reign of Queen Anne. The Institute's library holds an unrivalled collection of printed primary sources for British history, all readily available on open shelf; the British Museum (later the British Library) lay close by and the search rooms of the Public Record Office were then only a 20-minute walk away in Chancery Lane. The fact that the History of Parliament Trust, the Institute's tenant in its annexe in Tavistock Square, was at that time starting work on the section covering the house of commons 1690–1715, was another source of stimulation for someone who was gradually becoming fascinated by the history of post-revolution England.

---

[1] Clyve Jones, 'The Correspondence of Henry Cromwell, 1655–1659 …', University of Lancaster MLitt, 1969. Although the dissertation remained unpublished, it did give rise to one article ('Two Unpublished Letters of Oliver Cromwell', *Bulletin of the Institute of Historical Research*, xlvi (1973), 216–18), and much later was heavily used by Peter Gaunt (with full acknowledgment) in his own edition of *The Correspondence of Henry Cromwell, 1655–1659* (Camden, 5th ser., xxxi, 2008).

Clyve's interest was turned towards parliament in general, and the house of lords in particular, by involvement in a major editorial project undertaken jointly with Geoffrey Holmes, another of his professors at Lancaster. Holmes's magisterial study of *British Politics in the Age of Anne* had appeared in 1967, to great acclaim, and established him as the pre-eminent expert on the period. His and Clyve's edition of *The London Diaries of William Nicolson Bishop of Carlisle 1702–1718* would eventually be published in 1985, some 15 years after work began. While at the outset it was presumably Clyve's proven ability as an editor which secured him a place in the collaboration, by the time the book was completed there could be no doubt that it was, throughout, a genuinely collaborative effort. In fact, the name of Jones appeared first on the title page, in defiance of alphabetical order, and in recognition of the quantity and quality of Clyve's contribution, to text, footnotes, and the lengthy introduction.

The Nicolson diary edition is, in many respects, a model of its kind. The introduction sets Nicolson in his various contexts, as churchman and bishop, antiquarian and virtuoso,[2] and parliamentarian. There is also a substantial section on the history of the house of lords, which builds on the chapter on the Lords in Holmes's *British Politics*, and provides a detailed account of the topography of the House and the way in which proceedings were conducted. This incorporated some of Clyve's previously published conclusions about attendance, which were based on a close comparison between the published presence lists in the *Lords Journals*, and the manuscript minutes, preserved in what was then the House of Lords Record Office (now the Parliamentary Archives).[3] Together with other work appearing at about the same time, including the researches of John Sainty into divisions in the upper House and the use of proxies,[4] the *Nicolson Diary* may be said to have revolutionised the history of the early-18th-century house of lords. The introduction represented a major advance in the knowledge and understanding of the way in which the upper House functioned, while the publication of the diary itself, and the supporting detail provided in the extensive annotation, opened up a new window into its political history.

Until the publication of Holmes's book, historians of 18th-century politics had focused their attention on the house of commons. The work of the History of Parliament Trust – which has since begun to study the upper House and has, indeed, published a substantial five-volume section on the Lords between 1660 and 1715 – was at that time entirely devoted to the Commons. What was then the standard work on the house of lords, by A.S. Turberville, dated from as far back as 1927, and had not been particularly well received even when it was first published.[5] Holmes had successfully rehabilitated the upper House, pointing up its importance in the party struggles of Queen Anne's reign. He argued that in many respects this period was a golden age for the Lords: the leaders of the two parties were to be found there; and the great debates and the critical engagements in the war between whigs and tories took place in the upper House rather than the lower – on the Tack in

[2] This short section was contributed by Professor Joseph M. Levine.

[3] 'Seating Problems of the House of Lords in the Early Eighteenth Century: The Evidence of the Manuscript Minutes', *Bulletin of the Institute of Historical Research*, li (1978), 132–45. Details of all Clyve's publications can be found in the bibliography below, pp. 220–7.

[4] John Sainty and David Dewar, *Divisions in the House of Lords: An Analytical List 1685 to 1857* (House of Lords Record Office, Occasional Publications, 2, 1976); J.C. Sainty, 'Proxy Records of the House of Lords, 1510–1733', *Parliamentary History*, i (1982), 161–5.

[5] A.S. Turberville, *The House of Lords in the XVIIIth Century* (Oxford, 1927).

November 1704, the Anglo-Scottish Union, the Sacheverell impeachment, and the peace of Utrecht.[6] The text of the *Nicolson Diaries*, with its frequent references to Lords' debates, fleshed out by a very full critical apparatus, enabled this importance to be more clearly appreciated.

One of the most remarkable aspects of the Nicolson edition was the range of manuscript material which had been consulted; collections of papers in national and local repositories, institutional libraries, record offices, and country-house muniment rooms, including a significant number of collections held in Scotland. In scouring Britain for archives, Clyve worked closely with the staff of the 1690–1715 section of the History of Parliament, including the present author, accompanying them on several provincial tours, to the north and west of England. Thanks to a visiting fellowship, he was also able to join members of the History's staff in a memorable trip to the USA, to consult the remarkable collections of manuscripts in the Huntington Library in California and smaller, but interesting deposits of papers in Kansas and at Yale. The work in Scottish archives, however, was very much his own. The results of this intense period of research were not only to be seen in the footnotes to the Nicolson diaries, but in a series of articles.

Clyve kept a particularly sharp eye open for new parliamentary lists: divisions, forecasts, assessments of party strength. The discovery and analysis of a number of new division lists in the 1960s, by historians interested primarily in the house of commons, had proved crucial in reinstating the importance of party divisions in Westminster politics, against the arguments of Robert Walcott, whose *English Politics in the Early Eighteenth Century* (1956) had sought unavailingly to replace a bipartisan political 'structure' with a more variegated picture in which the dynamic forces were not the whig and tory parties but a number of smaller, family-based 'connections'.[7] Clyve now began to compile information about Lords' lists for the period 1689–1714, adding more and more items to the pile every time he searched through a new collection. The high point was probably the discovery of no less than ten new lists for the first half of William III's reign in the Ailesbury papers at the Wiltshire Record Office, after the county archivist had attempted to forestall disappointment by announcing that from his own personal knowledge there would not be much of value to the parliamentary historian in that particular collection.

Lists, once discovered, had to be published. The first in what would become a stream of articles printing and analysing division lists appeared in the *Scottish Historical Review* in 1709. This kind of piece became typical of Clyve's output, bringing forward a new archival discovery, which transformed understanding of a particular episode in the history of the house of lords, or cast a different light on the organisation of parties and factions in the upper House, and demonstrating considerable forensic, as well as palaeographical, skills in decoding obscure annotations, and identifying obscurely referenced individuals. Leading on from the publication of individual lists or groups of lists, Clyve was the moving spirit among the group of historians who came together to produce a *Register of Parliamentary Lists* for the period 1660–1800, first published in 1979 as an 'occasional publication' by Leicester

[6] Robin Eagles, 'Geoffrey Holmes and the House of Lords Reconsidered', in *British Politics in the Age of Holmes*, ed. Clyve Jones (Oxford, 2009), 15–19.

[7] Henry Horwitz, 'The Structure of Parliamentary Politics', in *Britain after the Glorious Revolution*, ed. Geoffrey Holmes (1969), 96–114.

University's history department, and then extended chronologically and reissued in hard covers by Hambledon Press in 1995.

Clyve's close collaboration with the History of Parliament staff also resulted in a very different type of publication: the journal *Parliamentary History*, begun as a yearbook in 1982. Clyve served on the editorial committee from the outset, taking over as editor from Eveline Cruickshanks when the journal moved to a biannual format in 1987, and remaining in post for over a quarter of a century. Throughout his long scholarly career he has contributed many articles to the journal, but arguably the first to be published is still one of the most important. The inaugural issue contained an article co-authored by Clyve and Geoffrey Holmes, re-examining the parliamentary crisis of 1713. This session witnessed a major back-bench rebellion against the earl of Oxford's tory ministry and forced Oxford to reconstruct the political basis of his administration. Unsurprisingly perhaps, the argument of the article rested partly on the discovery of new lists, this time lists of members of the house of commons in the papers of the Scottish MP, George Baillie of Jerviswood, at Mellerstain House in Berwickshire. Clyve has long maintained – justifiably – that documentary sources for Scottish parliamentary families in the early 18th century are far richer than those in England, and the deployment of this Scottish material has formed a consistent thread running through his writings (reflected in this volume in essays by Graham Townend and Daniel Szechi). He has frequently returned to the material in Scottish archives, publishing several pieces based primarily on Scottish sources, as well as an edition of the correspondence of the Scottish representative peer, Lord Balmerino, and has done much to disentangle the complexities of Anglo-Scottish parliamentary politics in the aftermath of the treaty of union, especially the alignments and activities of the representative peers.

The analysis of the 1713 political crisis is also typical of Clyve's work in another important respect, because of its focus on parliamentary management, and more particularly, the way in which ministers went about securing for themselves a majority in the Lords. This has required not only an analysis of the composition of the upper House, but also a detailed examination of the relationships between governments and individuals. In a volume which he edited on *Party and Management in Parliament, 1660–1784* (published in 1984) he set out a clear statement of the means by which Robert Harley managed the house of lords between 1710 and 1714, building on the article which he and Geoffrey Holmes had written together on the crisis of 1713, and, of course, on the chapter on the Lords in Holmes's *magnum opus*. He was able to show once again the importance of the Scottish representative peers, and also of English 'poor lords' like the earl of Warrington, whose financial misfortunes he and John Beckett had already chronicled in a jointly-authored article. The scheme of management Harley created, and which Clyve anatomised, served the chief minister well until breaking down under the twin pressures of controversy over the peace of Utrecht and anxiety over the Hanoverian succession. In his conclusion, Clyve suggested that it had formed a pattern for the system subsequently developed by Sir Robert Walpole in order to reduce the upper House to compliance, and in a survey of the history of the Lords between 1701 and 1742 he set both Harley's and Walpole's administrations in a broader context, the gradual assertion of control by the executive over the upper House once the 'first age of party' had come to an end.[8]

[8]Clyve Jones, 'The House of Lords and the Growth of Parliamentary Stability', in *Britain in the First Age of Party, 1680–1750: Essays Presented to Geoffrey Holmes*, ed. Clyve Jones (1987), 109.

It has been a theme of all Clyve's writings that, however cleverly and indeed ruthlessly, a ministry might seek to discipline the members of the upper House, buying off the ambitious and the poverty-stricken with places and pensions, and drilling the bench of bishops into compliance, the Lords could never be taken for granted. In his later writing he has taken his detailed narrative of parliamentary management forward into the reigns of the first two Georges. There has been a forensic investigation into the circumstances lying behind the defeat of Lord Sunderland's Peerage Bill in 1719, an important analysis of the membership and activities of the 'Country' opposition in the upper House, 1720–3, and articles and essays on Walpole's management of the Lords, during and after the furore against his excise proposals in 1733, and in the final crisis which precipitated his fall from power in 1742. Taken together, these various pieces form a convincing narrative of politics and management in the upper House across the first half of the 18th century.

The length of the bibliography of Clyve's work which is appended to the essays in this volume should be evidence enough of his contribution to the subject. It also makes painfully clear that any attempt to do justice to the range of his interests and his publications would require a very great deal of space. Besides the *Nicolson Diaries*, he has been responsible (with Stephen Taylor) for another major edition of parliamentary materials, the papers of Robert Harley's grandson, Edward, 3rd earl of Oxford, and the whig MP, William Hay. He has also edited (sometimes in collaboration) no less than 11 collections of original essays on parliamentary history, as well as the *Short History of Parliament* published by Boydell in 2009. The vast (and continuing) flow of articles comprises not only pieces on the politics of the house of lords, but on procedural matters, and on the social life of members. He has even been involved in the heated controversy over the role of jacobitism in early Hanoverian politics, taking a typically careful and considered position in relation to allegations that whig politicians like the 3rd earl of Sunderland or the lord chancellor, William Cowper, entertained jacobite sympathies. He has never lost his fascination with Queen Anne's reign, nor with Scottish politics, and in some of his most recent work has returned to these former hunting grounds.

Certain characteristics are visible throughout this remarkable body of work despite its chronological range and varied subject matter: a strong emphasis on archival research, and a determination that the results of this research should be made available to the scholarly community; a deep familiarity with individuals and events; a scrupulous attention to context, and at an awareness of broader developments in his chosen period in the history of parliament, and of the house of lords in particular.

Clyve retired in 2008, by which time his contribution to historical research had been recognized by promotion to a readership in modern history at the University of London. He had also been awarded a DLitt by the University of Lancaster in 1995, and in retirement became an honorary fellow of the Institute of Historical Research, whose library had contributed so much to his work. He handed over the reins of *Parliamentary History* in 2014, though staying on as a member of the editorial committee, and as editor of the Texts & Studies Series. In retirement he continues to research, to write and to publish: his latest article, examining the way peers were involved in lobbying members of the house of commons in one particular contested election in 1735, appeared in *Parliamentary History* last year. Typically, it was based on a tranche of recently discovered material (from a further deposit of Ailesbury papers in what is no longer the Wiltshire Record Office but the

Wiltshire and Swindon History Centre); at its core was a set of parliamentary lists, which were tabulated and analysed; and, of course, what it had to say was entirely new.

This volume of essays is presented to Clyve by his friends (including some former collaborators) in admiration and gratitude, and in recognition of the remarkable contribution he has made over four decades, both to parliamentary history, and to *Parliamentary History*.

The Duke's Parrot: The Earl of Leicester, the King's Children and the English Revolution[*]

JASON PEACEY

This article examines neglected evidence regarding the ongoing captivity of the children of Charles I, at the hands of the republican regime, long after the regicide in January 1649. While it is well known that the Long Parliament was anxious to attend to the education of the royal children, and to exert authority over their upbringing, and also that there were rumours during the 1640s about plans to install the youngest prince, the duke of Gloucester, on the throne in place of a deposed king, little attention has been paid to voluminous and intriguing evidence about their fate during the interregnum. The aim of this essay is to survey such sources, and to recover evidence of a political and parliamentary debate about the children's fate, not least in a situation where it was thought possible that they might provide a rallying point for royalists, and a security threat. That debates about their fate were protracted and convoluted is used to flesh out rather sketchy evidence – much commented upon by historians, but not taken very seriously – that there was an ongoing debate over a possible monarchical settlement until 1653.

Keywords: Charles I; Henry, duke of Gloucester; monarchy; political factions; Princess Elizabeth Stuart; regicide; republic

1

On 30 July 1649, a servant of the countess of Leicester, Miles Smyth, recorded in his accounts having paid one Tom Elliott 1s. 6d. 'for carrying the duke's parrot from Sion to Southwark'. 'The duke' was Henry, duke of Gloucester, the third son of the recently executed Charles I, and the transportation of the parrot came about as the nine-year-old duke, like his 13-year-old sister, Princess Elizabeth, was transferred from the control of the earl of Northumberland to the care of the earl's sister, the countess of Leicester, at Penshurst in Kent. It is but one entry in a fascinating set of accounts that shed remarkable light upon the children's life between their arrival at Penshurst on 14 June 1649 and their subsequent move to the care of Anthony Mildmay at Carisbrooke Castle, in early August 1650. It is possible to observe repeated payments for 'the princess to play' (usually at £2), as well as payments to get her supplies of cake, oranges, and lemons. Her wardrobe was replenished, which meant that her petticoats were mended, and that purchases were made of scarlet galloon (12s.), scarves, powder, bodices, shoes, combs, gloves, ribbons, and other 'stuffs'. In March 1650, Mrs Briott was paid 18s. to supply Elizabeth with a gorget, cuffs, peaks, and a border. The princess was also provided with pins, serge, and silk by 'Robin the Welshman', so that she could do her

[*]The author wishes to thank Jack Sargeant for generously sharing some references regarding the fate of the king's children during the 1640s.

sewing, and then with a battledore and shuttlecocks so that she could play with her brother and the young Henry Sidney, the future earl of Romney, who was only a few months younger than the duke. Elizabeth's more lavish tastes, meanwhile, were accommodated by payments to mend her watch (2s.), to buy crystal (£1 15s.), and perhaps also to buy jewellery. The sum of £50 was paid to one Mr Crompton for 20 diamonds, for setting a diamond and a great ruby, and for polishing rings. In November 1650, a further £28 was spent on a ruby ring set with diamonds.

The duke, meanwhile, was provided with all manner of goods, from the trivial to the luxurious. These included 'a comb and a puff', laced bodices (over £1), shoes, stockings, gloves, and a leather cap, as well as periwigs, complete with boxes, powder, and combs. In November 1649 he received a 'sad coloured cloth coat', a black suit and a velvet coat (£13 8s. 6d.), and in March 1650 two new suits and a cloak (£10 1s.), and then a black serge suit in July 1650 (£3 9s.). His old hat was lined, and he was given a new beaver hat with a case (£2 16s.), and then another one a few months later (£2 12s.). He was given knives, bowls, and a standish. Mr Peaker was paid £1 for shaving him. Attention was paid to his education; his tutor, Richard Lovell, whom Clarendon called 'an honest man', apparently ensured that he was 'well taught in that learning that was fit for his years'. Lovell spent £2 8s. 4d. on books for his young charge in October 1649, and a further £1 in August 1649, and also acquired a pair of globes and 13 maps, at a cost of £2 2s. At the same time, the duke engaged in a range of other pursuits. His pistol was mended, and he was given a bow, quiver, and arrows, the latter at a cost of 30s. He received riding boots and spurs in November 1649 (£1 12s.). He hunted deer, and was given a greyhound (the messenger who brought the dog received 5s.). The duke and princess were also entertained with jugglers and fiddlers, treated to at least one masque (which cost at least £5), and made at least one trip to the bowling green. They each had their own servants, including footmen, grooms, and laundry maids, who were provided with equipment (smoothing irons), repaid their expenses (such as for travelling to Cobham and Petworth), and paid their wages (over £120 per annum), and also provided with suits, livery, and laced coats, hats, stockings, and shoes, all of which cost over £40.[1]

Smyth's accounts, in other words, provide an intriguing picture of the way in which the duke of Gloucester and Princess Elizabeth were maintained in the months after the execution of their father, Charles I. They also open up interesting issues relating to the politics and culture of the English republic, which have received little attention, and which relate very closely to the extraordinarily valuable work that Clyve Jones has done to address the role of the nobility in early modern politics. The duke and his sister have been more or less overlooked, at least until quite recently, perhaps because both met with early deaths. Familiar, of course, is the story about the duke being granted access to his imprisoned father on 7 January 1649, and it is also known that in the days between Charles I's execution and his burial, the young republic provided the duke with two chambers hung with black cloth (1 February 1649). We know that Elizabeth died in the summer of 1650, and that Henry, having eventually made his way to the Continent, returned to England with his elder brother, Charles II, in May 1660, took his seat in the house of lords, only to die of smallpox

---

[1] Penshurst Place, Kent, MS 398 (BL, M772/15): Miles Smyth accounts, 1648–50. Lovell had been tutor to the earl of Sunderland, the countess of Leicester's grandson. See Edward Hyde, earl of Clarendon, *The History of the Rebellion and Civil Wars in England*, ed. W.D. Macray (6 vols, Oxford, 1888), v, 335.

in the following September.[2] What is less well understood, however, is the thinking behind their treatment by the Commonwealth regime after the death of Charles I, the decisions that were made, and what these might mean, not least given that the children – like Charles's other offspring – had long been a political issue of real importance.

What seems clear is that the fate of the king's children had been in play since the early 1640s, when the 'Ten Propositions' demanded 'that some persons of public trust and well-affected in religion may be placed about the prince who may take some care of his education, and of the rest of his children, especially in matters of religion and liberty', and when the 'Nineteen Propositions' insisted that 'he or they unto whom the government and education of the king's children shall be committed shall be approved of by both houses of parliament'.[3] As contemporaries recognized, the royal children constituted a bargaining chip, and when the Venetian ambassador, Giustinian, noted, in November 1642, that the 'little duke of Gloucester' and his sister had been moved from the fringes of London to a house at the heart of the capital, he mocked the idea that this had been done to protect them from harm amid possible fighting as a 'specious pretence'. He detected, indeed, a 'secret design' on the part of parliamentarians:

> to avail themselves of these innocent victims as hostages if the king comes back victorious to his residence here, as they feel persuaded that the precious pledge of these children will serve them in the utmost peril as an opening to obtain a pardon from his majesty more easily, as well as safety for the persons and the fortunes as well of the rebels.[4]

What is also clear is that decisions about who should look after the king's children once war broke out were carefully thought through. Initially, the Commons had proposed that they should be looked after by Lady Vere, 'an old lady much in their favour' according to Clarendon, only for the house of lords to object, and for it to become clear that she was 'not at all ambitious of that charge'. As such, it was agreed that the children should fall under the care of the countess of Dorset, the wife of a moderate royalist peer, before eventually being entrusted, in March 1645, to the earl of Northumberland, a parliamentarian grandee of huge importance, complete with a maintenance of £3,000 per annum.[5] In keeping with the Nineteen Propositions, moreover, plans were laid for the royal children to have a godly education. During the mid 1640s, therefore, their household servants included a raft of puritan divines, such as Obadiah Sedgwick, Joseph Caryll, Jeremiah Whitaker, William Greenhill, William Spurstow, Samuel Torshell, and Stephen Marshall, the latter of whom was noted in the royalist press as having delivered monthly lectures to the captive children.[6]

Given such evidence about the importance that parliamentarians attached to the king's children and their governance, there are grounds for revisiting the fate of the only two members of the royal family who remained under parliamentarian control following the

---

[2] *CSP Ven., 1647–52*, p. 90; ODNB.

[3] S.R. Gardiner, *The Constitutional Documents of the Puritan Revolution, 1625–1660* (Oxford, 1906), 165, 251.

[4] *CSP Ven., 1642–3*, pp. 192–3.

[5] S.R. Gardiner, *History of the Great Civil War, 1642–1649* (4 vols, 1901), ii, 189; *LJ*, vii, 279, 327. For payments to Cornelius Holland as paymaster of the princes' household from December 1643 to April 1644, see TNA, SC 6/Chas.1/1661, m.4d.

[6] Parliamentary Archives, HL/PO/JO/10/1/167, HL/PO/JO/10/1/184; *Mercurius Aulicus*, 57 (Feb. 1644), 805.

escape of the duke of York from St James's Palace in the spring of 1648, particularly given that the duke of Gloucester remained in custody long after the execution of Charles I, until his eventual release in early 1653. By tracing the story of the royal children after January 1649 – when Gloucester was allowed to visit his father, on the same day that parliament ordered that nobody was to be proclaimed king 'without the free consent of the people in parliament'[7] – it will be possible to suggest that the complex dynamic of their captivity reflected serious – if cloudy – debates about their fate. These debates, moreover, bear serious scrutiny in the light of recent historiography regarding events leading up to the regicide, and in order to question problematic accounts offered by Venetian onlookers and contemporary royalists like the earl of Clarendon.

2

Clarendon's account of the duke of Gloucester and Princess Elizabeth revolved around the idea that, following the escape of the duke of York 'the parliament would not suffer, nor did the earl desire, that the rest should remain longer under his government', and that the children were immediately treated with less respect than they warranted.[8] What actually seems clear is that this is a dramatic oversimplification. Northumberland was cleared of any blame for the duke of York's escape, and remained governor of the remaining royal children until after the regicide.[9] More important, the months after the death of Charles I were marked by real uncertainty regarding the fate of the king's younger children. On 1 February, the committee dealing with the issue of the king's body was ordered to provide two chambers, hung with black, for Gloucester.[10] On 23 February 1649, Sir Henry Mildmay was ordered to report regarding the issue of their allowance, but what is remarkable is how little was said or done about them during the weeks that followed, even as it was finally decided to abolish the monarchy on 17 March.[11] Only in early April did the question of what to do with the prince and princess arise in earnest, following the decision by Northumberland to resign as their guardian, in a letter which was ordered to be reported to the Commons by Lord Lisle on 9 April.[12] That there was uncertainty about how to proceed at this juncture seems clear from the fact that this report was actually only delivered on 24 April, when the Commons resolved to consider it the following day as a matter of real importance, 'nothing to intervene'.[13] At this point – and perhaps in response to more than one letter from Princess Elizabeth – it was agreed to continue paying £3,000 per annum for the maintenance and education of the two royal children, while the committee of revenue was to consider what money remained due to Northumberland and to the children's servants for wages and arrears.[14]

[7] *CJ*, vi, 124.
[8] Clarendon, *Hist. Rebellion*, ed. Macray, v, 335.
[9] *CSP Ven., 1647–52*, p. 61.
[10] *CJ*, vi, 128.
[11] *CJ*, vi, 149.
[12] *CSP Dom. 1649–50*, p. 76.
[13] *CJ*, vi, 193.
[14] *CSP Dom., 1649–50*, p. 107; *CJ*, vi, 194–5. Evidence refers to her letters of 22 January and 2 April. The idea that the princess asked for a pension was mentioned by the Venetian ambassador: *CSP Ven., 1647–52*, p. 107.

Apart from the fact that there is no evidence of any discussion about the wisdom or necessity of the republic providing for the children of the executed king, what also emerges at this point is that at least some thought was given to the possibility of allowing the children to travel to their family on the Continent, with or without ongoing financial support from parliament and council of state. Whether or not Elizabeth asked for a pension, therefore, she may also have asked for liberty, and when these letters were considered on 25 April the question was posed that she at least should be allowed to travel abroad. That this was contentious, however, is evident from the fact that the House promptly divided, and that a vote was forced. On this occasion the yeas (whose votes were recorded by Sir William Masham and Sir William Allenson) were narrowly defeated by the noes (whose votes were reported by Sir Michael Livesey and Sir William Brereton), 29 to 24. It was decided, albeit only narrowly, that Elizabeth should stay under parliamentary control, and it is significant that there seems to have been no question at this stage that the duke should be allowed out of the country.[15]

Thereafter, however, uncertainty remained. The initial idea was that the two children should be placed under the care of Sir Edward Harrington, for whom the council started to prepare instructions, while Lord Lisle was asked to notify the earl of Northumberland.[16] Harrington, however, declined the role, pleading sickness (27 April),[17] and it was not until 24 May that it was decided that the children should be sent to Penshurst, under the care of Northumberland's sister, the countess of Leicester, who would receive their maintenance money, instructions once again being given to Lord Lisle to convey the news to his mother, the countess, and his uncle, Northumberland.[18] The Penshurst accounts record payment of 7s. for a copy of the order of 24 May, and both Northumberland and the countess engaged in negotiations with the committee of revenue (11 June).[19] There then ensued inevitable bureaucracy, noted in the Penshurst accounts in terms of payments to clerks and secretaries for copies of orders, and in terms of the cost of making repeated journeys by water to Westminster.[20] Eventually, however, the children were, indeed, taken to Penshurst, on 14 June, as noted in Leicester's diary,[21] a job that involved transporting 77 hundredweight of goods, at a cost of almost £10.[22] Thereafter, the accounts reveal regular receipts of £250 per month, beginning on 16 June, transactions that were handled by a trusty servant called William Hawkins, whose legal and clerical fees and gratuities – to Cozens and his clerk, and to Mr Sherwyn – were also recorded.[23]

Such evidence alone is insufficient to establish the thinking behind the decision to keep both children in England, although it is noteworthy that the earl of Leicester considered the

---

[15] *CJ*, vi, 194–5.

[16] *CJ*, vi, 195.

[17] *CJ*, vi, 196.

[18] *CJ*, vi, 215–16.

[19] Penshurst, MS 398; *CJ*, vi, 228–8.

[20] Penshurst, MS 398.

[21] *Sydney Papers*, ed. Robert Blencowe (1825), 75; HMC, *De L'Isle and Dudley MSS*, vi, 589.

[22] Penshurst, MS 398.

[23] Penshurst, MS 398. It is unclear whether *all* payments in the Penshurst accounts came from government money.

business 'troublesome', and referred to a 'huge storm' over the costs involved.[24] Fortunately, other evidence about their treatment at Penshurst makes it possible to at least go some way towards dealing with such issues. First, it is possible to offer qualified support for Clarendon's claim about the way in which the royal children were treated. Clarendon claimed that previously the children had been awarded money 'as might well defray their expenses with that respect that was due to their births', and that Northumberland 'received and treated them in all respects as was suitable to their birth and his own duty', even if he could 'give them no more liberty to go abroad than he was in his instructions from the parliament permitted to do'.[25] Clarendon also added that this was 'performed towards them as long as the king their father lived', and that thereafter this allowance was 'retrenched', so that their attendants and servants might be lessened. This seems not to have been the case in financial terms, although Clarendon correctly noted that 'order was given that they should be treated without any addition of titles, and that they should sit at their meat as the children of the family did, and all at one table'. Here Clarendon picked up on instructions issued on 13 June 1649, whereby the children were to sit with the earl and countess 'at their table, as part of their family, and not otherwise', and that 'no other observance or ceremony be used to the late king's children, than is used to noblemen's children of this nation'.[26] Clarendon's comment was that the royal children were 'carefully looked to, and treated with as much respect as the lady pretended she durst pay to them', and what seems fairly clear is that, lavish though the lifestyle of the duke and princess seems to have been, they were treated as *noble* rather than *royal* children.[27] It is notable that the kind of money that was spent on them was similar to, done in the same way as, and paid at the same time as, money spent on young Henry Sidney. The two young boys, indeed, were brought up in the same way; they not only played together, but received the same clothes and toys, and the same education. Of course, Penshurst was a grand house, and the earl and countess certainly lived a lavish lifestyle, as is clear from other entries in the accounts, not least in relation to art work. On 7 May 1649, therefore, one Mr Geldrup was paid £7 for a copy of the earl of Sunderland's picture, while Mr Stone was paid £12 for 'a copy of the large Venus'. Between April and December, moreover, the family paid Sir Peter Lely £25 for two pictures of Henry Sidney.[28]

If the duke and princess were deliberately treated as members of the nobility, but not as royalty, then what also seems clear is that the decision to place them at Penshurst reflected nervousness about their potential visibility. Here, too, however, Clarendon's account was rather simplistic. He was wrong to say that the children were moved 'as soon as the king was murdered', although perhaps right to claim that the order 'that the children should be removed into the country' reflected a concern 'that they might not be the objects of respect, to draw the eyes and application of people towards them'.[29] Here, therefore, it seems plausible to conclude that the move to Penshurst was an attempt to restrict the visibility of the royal children, in the face of their capacity to elicit sympathy. Indeed, it is possible that such concerns had been evident much earlier. A recommendation by the Lords in

[24] HMC, *De L'Isle and Dudley MSS*, vi, 558.

[25] Clarendon, *Hist. Rebellion*, ed. Macray, iv, 237.

[26] *CJ*, vi, 231.

[27] Clarendon, *Hist. Rebellion*, ed. Macray, v, 335.

[28] Penshurst, MS 398.

[29] Clarendon, *Hist. Rebellion*, ed. Macray, v, 335.

July 1647, that the children should be removed from London to one of Northumberland's country residences (Syon House), was ostensibly made in the interest of their health, but this may merely have been a veil for concerns about their popularity. Living at Syon made it possible for them to visit the king at Hampton Court, but also placed them out of sight at a particularly tense moment in the capital, and evidence from May 1648 reveals that they were capable of drawing a crowd in places like Hyde Park, where many people apparently came to kiss their hands.[30]

Such evidence suggests that Clarendon's account was rather simplistic, and that the authorities were grappling with something of a conundrum, rather than merely downgrading the children's status and preventing them from attracting public attention and popular sympathy. Parliament and the council of state made conscious decisions about what kind of respect to show to the royal children, and to categorise them as members of the nobility (but nothing more), and there does, indeed, seem to have been a concern that they might attract attention from a public still adapting to the new republic, and become rallying points for royalist agitation. Nevertheless, the delay in making decisions about what to do with them until late May 1649 also signals uncertainty about how best to proceed, and about what a long-term solution might be. According to the Venetian ambassador, the decision to send the children to Penshurst was a temporary measure, 'until other arrangements were made by the Commons'.[31] There was at least some consideration given to the possibility of their being released, although it is notable that this was more obviously considered to be an option for Princess Elizabeth than for the young prince, and there was much more obviously a resolve to keep Gloucester in England. Indeed, the significance of a curious story told by Lord Hatton, about delayed attempts to effect the duke's escape in January 1650, reflects not just on the strange behaviour of key courtiers – Hatton wrote of 'strange diffidence of those about the king', and of one 'of nearest trust' to the duke complaining that an attempt being 'spoiled' – but also on the attitude of the republican government. Hatton recorded that notice was given to the earl of Leicester to 'look about him and take heed of a design in this kind' – by someone 'in place about his majesty' – which would seem to signal a resolve on the part of the duke's captors to keep him in their custody.[32] Such themes, and a sense of contemporary debate about what to do with the duke of Gloucester, come into sharper focus by exploring the next phase of his captivity.

3

That Penshurst was considered to be an imperfect solution to questions surrounding the duke of Gloucester is clear from the events in the summer of 1650, which saw the royal children moved from Penshurst to Carisbrooke Castle on the Isle of Wight, although once

---

[30] *Perfect Occurrences*, xxix (16–23 July 1647), sig. Ff2v; Clarendon, *Hist. Rebellion*, ed. Macray, iv, 250; *Calendar of the Clarendon State Papers*, ed. W.D. Macray *et al*. (5 vols, Oxford, 1872–1970), i, 318; *CSP Ven.*, *1647–52*, pp. 59–60.

[31] *CSP Ven.*, *1647–52*, p. 107.

[32] *The Nicholas Papers*, ed. G.F. Warner (4 vols, Camden, new ser., xl, l, lvii, 3rd ser., xxxi, 1886–1920), i, 165. Hatton described this as 'a business [that] hath slept some while in my hands, but I have not been idle in it, concerning duke of Gloucester', and he blamed the intervention of an unnamed knight, who pretended to be employed by Charles II. That Leicester may have been concerned about the impact of his playing host to the duke on his own fortunes by early 1650 seems clear: HMC, *De L'Isle and Dudley MSS*, vi, 473.

again the evidence suggests that Clarendon's account is more or less deficient, that this phase in their captivity raises important issues and challenges, and that the authorities were uncertain, and perhaps conflicted, about what to do. The new regime certainly made some fascinating decisions, influenced by concerns about security, as well as by considerations about whether or not to keep the children – and particularly the duke – in captivity.

Most obviously, the republican government demonstrated ongoing concern about the risk that the duke would provide a rallying point for royalists, not least in the wake of the arrival of Charles II in Scotland on 23 June 1650. On 24 July, the Commons heard a report from the council of state – delivered by Sir Henry Mildmay – to the effect that because of 'many designs now on foot, if any stirrings or insurrections should happen, the public peace would be much more endangered, by occasion of the late king's children, who are here remaining, who may be made use of to the prejudice of the public'. The council urged parliament to think of a 'remedy'. What is significant, however, is that at this stage it was debated whether both Elizabeth and Henry should be 'removed beyond the seas, out of the limits of this commonwealth'. Indeed, this was duly agreed, and the council was ordered to consider a 'fit place' and suitable maintenance 'beyond seas'.[33] Only subsequently was it decided – on 27 July – that they should be sent to Carisbrooke, and placed in the custody of Sir Henry Mildmay's brother, Anthony Mildmay, with a similar maintenance and with up to eight servants (of the children's own choosing), after instructions had been issued, and after both the countess of Leicester and the earl of Northumberland had been notified. Arrangements for their transportation and maintenance were discussed in special sessions of the council in the days that followed, and Major General Thomas Harrison was deputed to make arrangements, 'the port, way, manner and convoy being wholly left to him'. Intriguingly, this order was passed on the very same day that statues of both James I and Charles I were ordered to be removed from London 'by having their head taken off'. Ultimately this involved Mildmay collecting the children from Penshurst on 9 August, and conveying them by two coaches, with six horses apiece, 'for their better accommodation', and it was noted that this was all to be done 'privately' and without 'ceremony', with an eye to security.[34]

As with the move to Penshurst, Clarendon saw this transfer to Carisbrooke as part of a calculated process by which the status of the royal children was downgraded. Noting that they were to be provided with maintenance, therefore, Clarendon claimed that 'in truth' this was given to Mildmay 'as a boon to him'.[35] In fact, it seems clear that the state merely transferred to Mildmay the same funds that had been assigned to Northumberland – £3,000 per annum – along with all the goods that had been supplied for them at Penshurst. Once again, Clarendon was closer to the mark in noting that strict requirements were put in place 'that no person should be permitted to kiss their hands, or that they should be otherwise treated than as the children of a *gentleman*'. What this meant in practice, according to Clarendon, was that Mildmay, in observing his instructions 'very strictly', referred to the

---

[33] *CJ*, vi, 231, 446; *CSP Dom.*, *1650*, p. 250.

[34] *CSP Dom.*, *1650*, pp. 255–6, 257–8, 259, 261, 263, 270, 274. Plate, hangings, bedding and other stuff at Penshurst belonging to state were to be returned. The earl of Leicester noted their departure in his diary: *Sydney Papers*, ed. Blencowe, 103; HMC, *De L'Isle and Dudley MSS*, vi, 559, 599. Later, Paulucci could note that 'the present place of his confinement remains a secret': *CSP Ven.*, *1647–52*, p. 325.

[35] Clarendon, *Hist. Rebellion*, ed. Macray, v, 335.

duke as 'Mr Harry'.[36] Mildmay's official instructions had, indeed, indicated that he was 'not to suffer any other ceremony … than what is fit for and due to a gentleman, neither at table, nor in the journey, nor otherwise'. The children were to be placed under guard, to be supplied by the governor of the Isle of Wight, Colonel William Sydenham, while Mildmay was empowered to displace any servants as he saw fit.[37]

Beyond this issue of their treatment, evidence from the months that followed suggests that the authorities remained conflicted over where exactly the children should reside, whether or not to grant them liberty, and whether or not to treat the two siblings differently. On 20 August, at the same time as the council responded to a letter from Anthony Mildmay by ordering an inventory of all the goods that had been sent to Penshurst by Northumberland, in order to ensure that the children would have 'things necessary, provided all be included in the sum of £3,000 per annum', Sir Henry Mildmay was ordered to move them 'to such place as they are most willing to go, they being appointed by parliament to be transported out of the limits of the commonwealth'. Perhaps Carisbrooke, in other words, was only seen as a temporary residence.[38]

In the face of Elizabeth's illness, for example, it was certainly thought possible that she might be released. On 5 September 1650, therefore, after the victory over the Scots, it was reported to parliament that since her transfer to Carisbrooke, Elizabeth's health had deteriorated seriously, and she was described as being 'indisposed'. The council of state agreed to her request to be able to go to her sister, the princess of Orange, and ordered that she should receive £1,000 per annum, 'so long as she shall behave inoffensively to the parliament and commonwealth'.[39] That this did not in fact happen merely reflected her worsening condition, which prompted Mildmay to send for her doctor, despite there being 'little hope of life amid many signs of imminent death'. Elizabeth died within a matter of days, and was buried on 24 September, the committee of revenue being ordered to make arrangements for the funeral, which saw the duke of Gloucester and the royal servants being provided with mourning attire.[40]

Interestingly, however, there seems to have been at least some support by this stage for the idea of letting Henry leave, too. On 5 September, therefore, it was decided that Henry should be sent to his brother, Charles II, in Scotland and have £1,000 per annum on similar terms to his sister, 'so long as he behave inoffensively'.[41] This might, indeed, have happened, one suspects, had it not been for the timing. Thus, while Sir Henry Mildmay reported the council's view to the Commons on 11 September, parliament evidently thought it more appropriate, in the wake of the Battle of Dunbar, to send the young duke to the University of Heidelberg, accompanied by three servants of his choice, and supported by £1,500 per annum.[42] A council committee, comprised of Mildmay, Thomas Chaloner, and Thomas Scot, was charged with finding the 'best way' to achieve this, and to organise instructions

---

[36] Clarendon, *Hist. Rebellion*, ed. Macray, v, 335–6 (emphasis added).

[37] *CSP Dom., 1650*, pp. 258, 261.

[38] *CSP Dom., 1650*, p. 295.

[39] *CJ*, vi, 465–6; *CSP Dom., 1650*, p. 327.

[40] *CJ*, vi, 465–6; *CSP Dom., 1650*, p. 331. For an indication of her popularity, see the following ballad which marked her death: *The Lamenting Ladies Last Farewel* (1650).

[41] *CSP Dom., 1650*, p. 328. See HMC, *De L'Isle and Dudley MSS*, vi, 485.

[42] *CJ*, vi, 465–6; *CSP Dom., 1650*, p. 335.

and financial arrangements, while the admiralty committee was ordered to provide a ship.[43] Subsequently, on 26 September, Mildmay was asked to confer with Fauconbridge regarding the finances, while Walter Frost was ordered to contact local merchants in Heidelberg about arranging bills of exchange, in consultation with Mildmay, Chaloner, and William Heveningham.[44] This plan was still on the cards in early October 1650, when the council agreed to allow one Mr Fitzwilliams to accompany the duke to Heidelberg, when the orders were renewed for the admiralty committee to find a suitable ship, and when Thomas Scot, Edmund Ludlow, and Sir William Constable were added to the committee to oversee the duke's departure (11 October).[45] By 18 October, however, when Chaloner was ordered to report to parliament on progress regarding such proceedings, the council had decided that the situation north of the border had changed sufficiently for the duke to be sent to Scotland after all.[46] Perhaps such thinking was encouraged by a letter from Anthony Mildmay, in mid-November 1650, in which he referred to the Isle of Wight as a 'bleak and cold' place in winter, and to the fact that the poor air might be prejudicial to the duke's health.[47] More likely is the possibility that concerns remained about the duke as a security threat. On 30 November, therefore, the council signalled its intention to write to Anthony Mildmay to express concern that the duke's 'going up and down in the Isle of Wight may be of dangerous consequence to the peace of the nation in regard of the insurrections already begun'. As such, he was ordered to be kept within Carisbrooke Castle.[48]

Even at this stage the duke was not released; he remained at Carisbrooke, and Mildmay continued to receive his allowance, although ongoing concerns about his behaviour, and about the possibility that he might attract unwanted attention occasionally led to renewed interest in the possibility that he should be 'disposed of to some other place than the Isle of Wight', including Scarborough, as in early June 1651 and again in the following August.[49] In late November 1651, the council reported to parliament that if the Commons 'think fit to continue him there' something would need to be done to provide him with 'necessary accommodation', given the zeal with which the contractors for the sale of the late king's goods had been asset-stripping the castle.[50]

Such evidence seems to indicate uncertainty and divided opinions over the duke's fate, although perhaps not quite the dynamic that Clarendon tried to fathom in the run-up to Gloucester's eventual release in early 1653. In seeking to explain this outcome, therefore, Clarendon mused that it reflected the fact that Cromwell was 'jealous' that the duke – whom he described as 'a prince of extraordinary hope, both from the comeliness and gracefulness of his persons and the vivacity and vigour of his wit and understanding' – might 'be made use of by the discontented party of his own army to give him trouble'. Clarendon also considered the possibility, however, that Cromwell merely sought to 'show the contempt he

---

[43] *CSP Dom.*, *1650*, p. 344.

[44] *CSP Dom.*, *1650*, pp. 357, 366.

[45] *CSP Dom.*, *1650*, pp. 368, 379, 394.

[46] *CSP Dom.*, *1650*, pp. 392, 405.

[47] *CSP Dom.*, *1650*, p. 431. This letter was sent along with Mildmay's accounts for £312 spent moving the children from Penshurst to Carisbrooke: *CSP Dom.*, *1650*, pp. 440–1; TNA, SP 18/11, ff. 132–3.

[48] *CSP Dom.*, *1650*, p. 449.

[49] *CSP Dom.*, *1651*, pp. 33, 205, 209, 212, 235, 311.

[50] *CSP Dom.*, *1651–2*, p. 29.

had of the royal family, by sending another of it into the world to try his fortune'. Whatever the logic of Clarendon's reasoning, his account is interesting because of his suggestion that Cromwell did 'declare one day to his council that he was well content that the son of the late king … should have liberty to transport himself into any parts beyond the seas as he should desire', and because this was said to have been 'much wondered at, and not believed, and many thought it a presage of a worse inclination'. As such, Clarendon noted, 'for some time there was no more speech of it'.[51] Thereafter, Clarendon claimed, the impetus for releasing the duke came most obviously from the prisoner himself, who was informed about such machinations 'by those who wished his liberty', people who encouraged him to 'prosecute the obtaining that order and release'. As such, according to Clarendon, the duke sent Lovell to London, 'to be advised by friends what he should do to procure such an order and warrant', adding that Lovell 'did so dextrously solicit it' that he eventually secured precisely such a warrant on 17 January 1653, together with £500.[52]

As on other occasions, Clarendon's account is intriguing, but not entirely convincing. Lovell had certainly demonstrated a willingness to lobby on the duke's behalf. In October 1650, for example, the council of state ordered Chaloner and Scot to consider a petition from Lovell and John Griffith, and to grant them an allowance during their stay in London, out of the £1,500 which had been assigned to effect the duke's transportation overseas.[53] In March 1652, Lovell had also complained about delays in paying the duke's maintenance, saying that this caused 'great difficulty in making daily provision', and thereby effecting the payment of arrears.[54] However, it seems likely that the machinations to which Clarendon referred involved hard thinking on the part of Cromwell and his colleagues, and decisions that proved difficult and perhaps divisive. In what may have been the incident to which Clarendon referred, the council resolved, on 7 September 1652, to consider how to dispose of the duke, although the matter did not resurface until 6 December, when the lord president was ordered to move parliament that 'considering the state of affairs' the duke should be moved 'to some other place', as the Commons saw fit.[55] It was at this stage that the idea really gained momentum. On 7 December, parliament issued an order for the duke to be removed from the Isle of Wight; three days later the matter was taken up by the council; and on 13 December, the committee for foreign affairs was ordered to consider the place to which the prisoner should be sent, and what accommodation would be fit.[56] Within a matter of days the council had resolved to ask the duke himself 'the place in France or Flanders where he desires to be landed and the persons he chooses to attend him', and its committees considered issues relating to money and transport, and resolved to provide him with £400 to cover the cost of his journey to Dunkirk or Ostend, and to pay any unpaid bills on the Isle of Wight. The duke was also to have Antwerp bills of exchange to the value of £1,000, alongside a ship and four servants, as well as 'necessaries', and the duke authorised Lovell to receive such money on his behalf, and to organise the journey, with

[51] Clarendon, *Hist. Rebellion*, ed. Macray, v, 336.
[52] Clarendon, *Hist. Rebellion*, ed. Macray, v, 336.
[53] *CSP Dom., 1650*, pp. 394, 405.
[54] *CSP Dom., 1651–2*, p. 170.
[55] *CSP Dom., 1651–2*, p. 394; *1652–3*, p. 12.
[56] *CJ*, vii, 226; *CSP Dom., 1652–3*, pp. 20, 23.

the approval of Mildmay and Sydenham.[57] What Clarendon did not consider, but what the Venetian ambassador certainly noticed, was that this flurry of activity coincided with fears regarding a possible Dutch attack on the Isle of Wight. On 27 December, the ambassador noted that, although the island was 'in a good state of defence':

> they have considered it advisable to order the removal thence of the duke of Gloucester … who has been kept prisoner there a long while. It is not known what they mean to do with him now. Some say that he will be allowed, if he likes, to go to his cousin, the Count Palatine in Germany, parliament paying him an annual pension. Others assert that they mean to give him £1,000 sterling and desire him to leave England and go where he pleases.[58]

At precisely this time the council considered Sydenham's proposals for improving the island's fortifications.[59]

Even at this late stage, however, things did not run entirely smoothly, despite efforts to secure a vessel with the help of the admiralty committee, the passing of an order to issue the duke with a pass (on 14 January) and to organise his finances, and the issuing of such a warrant on 17 January.[60] As late as the first week of February, therefore, Sydenham was forced to report to the council that, although Lovell had procured a vessel to take the duke to Flanders, Anthony Mildmay refused to release him, claiming not to have been formally discharged of his trust. Referring to 'this unexpected forcible stop', Sydenham explained that Mildmay was keeping the duke locked up within his own lodgings, and he obviously sought to deny any responsibility. Indeed, he also enclosed a letter to the council from the duke himself, who acknowledged the 'many favours' he had received, and expressed thanks for being allowed to travel abroad, but who asked that the council would be 'pleased to assert your own act'. The duke explained that Mildmay:

> has not only taken resolution to stay me and to that purpose refused to accommodate me with a bed, or blanket, or any utensil to carry on shipboard, but locks his door upon me, and denies me to talk about the castle, or to enjoy that liberty which you have always granted me, unless he be forced to it by arms or a particular order from you.

He noted that Mildmay had seen a copy of the council's warrant, 'but is not satisfied'.[61] As a result, the council decided to write to Mildmay on 4 February, ordering him not to 'hold Henry Stuart in restraint'. Eight days later Sydenham was able to report that the council's orders had been executed, and that the duke had set sail from Cowes the previous day.[62]

This curious episode is important because it shines a light on issues that had almost certainly been in play since the spring of 1649. First, Sydenham confirmed fears that had

[57] *CSP Dom., 1652–3*, pp. 27, 47, 53–4, 56–7, 65; TNA, SP 18/26, f. 108.
[58] *CSP Ven., 1647–52*, p. 325.
[59] *CSP Dom., 1652–3*, p. 56.
[60] *CSP Dom., 1652–3*, pp. 102–3, 464. This authorised the duke to pass to any port in Flanders in any vessel he chose.
[61] *CSP Dom., 1652–3*, pp. 141–2.
[62] *CSP Dom., 1652–3*, pp. 146, 162.

always surrounded a captive member of the Stuart family, namely that he would provide a rallying point for royalist sympathisers. Thus, while Sydenham sought to ensure the government that the duke slipped away 'without much notice or observance', he was forced to admit that 'some private men of war in the road were more free in their salutes than became them'.[63] Such expressions of respect for the duke duly provoked an investigation by the council into who might have been responsible.[64] Indeed, nervousness about the duke persisted even after his departure from the Isle of Wight, not least when Lovell approached the mayor of Dover on 14 February for permission to come ashore and take refreshment, the duke having become ill as a result of contrary winds and a 'distemper at sea'. The mayor, William Cullen, as well as the town's governor, agreed to this request, but only after Lovell promised that the duke would rest privately at the house of one Mr Delavall, and that nobody would be allowed to visit him, 'whereby anything should be done prejudicial to the commonwealth'. It is also interesting that, having granted the duke this civility, Cullen sought reassurance from the council that he had not done anything untoward. Second, the duke's letter to the council indicated more than just that Mildmay was being punctilious in the absence of the original warrant, and intimated awareness that the issue of his release had 'long endured dispute and now suffers resistance also', and that there were 'many threats to hinder my going'.[65]

4

Eventually, of course, the duke made it to Dunkirk, before heading to Antwerp and The Hague, amid reports that he had been 'exiled by parliament there on pain of death if he ventures to return', and that he had been sent out of the country 'to prevent any possible inconvenience that his presence … might cause the commonwealth'.[66] What quickly became apparent was what parliamentarians had always feared: that without proper guidance Gloucester would fall into the clutches of papists and be converted to catholicism, and even be made a cardinal. By May he had reached Paris, to be greeted by his mother 'who left him in England a mere baby'. When Charles II discovered how Henrietta Maria intended to have his brother educated, he sent Ormond to try and dissuade her, prompting the Venetian ambassador to suspect that 'the project will be dropped, and the princes of the house of Stuart, after having been expelled from the kingdoms of this world, will now submit to banishment from the kingdom of heaven'.[67] What merits reflection, however, is what to make of this complex and protracted story of the process which culminated in the duke being reunited with his less than united family.

What seems clear is that whatever role was played by 'civility' in supporting young members of the royal family who had played no part in the civil wars, there was a deeper significance to decisions about where the duke and princess should be detained, and to whom

[63] *CSP Dom., 1652–3*, p. 162.
[64] *CSP Dom., 1652–3*, p. 163.
[65] *CSP Dom., 1652–3*, p. 164.
[66] *CSP Dom., 1652–3*, pp. 221–2; *Nicholas Papers*, ed. Warner, ii, 5; *CSP Ven., 1653–4*, pp. 38, 43, 54. See the duke's letter to Hyde thanking him for his kindness and expressing thankfulness for his escape from England: *Cal. Clarendon SP*, ed. Macray et al., ii, 187.
[67] *CSP Ven., 1653–4*, pp. 77–8, 283; *Nicholas Papers*, ed. Warner, ii, 7, 8, 11.

their care should be entrusted. There can also be no doubt that the republican regime thought carefully about how the royal children should be treated, and about how much respect they should be afforded, and it is hard not to conclude that the machinations surrounding their captivity revealed uncertainty over whether to detain them or release them. What emerges is that, given the fear that they might become a rallying point for disaffected royalists, and that keeping them hidden was more or less difficult, not to say expensive, it might have been easier to let them go. At certain points at least some contemporaries thought that this would be the best option. All of which begs the question: what possible reason was there to keep them in custody?

My suggestion is that answering this question requires reflecting on earlier ideas and rumours regarding the duke, which had been common currency since the early 1640s, and which involved the notion that he could be placed on the throne as a puppet king in place of a deposed (or indeed executed) Charles I. As early as October 1643 the earl of Bath reported a story that parliamentarians planned to make the duke 'constable of England' and 'then manage the war in his name', while the royalist press even suggested that Henry Marten threatened to seize the crown jewels in order to 'crown his majesties youngest son'.[68] Later, in March 1645, the Venetian ambassador reported that if Charles I refused to come to terms, parliamentarian leaders would place the crown on the young duke's head, and make Northumberland protector.[69] This was an idea that refused to die, and in January 1646, as news of the Glamorgan treaty provoked strong words against the king in parliament, thoughts turned again to the possibility of deposing Charles. According to the French ambassador, it was mooted that the prince of Wales would be declared an enemy of the state, and that if the duke of York refused an official summons to return to London, the 'little duke of Gloucester' would be crowned, under the protectorate of the earl of Northumberland.[70] In the following July, another French ambassador arrived in London to reports that the Independents would set the duke on the throne for a year or two, before declaring a republic.[71] Such rumours were what underpinned Charles I's warning to his youngest son, that he might become 'an instrument' to achieve the 'wicked designs' of Independent grandees, and that if Charles himself was killed 'they might possibly … make him king, that under him, whilst his age would not permit him to judge and act for himself, they might remove many obstructions which lay in their way, and form and unite their councils, and then they would destroy him too'.[72]

Such rumours and stories persisted into the late 1640s, not least as the escape of the duke of York led parliamentarians to reiterate their support for a monarchical government,[73] and as contemporaries noted that 'they have not decided how, by what particular means they shall reach this end and whether they shall have for king … the duke of Gloucester, his third

---

[68] Kent History and Library Centre, Maidstone, U269, C267/14; *Mercurius Aulicus*, 23 (4–10 Oct. 1643), 301–2.

[69] BL, Add. MS 27962K, f. 417; Gardiner, *Hist. Civil War*, ii, 189.

[70] *The Diplomatic Correspondence of Jean de Montereul*, ed. J.G. Fotheringham (2 vols, Edinburgh, 1898–9), i, 117; Gardiner, *Hist. Civil War*, iii, 42–3.

[71] Gardiner, *Hist. Civil War*, iii, 130.

[72] Clarendon, *Hist. Rebellion*, ed. Macray, iv, 252. This was why Charles told the duke not to 'accept or suffer himself to be made king whilst either of his elder brothers lived': Clarendon, *Hist. Rebellion*, ed. Macray, iv, 252.

[73] *Mercurius Elencticus*, 23 (26 Apr.–3 May 1648), 179.

son, eight years of age and who is in their hands'.[74] It might not have been coincidental that on this occasion such stories about the potential for the duke to replace a deposed king emerged at the same time as evidence about the duke's popularity, and in June 1648 one pamphleteer mused that parliament might 'set up Gloucester … as a cipher to please the people'.[75]

By the winter of 1648–9, however, the thinking may have changed somewhat, and the recent revival of interest in the regicide has raised questions about the motives of those involved in the king's trial, and about whether formal proceedings would necessarily end in his execution, let alone to the abolition of monarchy.[76] One result of such debates has been consideration of the possibility that Charles's prosecutors sought, or perhaps threatened, his replacement with the duke of Gloucester, and that this influenced the way in which the king behaved during these crucial weeks. On this account, talk of a Henrician succession represented an attempt to weaken the resolve of the king, who understood that crowning his youngest son would 'entrench grandee parliamentarian interests and put in place a child king in whose name any number of affronts to the ancient constitution might be committed'.[77] Thus, the *Army Remonstrance* intimated that the king could be replaced by another member of his family,[78] and during November 1648 news reports reflected on the possibility – 'some mutter, and it is believed' – that the duke would be set upon the throne, and that during his minority 'great ones will make themselves protectors'.[79] Whitelocke later reflected on a 'secret conclave' that took place in Speaker Lenthall's chamber on 23 December 1648, where the idea resurfaced, and on 6 January 1649 Whitelocke was informed by Ralph Darnall, a parliamentary clerk, that there were stories about people 'drinking to Harry the ninth', even if some believed that such stories and ideas were merely intended to 'fright' the king.[80] Such ideas, of course, were controversial, and it was also noted that many key people would not 'submit' to a crowned duke of Gloucester. Nevertheless, pamphlets from this period certainly claimed that removing the king would require setting up a new monarch, and noted that: 'we have one precious flower and blossom to fix our eyes upon, the duke of Gloucester … who in all probability will speedily be advanced to great honours and dignities, to the great acclamation of the whole kingdom'.[81] As late as 8 January, one report suggested that Gloucester would be kept in custody 'as a reserve in case the prince and duke of York should prevail so far as to raise any considerable party in the kingdom'.[82] Indeed, on 26 January, one well-informed royalist intelligencer noted that the

---

[74] *CSP Ven., 1647–52*, pp. 59–60.

[75] *Cal. Clarendon SP*, ed. Macray et al., i, 318; *Westminster Projects*, 6 (1648), 6.

[76] Sean Kelsey, 'The Trial of Charles I', *English Historical Review*, cxviii (2003), 583–616; Sean Kelsey, 'The Death of Charles I', *Historical Journal*, xlv (2002), 727–54; Sean Kelsey, 'Staging the Trial of Charles I', in *The Regicides and the Execution of Charles I*, ed. Jason Peacey (Basingstoke, 2001), 71–93; Clive Holmes, 'The Trial and Execution of Charles I', *Historical Journal*, liii (2010), 289–316.

[77] Sean Kelsey, ' "The Now King of England": Conscience, Duty and the Death of Charles I', *English Historical Review*, cxxxii (2017), 1099–100.

[78] *A Remonstrance from the Army* (1648), 65–7; *An Abridgment of the Late Remonstrance* (1648), 3, 6.

[79] Bodl., MS Clarendon 31, f. 312; BL, Add. MS 78221, f. 24.

[80] David Underdown, *Pride's Purge: Politics in the Puritan Revolution* (Oxford, 1971), 170, 183; Bulstrode Whitelocke, *Memorials of the English Affairs* (4 vols, Oxford, 1853), iii, 479–81; Longleat House, Wilts., Whitelocke papers, x, f. 1; *Mercurius Pragmaticus*, 40/41 (26 Dec. 1648–9 Jan. 1649), sig. Fff3.

[81] *The Queens Majesties Letter to the Parliament of England* (1649), 3, 5.

[82] Bodl., MS Clarendon 34, f. 72v.

children were to be looked after by Sir Henry Mildmay, with the comment that the king's enemies would not 'exchange a king in their power for a king (meaning the prince) out of their power'.[83] For Sean Kelsey, Charles I's fear that he might be replaced by the young duke might have encouraged him to consider coming to terms with the new regime, and even recognizing the authority of the high court of justice, as perhaps the best way of protecting the monarchy.[84]

The significance of such ideas and stories about a Henrician succession is that they help to make sense of the complex and shifting story of the duke's captivity *after* the regicide. It has been suggested that 'support for the inauguration of a new reign', which might be thought to have been real until the 30 January 1649, 'was not totally eclipsed until the office of king was finally abolished in March 1649', and Kelsey has argued that the determination to prevent a new king from being proclaimed after the regicide reflected concern that this was precisely what might happen by parliamentarians, rather than just royalists.[85] However, having insisted that nobody should be proclaimed king 'without the consent of the people in parliament' – on the very day that the young duke was granted access to his father (7 January 1649) – it seems clear that talk of monarchy, and perhaps even of the duke being crowned, persisted during the entire period that he was held in captivity. Naturally, such an idea would have been profoundly divisive, and as such it is possible that the events relating to the duke's captivity need to be set against the shifting political landscape of republican England, and the waxing and waning of both radical and moderate forces within the republic.

It might be noteworthy that so much of the business relating to the royal children was handled by a small group of powerful grandees, who had been prominent within parliamentarian ranks during the 1640s, who remained prominent during the Rump, and who cannot be regarded as having occupied the radical fringes of contemporary thought. These included Northumberland, his sister, the countess of Leicester, and her son, Lord Lisle, as well as the former courtier, Sir Henry Mildmay, and his brother, Anthony. Sir Henry Mildmay is intriguing as someone who, having opposed a personal treaty with the king in late 1648 – apparently saying that the king was 'no more to be trusted than a lion that had been enraged and let loose again at liberty' – withdrew from the high court of justice in January 1649 and refused to sign the death warrant, but then served on all but one of the republican councils of state. Given the conservatism of this group, it might make sense to suggest that the actions to remove the royal children to Penshurst represented a defensive move prompted by discontent within the army, and debates over the constitution which eventually saw votes to end monarchy (February), and then the passage of an act abolishing the institution, before it was finally resolved that England would be a free state, in May 1649.

It might also be noteworthy that the decision to move the duke to Carisbrooke coincided not just with the with arrival of Charles II in Scotland, and heightened concerns about royalist activity, but also – very precisely – with provocative decisions to destroy statues of Charles I around London, one of which saw 'the head taken off, and the sceptre out of

---

[83] Bodl., MS Clarendon 34, ff. 86–7.

[84] Kelsey, ' "The Now King of England" ', 1098–9, 1100–1, 1104.

[85] Sean Kelsey, 'The Foundation of the Council of State', in *Parliament at Work*, ed. C.R. Kyle and Jason Peacey (Woodbridge, 2002), 138–41; Kelsey, ' "The Now King of England" ', 1100.

his hand', to be replaced by the inscription '*exit tyrannus, regum ultimus, anno primo libertatis Angliae 1648*'. This, too, may have been a defensive move, prompted by both security fears and heightened radicalism, and it is significant that the move to Carisbrooke was made in the face of calls for the duke to be moved beyond the limits of the Commonwealth. Likewise, it seems plausible to argue that moves to release the duke — either by sending him to Scotland or to Heidelberg — reflected the resurgent fortunes of political radicals in the wake of the Battle of Dunbar, not least given the involvement of a radical group of prominent republicans, such as Chaloner, Scot, and Ludlow. Paradoxical as it might seem, it was radicals and republicans who were most obviously involved in attempts to release the duke, and political conservatives who sought to keep him in captivity. However, the logic of both positions can perhaps be rationalised: the former wanted to prevent any possibility of the duke being installed on the throne; the latter may have been considering precisely this option.

Also striking is that another period of radical resurgence — in the wake of the Battle of Worcester in September 1651 — seems to have provoked thoughts in at least some quarters about the desirability of a form of monarchical settlement, and debates that are said to have taken place involving Cromwell, a range of conservative Rumpers (like Whitelocke, Widdrington, and St John), as well as more radical figures from the army (Harrison, Fleetwood, Whalley, and Disborow). On this occasion, Whitelocke claimed that Cromwell asked 'whether a republic or a mixed monarchical government will be best to be settled', and while the soldiers opposed any move towards monarchy, Whitelocke claimed to have said that 'the laws of England are so interwoven with the power and practice of monarchy that to settle a government without something of monarchy in it would make so great an alteration in the proceeding of our law that you have scarce time to rectify nor can we well foresee the inconvenience which will arise thereby'. Cromwell agreed with St John on the desirability of having 'something of monarchical power', noting that 'this will be a business of more than ordinary difficulty', but that 'if it may be done with safety … it would be very effectual'. On this occasion Whitelocke apparently mentioned that the duke of Gloucester was 'still among us, and too young to have been in arms against us, or infected with the principles of our enemies'. At least some of those present supported the idea that the duke should 'be made king'.[86] This meeting — the precise dating of which is unclear — perhaps took place at one of those moments where the possibility of releasing the duke resurfaced, but even more remarkable is the fact that at the precise moment when the council raised the issue of the duke's fate in early September 1652, Cromwell was said to have been preparing to dissolve parliament, call a new representative, and 'by the assistance and countenance of it get the duke of Gloucester to be crowned and himself to be declared protector'.[87] As Worden has noted, nothing came of this idea, 'and the issue of monarchy was quietly dropped', but perhaps it at least helped to provoke the subsequent move to release the duke in the winter of 1652–3, during yet another period when radicalism seemed to be on the rise.[88]

---

[86] Blair Worden, *The Rump Parliament, 1648–1653* (Cambridge, 1974), 276–7; *The Writings and Speeches of Oliver Cromwell*, ed. W.C. Abbott (4 vols, Cambridge, MA, 1937–47), ii, 505–7; Whitelocke, *Memorials*, iii, 372—4; Underdown, *Pride's Purge*, 292.

[87] *Nicholas Papers*, ed. Warner, i, 310.

[88] Worden, *Rump Parliament*, 277.

In other words, it seems plausible to suggest that the complex story of the captivity of the duke of Gloucester reflected divisions over the constitution that continued beyond the spring of 1649, and throughout a period of 'contingency, uncertainty and improvisation'.[89] This saw radicals more or less eager to release him and send him beyond the limits of the Commonwealth, Cromwell at least contemplating some kind of monarchical settlement, and moderate or conservative interests keen to keep him within the Commonwealth, in case an opportunity arose to effect a constitution with 'something of monarchy' in it, even if only a puppet king. Intriguingly, Charles II's anger at the prospect of the duke being educated as a catholic reflected his concern that 'if the report reaches England, or if any schisms or change of government should occur, the fact would forever prevent the return of his family to their hereditary dominions'. Perhaps Charles II, too, entertained the vain hope of seeing the 'little duke' on the English throne.[90]

[89] Kelsey, ' "The Now King of England" ', 1108.
[90] *CSP Ven., 1653–4*, p. 283.

The 'Little Palaces' of St James's: Ladies, Lords, and Political Association under the later Stuarts

FRANCES HARRIS

Clubs, coffee houses, and taverns, the most widely studied sites of political gathering in later Stuart London, largely excluded women. This essay argues that places of 'intermixed conversation' which existed alongside them should also be taken into account, and considers several examples of regular, semi-private assemblies, chiefly hosted by elite women (including duchesse de Mazarin, Lady Pulteney, and Barbara Villiers, Lady Fitzhardinge) and frequented by both sexes for the overt purpose of card playing, which were also significant places of political association at this period.

Keywords: assemblies; card playing; Charles Montagu, Lord Halifax; clubs; coffee houses; duchesse de Mazarin; gambling; Lady Fitzhardinge; Lady Pulteney; Sidney, Lord Godolphin

Historians of political culture under the later Stuarts still admit women rather sparingly; much, in fact, as women themselves were admitted at the time to the Palace of Westminster and the smoke-filled rooms of its nearby taverns, clubs, and coffee houses, the places of political association which have received most attention from historians. When women's political involvement is addressed it is most often as a separate activity; interventions in print culture, patronage, or electioneering, for example.[1] This is surprising, since contemporaries took it for granted that women's *joint* involvement was at least as significant in influencing political action as the predominantly masculine forms of association of the emerging public sphere; James II would never be able to depend on his army to establish Roman catholicism, the Lord Keeper Guilford commented matter-of-factly, because:

> the people would grow upon it or wear it out by their intermixed conversation. Men naturally fall in with parties and their interests among whom they live, and they will not bear the reproaches of their women and pot-companions without falling into harmony with them. That it was utterly impossible to bring the people to reconciliation with his persuasion; and that the more they were urged … the worse they would be.[2]

---

[1] Lois Schwoerer, 'Women and the Glorious Revolution', *Albion*, xviii (1986), 195–218; Ingrid H. Tague, *Women of Quality, Accepting and Contesting Ideals of Feminity 1690–1760* (Woodbridge, 2002), 194–6; Elaine Chalus, '"Ladies are Often Very Good Scaffolding": Women and Politics in the Age of Anne', in *British Politics in the Age of Holmes*, ed. Clyve Jones (Oxford, 2009), 150–65; but see Melina Zook, *Protestantism, Politics, and Women in Britain 1660–1714* (Basingstoke, 2013).

[2] Roger North, *The Lives of … Francis North, Lord Guilford … Sir Dudley North and … Dr John North*, ed. Augustus Jessopp (1890), i, 359.

There were plenty of venues outside the family circle where this conversation could take place. A French visitor to London at the beginning of James II's reign noted that many elite Londoners chose to spend their afternoons and evenings not in taverns and public houses, but at '*maisons particuliers*' in the company of select groups of friends, male and female; this was in contrast, he noted, to continental ritual of formal visiting which the English found tedious and reserved for such occasions as congratulation on marriage or condolence on bereavement.[3] Though the custom among women of fashion of having a 'day' for receiving their circle of male and female acquaintance is usually said to have begun in Queen Anne's reign, already at the Restoration court a number of elite women kept open house for favoured visitors at stated times. When the young Sidney Godolphin complained of not being able to avoid the bad company of the king's bedchamber, his future wife told him to spend more time in 'making thos visits … I hope you will allow to be harmless: I mean [to] my la[dy] Su[nderland], my La[dy] Fa[lmouth], my La[dy] Haryet H[yde], my La[dy] Dutches of Munmouth, my La[dy] Dutches of Buck[ingham]', as well as the Lord Chamberlain and John Harvey, the queen's treasurer, 'when he is not drunk'.[4] Of the women mentioned here, Lady Sunderland and Lady Harriet Hyde were wives of men of ministerial ambition, Lady Falmouth was a high-status court widow and the two duchesses were the wives of notoriously erring husbands concerned to maintain their independent status. They were soon joined by Lady Sophia Bulkeley, younger sister of Frances Stewart, duchess of Richmond, whose upbringing at the court of the queen mother in Paris made her well-practised in salon hospitality, and Arlington's daughter, the duchess of Grafton. Lady Sophia, who was granted the precedence of an earl's daughter to enable her to serve Mary of Modena as lady of the bedchamber, went into exile with her mistress at the revolution, but the duchess of Grafton, whose husband took an active part on William's side but was killed in action shortly afterwards, was prominent in London elite society in her own right before and after her widowhood.

In 1676 there was another notable addition to their number. The Franco-Italian adventuress, Hortense Mancini, duchesse de Mazarin, arrived at court, heralded by her own account in print of the picaresque career which had led to her taking refuge in England. 'All the world knows her storie', John Evelyn commented, 'Niece to the great Cardinal Mazarine & married to the Richest subject in Europ, as is said: she was born at Rome, educated in France, an extraordinary Beauty & Witt, but dissolute, & impatient of Matrimonial restraint, so as to be abandoned by her husband, [and] came to England for shelter.[5] Initially, as a cousin of the duchess of York, Mazarin was lodged in St James's Palace, but when it became clear that she intended to stay indefinitely, the duke of York bought a house that one of his courtiers had built adjacent to St James's Palace, and presented it to her.[6] It was one of a group of rather undistinguished dwellings fronting on the lane which separated the palace from its stableyard; Mazarin's was described as 'a brick tenement … having two clear stories besides cellars and garrets, four rooms of a floor but small and irregularly built, about 40 foot in depth, including a small yard of 10 foot deep in the back part and about 60

[3] Marquis d'Auvers, *Un Voyageur Français à Londres en 1685*, ed. Georges Roth (Paris, 1968), 70–1.

[4] BL, Add. MS 79501, f. 98: Margaret Blagge to Sidney Godolphin, 'Friday night' [Sept.–Oct. 1673?].

[5] John Evelyn, *Diary*, ed. E.S. de Beer (6 vols, Oxford, 1955), iv, 97; v, 330; '*The Wandering Life I Led*': *Essays on Hortense Mancini, Duchess Mazarin*, ed. Susan Shifrin (Newcastle upon Tyne, 2009), esp. 2–47.

[6] '*Wandering Life*', ed. Shifrin, 164, 195; HMC, *Rutland MSS*, 28–9.

foot in front'. The houses on either side were occupied by one of the duchess's bedchamber women, Margaret Dawson, afterwards a conspicuous jacobite, and by Christian Harrell, a doctor of medicine, 'but of what university is not known', who attended Charles II and Nell Gwyn on their deathbeds, while opposite lived Eleanor Oglethorpe, a former servant of the duchess of Portsmouth who also served James II as an occasional clandestine mistress.[7] Nevertheless, Mazarin's house was soon a well-known place of resort and 'the end of the Walk by Madam Mazarine's lodgings', a place of assignation no one could mistake.[8] The émigré Saint-Évremond, 'the most famous Frenchman in England' and one of her most regular visitors, dubbed it '*le petit palais*'. It has been called the nearest thing in England to a Parisian salon and quite unique.[9] In fact it was rather more raffish than a salon and except perhaps for its cosmopolitanism, by no means unique.

It was Mrs Jane Middleton, rather than the higher-ranking court hostesses already mentioned, who emerged as Mazarin's chief rival. In contrast to the exotic duchesse, Jane Middleton was the archetypal English beauty, 'all white and golden'. Her relations with the men who paid their homage at her house in Charles Street (among them the chief treasury minister, Laurence Hyde, earl of Rochester) were matter for gossip.[10] But the real nature of the competition between the two women is better caught by another letter from Margaret Godolphin to her husband:

> I dined at my Lady Sunderland's yesterday, where I saw M St Evremont, who did not know me, upon which my Lord Sunderland raileyd him much and told him he did those things on purpose to make a sacrifice to Madam Mazerin, at which M de Reveney [Henri Massue de Ruvigny, afterwards earl of Galway] who was ther also, was much deverted for he is all for Mrs Midleton and was glad to see one that had forsaken her so treated.[11]

What had begun as a friendly rivalry between two contrasting beauties was soon an indicator of political allegiances. Mazarin was so unnerved by anti-catholic hostility during the Exclusion Crisis that at one point she considered leaving the country, while Jane Middleton, whose sister, Eleanor Needham, was the long-standing mistress of the duke of Monmouth, sided with the proto-whigs and became so outspoken a critic of the court that the queen finally ordered her out of the drawing room. 'Her answer was, that she would go out, & that she would never see her again till she could see her in the Presses of Westminster for two pence', the duchess of Marlborough remembered years later, adding that 'this Answer in those times was approv'd of much'.[12]

During the reign of James II, Mazarin's position was protected, but after the revolution her fortunes declined. She was not required to leave the country, but she did have to quit St James's. Increasingly in debt, she moved first to Kensington, then to a small house in Chelsea, maintaining herself by keeping it as a private gambling establishment, where a

[7] '*Wandering Life*', ed. Shifrin, 84, 197; Arthur Dasent, *The Story of Stafford House* (1921), 24–6.
[8] Gesa Stedman, *Cultural Exchange in Seventeenth Century France and England* (Farnham, 2013), 98.
[9] '*Wandering Life*', ed. Shifrin, 170–1.
[10] S.M. Wynne, 'Jane Myddelton [*née* Needham]', *ODNB*.
[11] BL, Add. MS 79501, f. 102: Margaret Godolphin to Sidney Godolphin, 31 May [1678].
[12] BL, Add. MS 63650, f. 70: Sarah, duchess of Marlborough, to Lady Longueville, 18 Mar. 1729.

set-price dinner was provided along with access to the gaming tables. She drew some of her former habitués after her: Saint-Evremond, Lord Galway, and Ralph, Lord Montagu among them. Godolphin, the most durable treasury minister of his generation, commonly dined there as well, it was noticed, 'paid his half guinea' and spent the rest of the day at play. It was not until after Mazarin's death in 1699 that he returned to the West End, frequenting the similar establishment at the Pall Mall house of the country MP, Sir Henry Dutton Colt, at this period a bachelor whose niece apparently kept house for him.[13]

Not far away in St James's Street, the large house of Grace, Lady Pulteney, widow of the West End property developer, Sir William Pulteney, was a similar place of resort. The jacobite, Lord Ailesbury, a regular visitor in James II's reign, recalled an evening spent there in 1692 in company with Sunderland, Shrewsbury, Godolphin, Romney, and Sir Thomas Felton:

> During the play I sat most of the time by the fire with Mr Henry Guy, a substantial good friend of the house, and Secretary of the Treasury, and we being old friends in the former reigns, we continued the same, and talking over many things he owned to me that King Charles the Second in his most profuse time spent not on the Civil List far to what the present King [William] did … The cards money generally defrayed the supper, and what we had heretofore and now this night was neat and good, and we were very merry at supper, and all most obliging to me.[14]

Henry Guy, a childless bachelor, had been Pulteney's business partner and his devotion to Pulteney's wife was common knowledge.[15] In due course he adopted their children as his heirs, with what far-reaching consequences is clear when it is remembered that this fortune helped William Pulteney, earl of Bath, to establish himself as Walpole's chief opponent. Ailesbury's account also makes quite explicit the way in which these gatherings differed from simple private hospitality. Mazarin, whose finances were always precarious, made her house into a private gambling establishment in order to keep herself, but even a wealthy widow such as Lady Pulteney expected the gatherings at her house to be self-financing. It is also clear that 'play' was not the only, or even their chief purpose; rather the house provided a safe meeting place in uncertain times for political associates of very differing allegiances, where they could speak freely without being observed or overheard. It is a neat illustration of the interpenetration of public and private at such places, that after Lady Pulteney's death in 1704 her son leased the house to a vintner and it became the Thatched House Tavern.[16]

Meanwhile Mazarin's house adjoining St James's Palace had kept its function under a different hostess. After the revolution the nominal leaseholder was William Cavendish, duke of Devonshire.[17] Described as 'the finest and handsomest gentleman of his time, [who] loves the ladies and play', he bestowed Mazarin's old dwelling on Barbara Villiers, Lady

---

[13] 'Wandering Life', ed. Shifrin, 184; C.H. Hartmann, *The Vagabond Duchess* (1926), 263; BL, Add. MS 9199, f. 85: notes by Henry Etough; *The History of Parliament: The House of Commons, 1690–1715*, ed. Eveline Cruickshanks, Stuart Handley and D.W. Hayton (5 vols, Cambridge, 2002) [hereafter cited as *HPC, 1690–1715*], iii, 654–5.

[14] *Memoirs of Thomas, Earl of Ailesbury Written by Himself* (Roxburghe Club, 1890), 303–4.

[15] BL, Stowe MS 751, f. 129: Sarah, duchess of Marlborough to James Craggs, 1 Sept. 1716.

[16] *The Parish of St James Westminster, Part I*, ed. F.H.W. Sheppard (Survey of London, xxix, 1960), 466.

[17] 'Wandering Life', ed. Shifrin, 197; TNA, E 367/3582: lease to Devonshire of a house and grounds near St James's Palace, 1692–3.

Fitzhardinge, governess of Princess Anne's son, sister of the king's mistress, Betty Villiers, and reputedly his own mistress;[18] it appears that part of his lodgings as lord steward at Windsor was made over to her as well.[19] 'As witty and pleasant lady as any in England', she was married to an MP, 'a man of wit and pleasant conversation' in his own right, who had something of a reputation as a critic and a dramatist.[20] Their two daughters also became noted wits and beauties, the eldest, married in 1706 to Walter Chetwynd MP, later becoming a noted assembly hostess herself.[21] This constellation of personalities ensured that the '*petit palais*' of St James's remained a natural gathering place for men and women with the same interest in wit and politics.

As in Mazarin's time there were always card tables; the tory satirist, Delarivier Manley, described Lady Fitzhardinge as 'a handsome, hospitable lady that keeps a bank and cards for all idle and avaricious people, either to sling away or improve their money'.[22] Sometimes there would be dancing and music as well, though the latter might be nothing more sophisticated than ballad singing ('let me make the ballads of a nation, and I care not who makes the laws', Andrew Fletcher of Saltoun was reported to have said). Of the Kit-Cats, Devonshire, Halifax, Congreve, and Maynwaring were habitués; among the women the duchess of Marlborough mentions Lady Oxford and her daughter, the duchess of St Albans, Lady Sandwich, Jane Hammond (wife of Anthony Hammond MP and later sister-in-law of the Fitzhardinge's younger daughter), and a certain Mrs Ramsay. Lady Sandwich was the daughter of John Wilmot, earl of Rochester, who had been left effectively independent by the mental incapacity of her husband and was more than capable of sustaining this position in any society; Saint-Evremond thought she had 'more wit than her father had' and Lord Chesterfield, who knew her in old age, described her as having 'the strongest parts of any woman I ever knew in my life'.[23] Mrs Ramsay had been companion to the duchess of Grafton before the duchess's remarriage in middle age to the tory MP, Sir Thomas Hanmer, when she appears to have transferred to Lady Fitzhardinge's household. Of Dutch extraction and the widow of a high-ranking Scots army officer, she was one of a group of 'female wits' (the whig friends, Anne Long and Catherine Barton among them), who remain rather shadowy figures because they left no writings to be recovered by later feminist scholars: independent women, who were equally at home in male or female society. Mrs Ramsay became a friend of Swift among others.[24]

Sarah, duchess of Marlborough, and Barbara Fitzhardinge had been intimate friends in their young days, so much so that at one point Anne became acutely jealous of 'that

[18] *Poems on Affairs of State; Augustan Satirical Verse 1660–1714*, ed. G. deForest Lord *et al.* (7 vols, New Haven, CT, 1963–75), vi, 158; *The London Diaries of William Nicolson, Bishop of Carlisle, 1702–1718*, ed. Clyve Jones and Geoffrey Holmes (Oxford, 1985), 267 (which confirms the identity of the house by mentioning that Queen Anne was able to observe the parade of French standards captured at the Battle of Blenheim from the window as it filed through St James's stable-yard).

[19] *The Marlborough-Godolphin Correspondence*, ed. Henry L. Snyder (3 vols, Oxford, 1975), iii, 1110.

[20] Jenkin Lewis, *Memoirs of Prince William Henry, Duke of Glocester* (1789), 27; *HPC, 1690–1715*, iii, 187–9; Delarivier Manley, *The New Atalantis*, ed. Ros Ballaster (1991), 111.

[21] *The Tatler*, ed. G.A. Aitken (3 vols, 1898), i, 378.

[22] Manley, *New Atalantis*, 111.

[23] Bernard Falk, *The Way of the Montagues* [1947], 289–300.

[24] *Marlborough-Godolphin Correspondence*, ed. Snyder, ii, 688–9; *The Correspondence of Sir Thomas Hanmer …*, ed. Sir Henry Bunbury (1838), 102.

enchantress', as she dubbed her son's governess. But once Sarah's daughters were grown-up she distanced herself and tried to make them do so too, on the grounds that although Lady Fitzhardinge 'had a great deal of wit and humour that was diverting, her house was a dangerous place for young people'. Though Marlborough supported her, the daughters resisted. The eldest, Lady Harriet Godolphin, reminded her mother that Lady Fitzhardinge was 'one that people you think best of are very often with', and this was quite true. Godolphin left the treasury secretary, William Lowndes, to 'ply his coffee-house' before an important division in the house of commons, while he himself continued to frequent the *'petit palais'* just across the lane from his own house (formerly that of Eleanor Oglethorpe, which he had taken over and enlarged early in William's reign), and so did the duke of Marlborough as well, during the winters he was in England.[25] Lady Sunderland admitted that the conversation at Lady Fitzhardinge's was not always 'very desent'; nevertheless, 'I should be apt to differ with Papa in our never going there but as a formal visit, for when every body does play there some times, it does but get one a vast many Enemies to put oneself upon a foot above every body els.'[26]

Halifax might frequent Lady Fitzhardinge's on occasion, but he had his own plans for promoting 'intermixed conversation'. A brilliant, cultivated, but physically rather unprepossessing man, he had retired from the treasury to the post of auditor of the exchequer in 1699 and proceeded to remodel the auditor's house in New Palace Yard as a place of sophisticated hospitality, with a fine staircase, dining room, private concert room, and a library gallery furnished with Italian paintings and statuary which was described by one visitor as the most 'completely satisfactory in its kind' he had ever seen. Halifax's intention was to make it the headquarters for an 'assembly of *beaux esprits*' and a venue for the musical events which were another important form of intermixed partisan gathering; while the tories favoured the Italian, Marguerite L'Epine ('Margarita's singing assembled them, and a court whisper has broke 'em', St John commented of Godolphin's victory over the tory leaders early in Anne's reign), the whigs patronised her professional rival, Catherine Tofts, a Scotswoman who had been brought up in the household of Gilbert Burnet, bishop of Salisbury.[27] Whatever Halifax's much-debated relations with Catherine Barton, they were not such as to give the bishops and City men any qualms about accepting his hospitality. 'He had great interest in the city and used to make great entertainments, but always for some good purpose and they were extremely well-performed', the duchess of Marlborough testified, 'This got him a great many friends even among the ladies.' These might be moveable feasts on occasion, as when he and the duchess planned to take 'two coaches of ballad singers' on a summer visit to Lord Bradford's Twickenham house: 'if Your Grace will

[25] Sir Tresham Lever, *Godolphin: His Life and Times* (1951), 150–1; Henry L. Snyder, 'The Defeat of the Occasional Conformity Bill and the Tack', *Bulletin of the Institute of Historical Research*, xli (1968), 175; *Marlborough-Godolphin Correspondence*, ed. Snyder, i, 129; ii, 690.

[26] BL, Add. MS 61442, ff. 22–5: Lady Sunderland to duchess of Marlborough, 3, 6 Oct. [1707?]; in the correspondence of Queen Anne and Sarah Lady Fitzhardinge was nicknamed 'the Nag's Head', probably in reference to the famous tavern in the Haymarket: see David Green, *Sarah, Duchess of Marlborough* (1967), 64, and C.L. Kingsford, *The Early History of Piccadilly, Leicester Square [and] Soho* (Cambridge, 1925), 93.

[27] *London Diaries of William Nicolson*, ed. Jones and Holmes, 146; Susan Spens, *George Stepney 1663–1707: Diplomat and Poet* (Cambridge, 1997), 309; Frances Harris, *The General in Winter: The Marlborough-Godolphin Friendship and the Reign of Anne* (Oxford, 2017), 140; Olive Baldwin and Thelma Wilson, 'The Harmonious Unfortunate: New Light on Catherine Tofts', *Cambridge Opera Journal*, xxii (2011), 217–34.

take care of the land service I will charge myself with providing hautbois, crimp cards and barges'.[28]

Card playing continued to be an invariable part of these gatherings, whether in the form of games of skill and strategy such as the fashionable crimp, or high-stakes games of chance such as basset, said to have been introduced into England by a croupier who worked for Mazarin.[29] The establishment of a basset table in a private house effectively made it a place of public resort; in Susanna Centlivre's *The Basset-Table* of 1705, Lady Reveller, 'a coquettish widow' living in the house of her uncle Sir Richard Plainman, is berated by him:

> Can you who keeps a Basset Table, a public gaming-house, be insensible of the shame on't? I have often told you how much the vast concourse of people which day and night make my house their rendezvous incommode my health. Your apartment is a parade of men of all ranks, from the duke to the fiddler ... everyone has his several ends in meeting there, from the lord to the sharper, each has his separate interests to pursue.[30]

In this respect there was little distinction between a private house and the predominantly masculine haunts of the public sphere. 'The clubs and coffee-houses and cabaret [tavern] meetings are infected', Delarivier Manley lamented, 'If gambling thus obtain, down with the nurseries of liberal arts ... for who would study to write, when there are found none to hear or read? ... if empty theatres be his reward, a solitary house his laurel, whilst each gaming table's crowded to the brim'; women were becoming 'neglectful mothers' and 'insupportable wives', 'exchanging all their charms for gold to lavish at the basset table'; 'such is the infatuation that even the busy and the wise ... are possessed'.[31]

Though later in the 18th century a young Horace Walpole professed himself shocked at the numbers of aristocratic women in Paris who lived off the profits of private gambling establishments, there had clearly been prominent examples in London for years. The concern was that professional gamesters or sharpers might infiltrate these venues, preying on the inexperienced to the point of weakening the government.[32] In 1709, the newly-established *Tatler* devoted several issues to this evil and the following winter, parliament began to take an interest. Prudent hostesses had an eye to these developments. From her house in St James's Square early in 1710, Lady Hervey scribbled a note to her husband: 'This opera is done so early that I shall play at Crimp after; therefore I desire you woud ask Lord Treasurer and Lord Carlisle, and, if either of them fail, the Duke of Bolton or Lord Ryalton'; and she added the postscript: 'Pray send me an answer to this, and how the Gaming bill has gone.'[33] In fact to some, gaming had simply become an analogue of politics. Godolphin was well known as an expert gamester; when out of office towards the end of William's

[28] Harris, *General in Winter*, 146; *The London Letters of Samuel Molyneux, 1712–13*, ed. Paul Holden and Anne Saunders (London Topographical Society, clxxii, 2011), 43–4; BL, Add. MS 61458, f. 177: Halifax to Sarah, duchess of Marlborough, [early 1705].

[29] David Parlett, *History of Card Games* (Oxford, 1990), 77; Hartmann, *Vagabond Duchess*, 230.

[30] Susanna Centlivre, *The Basset Table*, act 1, scene i.

[31] Manley, *New Atalantis*, 187.

[32] Donna T. Andrew, *Aristocratic Vice: The Attack on Duelling, Suicide, Adultery and Gambling in Eighteenth Century England* (New Haven, CT, 2013), 178–89, esp. 182.

[33] *Letter-Books of John Hervey, First Earl of Bristol* ... (3 vols, Wells, 1894), i, 265.

reign he had depended on his winnings for a good part of his income.[34] In mixed company he favoured crimp, an early variant of poker in which victory would go to the player who, by 'his composed countenance, and subtle manner of overawing the other', could make his hand out to be better than it was.[35] Maynwaring called Godolphin's strategy of playing one party off against another a kind of crimp, and one of Harley's nicknames for him was 'the sharper'.[36]

Gaming might be common to all these gatherings, but their essential purpose remained the same: the exchange of news, gossip and opinion, the rallying of supporters and the disparagement of opponents, with the women as much engaged as the men; 'we swarmed with politic would-bes of the female sex', Ailesbury commented sardonically.[37] A private venue simply meant that the company would be more select and the talk more confidential, with card tables sometimes providing a cover for high-level strategy meetings; in September 1710, Sunderland, having been closeted with Wharton, 'came out among the gamesters very sanguin' (though on no good grounds, as it turned out) about the whigs' election prospects.[38] Of course, none of the coffee houses and few of the clubs, still less the private assemblies, were institutions of record. But the glimpses and snatches we do have of what went on at the latter are suggestive: Mrs Ramsay's uninhibited talk of the Hanoverian court's discontent at Queen Anne's refusal to invite them to England which was significant enough to cause Godolphin uneasiness;[39] the duchess of Marlborough entertaining the company at Lady Fitzhardinge's 'by telling them what a godly praying idiot the queen was', and naïvely imagining it would go no further;[40] Maynwaring taking his cue to begin a ballad-mongering campaign against Abigail Masham ('from the time I heard you mention it I have thought of nothing else', he scribbled to the duchess of Marlborough afterwards).[41] When Lady Fitzhardinge died unexpectedly in October 1708 she had no single successor. Instead, her clientele dispersed to a proliferation of rival assemblies: Lady Hervey's and the duchess of Marlborough's in opposition to those of the duchess of Shrewsbury, Lady Betty Germain, and Lady Masham herself.[42]

As with so much else in this divided society, the issue of 'intermixed conversation' polarised opinion. Men who frequented these assemblies and paid court to their hostesses were liable to be called foppish and effeminate, while they, in turn, blamed excluders of

[34] Harris, *General in Winter*, 83.

[35] Parlett, *Card Games*, 85, 103. Crimp, though often mentioned in literary sources, is not included in standard English gaming manuals; I am grateful to Edward Copisarow and Thierry de Paulis for the information that it originated in Germany and was a three-card 'vying' game related to brag (and the French brelan), and later poker.

[36] Harris, *General in Winter*, 254, 235.

[37] *Ailesbury Memoirs*, 307. For two striking examples, see Frances Harris, 'Revolution Correspondence: Elizabeth Packer Geddes and Elizabeth Burnet', in *Women, Identities and Communities in Early Modern Europe*, ed. Stephanie Tarbin and Susan Broomhall (Aldershot, 2008), 171–7.

[38] *Marlborough-Godolphin Correspondence*, ed. Snyder, iii, 1631–2.

[39] *Marlborough-Godolphin Correspondence*, ed. Snyder, ii, 688–9.

[40] *Bishop Burnet's History of His Own Time* (6 vols, Oxford, 1833), v, 454: Dartmouth's note.

[41] BL, Add. MS 61459, ff. 32, 41: Maynwaring to Sarah, duchess of Marlborough, [22 Apr., 1 May 1708].

[42] *The Wentworth Papers 1705–1739 ...*, ed. J.J. Cartwright (1883), 208; *The Correspondence of Sir James Clavering*, ed. H.T. Dickinson (Surtees Society, clxxviii, 1967), 103; Hannah Greig, *The Beau Monde: Fashionable Society in Georgian London* (Oxford, 2013), 38–9.

women for the degeneration of conversation and manners since the time of Charles I.[43] But it goes without saying that men such as Halifax, Maynwaring, and Godolphin did not frequent Lady Fitzhardinge's house to play Witwoud and Petulant to her Lady Wishfort or her daughter's Millamant; nor did her assemblies (or Mazarin's, or Lady Pulteney's) in any way aspire to Caroline high-mindedness. But then neither, it has been pointed out, were clubs, taverns and coffee houses always the scenes of civilized and rational debate they aspired to be and have sometimes been represented.[44] What they all were in their different ways were venues of cultural and political significance in a divided society which well understood how to make use of the fluid boundaries between the public and the private and the parts women might play there. It is time for historians to follow suit.

[43] Brian Cowan, 'What Was Masculine about the Public Sphere? Gender and the Coffeehouse Milieu in Post-Restoration England', *History Workshop Journal*, li (2001), 127–57; Jonathan Swift, 'Hints Towards an Essay on Conversation', in *The Prose Writings of Jonathan Swift*, ed. Herbert Davis *et al.* (16 vols, Oxford, 1939–74), iv, 94–5.

[44] Mark Knights, *Representation and Misrepresentation in Later Stuart Britain: Partisanship and Political Culture* (Oxford, 2004), 248–56.

Republicans, Unionists and Jacobites: The 1st Marquess of Tweeddale and the Restoration of the British Parliament[*]

GRAHAM TOWNEND

Although John Hay, 1st marquess of Tweeddale, contributed significantly to both the ruthless overthrow of Charles I, and the establishment of the first British parliament in the 1650s, most of his political career was concerned with attempting to re-establish this parliament after it was dissolved at the restoration of Charles II. His first attempt ended in defeat at the hands of the king and the duke of Lauderdale in 1670, but following the overthrow of James VII and II in 1688, Tweeddale tried to persuade the prince of Orange to unite Scotland and England. The prince, however, showed much more interest in securing the crown of Scotland than uniting the two kingdoms. Tweeddale, as lord high commissioner to the Scottish parliament in 1695, responded by passing legislation designed to provoke the English parliament into accepting union. He was also engaged in a jacobite intrigue to restore King James. Tweeddale intended that the restored monarch would be little more than a puppet, who could be used to legitimise what was effectively a republican regime in all but name. By this means the restored parliament would avoid the unpopularity which brought down the first British parliament in 1660. Tweeddale's scheme came to nought, but the technique he employed to manipulate the English parliament, and exploit the jacobite threat, contributed to the restoration of the British parliament ten years after his death.

Keywords: British parliament; Company of Scotland; jacobitism; James Johnston; John, Lord Somers; King James VII and II; King William II and III; marquess of Tweeddale; republicanism; Scottish parliament; union of England and Scotland; unionism; 2nd earl of Sunderland; 3rd duke of Hamilton

In his published articles and editions of political correspondence, Clyve Jones has made a very important contribution to the study of the development of British politics in the years immediately after the union of England and Scotland. Encouraged by the late Geoffrey Holmes, Clyve spent many years researching in public and private archives in Scotland. His mastery of these sources enabled him to demonstrate not only the importance of the Scottish dimension in British politics after 1707, but also that a familiarity with the rich material in Scottish archives is essential to understanding political changes in England at this time. Although Clyve's work has been primarily concerned with the years after the Union, the rich manuscript evidence in Scottish archives can be also used to demonstrate the development of British politics before 1707.

[*]I would like to thank David Brown and David Hayton for their comments on an earlier draft of this essay. Punctuation and spelling has been modernised in quotations. Unless otherwise stated, all dates are in old style.

While historians have noted the marquess of Tweeddale's involvement in the history of the British parliament, there has been little attempt to examine his contribution in any detail. William Ferguson observed in 1977, when writing about the unsuccessful union attempt of 1670, that: 'Tweeddale was keen on a union and may indeed have introduced the idea to the king; and certainly it is suggestive that the estrangement between Lauderdale and Tweeddale dates from the middle of the subsequent negotiations.'[1] Almost 30 years later, Christopher Whatley and Derek Patrick noted that after the Glorious Revolution 'the initial move for a union seems to have been made at the end of 1688, initiated by the marquess of Tweeddale who ... had been involved in the abortive negotiations for a union in 1670'.[2] Whatley and Patrick added a little more detail to this in a subsequent article, when they observed that Tweeddale 'was behind an address from East Lothian' in 1689 urging the prince of Orange to promote the union of England and Scotland.[3] Maurice Lee has also examined Tweeddale's connection with Lauderdale. As well as confirming Ferguson's suspicion that the failure of the union negotiations in 1670 marked a turning point in the relationship between Tweeddale and Lauderdale, Lee also provided a brief, but very perceptive, assessment of Tweeddale. He observed that

> since his days as a member of the parliaments of the Protectorate Tweeddale had believed in union ... He never stopped believing in it. When union again looked to be possible in the wake of the revolution of 1689 he pushed hard for it, only to be defeated by English indifference. He did not live to see it come about, but it seems likely that he would have applauded it, and been a far more effective advocate than his well-meaning but inept son.[4]

While acknowledging the significance of Lee's verdict, this essay will suggest that overall it was Tweeddale who made the most important contribution to both the establishment of the British parliament under Cromwell and its restoration in 1707.

When Charles I came to Scotland for his coronation in 1633, he visited Seton Palace in East Lothian where he met John Hay, Lord Yester, the seven-year-old son of the 1st earl of Tweeddale. Looking at the boy, the king 'took special notice of him, and kissing him said God make you a better man than your father'.[5] The king's hopes were tragically unfulfilled. After the shattering royalist defeats in the first civil war, Charles left Oxford and surrendered himself to his Scottish enemies at Newark. He was then sent north to Newcastle where he was held prisoner. During his confinement the king

> was pleased to allow the Master of Yester several opportunities of speaking to him, and upon his return from Scotland, from a meeting of the assembly there, he took account

---

[1] William Ferguson, *Scotland's Relations with England: A Survey to 1707* (Edinburgh, 1977), 155.

[2] C.A. Whatley with Derek Patrick, *The Scots and the Union* (Edinburgh, 2006), 91.

[3] D.J. Patrick and C.A. Whatley, 'Persistence, Principle and Patriotism in the Making of the Union of 1707: The Revolution, the Scottish Parliament and the *Squadrone Volante*', *History*, xcii (2007), 172.

[4] Maurice Lee jr, *'Dearest Brother': Lauderdale, Tweeddale and Scottish Politics, 1660–1674* (Edinburgh, 2010), 244–5.

[5] National Library of Scotland [hereafter cited as NLS], MS 7109, f. 1.

of all matters in that country from him, and used to call him ruling elder, especially after the king's hearing a sermon talking with him about it as he liked and disliked it.[6]

Yester had already shown his capacity for betrayal, when he abandoned the royalist forces for the parliamentarian army at the Battle of Marston Moor in 1644, and having spoken to the king, he returned to Scotland, where he misled the Scottish parliament into believing that the king wanted the Scots to raise an army and invade England. On Yester's suggestion, parliament agreed 'that an army should be raised for rescuing the king and bringing him to London with honour, freedom, and safety, which was called the engagement'.[7]

Seemingly this was 'the greatest and best army that ever was raised in Scotland, and best provided with money, in which army the Lord Yester had the regiment of foot of East Lothian and Tweeddale, being thirteen hundred men'.[8] Carlisle was chosen as the rendezvous for the Scots army, but while the troops under his command marched towards north-west England, at Selkirk 'my Lord Yester, having gone so far with his regiment was necessitated to return home to his lady at the Neidpath'.[9] After his wife had given birth to a son, and the child was christened, Yester prepared to join the army again, but 'the news of the defeat of the Scots at Preston, a few days after their entering England, prevented his going'.[10] The Scottish invasion of England provided the New Model Army with the pretext it required for demanding that the king be executed for waging war on the people of England.

Having helped to depose King Charles I, Yester and his associates then turned their attention to the prince of Wales, then in exile on the continent. Sir Archibald Johnston of Wariston encouraged Prince Charles to come to Scotland, and Yester spent much time ingratiating himself into his favour. The prince was crowned King Charles II at Scone Palace 'with all possible solemnity, my Lord Yester being one that carried the pale from the house to the church'.[11] Another army was raised for a second invasion of England, but Yester, again, avoided accompanying it. Instead he took refuge in the Highlands with his family. They were subsequently sent home while he remained in hiding until he eventually heard that 'the Scots army was defeated at Worcester and the king had escaped, as was thought to France, and the duke of Hamilton killed and the rest of the nobility of Scotland taken prisoners'.[12] Yester remained in hiding until his wife obtained permission for him to return home from the parliamentarian army in Scotland. Lady Yester 'wrote to Colonel Fenwick (from whom she had a pass when she came south) that she might have on[e] to her lord, who was disposed to come home, which, with little difficulty was procured and sent to her'.[13]

The leaders of the republican regime in England responded to these successive invasions, instigated by Yester and his associates, with 'a tender of an union of the people of Scotland

---

[6]NLS, MS 7109, f. 9.
[7]NLS, MS 7109, f. 10.
[8]NLS, MS 7109, ff. 10–11.
[9]NLS, MS 7109, f. 11.
[10]NLS, MS 7109, f. 11.
[11]NLS, MS 7109, f. 14.
[12]NLS, MS 7109, f. 16.
[13]NLS, MS 7109, f. 17.

into one commonwealth with England sent down with commissioners, who residing at Dalkeith, issued their orders to the several shires to send commissioners in their names to consent to the tender of this union, which being generally agreed to there was an act of union published'.[14]

When Oliver Cromwell summoned the third parliament of the three kingdoms, which met on 17 September 1656, Yester, who had succeeded his father as 2nd earl of Tweeddale, 'was chosen commissioner for the shire of East Lothian, being much pressed by the generality of his friends and acquaintance'.[15] Two years later he was, again, present in the house of commons, on 27 January 1658, for the meeting of Richard Cromwell's parliament of both nations and at the end of January 1659, was listed among the Scots members 'elected to serve in the present parliament now assembled at Westminster'.[16]

Although the British parliament was dissolved at the return of Charles II in 1660, Tweeddale wanted it restored as soon as possible. Unfortunately for him the king did not share his urgency, but eventually in the summer of 1669, Tweeddale went to London where the king 'having called some of his privy councillors of both kingdoms did communicate to them the desire he had of a nearer and more complete union of his kingdoms of Scotland and England'.[17] As a preliminary, the Scottish parliament was summoned to meet at Edinburgh on 19 October 1669. When the king's letter to parliament was read that day, it recommended the 'bringing of these two kingdoms of Scotland and England to as close and strict an union as is possible'[18] as the best way to promote the happiness of his people. Having considered the letter, parliament expressed, on 31 October, its 'hearty concurrence' with the proposed union, and willingness to appoint commissioners to negotiate with their English counterparts.[19] The Scottish parliament was then adjourned.

When it met again, on 22 July 1670, the king's letter announced that the English parliament had appointed commissioners to negotiate a union and reminded the Scots that they had already expressed their willingness to do likewise. On 30 July, the Scottish parliament passed an act 'authorising certain commissioners of the kingdom of Scotland to treat with commissioners of England for the well of both Kingdoms'.[20]

Tweeddale was appointed one of the Scottish commissioners, but before they met at London he 'was commanded by the king to go to Glasgow to attend the meeting between Archbishop Leighton, and some of his clergy with others of the Presbyterian persuasion'.[21] This conference achieved little, but it meant that Tweeddale missed the first five meetings of the Scottish and English commissioners in the exchequer chamber at Westminster and also at Somerset House. Tweeddale attended the meetings at Somerset House on 20 and 22 October, but then, much to his dismay, witnessed the collapse of the negotiations on 1 November.

[14] NLS, MS 7109, f. 11.

[15] NLS, MS 7109, f. 11.

[16] *Acts of the Parliaments of Scotland* (12 vols, Edinburgh, 1824) [hereafter cited as *APS*], vi, pt 2, p. 778.

[17] NLS, MS 7109, f. 30.

[18] *APS*, vii, 551.

[19] *APS*, vii, 553.

[20] *APS*, viii, 6.

[21] NLS, MS 7109, f. 30.

When Lauderdale communicated the agreement of the Scottish commissioners to the king's proposal, presented to the commissioners on 17 September 1670, for 'reducing of both parliaments into One',[22] the English lord keeper, Sir Orlando Bridgeman, asked what proportion of Scots would sit in the united parliament. Lauderdale's answer was that, as the Scots commissioners 'came to this treaty by the authority of the parliament of Scotland and were named by his Majesty … they did not see how their number shall be less than now it is in the parliament of Scotland',[23] to which Bridgeman replied that the Scots 'having proposed a thing which the commissioners for England could not expect, it would be fit to take some time to consider thereof'.[24]

Although the commissioners were due to meet again on 8 November, it was clear that the English would not accept the incorporation of the entire Scottish parliament into the new assembly, so the king intervened and ordered an adjournment until the end of March 1671. This effectively terminated the attempt to unite Scotland and England. Angry and frustrated by this disappointment, Tweeddale had to endure 17 years of dissatisfaction until another opportunity presented itself, with the prince of Orange's invasion of England in November 1688 forcing King James VII and II into exile in France.

Writing from Edinburgh on 1 January 1689, Tweeddale informed his eldest son, Lord Yester, that:

by the last post on Saturday I sent you the address of East Lothian to the prince of Orange under a cover to Mr Fouls with 53 hands at it, whereof 21 are burgesses and 32 gentlemen. You are desired to get all the hands you can to it and to carry as many of those of the shire who are there as you think fit with you to the presenting it.[25]

Tweeddale had drawn up a rough draft of the address which urged the prince to

take it into your consideration by what ways and means these kingdoms of Scotland and England may be united in a more strict and inseparable union than they have been as yet, that we be not hereafter left open by the advantage may be taken of our distinct and different laws and customs and exercise of government.[26]

A more formal copy was then drafted and sent to Yester at London.

On 8 January 1689, Yester informed his father that after receiving the East Lothian address he had made great efforts to add further signatures to it and, on the evening of 2 January had 'waited on … as the prince came from supper, having Ormiston and Gosford with me, and gave it withal telling his highness that when he had read it if he thought it for his service that the heads were put in the Gazette his order should be obeyed'.[27]

[22] *The Cromwellian Union* … , ed. C.S. Terry (Scottish History Society, xl, Edinburgh, 1902), 197.
[23] *Cromwellian Union*, ed. Terry, 206.
[24] *Cromwellian Union*, ed. Terry, 206.
[25] NLS, MS 7026, f. 98: [Tweeddale] to [Lord Yester], 1 Jan. 1689.
[26] NLS, MS 7026, f. 94b: 'The humble address of the noblemen, gentlemen and royal burghs within the shire of East Lothian'; see also MS 7026, f. 94a.
[27] NLS, Mf. MS 192: [Yester] to Tweeddale, 8 Jan. 1689.

While waiting for the prince's response, Tweeddale began lobbying prominent English politicians about the possibility of uniting Scotland and England. Writing from Edinburgh on 29 January 1689 he observed that the Union

> may be somewhat uneasy at first, as all new forms are at first setting up, but in a few years please much better than the old ones, especially if abused and corrupted. In my apprehensions the flourishing and security of both kingdoms lies in it, and now or never it is to be endeavoured and brought about after we have seen and felt the ill consequences of breaking up of the last treaty and the advantage taken since by our common enemies of our different circumstances, laws and customs and form of government, endeavouring to introduce popery by arbitrary government.[28]

Tweeddale, however, was alarmed when his son informed him that the prince had met a large group of Scots politicians, led by the duke of Hamilton, where it had been agreed to summon a convention parliament at Edinburgh to settle the government of Scotland. Fearing that the Scottish convention would degenerate into interminable debates about different forms of government, he thought this danger could be avoided if the convention parliament in England, during their debates about settling the crown and government of England on the prince, could

> either by a letter, or rather by commissioners make a proposition and tender of union to us upon our first sitting, and desire we may appoint commissioners to treat with such as they should name about this union, who might be empowered to bring all matters relating to it to a full conclusion and make a report thereof to the respective conventions for their approbation thereto.[29]

Tweeddale told his son to

> communicate this to the Prince and, if he allows then to communicate it to the Marquess of Halifax, President of the house of lords and my Lord Fauconberg, who was one of the commissioners in the last treaty of the union and to Mr Powel [Henry Powle], Speaker of the house of commons and to Sir James Hays, to which 4 I have wrote. And to any other the prince allows you speak of it. If the prince entertain the motion, he will give you his further commands about it, for the whole success thereof must depend on his highness. And in my humble opinion none of our countrymen must know anything of it, but as he is pleased to communicate it to them and not at all from this.[30]

Tweeddale had been encouraged to believe that the English would be favourably inclined towards a union by Yester's letter of 7 February, where he had written, in regard to the Union, that:

> this is the fairest occasion ever can offer, the apprehensions whereof, if right managed with this people in this conjuncture, will procure us a treaty upon easier and better

---

[28] NLS, MS 7026, f. 116: Tweeddale to 'My Lord', 29 Jan. 1689.
[29] NLS, MS 7026, f. 134: [Tweeddale] to [Yester], 14 Feb. 1689.
[30] NLS, MS 7026, f. 134: [Tweeddale] to [Yester], 14 Feb. 1689.

terms then ever could have been expected. For as affairs now stand a separation is as dangerous for them as for us and a union as much their interest as ours. That they think so is evidently what was said in the house of peers, where of I gave you account, and much to the same purpose was spoke in the house of commons.[31]

Sir James Hayes also hoped, as he wrote to Tweeddale from London on 23 February 1689, that both houses of parliament would embrace the Union, but was concerned 'that my Lord duke of Hamilton (who went hence upon Thursday morning last) hath endeavoured to leave contrary impressions upon the king's mind'.[32] Hayes's suspicion was confirmed by Yester, who informed his father that Hamilton 'will neither be for making the union the first step, for he frankly told us we behoved to follow the methods of England had taken, the king, the queen and Princess Anne having spoke to him to that purpose'.[33]

Tweeddale shared this concern about Hamilton when he wrote to Yester on 28 February 1689. He remained optimistic that the Union would succeed unless

> Duke Hamilton, his speaking of it with the king, occasion not some prejudice for you know he speaks with great earnestness against anything he likes not. Sir James Hay … writes to me that the duke he had given ill impressions of it to the king. Sir James will tell you how he had that information, but it seems the duke is very well with the king and has undertaken much.[34]

On 16 March Tweeddale wrote again to his son informing him that:

> yesternight Sir John Dalrymple was with me above an hour … I perceive by the king's letter the Viscount Fauconberg has not been wanting to what he undertook and has given good impressions of the union to him. And Sir John assures me that he has done likewise and now by this encouragement the union may succeed.[35]

The convention parliament met at Edinburgh on 15 March 1689. The next day the prince of Orange's letter to the estates was read in which he gracefully acknowledged how the nobility and gentry whom he had met at London in January, had urged him to take the government of Scotland upon himself and call a meeting of the estates. He encouraged them to establish the government upon lasting foundations and, with regard to the Union, observed that, like so many of the nobility and gentry he had met at London, he believed that it would contribute to the peace and happiness of both Scotland and England, and was 'resolved to use our utmost endeavours in advancing everything which may conduce to effectuating the same'.[36]

The reply was presented to the estates on 22 March. It expressed thanks for the summoning of the estates and promised to do everything possible to secure the protestant religion

[31] NLS, Mf. MS 192: [Yester] to Tweeddale, 7 Feb. 1689.

[32] NLS, MS 7011, f. 171: Ja[mes] Hayes to Tweeddale, 23 Feb. 1689.

[33] NLS, Mf. MS 192: typed note of letter of 23 Feb. [1689?].

[34] NLS, MS 7026, f. 147: [Tweeddale] to Yester, 28 Feb. 1689.

[35] NLS, MS 7026, f. 160: [Tweeddale] to [Yester], 16 Mar. 1689.

[36] *APS*, ix, 9.

and to establish the government, laws and liberties of the kingdom. It also observed that as 'to the proposal of the union we doubt not your majesty will so dispose that matter that there may be an equal readiness in the kingdom of England to accomplish it as one of the best means for securing the happiness of these nations and settling a lasting peace'.[37]

A committee made up of eight representatives from each of the three estates was appointed on 26 March to settle the government of Scotland. The question of the Union was raised in this committee on 30 March by Sir John Dalrymple, but the reaction, as Tweeddale observed, was very discouraging. He wrote to Yester the same day describing the committee's proceedings where 'Sir John Dalrymple in a long discourse following out that design you and his father had been talking of, was so run down that he was necessitate to pursue it no further.'[38]

Tweeddale took some comfort from the willingness of the committee to allow him, and an extra member from each of the other two estates, to attend its meetings, and on 2 April 1689 wrote to Yester to confirm that:

this day all is finished for a dispatch to the king the instrument of government, petition of right, grievances and a long letter to his majesty, with which I am sure you will be well pleased, especially as to what concerns the union, wherein they have declared their willing to be united into one kingdom, and being one people to be represented in one parliament as they are under one head and sovereign, their reserving to the them to government of the church as it shall be settled the time of the union.[39]

After the committee had met on 4 April, Tweeddale wrote to his son that he expected that the instrument of government, which was to be presented to the king and queen of England, would be drawn up the following day. If anything was proposed about

the union therein, it will be expected an answer will be returned then with the acceptance of the crown, far from the terms of a condition, but frankly reserving the number and naming of the commissioners to the king, as they were to King Charles the second, and offering to stand to the king's award and determination in all points of the said union wherein the deputes appointed to treat thereupon shall not agree.[40]

Tweeddale explained that: 'I writ these things before they come to pass, that you may prepare with all the friends and acquaintances you have, Scots and English, that your father may be named by the King one of the commissioners of the union, since he is to go to London … in his way to the Bath.'[41]

The 'declaration of the estates … containing the Claim of Right and the offer of the crown to their majesties William and Mary, king and queen of England' was approved on 11 April 1689.[42] Within 24 hours the estates allowed 'the earl of Tweeddale to pass into

[37] *APS*, ix. 20.

[38] NLS, MS 7026, f. 176: [Tweeddale] to Yester, 30 Mar. 1689.

[39] NLS, MS 7026, f. 179: [Tweeddale] to Yester, 2 Apr. 1689.

[40] NLS, MS 7026, f. 184: [Tweeddale] to Yester, 4 Apr. 1689.

[41] NLS, MS 7026, f. 184: [Tweeddale] to Yester, 4 Apr. 1689.

[42] *APS*, ix, 37.

England for his health'.[43] Almost a fortnight later, on 23 April, an act was passed nominating commissioners, including Tweeddale, to treat for a union with commissioners appointed by the English parliament.

The next day, three commissioners, the earl of Argyll, Sir James Montgomery of Skelmorlie, and Sir John Dalrymple, were appointed to offer the Scottish crown to William and Mary. These three carried with them a letter from the estates expressing the hope

> that as both kingdoms are united in one head and sovereign so they may become one body politic, one nation to be represented in one parliament, and to testify our readiness to comply with your majesty in that matter, we have nominated commissioners to treat the terms of an entire and perpetual union betwixt the two kingdoms, with reservation to us of our church government, as it shall be established at the time of the union. These commissioners do wait your majesty's approbation and call, that they may meet and treat with the commissioners to be appointed for England and what time and place your majesty shall appoint.[44]

On 26 April, the estates issued an order instructing 'all the Scots nobility and persons of quality who are at present at London or about the court, especially the members of the meeting of the estates, be advertised to attend his majesty when the commissioners for this Kingdom shall wait on him with the offer of the crown'.[45] Tweeddale took advantage of the opportunity presented to him to attend the Banqueting House at Whitehall on 11 May when Argyll, Skelmorlie, and Dalrymple offered the crown of Scotland to William and Mary.

Writing to the duke of Hamilton the next day, Argyll and Skelmorlie recounted that:

> yesterday we disburdened ourselves of the crown which was done on the Banqueting House with great solemnity. The king and queen swore the oath. The king himself swore it with that gravity and seriousness that we had never seen expressed in the taking any oath before. When he came to that part of the oath anent rooting out heretics, he told us that by it he did not understand himself obliged to persecute any upon account of religion and took us three witnesses upon it. After all was over, he commanded us to make no return to the States of his having taken the oath till further orders.[46]

Four days later, however, Sir John Dalrymple wrote a more troubling letter to Hamilton. The estates had originally required the commissioners to present to the king the letter about the Union together with the list of grievances for which redress was sought and the address for turning the convention into a parliament. Now Dalrymple told Hamilton that:

> though I came here on the Wednesday, yet my brethren went without me to Hampton Court where they delivered the letter and what else was committed to us … I cannot

---

[43] *APS*, ix, 43.
[44] *APS*, ix, 60.
[45] *APS*, ix, 66.
[46] HMC, *Hamilton MSS*, i, 182.

say what they represented to the king, or whether there was any mention of these things your grace was pleased to charge us with at parting.[47]

The king, however, had already decided against uniting Scotland and England. Dalrymple told Hamilton that:

> I found the king was determined in the matter and that your grace had signified some part of your thoughts to his majesty by letter. Some of the English were jealous it might import some disparagement to their procedure if we did not follow that same course as not to be secure or legal. I confess to your grace I have never meddled or spoken word to the king in any matter. By the stop that's made your grace may easily see that my father or I could have little interest in it. Therefore, since I do pretend to nothing but my own private employment, and that I have been very ill used by my colleagues, I keep myself very abstract.[48]

Tweeddale was incensed by the king's failure to embrace the Union. During the remainder of his stay in England he set about planning how to force William to change his mind. Together with the marquess of Carmarthen, Tweeddale began laying the foundations of a strong unionist party in England. He also took a close interest in the fortunes of James Johnston, the son of his old associate, Sir Archibald Johnston of Wariston who, like him, had sat in the British parliament under Cromwell.

At this time Johnston was closely involved with the 1st duke of Queensberry, as Tweeddale revealed when writing to Yester on 20 December 1688: 'it is said that Queensberry makes much use of one Mr Johnston, who was Secretary to Colonel Sidney and your son's knew well to be of good parts and it is upon Mr Fall, principal of Glasgow College, his acquaintance'.[49] Yester had also noticed that when the Scots nobility and gentry in London met in the Council Chamber at Whitehall on 9 January 1689, to settle the heads of an address to the prince of Orange, the clerks responsible for drawing up the document were 'Commissary Monro and Mr Johnston, Wariston's son'.[50]

Tweeddale had long suspected that Sir John Dalrymple had lied when telling him that he, Dalrymple, had encouraged the king to unite Scotland and England in 1689. He believed that Johnston would be well suited to spying on Dalrymple and to this end sought Carmarthen's help. Johnston was appointed as the king's envoy to Berlin in the spring of 1690, but was in the Spanish Netherlands in January 1691 when he received a letter from Tweeddale announcing that Dalrymple, now one of the Scottish secretaries of state, had left England with the king. Johnston reached The Hague on 17 February from where, on 21 March, he informed Tweeddale that he had followed his instructions about Dalrymple and tried to live

> as well with him as he would allow me to do and have endeavoured to do him such little services as he seems to stand mightily in need of, much more indeed than I imagined,

[47] National Records of Scotland [hereafter cited as NRS], Hamilton MSS, GD 406/1/3545: Sir John Dalrymple to the duke of Hamilton, 16 May 1689.

[48] NRS, GD 406/1/3545: Dalrymple to Hamilton, 16 May 1689.

[49] NLS, MS 7026, f. 88: [Tweeddale] to [Yester], 20 Dec. 1688.

[50] NLS, Mf. MS 192: [Yester] to Tweeddale, 8 Jan. 1689.

for I did not think that he had been so much a stranger to the way of living in the world, but all this is new to him.[51]

While Johnston continued spying, Tweeddale encouraged Carmarthen to appoint him as joint secretary of state for Scotland alongside Dalrymple. Johnston had been corresponding with Carmarthen since November 1690, a service which had brought him ample rewards. He told Tweeddale in March 1691 that 'strangers have done me good offices with the king without my knowledge, but I asked nothing and did nothing'.[52] Johnston's progress continued throughout 1691 and on 27 February 1692, the earl of Selkirk advised his father, the duke of Hamilton, 'that this day Mr Johnston kissed the Kings hand for the secretary's place and is to stay here and Master of Stair [Dalrymple] is to go over with the King'.[53]

Although little direct progress was made towards uniting Scotland and England during the next three years, Tweeddale could take comfort from the misfortunes which began to beset the two men he regarded as the leaders of the Scottish opposition to union. The first of these was Dalrymple. After his appointment as secretary of state, Johnston began investigating the massacre at Glencoe on 13 February 1692, and during the next 12 months produced evidence to suggest that Dalrymple had exceeded the king's instructions when ordering the attack on the MacDonalds. Johnston had no scruples about using this evidence to discredit Dalrymple and his family: in a letter of 11 July 1693 he wrote that with 'the Glencoe affair in my hands, I'll lash them into good behaviour, cost what it will'.[54]

Tweeddale was also encouraged by the unexpected death of the duke of Hamilton at Holyroodhouse on 18 April 1694. Hamilton had been the leader of the opposition to the Union in the Scottish parliament in 1669, as Lauderdale acknowledged in a letter to Hamilton in November 1670, in which he noted that 'the treaty of Union, which your grace opposed so zealously when it was commanded by the King, is now adjourned'.[55] Hamilton had repeated his opposition to union in 1689, and his death persuaded Tweeddale that it was now time to revive the project. He had, however, to wait another year until the meeting of the fifth session of the first parliament of King William, at Edinburgh on 9 May 1695. Tweeddale was named as lord high commissioner and Johnston lord secretary.

Under Johnston's management, much of parliament's time was taken up with the report of the commission of inquiry into Glencoe, which allowed him to honour the pledge he had made in 1693 to scourge Sir John Dalrymple. There was also an attempt to impeach the earl of Breadalbane. These proceedings helped to divert attention from Tweeddale's intention to establish a Scottish trading company without the king's consent.

The first indication of Tweeddale's scheme came in the speech he made to parliament as lord high commissioner on 9 May 1695:

if you find it will tend to the advancement of trade, that an act be passed for the encouragement of such as shall acquire and establish a plantation in Africa or America, or any other part of the world, where plantations may be lawfully acquired, his majesty is

[51] NLS, MS 14408, f. 13: [James Johnston] to [Tweeddale], 17 Mar. [1691].
[52] NLS, MS 14408, f. 13: [Johnston] to [Tweeddale], 17 Mar. [1691].
[53] NRS, GD 406/1/11049: [Selkirk] to [Hamilton], 27 Feb. 1692.
[54] NRS, SP 3/1: [Johnston] to William Carstares, 11 July [1693].
[55] NRS, GD 406/1/2703: Lauderdale to Hamilton, 24 Nov. 1670.

willing to declare, that he will grant to the subjects of this kingdom, in favours of those plantations, such rights and privileges as he doth grant in like cases to the subjects of his other dominions.[56]

This recommendation was accepted and on 12 June 1695, the 'draft of an act for encouraging trade, [was] read and remitted to the committee of trade'.[57] The draft, however, was nothing more than the 'act for encouraging of foreign trade',[58] which had originally been passed by parliament on 14 June 1693. Under its terms Scottish companies could trade with 'kingdoms, countries, or parts of the world, not being in war with their majesties ... and particularly, besides the kingdoms and countries of Europe, to the east and west indies, to the straits, and trade in the Mediterranean, or upon the coast of Africa or northern parts'.[59] Parliament then took the unusual step of ordering 'the committee of trade to meet in the Abbey'.[60]

Next day the committee assembled at Holyrood Abbey, where it was free to make substantial additions to the original legislation. A new act was drawn up for incorporating a joint stock company, 'by the name of the Company of Scotland Trading to Africa and Indies', whose 'ships vessels, merchandise, goods, and other effects whatsoever ... shall be free of all manner of restraints or prohibitions, and of all customs, taxes, cesses, supplies, or other duties imposed, or to be imposed, by Act of Parliament, or otherwise, for and during the space of twenty one years'.[61] The committee reported back to parliament on 26 June and the act was quickly 'read, voted, and approved'.[62]

The next day, the lord provost of Edinburgh, Sir Robert Cheesley, wrote to William Paterson with the news that parliament had approved the act establishing the Company of Scotland. As one of the founders of both the Bank of Scotland and Bank of England, Paterson, who was also named as one of the undertakers in the act establishing the company, exercised a powerful influence over the development of the company. He and his London associates had sent Cheesley their thoughts about the company, and now, writing in response to Cheesley's letter of 27 June, Paterson suggested that the several preliminaries relating to the company 'ought first to be concerted in a meeting in London about the end of October ... where most of the persons named in the act ought to be present'.[63]

At the beginning of September, however, Paterson conceded that there had been a significant change of circumstances. He explained to Cheesley that the

business here hath taken more air than we expected so soon, and what was a reason for use before to delay our business some time, proves now an argument for us to hasten it, because it is now as public as it can well be, and our politicians here seem inclined rather

[56] *APS*, ix, appendix, 95.

[57] *APS*, ix, 367.

[58] *APS*, ix, 314.

[59] *APS*, ix, 315.

[60] *APS*, ix, 369.

[61] *APS*, ix, 377, 380.

[62] *APS*, ix, 377.

[63] *The Darien Papers* (Edinburgh, 1849), 1.

to endeavour that England should follow our example as much as may be in encouraging foreign trade.[64]

It was not long before the Company of Scotland began to have the impact that Tweeddale had anticipated. James Johnston's brother, Alexander, informed Tweeddale, on 12 September 1695, that the English secretaries of state, the duke of Shrewsbury, and Sir William Trumbull, together with several prominent members of the house of commons, had asked him for copies of the act establishing the Scottish company. Although Alexander Johnston told them he was unable to comply, he was now sufficiently acquainted with English discontent to advise Tweeddale that: 'I understand their great objection is the exception of customs for so many years, whereby you may undersell them and so bring the whole trade to their selves and the customs here will be sunk to the King.'[65]

By the end of September this fear had generated such hostility that at a meeting of the company's undertakers at London it was agreed, in response to some malicious misrepresentations of their purpose, regarding the interest of England, that: 'the members of this company do, upon all occasions speak with due respect of the power of the government and people of England'.[66] A further instruction followed on 22 October, that: 'all discourses and transactions passed here relating to the company, shall be inviolably kept secret from all other persons whatsoever'.[67]

The same meeting also agreed that the company should begin to take subscriptions and that: 'the joint stock, or capital fund, of this company do consist of six hundred-thousand pound sterling'.[68] The storm of investment in the company, however, was so intense that measures had to be taken to prevent the original capital stock from being overwhelmed by the number of subscriptions. The remedy was to oblige subscribers to pay 'one quarter-part of the sums subscribed for, at the time of subscription'.[69]

On 9 November, it was also agreed that copies of the company's journal be sent to Scotland and, almost a fortnight later, on 22 November, the same day on which the English parliament met, there was a meeting of the undertakers, with Paterson acting as chairman. When the subscription books were examined it was found 'that the complete sum of £300,000 is subscribed therein; ordered, that the said book be closed'.[70] Finally, on 3 December, the undertakers resolved that: 'all necessary directions be given, forthwith, for carrying on the subscription in Scotland'.[71]

By the time that the company's undertakers hurried back to Scotland, English opposition to Tweeddale and Johnston had consolidated around Robert Spencer, 2nd earl of Sunderland. During Charles II's reign, Sunderland, under the guidance of Lauderdale, who often visited Sunderland's family home at Althorp in Northamptonshire when travelling between London and Scotland, had developed a formidable understanding of Scottish politics

[64] *Darien Papers*, 6.
[65] NLS, MS 7019, f. 36: Alexander Johnston to Tweeddale, 12 Sept. 1695.
[66] *CJ*, xi, 401.
[67] *CJ*, xi, 401.
[68] *CJ*, xi, 402.
[69] *CJ*, xi, 402.
[70] *CJ*, xi, 404.
[71] *CJ*, xi, 405.

and a strong dislike of unionism. Lauderdale showed Sunderland how to frustrate unionist ambitions while appearing to embrace their principles. It was a technique which Lauderdale had himself employed in November 1670 when he deliberately sabotaged the union negotiations at Somerset House by simply asking too much of the English commissioners.

After Lauderdale's death, Sunderland and the duke of Hamilton drew together to forestall any attempt to unite Scotland and England. Sunderland's friendship with Hamilton's eldest son, James, earl of Arran, reinforced this bond, and when Sunderland wrote to Arran from Whitehall, on 20 June 1685, he confirmed the strength of his connection with Hamilton by observing that: 'your father has come and we are all one'.[72] The link grew even tighter in January 1688 when Arran married Sunderland's eldest daughter, Lady Anne Spencer.

On the prince of Orange's landing in England in 1688, Sunderland fled into exile in the Netherlands, leaving Hamilton and Sir John Dalrymple to persuade the prince not to endorse Tweeddale's attempt to unite Scotland and England. Sunderland returned to England in 1690, just as Hamilton and the king were becoming increasingly disenchanted with each other. Encouraged by Carmarthen and James Johnston, the king had come to rely more on Tweeddale than on Hamilton, whom he appointed as lord high chancellor of Scotland in 1692. The following year, Hamilton expressed concern about Tweeddale's influence. Writing to his wife on 21 October 1693 from London, he told her that: 'I see our chancellor grows more and more absolute if a stop be not put to his career.'[73]

Tweeddale's rise coincided with Sunderland's growing influence at court. On 23 August 1693, Johnston wrote to Hamilton that it 'is no more doubted but that there will be great changes here and that my Lord Sunderland will come into the Cabinet'.[74] Johnston sent a similar message eight days later when he told the earl of Annandale that: 'I doubt not but my Lord Sunderland will be the man this winter, and it's like the change will be not only of men but of measures. I see not how the business will do else.'[75]

Hamilton hoped that Sunderland would be able to convey to the king his concern about Tweeddale, and on 19 October told his wife that: 'I saw my Lord Sunderland but has not had time to discourse fully with him.'[76] Opportunities for further discussion about Tweeddale, either directly with Sunderland, or through Arran, presented themselves in December 1693. Sunderland and his wife were both alarmed to hear of the illness of their granddaughter, Lady Mary Hamilton, and when Hamilton acknowledged his wife's letter of 14 December, which brought news of a recovery, he said how glad he was to hear that 'the child continues to recover … my Lord and Lady Sunderland seemed very concerned for her'.[77] Nine days later Hamilton informed his wife that their son, Arran, 'appeared abroad yesterday and dined with Lord Sunderland and come to me after dinner and stayed most of the afternoon'.[78]

Sunderland and Arran had met briefly when the news of Hamilton's death reached London in April 1694. Arran then set out for Scotland while Sunderland went to Althorp. He wrote to Arran on 4 June 1694 confirming that: 'I received a letter from you with great

[72]NRS, GD 406/1/7657: [Sunderland] to Arran, 20 June [1685].

[73]NRS, GD 406/1/7303: [Hamilton] to [duchess of Hamilton], 21 Oct. 1693.

[74]NRS, SP 3/1: [Johnston] to Hamilton, 24 Aug. [1694].

[75]NRS, SP 3/1: [Johnston] to Annandale, 31 Aug. [1693].

[76]NRS, GD 406/1/7302: [Hamilton] to [duchess of Hamilton], 19 Oct. 1693.

[77]NRS, GD 406/1/7357: [Hamilton] to [duchess of Hamilton], 14 Dec. 1693.

[78]NRS, GD 406/1/7361: [Hamilton] to [duchess of Hamilton], 23 Dec. 1693.

satisfaction, finding by it that you were well arrived in Scotland. I shall be at London the 19 of this month.'[79] Sunderland had to delay his journey until the end of the month and extended his stay there beyond the 'week or ten days' he had initially intended.[80] It was from London that he wrote to Arran on 18 July 1694, thanking him for his letter of 7 July, but also expressing the concern that:

> you will not have finished your business in Scotland a great while, but when it is, I hope we shall see you at Althorp whither I intend to go the whole summer. You know I never write news, so that I must refer you to the Gazette. Pray present my most humble service to my Lady Duchess and kiss Lady Mary for me.[81]

Sunderland was relieved to discover that, particularly after the death of Queen Mary in December 1694, the king had become increasingly suspicious of Tweeddale and Johnston. During the summer of 1695 the news of the proceedings of the Scottish parliament did nothing to allay his doubts, and when William returned to England from The Hague on 10 October 1695, he was ready to follow Sunderland's advice closely.

This change was immediately noticed by Johnston. Uncertain of the king's intentions, Johnston wrote to Tweeddale on 12 October 1695 admitting that: 'I can only tell you that I have kissed the king's hand and that is all.'[82] Johnston was also ignorant of William's decision to visit Sunderland at Althorp, and was equally surprised when he was summoned to join the king there. None the less, Johnston was still confident that William could be forced to consider uniting Scotland with England when the English parliament met. He wrote to Tweeddale, on 9 November 1695, that when the Scottish act establishing the Company of Scotland came to be considered, Carmarthen, now duke of Leeds, and 'others of that side, will make in parliament all the stir they can about it and the other side will rather concur than oppose, and the King at last cannot refuse them here such an act which will be a great loss to him in his customs'.[83]

Believing that the king would not find it easy to resolve the trade disagreement between his Scottish and English parliaments, Johnston prepared a solution which he could offer to settle this dispute. The day before the English parliament was due to meet he wrote to Tweeddale explaining that

> the duke of Shrewsbury, the lord keeper, the archbishop [of Canterbury], Sir William Trumbull, Lord Sunderland and many others have spoken to me … most of them upon the Kings account will do what they can to calm matters, and would gladly catch at any expedients fit for their purpose, and … I can think of nothing better than that commissioners be named for adjusting trade between the two nations.[84]

The king delivered his speech to the English parliament on Friday, 22 November, and 11 days later the house of lords considered its response in a committee on the state of the

[79] NRS, GD 406/1/3920: Sunderland to [Arran], 4 June 1694.
[80] NRS, GD 406/1/7029: Sunderland to [Arran], 23 June 1694.
[81] NRS, GD 406/1/7033: [Sunderland] to [Arran], 18 July 1694.
[82] NLS, MS 14408, f. 405: Johnston to Tweeddale, 12 Oct. 1695.
[83] NLS, MS 14408, f. 415: [Johnston] to [Tweeddale], 9 Nov. 1695.
[84] NLS, MS 14408, f. 419: [Johnston] to [Tweeddale], 21 Nov. 1695.

nation. As Viscount Fauconberg informed Tweeddale, the debate in the committee was 'very warm and unanimous upon the subject of your act, procured for the east and West Indies trade, with exemptions unheard of, and no limitation'.[85] When the House resumed, the earl of Huntingdon reported the committee's opinion that the

> merchants trading to the East and West Indies, and Africa, as likewise the commission-
> ers of the customs, do attend this house on Thursday next, at ten of the clock in the
> forenoon, to give an account wherein the act of parliament lately made in Scotland,
> for a company trading to Africa and the Indies, may be prejudicial to the trade of this
> kingdom into those parts.[86]

The same day, according to Lord Elcho, there

> was a Scottish council held at Kensington … where the king was very ill pleased with
> Johnston's proceedings in parliament. In particular, he challenged the bringing these
> things before the parliament as follows viz: the business of Glencoe, my Lord Breadal-
> bane's impeachment and their proceedings in the business of the East Indian company
> without his knowledge.[87]

This was not the first sign of dissatisfaction at Tweeddale's management of the Scottish parliament. On 11 July 1695, Robert Pringle, under secretary of state for Scotland, had written to Tweeddale from Namur, where he was attending the king, about the decision to communicate to parliament the commission of enquiry's report about Glencoe. Pringle remarked that if

> your grace had, with the last post acquainted me with the desire you then made to
> the king, for liberty to communicate the report to the parliament, I could have moved
> him to it, at least have given you his mind. But at the same time your grace lets me
> know you have writ for an order to communicate that report, the king by other letters
> is informed that the commission had already determined it should be communicated
> without waiting his mind.[88]

Pringle also revealed that:

> I have but too much reason to believe the king is very much dissatisfied with the par-
> liament's proceeding in reference to my Lord Breadalbane. The impeaching of the earl
> upon articles which the king and his council had in their hands 3 years ago seems to
> him to be very improbable that he scarce yet seems to believe the matter of fact. And
> though there had some discovery been made of some recent guilt of the earl, yet even in
> that case good manners and respect to his majesty might have obliged the parliament to

---

[85] NLS, MS 7019, f. 147: Fauconberg to [Tweeddale], 3 Dec. 1695.
[86] *LJ*, xv, 603.
[87] NRS, Leven and Melville MSS, GD 26/13/93: Elcho to [countess of Leven], 5 Dec. 1695.
[88] NLS, MS 7018, f. 108: Pringle to [Tweeddale], 11 July 1695.

give the king notice before any orders had been given about his trial, much more when the impeachment proceeds upon articles, which the king having seen, did pass from.[89]

Pringle also expressed his concern about Tweeddale's decision to extend the length of the session without the king's permission. He told Tweeddale that: 'the king was very much surprised to find the parliament was to sit after the time he had allowed. I could give no answer, but that I doubted not but your grace would in your letters satisfy his majesty.'[90] Although the king did eventually approve Tweeddale's decision, Pringle was still 'very much afraid, yea confident, the king will not so readily approve of your continuing the parliament without his order'.[91]

Pringle's expectation that the king would be displeased was hardly surprising. Even though there appear to have been some mitigating circumstances, Tweeddale's decision to allow parliament to sit without the king's permission was still treasonable. Johnston told the duke of Shrewsbury that the

orders for continuing the parliament being lost in the packet boat that is missing, and the letters that came after bearing only in general that such orders were sent without mentioning the time, and we only having asked the half of July, we could not but conclude that the time allowed did not exceed the time asked; and even the sitting without them, though they were granted, being treason, the commissioner was necessitated to end the parliament somewhat abruptly.[92]

However, despite these provocations Pringle thought that the king might not be too displeased with Tweeddale's management of the Scottish parliament. On 1 August 1695, he told Tweeddale that he believed that the king had

no reason to be dissatisfied with the close of the parliament, though he seemed to long for it much. And I am hopeful the good acts that are passed in it, both for the advantage of the nation and his own interest and service, will make him overlook what perhaps he has been displeased with.[93]

It was the act establishing the Company of Scotland which finally proved too much for the king. He expressed his annoyance on 3 December 1695, at a conference with leading Scottish politicians in London. Because he had not given permission for the act, the king expressed his anger. His remarks were communicated to Tweeddale by Annandale, who recounted that this act 'does vex and perplex the King more than can be imagined, and at our conference he did not appear warm as to anything except this act, for he said it was granting such powers and sovereignties as if there had been no king of Scotland'.[94]

Johnston, in an account of the meeting sent to Adam Cockburn of Ormiston, observed that the king 'spoke with great regard, both to the nation and parliament, and could not

---

[89] NLS, MS 7018, f. 108: Pringle to [Tweeddale], 11 July 1695.

[90] NLS, MS 7018, f. 120: Pringle to [Tweeddale], nd.

[91] NLS, MS 7018, f. 120: Pringle to [Tweeddale], nd.

[92] HMC, *Buccleuch MSS*, ii, pt 2, p. 201.

[93] NLS, MS 7018, f. 124: Pringle to [Tweeddale], 12 Aug. 1695 ns.

[94] NLS, MS 7019, f. 154: Annandale to Tweeddale, 9 Dec. 1695.

condemn even the Indian act, but said he was sorry, for the consequences of it was like to have, which he believed would not be even for the interest of Scotland'.[95] Johnston underlined these conciliatory remarks two days later. Writing to Tweeddale on 5 December 1695, Johnston revealed that: 'I was in the Closet about the Indian act. The king appeared rather vexed than angry he said they would oblige him to make an act against it. I said we could not complain of that each nation was to do for themselves.'[96] He also informed Tweeddale that Sunderland 'seems to be very well disposed as to our business. Pray give me what light you can into whatever passed betwixt the two nations or may be talked of in order to an union either of trading or of government. This is the season to let it out and the English seem very disposed to hear it.'[97]

On 9 December, almost a week after this meeting, the house of lords' committee appointed to examine the act of the Scottish parliament establishing the Company of Scotland sat again. When Huntingdon reported back, the company was ordered to lay its subscription books before the House. Orders were also issued requiring that all English trading companies should give in their opinions about 'what they conceive may be the proper means to remedy the inconveniencies arising by the late act of parliament made in Scotland for establishing an East India company there'.[98]

On 12 December 1695, the Lords' committee examined the subscription books of the Company of Scotland and the recommendations of the English trading companies. During these deliberations Johnston's cousin, Gilbert Burnet, bishop of Salisbury, proposed uniting Scotland and England. The same day Johnston wrote excitedly to Tweeddale announcing that the establishment of the Company of Scotland had 'exerted a wonderful disposition to an union. The bishop of Sarum's motion for it was received in the house of lords with universal applause, even my Lord Rochester seconded it.'[99]

Huntingdon's report to the House on 12 December, however, did not contain any reference to uniting Scotland and England. It merely recommended appointing a committee to draw up an address to the king representing 'the great prejudice, inconveniencies, and mischiefs, the act for establishing an East India company in Scotland may be to the trade of this kingdom'.[100] The following day Rochester reported from this committee. The draft address took exception to the clauses in the Scottish act exempting the Company of Scotland and its employees from paying taxes for 21 years. The consequence of this privilege, the address alleged, would be that Scottish merchants would be able to supply Europe with East India goods far more cheaply than their English counterparts. The address warned that these goods 'will unavoidably be brought by the Scotch into England, both by sea and land, to the vast prejudice of the English trade and navigation, and to the great detriment of your majesty in your customs'.[101] The house of commons readily endorsed the Lords' address the same day, and on 16 December 1695, members of both Houses went to Kensington to present it to the king.

[95] NLS, MS 7019, f. 154: Annandale to Tweeddale, 9 Dec. 1695.
[96] NLS, MS 14408, f. 430: Johnston to [Tweeddale], 5 Dec. 1695.
[97] NLS, MS 14408, f. 430: Johnston to [Tweeddale], 5 Dec. 1695.
[98] *LJ*, xv, 608.
[99] NLS, MS 14408, f. 433: Johnston to [Tweeddale], 12 Dec. 1695.
[100] *LJ*, xv, 610.
[101] *LJ*, xv, 611.

William's answer was short and sharp: 'I have been ill served in Scotland, but I hope some remedies may be found to prevent the inconveniencies which may arise from this act.'[102] When the Lords came to consider possible remedies, on 18 December 1695, the committee recommended that the king's English subjects avoid any involvement in the Company of Scotland and that the English parliament consider establishing an English East India company to compete with the Scots. There was no mention of union. Having witnessed the king's opposition to the Union in 1689, Tweeddale, suspected that William, like Charles II, would never accept a union of Scotland and England because he believed it would be an irrevocable step towards a republican regime.

Tweeddale was so determined to restore the British parliament that he was prepared to consider any means to achieve this end, even if it involved replacing King William with King James. Since he had anticipated William's continuing opposition after 1689, Tweeddale had begun to explore the jacobite option as early as 1690, and in this he knew he would have to rely heavily on James Johnston.

Because of his friendship with David Nairne, Johnston was able to provide a crucial link to the jacobite court at St Germain-en-Laye. Born at St Andrews in 1655, Nairne had been awarded a master's degree from the university in 1673 and the following year went to Leiden where he studied law for six months. He left Leiden in February 1675 and, as he recorded in his journal, 'went by Amsterdam to Franeker … and stayed near 6 months studying the law with David Douglas, Mr Johnston, Hugh Dalrymple, John Cockburn etc.'.[103] After leaving Franeker, Nairne

> crossed the Zuyder Zee between Harlingen and Amsterdam, stayed at Amsterdam some 8 or 10 days and went from thence to Utrecht, where I … stayed 14 months, continuing the study of civil law in company with Johnston, afterward the secretary of state … and several others.[104]

Utrecht University had been recommended to Johnston by his cousin, Gilbert Burnet. Like Nairne, Johnston also studied civil law

> and had the character of the greatest proficient that ever was in Utrecht. When he had finished his studies he went into Italy, where, making an acquaintance with my Lord Romney, he was by him instructed in the secrets of the revolution, and employed by that Lord to come into England, which he did successfully.[105]

Nairne, meanwhile, left Utrecht for France in 1676 and arrived at Paris in November. During the next 12 years he travelled widely in France, mastered the French language, married a Frenchwoman and converted to catholicism. When James II arrived at St Germain-en-Laye in 1689 Nairne

> went thither … to kiss the king's hand. Mr Inese presented me to the Earl of Melfort, and he carried me to the king, and being told I had been long in France and had the

---

[102] *LJ*, xv, 616.

[103] NLS, MS 14266, f. 2: journal of Sir David Nairne.

[104] NLS, MS 14266, f. 3.

[105] *Memoirs of the Secret Services of John Macky* (1733), 204.

French tongue perfectly well, and knowing my family, that very night he sent for me and employed me to translate a paper in French, which I sat up all night to do and carried it to him next morning, and ever since I continued in the Secretary's office.[106]

From St Germain, Nairne provided Johnston with valuable assistance. The misfortune which befell a French attempt to assist King James by invading England in the summer of 1692 can be directly attributed to Nairne's link with Johnston. Nairne recorded in his journal that on 21 May 1692: 'I went with the king to La Hogue to see the French fleet, which was come in that road and the English fleet pursuing them. The last came within half a canon shot of the castle of La Hogue where we were with the king … The English burnt the French ships at La Hogue.'[107] It was noted that Johnston had done 'great service in England … He discovered the La Hogue descent, and had better intelligence from France than any about the king. This gave him great credit at court.'[108]

While Nairne was an excellent source of intelligence for Johnston, Johnston could also be an excellent source of intelligence for Nairne. In return for valuable information about the jacobite court, Johnston was able to provide Nairne with valuable information about the English court and, by the summer of 1695, the two of them, at Tweeddale's instigation, were involved in a plan to restore King James.

Their scheming, however, had not gone unnoticed. On 3 December 1694, Nairne mentioned that a packet of letters, that were being sent to England, included 'mine to English covering the King's to E[arl] A[rran]'.[109] Having successfully infiltrated Arran into the jacobite movement, Sunderland was able to use him to frustrate the preparations being made for a jacobite rebellion.

On Tuesday, 23 August 1695, Nairne wrote in his journal that:

I copied a memorial in French, written by Mr Caryll, representing that there could be no safe peace for France as long as the prince of Orange was left master of England, and that the only true way to a lasting and honourable peace would be to ruin the prince of Orange and re-establish the king. That an attempt upon England would be very practicable after the campaign, when troops may be spared and when the king of France, in all appearance, will be stronger by sea, when the English will not be able to put 30 ships of line to sea in October.[110]

Then, on 10 September, Nairne recorded that among the letters, sent in the packet from St Germain to England, was 'the k[ing]'s to the E[arl] A[rran]'.[111] Arran conveyed the contents of this letter to Sunderland, who, upon William's return to England from the continent, on 10 October, warned him that his life was in danger and that he must leave Kensington Palace immediately. Sunderland's son, Charles, Lord Spencer, announced the

[106] NLS, MS 14266, f. 7.
[107] NLS, MS 14266, f. 42.
[108] *Macky Memoirs*, 205.
[109] NLS, MS 14266, f. 64.
[110] NLS, MS 14266, f. 87.
[111] NLS, MS 14266, f. 90.

impending journey to his brother-in-law, the duke of Newcastle, in a letter from London on 14 October. He wrote:

> to let your grace know that the king will be with you by the end of the next week intending to take a progress northward in this idle time before till the parliament meets. He intends to set out on Thursday for Newmarket. From thence he will be at Althorp on Monday next, where he will stay till Friday, and thence go to Nottingham, intending to hunt in Sherwood Forest. It's so sudden a resolution, that it will be troublesome to everybody to whose house he goes.[112]

Spencer also revealed that the

> people that go with him are the duke of Shrewsbury, my Lord Portland, my Lord Romney, my Lord Godolphin, Tom Wharton, Mr Montagu, Mr Felton, the gentlemen of the bedchamber, in waiting, and the captain of the guards and the duke of St Albans. Perhaps there may be some one or two more, but these are all I know of.[113]

Johnston was very surprised by this announcement, as he mentioned in his letter to Tweeddale of 15 October. He wrote that the 'king goes a progressing on Thursday for 3 weeks. I know nothing as yet.'[114] Two days later he revealed that a letter for adjourning the Scottish parliament

> was given in, but the king has left it unsigned. He said he would call me in yesterday, but at last told me that I must follow him into the country ... I know nothing of the king's mind. He has shunned much other business as well as ours. It's believed that Kensington has revived the memory of the queen and that makes him uneasy.[115]

On 21 October, Robert Pringle wrote to Tweeddale advising him that the 'secretary went this day to Althorp in Northamptonshire where the king is to be this night'.[116] Tweeddale was not unduly concerned, as he indicated when writing to Johnston on 24 October. He observed that: 'I ... am glad the King hath commanded you to follow him, *for possibly an opportunity may be had in the country as well as at Kensington, especially when you get the letter for adjourning our parliament.*'[117]

Johnston managed to smuggle out some news from Althorp to his brother Alexander, who wrote to Tweeddale on 26 October, that James was

> lodged in the house with his master (in my Lord Arran's father-in-law's house) at Althorp and is greatly obliged to his landlord and lady's civilities. I may add further that these little things (though not conclusive) renders some folks utterly Glencoe desperate. I have

---

[112]BL, Add. MS 70500, f. 330: Spencer to Newcastle, 14 Oct. 1695. I would like to thank Dr Clyve Jones for providing me with a transcript of this letter.

[113]BL, Add. MS 70500, f. 330: Spencer to Newcastle, 14 Oct. 1695.

[114]NLS, MS 14408, f. 407: Johnston to Tweeddale, 15 Oct. 1695.

[115]NLS, MS 14408, f. 409: Johnston to Tweeddale, 17 Oct. 1695.

[116]NLS, MS 7019, f. 105: Pringle to Tweeddale, 21 Oct. 1695.

[117]NLS, MS 7029, f. 97: [Tweeddale] to Johnston, 24 Oct. 1695 (emphasis added).

reason to believe the conclusion will correspond with the premises. God grant it prove so. The truth is my friend eats every meal with his master in that house where few are admitted.[118]

On his return to London, Johnston informed Tweeddale that:

I stayed near a week at my Lord Sunderland's house with the king and had all the good countenance I could desire, but only a minute or two for business. My Lord Shrewsbury says that barring matters of form, he has had no business with him since he came, and my Lord Sunderland thought it against rules to speak to the king of business in his own house.[119]

The fact that the king had also declined to discuss business with Shrewsbury, the English secretary of state for the southern department, was not without significance. The previous August, Shrewsbury had written to Tweeddale expressing his commitment to the Union, when remarking that the

affairs of Scotland, no doubt, have a very near relation to those of England. We are the same island, have the same secret and open enemies, are embarked in the same cause, and one must be very short sighted not to perceive we cannot long remain quiet if disturbances arise among you.[120]

On 19 November, Shrewsbury wrote to Tweeddale suggesting that:

it may be very necessary, your lordship should be here to inform his majesty upon several questions and difficulties that are like to arise among us, on occasion of an act passed in the parliament there for erecting a new East India Company. If your lordship therefore finds yourself in a condition to undertake such a journey, you will please to consider of it, and accordingly move the king for his leave to come up.[121]

Tweeddale replied that: 'I ... do fully acquiesce in your opinion I had much rather see the king than write to him. Nor shall the season of the year nor the fatigue and hazard of so long a journey deter me.'[122]

Johnston also believed that Tweeddale had to speak to the king in person to refute suggestions that had been made about the legality of the act establishing the Company of Scotland. On 12 December 1695, he wrote begging Tweeddale to

write to the king that you hope he will pardon you if, without leave, you come up to vindicate yourself ... I own the season of the year, but this is the most important conjuncture of your whole life and there is still room for this acts proving the greatest

---

[118]NLS, MS 7019, f. 109: Alexander Johnston to Tweeddale, 26 Oct. 1695.
[119]NLS, MS 14408, f. 413: Johnston to [Tweeddale], 31 Oct. 1695.
[120]NLS, MS 7018, f. 146: Shrewsbury to Tweeddale, 24 Aug. 1695.
[121]NLS, MS 7019, f. 133: Shrewsbury to Tweeddale, 19 Nov. 1695.
[122]NLS, MS 7029, f. 122: [Tweeddale] to Shrewsbury, 28 Nov. 1695.

blessing to Scotland that ever befell it, for it has excited here a wonderful disposition to an union.[123]

After he had waited on the king the previous evening, Johnston wrote excitedly to Tweeddale on 17 December: 'The king declares himself for the union and your friends have told him that no man knows it so well as you.'[124] He did, however admit, that: 'I know not the king's answer to the two Houses that has been at Kensington about our act.'[125] Writing to Tweeddale on 28 December Johnston mentioned that 'the king got yours on Thursday. He made me wait on but has not yet spoke to me. This is the day of the queen's death and he sees no body. I am told, and it seems probable, that he will do nothing in Scotch business in haste.'[126] There had been no improvement by 7 January 1696, when Johnston informed Tweeddale that: 'I have nothing to add, either to the king or others to what I have said for your coming up. What the king will do I know not, nor do I believe any other knows it … I suppose the king will wait, and do, what he finds necessary.'[127] Finally, on 28 January, Johnston reported that 'this night I had an hour of the king … though I could not get allowance to write to you that you might come up the king said at last that he thought he must consent to your coming up. I shall prefer my Lord Yester to ask this tomorrow, which will, if granted put all to rights.'[128]

Two days later there was a dramatic change in Johnston's correspondence. He explained to Tweeddale 'that I was much deceived in my last to you. You have indeed leave to come up, but it seems it is that you may not be condemned unheard, for all business is already done or resolved on. I am out.'[129] After considering Johnston's letters, Tweeddale decided that it would be best not to wait on the king. On 22 February he wrote to Yester to inform him: 'that my stay here hath been more necessary than leaving this place, though neither my health, nor the extreme stormy weather could well have suffered it'.[130] Tweeddale's reluctance to visit London would have been strongly influenced by the discovery of a plot to assassinate the king. Writing from London at midnight on 24 February, Lord John Murray, who had succeeded Johnston as one of the Scottish secretaries, advised Tweeddale that:

> yesterday morning was discovered a horrid conspiracy to murder our king as he was to come from hunting on Saturday, but his majesty getting some notice the day before did not go. At the same time there are accounts come that ten thousand men are on the coasts of France ready to be embarked for England, but I trust in God that any disappointment of their first wicked design will be a means to break their second.[131]

That the attempt to launch an invasion to restore King James came to nothing was largely owing to intelligence sent to James by Arran. When James and Arran corresponded, it was

---

[123]NLS, MS 14408, f. 434: Johnston to [Tweeddale], 12 Dec. 1695.

[124]NLS, MS 14408, f. 437: Johnston to Tweeddale, 17 Dec. 1695.

[125]NLS, MS 14408, f. 437: Johnston to Tweeddale, 17 Dec. 1695.

[126]NLS, MS 14408, f. 439: Johnston to Tweeddale, 28 Dec. 1695.

[127]NLS, MS 14408, f. 447: Johnston to Tweeddale, 7 Jan. 1695/6.

[128]NLS, MS 14408, f. 451: Johnston to Tweeddale, 23 Jan. 1696.

[129]NLS, MS 14408, f. 455: Johnston to Tweeddale, 30 Jan. 1696.

[130]NLS, MS 7030, f. 64v: [Tweeddale] to Yester, 22 Feb. 1696.

[131]NLS, MS 7020, f. 20: John Murray to [Tweeddale], 24 Feb. 1696.

usual practice for Nairne to decipher their letters. On Friday 24 January 1696, Nairne recorded in his journal that: 'the King gave me e[arl] A[rran]'s letter to uncipher'.[132] On Thursday 13 February, however, the king did not ask Nairne to decipher a letter he had received from Arran. Nairne wrote that: 'I carried E[arl] A[rran]'s letter unciphered to the K[ing].'[133] Five days later, Nairne wrote that the 'K[ing] parted from Saint Germ[ain] … and ordered me to follow him post and to bring the ciphers with me'.[134] Once James had deciphered Arran's letter he knew how to respond to the presence of an English fleet lying off the French coast at Calais. Nairne recorded in his journal, on 27 February 1696, that:

> I was at the k[ing]'s levee, who ordered me to wait on after sermon. Then he called me in and gave me the declarations to keep and told me that if the English came towards Calais, he would not go to Dunkirk till he saw if they attempted anything, but when he went, he said he would take care that I should go with him.[135]

The same day, Nairne also mentioned that the English 'ships came and passed within cannon shot of the fort to the number of about 60 sail in all, whereof it was judged there was about 30 men of war … The fort fired several guns, but they fell short as did also some shot of theirs.'[136] Tension mounted as the English ships waited for James to embark from Calais. He did nothing, however. Nairne recorded that the ships 'lay at anchor all day. The K[ing] resolved to stay at Calais and send for his plate etc. and keep his own table.'[137]

The tension broke on Sunday, 28 February, when James's illegitimate son, the duke of Berwick, was ordered to leave Calais for St Germain. James himself set out for Dunkirk the next day and when the English fleet sailed home its commander, Admiral Edward Russell, discovered that he and other prominent politicians, including Shrewsbury, had been implicated in jacobite conspiracy by the revelations made by Sir John Fenwick, a man well known to both Nairne and Johnston. When the two of them had attended Utrecht University in 1675, Nairne had written in his journal that 'Sir Jo[hn] Fenwick's regiment was in garrison there that winter.'[138] Nairne also mentioned that he had quarrelled with two of Fenwick's lieutenants, 'but there was no hurt done on either side and we were all made friends again'.[139]

As the conspiracy unravelled in the light of Fenwick's disclosures, Tweeddale was replaced as lord chancellor of Scotland in May 1696. Although he died on 11 August 1697, his strategy of using the Scottish parliament to manipulate its English counterpart continued to work. It finally achieved success in 1704, two years after the death of King William and the succession of Queen Anne. When the parliament of Scotland met that year, the 2nd marquess of Tweeddale was appointed lord high commissioner and James Johnston lord clerk register. By employing some rather tortuous parliamentary management, they were

---

[132]NLS, MS 14266, f. 103.
[133]NLS, MS 14266, f. 105.
[134]NLS, MS 14266, f. 106.
[135]NLS, MS 14266, f. 107.
[136]NLS, MS 14266, f. 107.
[137]NLS, MS 14266, f. 108.
[138]NLS, MS 14266, f. 3.
[139]NLS, MS 14266, f. 3.

able to pass an act of security which stated that the Scots were not obliged to accept the Hanoverian succession at Queen Anne's death.

As anticipated, this legislation produced an angry response in the English parliament. During a debate in the house of lords on 6 December 1704, in a committee on the state of nation, Lord Halifax 'said the Act of Security was not the distemper itself but a symptom: that the Darien miscarriage was that which galled all the kingdom of Scotland … and he insinuated that the same person [meaning Secretary Johnston] was the adviser of both the Darien Act and this'.[140]

This time, however, the house of lords responded very differently to the act of security than it had done to the act establishing the Company of Scotland. Knowing that the English unionists had enjoyed a majority in the Lords since 1700, Lord Somers stood up confidently in the committee and proposed that the English parliament penalise the Scots for passing the act of security. 'Some laws might pass here for the cutting off of all their trade with England; which laws … might be limited … so as not to … continue longer than the humour lasted of their setting up a different prince.'[141]

As lord keeper during William's reign, Somers had been one of the leading politicians who had responded to the first marquess of Tweeddale's attempt to create a unionist party in England. Writing to Tweeddale on 10 August 1695, Annandale had mentioned that he had met Somers, the archbishop of Canterbury and Sir William Trumbull, where

I spoke fully and particularly … upon all our business and both of men and things. Nor do I think anything that passed in parliament did escape and I do believe, upon good grounds, I can assure your lordship that they have as just a sense of all our affairs as you can wish and are entirely satisfied, and pleased, with all the proceedings of our parliament.[142]

By the beginning of Anne's reign, Somers had established himself at the head of the whig junto and was ready to complete Tweeddale's plan to unite Scotland and England. He had established a clandestine contact with James Johnston and was privately delighted when the Scottish parliament passed the Act of Security. Intent on using it to drive both Houses of the English parliament towards union, Somers was very alarmed at the discovery of a letter, written by the earl of Sutherland, which complained of 'Mr Johnston's ill conduct and named several great men here who were his supporters, among whom was the Lord Somers'.[143]

Because he was planning to lead the attack on the Act of Security in the house of lords, Somers was acutely aware that he would be seriously compromised if it was known that he had secretly approved of Johnston's conduct in the Scottish parliament.

[140] *The London Diaries of William Nicolson, Bishop of Carlisle, 1702–1718*, ed. Clyve Jones and Geoffrey Holmes (Oxford, 1985), 245. By 'the Darien Act' Halifax meant the act establishing the Company of Scotland in 1695. It was this company which subsequently founded a Scottish colony at Darien on the Isthmus of Panama.
[141] *London Diaries of William Nicolson*, ed. Jones and Holmes, 245.
[142] NLS, MS 7019, f. 128: Annandale to Tweeddale, 10 Aug. 1695.
[143] NRS, GD 406/1/5127: Gavin Mason to [duke of Hamilton], 1 Aug. 1704.

When Sutherland's letter was shown to him, Somers alleged that

Mr Johnston had done him much wrong, for in truth, he had never given him any countenance or encouragement in anything. That his lordship always looked upon him as a light-headed man and that he had troubled him with his solicitations which he never was pleased with. And that of late he had ordered his servants, whenever Johnston came to see him, he was not at home.[144]

Somers's explanation seems to have been sufficiently convincing to allay any serious doubts among the junto whigs in the house of commons about his alleged liaison with Johnston. Both houses of parliament readily agreed to Somers's proposal to prohibit Scottish trade with England and deny the right of citizenship to any Scots living in England. Faced with this ultimatum, the Scottish parliament nominated commissioners to negotiate a union in 1705 as did the English parliament. These commissioners met at London in the spring of 1706 and agreed to a treaty which was presented to the Scottish parliament for approval in the autumn.

Initially, there was some danger that the articles of the treaty might be rejected because of disagreements among what was variously called the New Party or the Squadrone Volante. Some of these politicians believed it would be better if the Scots just acknowledged the Hanoverian succession rather than uniting with England. This disagreement was only re-solved at the last minute by the intervention of James Johnston. On 8 October 1706 the duke of Hamilton observed, in a letter to his mother, that

the Squadrone have kept up their sentiments with great cautiousness till this day. They have declared themselves all as one man for the union, and in the terms as you see them. They say this has been brought about by Mr Johnston upon a letter written to him by the duke of Marlborough to negotiate with them.[145]

Once the Squadrone committed itself unequivocally to the Union, the court party, led by the duke of Queensberry, was able to push the articles of the treaty through parliament with relative ease. Delighted by the progress that was being made, Somers wrote to Sutherland on 26 October 1706, thanking him for his letter and 'congratulating with you upon the account of your hopeful entrance upon the great affair which I hope we shall see terminate to the interest and security of both kingdoms'.[146] When writing to the earl of Marchmont, one of the leaders of the Squadrone, Somers acknowledged the contribution made by Marchmont's friends:

Your Lordship is pleased to take notice of the actings of that which is called the New Party. I think they have taken a part so noble, so truly worth of all praise, that I am never weary of commending them. Without the happiness of a personal acquaintance with any of them, I have all the honour and service for every one of them that I can express, and shall be always ready to express it, as well as I can, and show it upon every occasion.

[144]NRS, GD 406/1/5127: Mason to [Hamilton], 1 Aug. 1704.
[145]NRS, GD 406/1/7854: [Hamilton] to [dowager duchess of Hamilton], 8 Oct. 1706.
[146]NLS, Sutherland MSS, Dep. 313/532: Somers to Sutherland, 26 Oct. 1706.

Give me permission to say, without vanity, I have acted myself upon a like foot for several years.[147]

Once the Scottish parliament had ratified the treaty, Somers wrote again to Sutherland, on 22 January 1706, to assure him that: 'I do most heartily congratulate your Lordship upon the happy conclusion of the union. I wish and hope for good success here and I shall be heartily joyful to meet you in Parliament next winter.'[148] Somers's hopes for the success of the Union in the English parliament were not disappointed. It was passed with little opposition in either Lords or Commons, and, in accordance with Article 3 of the Treaty, which came into effect on 1 May 1707, the British parliament was restored. The article stipulated: 'that the United Kingdom of Great Britain be represented by one and the same parliament to be styled the Parliament of Great Britain'.[149]

All that was required now to completely fulfil the 1st marquess of Tweeddale's scheme was a successful jacobite restoration. The British parliament met on 23 October 1707, and its proceedings were dominated by the Squadrone's attempt, with the support of the junto, to provoke unrest in Scotland. Legislation was introduced to reorganise the court of justiciary, change the Scottish militia and abolish the Scottish privy council. The Scottish Militia Bill was so incendiary that when Queen Anne came to the house of lords on 11 March 1708 to approve legislation passed by parliament, she 'rejected that for Modelling the Militia in Scotland'.[150] The queen also informed the House that she had received intelligence that a squadron of French ships had left Dunkirk squadron and was sailing northwards off the English coast.

An attempt to raise a jacobite rebellion in Scotland had begun at the end of February 1708. James II's son, James Francis Edward, left St Germain for Dunkirk,[151] after which there followed a combination of almost farcical misfortunes which became the distinguishing feature of the numerous unsuccessful attempts to restore 'King James III'. On 27 February, Nairne wrote that the 'king's sickness, and the English fleet appearing made us lose a whole week at Dunkirk, and contrary winds, and mistakes of pilots keeping us 8 days a going to Scotland, gave the enemy time to come up to us'.[152] The Dunkirk squadron finally anchored in the Firth of Forth. Then, on Saturday, 14 March, as Nairne observed, 'we perceived the English fleet, so instead of going up the river to land we were forced to sail to the north'.[153] The French ships managed to outrun their opponents and intended to land at Inverness, but, as Nairne recorded:

violent contrary winds hindered us to advance. Our fleet was dispersed and having reason to believe the enemy would keep along the coast and be upon us before we could land all our troops and ammunition, the French, to whom the king left to do what they thought most for their masters service and his, did advise, and even press, his majesty to return

---

[147]NRS, Hume of Marchmont MSS, GD 158/1154: Somers to [Marchmont], 11 Dec. [1706].

[148]NLS, Dep. 313/532: Somers to Sutherland, 22 Jan. 1706/7.

[149]*APS*, xi, 406.

[150]*London Diaries of William Nicolson*, ed. Jones and Holmes, 461.

[151]NLS, MS 14266, f. 210.

[152]NLS, MS 14266, f. 210.

[153]NLS, MS 14266, f. 210.

back to Dunkirk, the wind being very fair then, and accordingly Monsieur Fourbin [the French admiral] gave the signal and orders, and changed his course.[154]

The Dunkirk squadron finally returned to its home port on Saturday, 27 March 1708.

Although the attempt to raise a jacobite rebellion in Scotland had ended in failure, it did not mark the end of the attempts to restore James Francis Edward Stuart to the throne of Great Britain. The following year the British parliament began approving legislation that was deeply unpopular in Scotland. In 1709 it passed the Treason Bill; in 1711 the Scottish linen bill and a resolution denying the duke of Hamilton the right to sit in the Lords by virtue of his British title as duke of Brandon; and in 1712 the Episcopal Toleration Bill. At Queen Anne's death in 1714, Scotland was, again, on the brink of rebellion. The failure of the jacobite uprising in 1715 owed much, as it had done in 1708, to the apparent incompetence of James Francis Edward Stuart. No sooner had the rebellion subsided, however, than the cycle of incitement began again. It was to be the continuing feature of British politics in the 18th century. This was the legacy of the 1st marquess of Tweeddale.

The valuable and extensive evidence available for British politics, in the National Records and National Library of Scotland, suggests that the 1st marquess of Tweeddale made the most significant contribution to the restoration of the British parliament in 1707. A man of republican principles, Tweeddale understood that a Scottish republic could not survive without English support. Once Charles I had been overthrown, Tweeddale knew that the republic would only endure if leading Scots politicians were prepared to take a share of the responsibility for maintaining it by accepting seats in the British parliament.

After the Restoration, Tweeddale tried to persuade successive monarchs that it was in their best interests to restore a British parliament. That he failed was largely due to the suspicion of both Charles II and William III that a British parliament would inevitably seek to undermine the authority of the crown. When persuasion failed, Tweeddale was prepared to manipulate the English parliament and resort to a jacobite restoration to achieve his aims. Although his attempt failed, his efforts provided a blueprint for success in 1707, when the re-establishment of the British parliament followed the Treaty of Union between Scotland and England. The issues of republicanism and jacobitism, however, remained unresolved and continued to play a significant part in British political history in the 18th century.

[154]NLS, MS 14266, f. 210.

Playing with Fire: The 4th Duke of Hamilton's Jacobite Politics and the Union

DANIEL SZECHI

James Hamilton, duke of Hamilton and the Scots jacobites are generally linked in analyses of the final years of the Scots polity. Indeed, Hamilton is often presented as the leader of the jacobite party in the Scottish parliament. Yet both contemporaries and historians have been unsure what to make of his on-again, off-again, conduct with respect to the exiled Stuarts and France. This has fuelled an ongoing debate about Hamilton's erratic and highly enigmatic behaviour during the winter of 1706–7, when the Union was passing the Scottish parliament. Was he genuinely opposing the Union? Was he duped by the court? Or was he, 'bought and sold for English gold'? This essay takes a fresh look at the duke and his part in the Union crisis in the light of new and previously underused jacobite sources with a view to better understanding Hamilton's aims, objectives, and influence with this crucial group. Only the jacobites and the Cameronians were potentially willing to take their opposition to the Union to God's Acre. But neither party immediately flew to arms in response to passage of a union they both believed was a betrayal of everything they held dear, and Hamilton was a major factor in their failure to do so. This essay thus takes a close look at the duke's part in preventing a major national uprising against the Union in the winter of 1706–7 and advances a new interpretation of his conduct and significance throughout the Union crisis.

Keywords: England; France; jacobites; politics; Scotland; union of England and Scotland; 4th duke of Hamilton

1

There has never been any doubt that James, 4th duke of Hamilton, was a key actor in Scottish politics in the years leading up to the Union of 1707. In many respects, opposition, as much as government, shapes policies and legislative outcomes, and as the (intermittently) principal leader of the Scottish parliamentary opposition in 1702–7 he played a major role in shaping the Union.[1] In contemporary parlance, he was one of the 'great men' of Scottish politics, and as far as the Scots political nation was concerned this meant that he was naturally a mercurial, self-aggrandising mass of ambition with the potential for both good and ill.[2]

---

[1] See, e.g., T.M. Devine, *The Scottish Nation: A History 1700–2000* (1999), 15; J.D. Mackie, *A History of Scotland*, ed. Bruce Lenman and Geoffrey Parker (2nd edn, 1991), 260; P.W.J. Riley, *The Union of England and Scotland* (Manchester, 1978), 126, 149.

[2] *'Scotland's Ruine': Lockhart of Carnwath's Memoirs of the Union*, ed. Daniel Szechi (Aberdeen, 1995), 22; National Records of Scotland [hereafter cited as NRS], Clerk of Penicuik papers, GD 18/6080, p. 30; GD 24/1/872/1/3, pp. 193, 195–6, 198: memoirs of the Morays.

And he certainly lived up to their expectations in the final years of the early modern Scots polity. Whether it was leading a secession from parliament and a tax strike in 1702, cosying up to the masters of English politics at Westminster in the hope of obtaining office in Scotland, ostentatiously leading the opposition in putting forward popular patriotic measures or indelicately hinting at his potential claim to the crown of Scotland, he played the part with enthusiasm.[3] Which is, perhaps, why many modern historians have found the man and his behaviour difficult to fathom. Sir Thomas Devine has characterised his behaviour as, 'contradictory' and observed that he was: 'weak and indecisive at key moments which might have been exploited to advantage. So ambiguous was his position that some speculated as to which side he was actually on.'[4] William Ferguson saw Hamilton as 'untrustworthy', 'a mystery', 'enigmatic', and 'inexplicable', and summarizes him as a, 'curious mixture of great ability flawed by egregious folly'.[5] Patrick Riley implicitly agreed, commenting that Hamilton's behaviour was 'curious' and 'odd' and that his reasoning is, 'impossible to divine'.[6] For Paul Scott, he was simply 'indecisive and unpredictable'.[7]

Just as it is the job of oppositions to oppose, it is the job of historians to explain, and despite his strange conduct, sudden shifts and puzzling vacillations, the profession's take on Hamilton has developed two clear (albeit naturally overlapping) strands of interpretation. One reads him as primarily driven by his need for money. Two historians who have written extensively on Hamilton per se have offered detailed support for this reading of the duke. In her biography of Anne Hamilton, dowager duchess of Hamilton at the time of the Union, Rosalind Marshall observes: 'He was always ready to snatch at anything which would bring him financial advantage or enhanced reputation, no matter how far fetched the scheme.'[8] Likewise Victor Stater sees the mature Hamilton as having, 'an aptitude for nothing but improvidence', which led directly to him becoming 'grasping' and developing an 'obsession with money'.[9] Many historians whose focus is more on the Union than the duke, agree. Devine has no doubt that Hamilton's politics were primarily debt-driven. For Michael Lynch, his crucial move in setting the Union on track (in 1705) was, 'the product of graft'. Scott forthrightly states that Hamilton was bribed to let the Union pass the Scots parliament. A little more cautiously, J.D. Mackie, some time ago, observed that the Union as we know it would not have passed 'had not Hamilton betrayed his supporters, presumably for money'.[10]

[3] Keith Brown, 'Party Politics and Parliament: Scotland's Last Election and Its Aftermath, 1702–3', in *The History of the Scottish Parliament. Volume 2: Parliament and Politics in Scotland, 1567–1707*, ed. Keith Brown and Alastair J. Mann (Edinburgh, 2005), 249–52, 268–9; Victor Stater, *Duke Hamilton is Dead! A Story of Aristocratic Life and Death in Stuart Britain* (New York, 1999), 109–19; Rosalind K. Marshall, 'Hamilton, James, fourth duke of Hamilton and first duke of Brandon (1658–1712)', *ODNB*.

[4] Devine, *Scottish Nation*, 11, 15.

[5] William Ferguson, *Scotland: 1689 to the Present* (Edinburgh, 1968), 55; William Ferguson, *Scotland's Relations with England: A Survey to 1707* (Edinburgh, 1977), 190, 229, 231.

[6] Riley, *Union*, 75, 149, 286.

[7] Paul Scott, *Andrew Fletcher and the Treaty of Union* (Edinburgh, 1992), 118.

[8] Rosalind K. Marshall, *The Days of Duchess Anne: Life in the Household of the Duchess of Hamilton 1656–1716* (New York, 1974), 222, and also 135, 136, 171, 176. Dr Marshall's *ODNB* entry is a little more cautious on this issue.

[9] Stater, *Duke Hamilton is Dead!*, 108.

[10] Devine, *Scottish Nation*, 15; Michael Lynch, *Scotland: A New History* (rev. edn, 1992), 312; Scott, *Andrew Fletcher*, 78, 119; Mackie, *History of Scotland*, 260.

The second strand of interpretation sees the duke as being primarily driven by ambition: he wanted high office and power as a mark of his status as Scotland's premier aristocrat (though the money that high office would bring with it was doubtless a strong added incentive). Ferguson and Riley disagree fundamentally in their analyses of the Union crisis, but they are in accord with regard to the significance of ambition in explaining Hamilton's conduct. For Ferguson early-18th-century Scots politics was driven by 'envy and greed', and in Hamilton's case this led directly to his determination to bring down James Douglas, duke of Queensberry and contemporary Scotland's dominant magnate, and replace him in office.[11] Riley essentially agreed, observing that the duke sought 'to dominate Scottish politics', and more generally 'had an obligation to his house and following to assert himself, showing that he played second fiddle to nobody. A magnate had either to be dominant within the court or mighty in opposition.'[12]

This view is shared by the two most important and deeply researched analyses of the Union crisis that came out at the time of the tercentenary commemoration in 2007: Allan Macinnes's *Union and Empire* (2007) and Christopher Whatley's *The Scots and the Union* (2006).[13] Macinnes does not doubt that Hamilton was generally driven more by ambition than money, yet strikes a different note in that he is, for the most part, more sympathetic to the duke than Ferguson and Riley, allowing that Hamilton faced unending problems trying to coax the fractious opposition into united action versus the government and positing that this goes a long way towards explaining the duke's shilly-shallying and failures of leadership.[14] Whatley agrees that Hamilton's key objective 'was to be top dog in Scotland and to have the preference of the reigning monarch'. Yet he, too, is more sympathetic to the duke than has generally been the case, but for very different reasons. For Whatley, although financial cupidity also explains a lot about the duke's conduct, he sees Hamilton as being fundamentally compromised by the fact that in private the duke could see the advantages of the Union for Scotland and was thus reluctant to sabotage it entirely.[15]

2

The upshot of all this is that while we now have a pretty good understanding of the Union crisis and its dynamics, Hamilton's part in it remains more than a little puzzling. Why was he behaving so erratically and inconsistently? We do not have a satisfactory answer, and the problem, I would suggest, lies with the sources relied on by most of the historians who have written on the subject. Naturally enough, the two strands of interpretation outlined above have been overwhelmingly based on the surviving correspondence, memoranda, and memoirs left by the principal aristocratic and ministerial actors and other witnesses to the events in question. These are the gold standard for early modern politico-historical analysis

[11] Ferguson, *Scotland's Relations with England*, 189.

[12] Riley, *Union*, 88, 150.

[13] Allan I. Macinnes, *Union and Empire: The Making of the United Kingdom in 1707* (Cambridge, 2007); C.A. Whatley with Derek Patrick, *The Scots and the Union* (Edinburgh, 2006).

[14] Macinnes, *Union and Empire*, 89, 274, 305, but cf. 316.

[15] Whatley, *Scots and the Union*, 56, see also 249, 332.

and are, quite rightly, the first and most important bodies of evidence that a researcher in the field will go to when beginning a project on the politics of the Union. But there is one set of sources that has generally been either ignored, or greatly under-utilised: with the exception of George Lockhart of Carnwath's *Memoirs Concerning the Affairs of Scotland from Queen Anne's Accession to the Throne to the Commencement of the Union of the Two Kingdoms of Scotland and England in May 1707*, use of which is ubiquitous, other jacobite and French sources have been remarkably little used. In addition, in recent years new jacobite sources have been discovered or rediscovered. This is particularly important in Hamilton's case because we have known for a long time that he was playing in both the conventional political world and the underground world of jacobite politics, and obviously his machinations in one could influence his conduct in the other.

So what are these neglected/new jacobite and French sources? The most important under-utilised source is William Dunn Macray's 19th-century edition of the correspondence of Colonel Nathaniel Hooke, an Irish soldier in French service.[16] Hooke was secretly sent to Scotland in 1705 and 1707 by the French government, with a view to scouting the possibility of provoking a jacobite rising there. In the course of these two missions he met and negotiated with the leaders of the Scots jacobites, and in 1705 – most significantly from the point of view of this essay – had several long, detailed discussions with Hamilton personally. Thereafter he remained in communication with the Scots jacobites, who often discussed their relations with Hamilton in their letters. Hooke's missions and his reports to Louis XIV's *Conseil d'en Haut*, the key body responsible for the co-ordination of French military strategy, have made an appearance here and there in the sources underpinning interpretations of events, but more often for their striking vignettes (for example, Hamilton insisting on meeting Hooke in dead of night in a pitch-dark room so he could honestly claim he had not seen him) than the detailed content of Hooke's discussions and negotiations.[17] Hooke's correspondence and memoranda also dominate the documents on Scotland held at the Archives des Affaires Étrangères at La Courneuve in Paris, but there are, too, additional documents there that are concerned with Scots politics and few of these have been taken into account in the historiography.

The jacobite court at St Germain was, of course, keenly interested in what was going on in Scotland and at one time had an extensive archive of correspondence, memoranda and other documents that might have shed a great deal of light on jacobite affairs and politics in general in the three kingdoms in this period. Unfortunately the destruction of most of its records for the period 1689–1713 during the French revolution, has not left a great deal beyond the documents in the Carte manuscripts in the Bodleian Library, a broad selection of which were published by James Macpherson in 1775.[18] These can be supplemented by a number of translated forwards from the Stuart shadow government

[16] *Correspondence of Colonel N. Hooke, Agent From the Court of France to the Scottish Jacobites, in the Years 1703–7* (2 vols, 1870).

[17] Ferguson, *Scotland's Relations with England*, 229; Bruce Lenman, *The Jacobite Risings in Britain 1689–1746* (1980), 87; Stater, *Duke Hamilton is Dead!*, 133-4. A notable exception is John Sibbald Gibson, who describes Hooke's discussions with Hamilton in detail: John Sibbald Gibson, *Playing the Scottish Card: The Franco-Jacobite Invasion of 1708* (Edinburgh, 1988), 48ff.

[18] James Macpherson, *Original Papers: Containing the Secret History of Great Britain, from the Restoration to the Accession of the House of Hanover ...* (2 vols, 1775); Edward Corp, 'An Inventory of the Archives of the Stuart Court at Saint-Germain-en-Laye, 1689–1718', *Archives*, xxiii (1998), 118–46.

to its French patron, which are to be found in the French archives, but neither body of evidence has much influenced the interpretation of what was going on in Scotland in 1702–7, quite possibly because of the hostility of some historians to jacobite sources *tout court*.[19] Likewise, the correspondence in the British Library between the jacobite regent (de facto) Queen Mary of Modena and the papal nuncio in Paris, Cardinal Filippo Antonio Gualterio.[20]

One particularly valuable survival from the jacobite court, only recently rediscovered by Professor Edward Corp, sheds a good deal of new light on the activities of the jacobite court and needs to be taken into account in future: the journal of David Nairne, under secretary to the jacobite secretary of state, Charles Middleton, earl of Middleton.[21] Just as valuable in a general sense is the jacobite family memoir written (almost certainly) by Maurice Moray of Abercairny, held by the National Records of Scotland. Recognized and retrieved in 2011 by Dr Frances Shaw, this includes a great deal of new material and specifically, accounts of the missions to Scotland of Maurice's brother, captain, later lieutenant colonel, John Moray (a Scots soldier in French service sent on secret missions to Scotland in 1703 and 1707).[22] Most valuable and significant of all for the purposes of this essay, though, is the superb run of letters between Father James Carnegy of the underground Scots catholic church and his superiors at the Scots College in Paris. These compose part of the Blairs Letters now held at Aberdeen University Library and are a unique survival from the destruction of the college in 1792.[23] They are replete with insider accounts of Scots jacobite politics and news of what was going on in Scottish politics in general, as understood on the streets and in the taverns of Edinburgh. The most important material in the letters is, however, written in a cant code for which the key has been lost. Close, systematic reading and detailed research into Carnegy's context does, however, allow the partial retrieval of the evidence contained in the letters, and I have been using these techniques to decipher the letters. Evidence from Carnegy's letters, especially those in which he discusses his personal conversations and correspondence with Hamilton, is central to the argument presented below.[24]

What follows is a reappraisal of Hamilton's conduct in 1702–7 in light of the two strands of interpretation outlined above. Specifically, I will look at the French/jacobite evidence relating to his financial cupidity and then explore the dynamics of his drive for power and office through his relations with the Scots jacobites, in the latter case particularly focusing on the period from summer 1705 to winter 1706–7, the height of the Union crisis. At core I will be addressing two questions: how financially driven were Hamilton's politics, and how far did his relationship with the Scots jacobites affect his political conduct?

---

[19] See, e.g., Paul Langford, *A Polite and Commercial People: England 1727–1783* (Oxford, 1989), 200.

[20] Notable exceptions to this are Stater, *Duke Hamilton is Dead!*, 128–9, and Whatley, *Scots and the Union*, 228, 280. Otherwise these have been little used since the early 20th century: Martin Haile [Marie Halle], *James Francis Edward: The Old Chevalier* (1907), 62–3; F.W. Head, *The Fallen Stuarts* (Cambridge, 1901).

[21] National Library of Scotland [hereafter cited as NLS], MS 14266: Sir David Nairne's journal.

[22] NRS, GD 24/1/872/1.

[23] Special Collections Library, University of Aberdeen, Scots Catholic Archives, Blairs Letters [hereafter cited as Blairs Letters].

[24] I hope eventually to e-publish a freely accessible database of these deciphered letters.

3

Of all the pastimes a nobleman from the highest ranks of the social elite could take up in the early 18th century, politics was potentially one of the most ruinous.[25] In early-18th-century Scotland the great expense of funding a suitable domicile and lifestyle in Edinburgh, the most expensive city in the country, was only the beginning. To be considered a great man, which Hamilton always aspired to be, one had to entertain lavishly, display yourself and your servants in public dressed in the latest fashion and deploy appropriate ostentation in terms of carriages, horses and accoutrements.[26] But most important of all, a great man had to help his 'friends'. This rarely took the form of straightforward cash payments. Scots magnates who were safely ensconced in government office for the most part got by through the judicious (or not) distribution of official patronage. Magnates like Hamilton, who spent their political lives in opposition, instead made contributions to their friends' election expenses, costs of living in Edinburgh and other incidental and particular matters. In addition, they patronised writers and artists and selected clergymen, gave money to the Edinburgh crowd, as well as various good causes, and so on.[27]

The net drain on an aristocrat's resources could be prodigious, and in Hamilton's case (because of his long-standing propensity to extravagance in every aspect of life) had reduced him to dire straits by 1702.[28] His need for money accordingly fuelled his engagement with the jacobite court and its patrons (primarily France, but also Spain and the papacy). The fact that Louis XIV was the most splendid king in Europe, with a carefully cultivated reputation for wealth and generosity – which the duke had witnessed and enjoyed as a young man while he was at Versailles – almost certainly further influenced Hamilton to demand very large sums indeed for his services.[29]

These features of Hamilton's attitude towards the exiled Stuarts became clear as early as 1702, when John Hamilton, Lord Belhaven, secretly visited St Germain.[30] A key part of Belhaven's negotiations with the de facto queen regent, Mary of Modena, was the transmission of a request that she would secure a substantial sum of money (probably £20,000 sterling[31]) for the use of the duke of Hamilton, ostensibly to fund the 'country' coalition opposed to Queen Anne's ministry in Scotland. The jacobite court did not have that kind of ready money and so Queen Mary asked Louis XIV if he could fund Hamilton. Louis was sympathetic, but given the cost of fighting the War of the Spanish Succession, was reluctant to be the sole provider, and urged the queen also to ask the pope for a subvention.

[25] See, e.g., Paul Hopkins, 'Lindsay, Colin, third earl of Balcarres (1652–1721)', *ODNB*; Reed Browning, 'Holles, Thomas Pelham- … first duke of Newcastle under Lyme (1693–1768)', *ODNB*; Lawrence B. Smith, 'Wharton, Philip James, duke of Wharton and jacobite duke of Northumberland (1698–1731)', *ODNB*.

[26] Keith M. Brown, *Noble Society in Scotland: Wealth, Family and Culture, from Reformation to Revolution* (Edinburgh, 2000), 84–91.

[27] Ronald M. Sunter, *Patronage and Politics in Scotland 1707–1832* (Edinburgh, 1986), 1–86, 199–210; Stater, *Duke Hamilton is Dead!*, 109, 119.

[28] Marshall, *Days of Duchess Anne*, 135, 136, 171, 176; Stater, *Duke Hamilton is Dead!*, 107–8.

[29] Marshall, *Days of Duchess Anne*, 138; Stater, *Duke Hamilton is Dead!*, 27–8.

[30] Daniel Szechi, *Britain's Lost Revolution? Jacobite Scotland and French Grand Strategy, 1701–8* (Manchester, 2015), 117.

[31] La Courneuve, Paris, Affaires Étrangères, Correspondence Politique (Angleterre) [hereafter cited as AECP (A)] 215, f. 81: — to [Torcy?], nd.

Queen Mary did exactly this and in early 1703 secured a sum of 100,000 *scudi* (equivalent to £28,707 sterling) from the papacy, for which the French government would act as a front (Clement XI was well aware of the political toxicity of any hint that the Scots opposition was being supported by papal gold).[32] By this time, however, Louis XIV and his ministers were apparently beginning to have doubts about Hamilton's sincerity, possibly because they had received a report (from Hooke) that the duke had taken money to support the Hanoverian succession from the dowager electress of Hanover, Sophia, who had been declared heir to Queen Anne by the English Act of Settlement.[33] The French secretary of state for foreign affairs, Jean-Baptiste Colbert de Croissy, marquis de Torcy, accordingly told Archbishop Gualterio, the papal nuncio to France, that the French government wanted to hold off sending the money to Hamilton until they were sure of him, and they, therefore, apparently awaited the report of a jacobite agent whom Queen Mary was sending to Scotland at the duke's request.[34]

The agent, Captain James Murray of Stanhope, returned to France early in 1704 and delivered his report to St Germain, from whence it was passed on to the French. Hamilton's demands had by this time grown to £25,000 sterling. In return for this

> he proposes … to take a share of it to himself, to assist him to defray the great expence which he will be obliged to make for maintaining his credit with his party; to distribute another share of it in augmenting and strengthening his party, and in preserving and confirming those who are already of it, according as he shall see necessary for the service of [James III and VIII]; and to employ the rest in purchasing arms.[35]

The duke also wanted the French to prepare an expeditionary force on the coast of northern France ready to sail as soon as it received word from him, and St Germain to supply the names of its principal supporters in England so that he could co-ordinate matters with them.

It is worth pausing at this point to reflect on what Hamilton was asking for. The money is straightforward, the rest was highly problematic – as the duke was probably well aware. There was no possibility of the French tying up a substantial body of troops on the coast of France doing nothing while they waited on Hamilton's pleasure. France was engaged in a titanic struggle with the Grand Alliance and the war was not going well.[36] Besides which, any such concentration of French troops on the coast close by the British Isles was likely to be soon discovered by British agents and a royal navy squadron despatched to make sure they never sailed, or to destroy the expedition if they did. St Germain was also not going to supply Hamilton with the names and addresses of its secret supporters in England. In the first place it would have been far too great a hostage to fortune, and, second, the exiled court regularly pledged itself not to reveal the names of those who were in contact with

---

[32] Haile, *James Francis Edward*, 62–3; Head, *Fallen Stuarts*, 130–2; BL, Add. MS 20293, ff. 7–8: Queen Mary to Gualterio, 12/23 Apr. 1703.

[33] *Hooke Correspondence*, i, 1–20.

[34] BL, Add. MS 20318, ff. 67–8, 69: Torcy to Gualterio, 11/22, 12/23 Apr. 1703.

[35] Macpherson, *Original Papers*, i, 666–8.

[36] David Chandler, *Marlborough as Military Commander* (2nd edn, 1979), 94–122; Nicholas Henderson, *Prince Eugen of Savoy: A Biography* (1964), 56–75.

it.[37] Delivering them to the duke would have been a gross breach of trust and would have compromised the possibility of the exiled Stuarts using those contacts when opportunity offered in the future. The upshot was that Hamilton was, in effect, making two demands that he almost certainly knew could not be conceded, and one – the demand for money – that could. This can fairly be described as a standard political negotiating ploy, then and now. If it worked, the French government and the jacobite shadow government would refuse the tricky elements among his demands and simply send him the money. Hamilton would thereby get £25,000 sterling to satisfy some of his creditors and distribute among the country coalition as he saw fit and very likely be committed to nothing more than talking (indirectly through St Germain, with nice comfortable delays) to the leaders of the English jacobites and to the French about an invasion, at some point, when matters were mutually convenient, in the future, sometime, whenever.

As so often in his career, the duke was being too clever by half, and the result was predictable. It is not clear how much French, papal or jacobite government money reached him, but whatever the amount it was certainly not enough to satisfy him.[38] For the rest of the period under review Hamilton regularly included a demand for large sums of money at every opportunity in his negotiations with the French government and its jacobite ally. He did so from 1703 primarily through James Carnegy, his principal contact with both the French and the jacobites. Thus in April 1703, after talking with Hamilton about the forthcoming session of the Scots parliament, Carnegy obligingly prodded his superiors:

> The Jacobits admire that the French king, whom they know has not forces to spare to send to Brittain, did not at least send some money to be distributed amongst our poor members, by which he would have easily caried all that the Hamilton faction desires, to witt, that the succession be setled on the next Protestant heir without naming the person.[39]

This, and Murray's report, does not appear to have produced the result Hamilton wanted and he began to talk about sending Carnegy to France as his emissary, presumably assuming that Versailles and St Germain would be more sympathetic to his case when presented by a catholic priest.[40] Finally, in November, the duke prompted Carnegy bluntly to tell his superiors that he, 'desirs litle Judeth [£25,000 sterling] may be sent to Joanna ["Alexander Gaven"]'.[41] Again this did not produce the result Hamilton wanted, as Queen Mary acknowledged in May 1705 when briefing Hooke before his first mission to Scotland ('she complained that no money has been sent to Hamilton to help him with his necessary expenses in the next session of Parliament').[42]

Hooke responded that: 'we are not yet sufficiently clear as to the Scots' intentions for us to take such a step in their favour'. Interestingly and tellingly, the queen chose to concede

---

[37] Macpherson, *Original Papers*, i, 702–3.

[38] Haile, *James Francis Edward*, 62–3; Head, *Fallen Stuarts*, 130.

[39] Blairs Letters, 2/82/11: to [Lewis Innes?], 24 Apr. 1703.

[40] Blairs Letters, 2/93/7: Carnegy to [Lewis Innes?], 26 Feb. 1704; 2/93/19, 2/94/5, 8: to [Thomas Innes], 26 July, 26 Aug., 14 Oct. 1704.

[41] Blairs Letters, 2/94/11: Carnegy to [Lewis Innes?], 7/18 Nov. 1704.

[42] *Hooke Correspondence*, i, 191: Hooke to Torcy, 25 May/5 June 1705 ('*Elle se plaignit de ce qu'on n'envoye point d'argent au Duc de Hamilton pour l'aider à faire les depenses necessaires pendant la seance du Parlement*').

the point, and, instead, shifted her ground to push for the immediate sending of an envoy from the French government to the Scots jacobites.[43] The duke was accordingly somewhat put out when he met his old acquaintance, Hooke, at Holyrood Palace in August 1705. At their first encounter Hamilton asserted that Queensberry had bought the services of a tranche of commissioners (MPs) from northern Scotland with a sum of money he had brought from London and that he (Hamilton) needed Louis XIV to send him money to buy votes, particularly from the commissioners for the burghs as this would enable him to block legislation enacting either the Hanoverian succession or the Union.[44] When Hooke coolly replied that, 'the king's service would scarcely be advanced even if he succeeded', Hamilton first blustered about his commitment to the jacobite cause and then enquired if the French king might be willing to restore the duchy of Châtellerault to the house of Hamilton (this would have been a considerable fillip to the duke's finances)?[45] Hooke was blandly non-committal, so at their next meeting Hamilton returned to the subject of a lump sum from Louis XIV that would enable him to buy votes in parliament. Hooke forthrightly observed that from what he had learned in Scotland, the duke's political strength was waning anyway and he might as well 'take off his mask and declare himself', that is to say rebel. Clearly taken aback, Hamilton said he would think about it.[46]

When they met again the duke went over to the offensive entirely. As Hooke feelingly reported, the next three nights were, 'nothing more than a continual dispute; he wanted one hundred thousand pounds sterling to move [Scots] affairs to a breach [with England]; but he would not engage himself to do anything'. As far as Hooke was concerned, 'this gave me good reason to believe that there was nothing to be done with him'.[47] In their final meeting, however, Hooke, again, dutifully pressed Hamilton as to when he might deliver on his promises if he was supplied with money and arms? 'When it is time', replied the duke. When asked by Hooke when that might be, he stumbled revealingly: 'I do not know … opportunities could arise and if they do we will profit from them, but you can count on it happening on the death of Queen Anne.'[48] Hooke then took his leave and shortly afterwards returned to France, only to find when he arrived that Hamilton had apparently convinced himself (on no grounds whatsoever according to Hooke) that Hooke had brought £10,000 from St Germain with him to Scotland specifically for the duke, and that he had then deliberately gone back to France without leaving it behind for Hamilton to spend. Carnegy reported that the duke was in 'a passion' about this.[49]

Hamilton's search for funding became more urgent as the treaty negotiations steadily progressed over the winter of 1705–6 and by May 1706, he was threatening not even to

[43] Hooke Correspondence, i, 191: Hooke to Torcy, 25 May/5 June 1705 (' … qu'on ne voit pas encore assez claire dans les intentions des Ecossois pour faire une telle demarche en leur faveur. La reyne approuva ma reponse').

[44] Hooke Correspondence, i, 385–6: Hooke's report, 6/17 Oct. 1705 ('le service du Roy ne sera gueres avancé quand il sera venu au bout de tout cela').

[45] Hooke Correspondence, i, 389, 392.

[46] Hooke Correspondence, i, 397: Hooke's report, 6/17 Oct. 1705 ('lever le masque et se declarer').

[47] Hooke Correspondence, i, 408: Hooke's report, 6/17 Oct. 1705 ('n'etoit que des disputes continuelles; il vouloit avoir cent mil livres sterlins pour disposer les affaires à une rupture; mais il ne vouloit pas s'engager à quelque chose que ce soit, ce qui me donna juste raison de croire qu'il n'y avoit rien à faire avec luy').

[48] Hooke Correspondence, i, 417: Hooke's report, 6/17 Oct. 1705 ('Lorsqu'il sera tems … Je ne sçais, … des accidens peuvent arriver; s'ils arrivent, nous en profiterons, mais vous pouvez compter que ce sera à la mort de la Reyne Anne').

[49] Hooke Correspondence, i, 281; Blairs Letters, 2/125/1: Carnegy to [Lewis Innes], 25 May 1706.

turn up for the next session of the Scottish parliament unless he was sent some money from France.[50] This produced no result, so in June he sent Captain Harry Straton (one of the jacobite court's principal agents in Scotland) to St Germain as his personal representative in a final attempt to wring some cash for the session out of his putative continental allies.[51] Straton was courteously received by the jacobite government-in-exile and, as well as debriefing him extensively on the state of affairs in Scotland and the possibility of a rising against the Union, they promptly lobbied the French government on the duke's behalf.[52] The year 1706, however, was an *annus mirabilis* for the Grand Alliance, and on the heels of the rout of French forces in Flanders at Ramillies in May, the French army in Italy was effectively destroyed at Turin in September and Bourbon control of Spain was in a state of collapse by the end of the year.[53] The French king and his ministers thus had other things on their minds than the affairs of Scotland. Straton came back empty-handed.

Hamilton was correspondingly reported by Carnegy to be 'much dejected' in September, on the eve of the final session of the Scots parliament, and possibly at the duke's instigation the priest added his own moiety to the pressure on St Germain and Versailles, pleading that: 'A litle [money] would go a great length and do both him and [Louis XIV] good service.'[54] It was to no avail, and Hamilton and his allies went into the Union debates with only their own resources with which to play the patronage game. The duke was, as usual, up to his eyes in debt, so there was some justice to his complaint that he was condemned that autumn 'to make brick without straw'.[55] Whatever his circumstances, however, he did not relax the pressure on St Germain and Versailles, and pleas for cash continued for the rest of the year.[56] Unbeknown to Hamilton, his efforts, and particularly his political machinations with respect to harnessing the Scots jacobites to his campaign against the Union, did produce a result. On 12 January 1707, Hooke contacted Lewis Innes, principal of the Scots College and almoner to Queen Mary, to ask him to send a letter to the duke via the Scots College's secret channels of communication. From this letter it is clear that there was now a plan to send Hamilton a sum of money. The problem from the duke's point of view was that the money was going to arrive with a French expeditionary force attached.[57]

4

This brings us to Hamilton's relationship with the Scots jacobites and the very salient question of how matters came to such a pass. Though the duke is sometimes credited

---

[50] Blairs Letters, 2/125/1: Carnegy to [Lewis Innes], 25 May 1706.

[51] NRS, GD 24/1/872/1/3, p. 198.

[52] NLS, MS 14266: Nairne journal, 9/20, 12/23 Aug., 23 Aug./3 Sept., 30 Aug./10 Sept., 3/14 Sept. 1706; Bodl., MS Carte 180, ff. 212–20: 'An Account of the Present State of Scotland in July 1706' [by Harry Straton], [12/23 Aug.] 1706; AECP (A) 221, f. 194: Middleton to Torcy, 24 Aug./4 Sept. 1706 (English translation in Macpherson, *Original Papers*, ii, 21–2).

[53] Chandler, *Marlborough as Military Commander*, 166–83; Henderson, *Prince Eugen*, 115–35.

[54] Blairs Letters, 2/125/9: Carnegy to [Lewis Innes], 3 Sept. 1706.

[55] Blairs Letters, 2/125/11, 13: Carnegy to [Lewis Innes], 24 Sept., 12 Oct. 1706.

[56] Blairs Letters, 2/125/13, 15, 18: Carnegy to [Lewis Innes], 12, 26 Oct., 9 Nov. 1706.

[57] *Hooke Correspondence*, ii, 107–8.

with being the leader of the Scots jacobites, this interpretation does not match the reality of what was, in fact, a highly volatile and suspicious relationship.[58]

The Scots jacobites fully acknowledged that because Hamilton was Scotland's premier nobleman and sprang from a great royalist dynasty they should be prepared to follow him. As Charles Hay, earl of Erroll, told Hooke in 1705, 'I would be happy … to have him at our head, for he is the premier peer in the kingdom and the people love him.'[59] The great majority, though, understood the dynamics of contemporary Scots politics well enough to know that blindly following any great man was liable to lead not just to personal, but to ideological, disappointment.[60] And the Scots jacobites were fundamentally ideologically driven. The key objective as far as they were concerned was always the restoration of James III and VIII in the jacobite line. But as the Union crisis developed this objective became intrinsically attached to a commitment to stopping the Union at all costs. Indeed, by late 1706 stopping the Union was more important to them than precipitating a rising to restore their king.[61] This is not to suggest that they lost sight of their ultimate objective, but rather that they were willing to defer it in order to preserve Scotland's nominal independence. If they succeeded in this, they believed, matters would eventually fall out in favour of the exiled king and all would be well with the world.

This created friction between the Scots jacobites and Hamilton from the outset, which is to say, from the point of view of this essay, the election of Queen Anne's one and only Scottish parliament in 1703. As at least the nominal leader of the country opposition to Queen Anne's government, the duke had to coax a fractious coalition of commissioners and peers into co-operating against the government of the day despite their differences with each other. As was always the way with such alignments in the 18th-century British Isles, the country coalition included men whose principal motivation was the furtherance of their religious principles (presbyterianism or episcopalianism in this case), disgruntled courtiers who wanted to use it as a ramp back into office, 'commonwealthmen' who were in effect closet republicans, and aspiring magnates with an eye to making a reputation for themselves.[62] The jacobites who came into the Scots parliament in 1703 in significant numbers for the first time since 1689, can only have represented a further, highly unwelcome, complication.

This became apparent from the start of the first session. Charles Home, earl of Home, was the man the 'cavaliers' (that is to say, the jacobites) regarded as their parliamentary leader until his death in August 1706 and he and other influential leaders were straightforwardly

---

[58] George Hilton Jones, *The Main Stream of Jacobitism* (Cambridge, MA, 1954), 74; W.A. Speck, *The Birth of Britain: A New Nation 1700–1710* (Oxford, 1994), 38, 59.

[59] *Hooke Correspondence*, i, 381: Hooke's report, 6/17 Oct. 1705 ('*Je serois … bien aise … de l'avoir à notre tête; il est le premier pair du royaume, [et] le peuple l'aime*').

[60] *'Scotland's Ruine'*, ed. Szechi, 214–15, 248; *The Lockhart Papers*, ed. Anthony Aufrere (2 vols, 1817), ii, 298–9, 338; NRS, GD 24/1/872/1/3, pp. 186, 224, 254; NLS, Wodrow MSS, Quarto 75, item vi, ff. 32–3, 41: Walter Stewart's, 'A short Account of the proceedings of The Last Session of the Scots Parliament, with some necessary Reflections thereupon [by a member of both that & the preceeding parliament]' [c.1716]. (I am grateful to Dr Karin Bowie for allowing me to see her transcript of this fascinating document.)

[61] Szechi, *Britain's Lost Revolution?*, 109–49.

[62] Brown, 'Party Politics and Parliament', 273–4; Geoffrey Holmes, *British Politics in the Age of Anne* (rev. edn, 1987), 116–47.

suspicious of Hamilton's motives.[63] Indeed, Home in particular had personally experienced the duke's unreliability in the course of the jacobite plotting in which they were both involved in the 1690s.[64] Thus when Alexander Montgomery, earl of Eglinton, specifically confronted the duke on the question of a restoration, telling him, 'Declare what you are for. If it be [James III and VIII] I'll venture all I have above ground in the quarrell', and Hamilton obfuscated, this confirmed the cavaliers' doubts about him.[65] They accordingly pursued their own agenda throughout the session of 1703. What they were specially interested in achieving was some kind of official, legal toleration for episcopalians, and to secure this, were willing to do deals with the ministry regarding a formal confirmation of the acts passed by the 1702 session of the Scots parliament[66] and vote for a suitably large cess to fund the government and the war-effort.[67] Hamilton and the country coalition were opposed to both, and many of the presbyterians in its ranks were, in addition, hostile to any kind of legal toleration for episcopalians. Clashes between the jacobites and the country party duly followed.[68] As Carnegy (who was already becoming a closet Hamiltonian) reported in early May:

> When our Parliament sat first down ther was nothing in it but Court and Country pairty, but since the Jacobits came in … they'll ruin all, for instead of joyning with Duke Hamilton, by which they would have caried what they pleased, they make a faction of their own, more opposit to Duke Hamilton than the Court.

The jacobites' reasoning was that they believed

> Hamilton has no design for their maister since he joyns with the Presbyterians who will never consent to his [James III and VIII] incoming, and he [Hamilton] sayes they have … no love for him since they sell him for episcopacy and, at the best, have no thoughts of him [James] till Queen Anne dye.[69]

Hamilton was duly forced onto the political defensive, and instead of grandly commanding the jacobites was obliged to bargain with them for their support for country measures.[70] The duke was in a quandary: the political arithmetic of the 1703 election meant that the country group could not outvote the court without jacobite support. Unless he could bring the jacobite party on board he was facing political impotence. Fortunately for Hamilton, the court opened the way to country/cavalier alliance by reneging on its pact with the

[63] Blairs Letters, 2/82/10, 15, 2/83/1: Carnegy to [Lewis Innes?], 13 Apr., [11 May, 22 May/2 June] 1703. Here I differ from Professor Ferguson, who regards Home as only the 'nominal' leader of the jacobites and in general as 'a mere puppet' of Hamilton's: Ferguson, *Scotland's Relations with England*, 204.

[64] Paul Hopkins, *Glencoe and the End of the Highland War* (2nd edn, Edinburgh, 1998), 240, 274, 356.

[65] Blairs Letters, 2/82/12: Carnegy to [Lewis Innes?], 1 May 1703.

[66] This was the last session of William II and III's 1689 parliament and took place after he was dead. Technically it was legal, but even many of those who sat in the session were uneasy about whether it was constitutional.

[67] Blairs Letters, 2/83/1: Carnegy to [Lewis Innes?], [22 May/2 June 1703]; Szechi, *Britain's Lost Revolution?*, 120–3.

[68] Blairs Letters, 2/83/1, 2: Carnegy to [Lewis Innes?], [22 May/2 June], 8/19 June 1703; '*Scotland's Ruine*', ed. Szechi, 28–36.

[69] Blairs Letters, 2/82/15: Carnegy to [Lewis Innes?], [11 May 1703].

[70] Blairs Letters, 2/83/1: Carnegy to [Lewis Innes?], [22 May/2 June 1703].

jacobites. The duke exploited the breach by publicly standing out and speaking against the court's proposal specifically to establish the Hanoverian succession in Scots law,[71] and was duly rewarded by the votes of the jacobite party, which immediately joined the country coalition and gave the court a thumping defeat on the issue.[72] Bringing in the jacobites, however, had consequences. Up until this point Hamilton had been able to present himself as all things to all men, and despite his former associations with jacobitism had been able to keep many parliamentarians on side who were primarily interested in defending and advancing the presbyterian interest, by virtue of his own public rhetoric and the respect they felt for his mother, the dowager duchess, a famously unflinching adherent and protector of the kirk.[73] Voting down the Hanoverian succession changed that. Many country party presbyterians were unhappy at associating with the jacobites, and even more uneasy about blocking the Hanoverian succession in Scotland. A major rift began to open up between them and the duke.[74]

At this point it is worth reflecting further on Hamilton's jacobite problem. The jacobites were difficult to deal with on multiple levels: ideological incompatibility with politicians committed to the revolution settlement, political naïvety, hostility to constitutional conventions, cliquishness, and so on.[75] For the purposes of this essay, however, I will focus on the ideological problem. The jacobites were ideologically driven and thus any pact with them had to appear to further their agenda. In other words, Hamilton had to convince them that he really was a jacobite and had the interests of the exiled Stuarts at heart. The difficulty here was that, despite their political inexperience, the jacobites in essence knew him and his ilk too well. In early-18th-century Scotland a magnate's principles were always flexible, and thus while the jacobites were happy to co-operate with the duke over blocking the Hanoverian succession and passing the Act of Security, their alliance with him and the country party only extended as far as they perceived a common interest. To further his ambition of becoming the greatest man in Scotland, Hamilton had to find a way to tie them in more securely while at the same time (hopefully) keeping the country party presbyterians on board.

If a great man had the nerve for it there was, though, a uniquely jacobite political vulnerability that could be exploited. For the jacobites' principles necessarily enjoined deference to the wishes of the exiled court. If they were directed to follow Hamilton by the queen regent they would, in general, obey her.[76] Hence the duke began to play a very dangerous game from 1703 onwards. What would most convincingly demonstrate his jacobite bona fides? Close involvement in jacobite military plotting. This was the other half of jacobite activity in Scotland between 1702 and 1709. What we may legitimately call the movement's political wing was happy to busy itself trying to advance the cause in the Scots

[71] The English Act of Settlement of 1701 had laid down that the electress of Hanover was to succeed Queen Anne in all three kingdoms, but (apart from outraging Scots of every political stripe) this had no standing in Scots law.

[72] Blairs Letters, 2/83/7: Carnegy to [Lewis Innes?], 31 July 1703.

[73] 'Scotland's Ruine', ed. Szechi, 28; Jeffrey Stephen, *Defending the Revolution: The Church of Scotland 1689–1716* (Farnham, 2013), 155–6.

[74] Blairs Letters, 2/83/7: Carnegy to [Lewis Innes?], 31 July 1703.

[75] Szechi, *Britain's Lost Revolution?*, 89–98.

[76] *Hooke Correspondence*, i, 380.

parliament, but only as an interim measure. The jacobites knew right well that they would in all likelihood have to go to war to secure a restoration, and from their point of view the international situation was, prima facie, distinctly promising. The outbreak of the War of the Spanish Succession in 1701 had opened up the possibility of a rising supported by the Bourbon powers, and the Scots jacobites began scouting the prospect even before the three kingdoms formally adhered to the Grand Alliance and declared war on France and Spain.[77]

From 1702 onwards there was a good deal of secret traffic in and out of Scotland as agents from St Germain and Scotland's jacobite community shuttled back and forth trying to negotiate a satisfactory plan for a rising.[78] Hamilton had, of course, been involved in jacobite plotting in the 1690s and was still intermittently and indirectly in communication with the exiled court, but for all intents and purposes it is probably fair to say that his commitment to the cause had lapsed around the time he returned to Scotland to re-enter conventional politics in 1699.[79] The key point here is that his experiences in the 1690s meant that he knew how jacobite conspiracies worked in terms of their inception, development, faltering, fading, and collapse (the general fate of most jacobite plots). We have, of course, no forthright statement by the duke as to how he planned to use the jacobites to achieve his personal objectives. But we do know how he actually handled them over the period 1704–7 and there is a distinct pattern. The remainder of this essay will argue that Hamilton used his involvement in jacobite military plotting both to convince the jacobites that he was sound and to sabotage their efforts to start an armed rising.

The evidence for the first part of this hypothesis is clear-cut. To establish his bona fides, from late 1703 onwards (after his encounter with Eglinton in late April), the duke readily agreed to lead a rising in favour of James III and VIII whenever he was asked by a Scots jacobite, an emissary from St Germain or a French agent. Thus Murray, whom Hamilton had indirectly asked St Germain to send as its emissary, reported that the duke was effectively willing to put himself in a state of readiness, prepared to rise, 'in case they come to a rupture'.[80] Likewise, when Captain John Moray of Abercairny, who was in Scotland at the same time on behalf of the French government, spoke to the duke about a French invasion combined with a jacobite rising, Hamilton evinced great interest and pleasure at the prospect and 'entred into it very heartily'.[81] In a private communication with Carnegy in late 1704 the duke 'crye[d] continually' for St Germain to send over arms to equip a rising and indicated he was disappointed that James 'comes not home' forthwith.[82] In April 1705, through an unnamed intermediary, Hamilton assured James Drummond, jacobite duke of Perth and chancellor of Scotland, that he was 'ready to take arms, and is of opinion that this is the best conjoncture to do something'.[83] And when Hooke met the duke in secret in August 1705 Hamilton began by assuring Hooke that he 'has always been a faithful servant

[77] Szechi, *Britain's Lost Revolution?*, 167–9.

[78] Szechi, *Britain's Lost Revolution?*, 169–75.

[79] Hopkins, *Glencoe*, 123–4, 220, 268–9, 273–4, 298, 355–6, 372–3, 420, 436, 462; P.W.J. Riley, *King William and the Scottish Politicians* (Edinburgh, 1979), 134–5; NLS, MS 14266: Nairne journal, 2/13, 4/15 June 1702.

[80] Macpherson, *Original Papers*, i, 668.

[81] Macpherson, *Original Papers*, i, 677–80.

[82] Blairs Letters, 2/94/8, 11: Carnegy to [Lewis Innes?], 14 Oct., 7/18 Nov. 1704.

[83] *Hooke Correspondence*, i, 166.

of [James III and VIII], and that he is so still', and that he thought 'this was a good moment to shake off England's yoke'.[84]

This approach to securing the jacobite party's support worked tolerably well in 1704 and almost to the end of the 1705 session of parliament. Queen Mary directed the jacobites to back Hamilton and because they now believed him to be (once again) one of them they were happy enough to obey.[85] The peculiar dynamics of the Scots parties and Scots parliamentary politics in these years also worked in his favour and as a result he was able to cut a grand figure.[86] The only fly in the ointment was that despite intermittent negotiations with the power-brokers in London (particularly Lord Treasurer Godolphin) the duke was unable to parlay this into a suitably honourable and lucrative government office, probably because he was too greedy and rather too obviously associating with jacobites.[87] This, possibly plus over-confidence in his ability to command the country, and jacobite opposition, led to Hamilton's notorious (and from his personal point of view, disastrous) false step on 1 September 1705, when he deliberately waited until late in a long day of business to propose that instead of the Scots parliament (as a whole or by estates) selecting the commissioners to be appointed to negotiate a treaty of union, the choice be left to Queen Anne.[88] This was as good as guaranteeing that the court would pack the union commission and that the negotiations would produce a result in the form of treaty. It was such a barefaced betrayal of both the country and jacobite parties that it completely destroyed his authority. Home and his two principal lieutenants among the jacobites, Erroll and William Keith, Earl Marischal, had already become unhappy with Hamilton's behaviour; now they were furious and did not conceal their anger from Hooke. Though the faithful Carnegy did his best to justify the duke's conduct he had to admit that Hamilton 'is called nothing now but rogue and raskell, and they [the jacobites] would not salute him as he went through the streets'.[89] Home and the rest also asked specifically that St Germain henceforth keep the duke in the dark about their negotiations with the jacobite court and France regarding a rising and invasion.[90] Ironically, if Hamilton did in fact take this step because he had some kind of informal assurance that he would be one of the commissioners for the Union, or would be rewarded with government office, he was himself, in turn, betrayed by his interlocutors.[91] The duke had sold his friends and allies and did not even get any pottage.

If the hypothesis asserted above is correct, the second half of Hamilton's strategy involved him systematically sabotaging any possibility of a jacobite rising actually happening. Before exploring the evidence for this, however, it is appropriate to reflect on the context, and in particular the evidence that the duke was playing a double game more generally with respect to the country party and its jacobite allies from the second half of 1705 onwards.

---

[84] *Hooke Correspondence*, i, 384, 387: Hooke's report, 6/17 Oct. 1705 ('*qu'il avoit toujours été fidele serviteur du Roy d'Angleterre, et qu'il l'est encore*'; '*j'avoue ... que l'occasion pourroit être bonne pour secouer le joug d'Angleterre*').

[85] Macpherson, *Original Papers*, i, 626; *Hooke Correspondence*, i, 380.

[86] Riley, *Union*, 96–161.

[87] Riley, *Union*, 126, 149–50.

[88] Whatley, *Scots and the Union*, 249–50.

[89] *Hooke Correspondence*, i, 282, 380, 381, 395, 399; Blairs Letters, 2/108/20: Carnegy to [Lewis Innes?], 17 Nov. 1705.

[90] *Hooke Correspondence*, i, 414.

[91] Riley, *Union*, 150.

Hamilton's delivering the choice of union commissioners to the court in September 1705 has already been noted, and his excuses for his behaviour were certainly feeble, but there is no direct evidence that the popularly accepted explanation – that he did a secret deal with Argyll to secure himself a seat on the commission which Queen Anne and her ministers in London subsequently refused to honour – is correct.[92] A friendly letter from Hamilton to the English secretary of state, Robert Harley, in the midst of the fraught debates on the Union, signed off 'So honest Mason, adieu', suggests a Freemasonic connection between the two men but is otherwise inconclusive.[93] The first Masonic lodges had been established in London by this time and the capital's movers and shakers were joining in numbers. That the duke might have met Harley at a Masonic event on one of his frequent trips to London, and become friendly with him, does not necessarily mean there were any secret dealings afoot. Far stronger evidence that Hamilton was quietly undermining the opposition to the Union while simultaneously presenting himself as the leader of the patriot cause comes from two bodies of evidence: John Clerk of Penicuik's insider knowledge of Hamilton's negotiations with the ministers in Scotland and the duke's behaviour on three crucial occasions when the opponents of the Union planned to take radical measures to bring to a halt the process of pushing the bill through the Scots parliament.

Clerk was a baron of the Scottish exchequer who was closely associated, both personally and professionally, with the queen's chief minister in Scotland, James Douglas, duke of Queensberry. He was also a convinced unionist and a historian/antiquarian who took great pride in his own reputation for honesty and integrity.[94] This was, he asserted, what moved him to write an unpublished answer to Lockhart's *Memoirs Concerning the Affairs of Scotland* vindicating the supporters of the Union as rational, pragmatic politicians with their country's best interests at heart.[95] As part of his preparation for writing this book, Clerk gave his personal copy of the *Memoirs* a close reading and wrote marginal comments and notes on Lockhart's narrative. These are very illuminating with respect to the final session of the Scots parliament. At one point Lockhart waxes lyrical about Hamilton's stirring and emotional defence of Scotland's sovereignty and independence. Clerk commented:

> This speech indeed of the Duke of Hamiltone was very handsomely expressed, and a great many more to the same purpose. And yet in all this he played the montebank extreamly, since at the same time that he was caballing at the head of the Tory side he was in secret with the Duke of Queensberry every night, or at least 2 or 3 times in a week.[96]

[92] For Hamilton's evolving raft of excuses for his behaviour, see *Hooke Correspondence*, i, 335, 343; ii, 20–1; Blairs Letters, 2/108/20: Carnegy to [Lewis Innes?], 17 Nov. 1705. Underlying these is the clear implication that Hamilton believed that the queen would name him one of the commissioners for the Union.

[93] HMC, *Portland MSS*, iv, 338–9.

[94] *Memoirs of the Life of Sir John Clerk of Penicuik, Baronet, Baron of the Exchequer, Extracted by Himself from His Own Journals, 1676–1755*, ed. John M. Gray (Scottish History Society, xiii, Edinburgh, 1892), 59, 66–7; Rosalind Mitchison, 'Clerk, Sir John, of Penicuik, second baronet (1676–1755)', *ODNB*.

[95] *History of the Union of Scotland and England by Sir John Clerk of Penicuik*, ed. and trans. Douglas Duncan (Scottish History Society, 5th ser., vi, Edinburgh, 1993), 1–8.

[96] NRS, GD 18/6080, p. 252.

What were the two men – who Clerk notes were never friends – discussing? Clerk does not impart any details, but does state that 'The Duke of Hamilton … was resolved to do nothing that might effectively mine [i.e., destroy] the Union.'[97]

Finally we come to the duke's conduct with respect to three moments when there was a distinct possibility that the process of passing the Union might have been seriously disrupted, if not stopped in its tracks (at least for the rest of the winter of 1706–7). The first came on 29 November, when agitation and plotting by a cabal of jacobites and militantly anti-union presbyterians set in motion a rising in Glasgow and western Scotland. The plan seems to have been for an initially plebeian-led march on Edinburgh, beginning in Glasgow. This was to be supported by a muster of the formidable personal following of John Murray, duke of Atholl, together with musters and demonstrations against the Union in the south-west, and was to be joined en route by Hamilton and other opponents of the Union.[98] The rising never got off the ground for a number of reasons, but undoubtedly a crucial one was that just before it was due to begin Hamilton, as putative leader of the anti-union forces inside and outside parliament, expressly ordered its cancellation.[99]

The second moment came in mid-December, after the opposition had agreed to summon to Edinburgh the heritor signatories of many of the hundreds of petitions against the Union. The court had rejected these petitions in part on the grounds that no one could be sure the signatories had actually signed them. When the signatories arrived the opposition would then present a final, national and – evoking as it would the National Covenant of 1638 – highly symbolic address against the Union that would also call for new elections. This was to be signed publicly by hundreds, if not thousands, of elite Scots, who would accompany its presentation to parliament. By surrounding the parliament with armed gentlemen who would also be confronting the proponents of the Union on the streets of the capital, this demonstration might also have acted to intimidate supporters of the Union. At the last moment, however, Hamilton demanded that the address include a clause pledging the signatories to support the Hanoverian succession. As he must have known that a good many of the heritors already gathered in Edinburgh, and many of those who were planning to come up, were jacobites, the duke, in effect, collapsed the whole scheme and on 27 December a proclamation against tumultuous meetings in the city dispersed the assembling heritors.[100]

The third and final moment came in January 1707. By this stage it was clear that unless the opposition did something dramatic the Union was certain to pass. Hamilton therefore came up with a plan whereby the opposition as a body would propose to vote the Hanoverian succession into Scots law on condition that the Union Bill was dropped. All elements of the opposition (including the jacobites) agreed to this. They believed (as seems highly likely) that the court would reject the measure in favour of continuing with the Union, at which point the opposition as a whole would secede from parliament, implicitly threatening civil

[97]NRS, GD 18/6080, p. 325.

[98]Whatley, *Scots and the Union*, 302-3; Karin Bowie, *Scottish Public Opinion and the Anglo-Scottish Union, 1699–1707* (Woodbridge, 2007), 147–8; NRS, GD 24/1/872/1/3, p. 208.

[99]Bowie, *Scottish Public Opinion*, 148.

[100]Whatley, *Scots and the Union*, 304–5; Bowie, *Scottish Public Opinion*, 149.

war if the court pushed on.[101] As Clerk noted: 'I belive this methode would have done.'[102] It all, however, came to naught. As the premier nobleman of Scotland and the most eminent leader of the opposition, the duke was scheduled to propose the measure in parliament. But on the day he initially refused to turn up because he had a toothache, then, after he was shamed into appearing, suddenly refused to be the proposer of the bill. Lockhart alleged that this was because Queensberry, either in person or by messenger, threatened him with retribution in England (presumably against Hamilton's English estates, which were mired in a long-running legal dispute).[103] Clerk observed: 'This is true.'[104]

There is, thus, very good evidence that Hamilton was playing a double game during 1706–7, quite possibly to make sure that whichever way the Union crisis was resolved he personally would come out ahead. This brings us back to the duke's relationship with the jacobites, for they, as we have already seen, had been trying to put together a military solution to the succession/Union crisis ever since 1702. And, as will be argued below, Hamilton had been discreetly sabotaging them since at least 1704. The duke generally did this in the simplest possible fashion: by intervening with excessive or impossible demands whenever it looked as if a plan might actually result in a rising and/or invasion. We have already seen how he effectively set up his demand for £25,000 sterling as the only acceptable part of his response to proposals for a rising and invasion under discussion in 1703–4. But Hamilton also told Murray that in his opinion 'all the enterprizes which do not succeed tend to ruin the affairs of his Majesty, and to destroy his friends, and for that reason that nothing should be undertaken but upon good foundation and after matters were properly concerted and all the necessary measures taken for procuring success'.[105] This was tantamount to giving himself a veto whenever he cared to exercise it. What was a 'good foundation'? When would matters be 'properly concerted'? And when would 'all the necessary measures' be complete? Only the duke would know. When Moray also raised with him the possibility of a rising, Hamilton handled it slightly differently, but stifled any near prospect of action just as effectively by being 'of opinion to put it off until they saw what turn affairs would take in [the Scots] Parliament, in order to act accordingly afterwards with the King's friends in England'.[106] Since Moray was discussing the potential plot with the duke in the winter of 1703–4, waiting until the next meeting of the Scots parliament meant delaying until late summer, which would put it completely out of synch with the military-strategic annual cycle of military operations and guarantee it could not happen until 1705 (and more likely winter 1705–6) at the earliest.[107] In addition, co-ordinating matters with the English jacobites added a further block to the possibility of anything actually happening. As Hamilton must have known, given his frequent visits to London and Lancashire, the English jacobite movement was effectively moribund, transfixed by both its liking for the piously anglican Queen Anne and its conviction that all it had to do was wait and the queen would

[101] Daniel Szechi, *George Lockhart of Carnwath 1689–1727: A Study in Jacobitism* (East Linton, 2002), 67–8.
[102] NRS, GD 18/6080, p. 294.
[103] *'Scotland's Ruine'*, ed. Szechi, 195–6.
[104] NRS, GD 18/6080, p. 326.
[105] Macpherson, *Original Papers*, i, 668.
[106] Macpherson, *Original Papers*, i, 678.
[107] Szechi, *Britain's Lost Revolution?*, 159–60.

restore her half-brother upon her death.[108] The English jacobites were, therefore, virtually guaranteed to reject any plan for a rising.[109]

The duke periodically reinforced his potential blocking mechanisms under cover of confirming his commitment to the jacobite cause, as in November 1704 when he told St Germain, through Carnegy, that he very much wished James would invade, but that the jacobite king needed to bring, 'a good quantity of ribbons [troops] of all sorts, silk [arms] and hair stuffs [money] to gain Ralph's wife [Scotland]'.[110] This fended off any immediate prospect of a rising until the summer of 1705. Then, for their own grand strategic reasons, Louis XIV and his ministers became interested in the prospect of a jacobite rising specifically centred in Scotland.[111] As Hooke told Queen Mary, by that time, however, they were not sure what the Scots jacobites' intentions were (Hamilton had muddied the waters sufficiently), and so the *Conseil d'en Haut* decided to send Hooke with orders to speak directly to the Scots jacobite leaders.[112]

When Hooke arrived he found that a plan by the duke of Gordon to organise a secret jacobite association pledged to prepare a rising and act together in co-ordinating an invasion with France had been brought to nothing because Hamilton had prevaricated and delayed and so disrupted it. The leaders of the Scots jacobites correctly interpreted this as deliberate obstruction and were most unhappy with the duke. Hooke, too, was troubled by Hamilton's conduct, but decided that he needed to talk to him personally to resolve the question now hanging over his commitment to a rising.[113] As we have already seen, Hamilton refused to commit himself to any kind of timetable or triggering event, and reinforced this in letters to Louis XIV and Queen Mary which Hooke carried back to France. 'The present situation of our affairs', the duke solemnly told Louis, 'is such that because of our jealousies and divisions – even among the well-intentioned – we are not in a condition to be able to come together to show our recognition of your Majesty, nor to take suitable measures.'[114] In his letter to Queen Mary, Hamilton similarly blamed his inability to act on the divisions among the well-intentioned (omitting to mention the fact that he was the one who had provoked those divisions), but, none the less, unctuously pledged: 'I never will desert your intrest, nor promise more than I can do, only I beg you to allow me my own method.'[115] Multiple meetings with the duke finally convinced Hooke that the jacobites' leaders were correct in reading Hamilton as deliberately obstructing a military adventure, and the French agent moved on to serious negotiations with them alone.[116]

---

[108] Szechi, *Britain's Lost Revolution?*, 84–6.

[109] The northern English catholics were an exception to this general passivity: see AECP (A) 214, f. 413: '*Memoire touchant les affaires d'Angleterre*', [Apr. 1703].

[110] Blairs Letters, 2/94/11: Carnegy to [Lewis Innes?], 7/18 Nov. 1704.

[111] Szechi, *Britain's Lost Revolution?*, 150–7, 172–3.

[112] *Hooke Correspondence*, i, 191.

[113] *Hooke Correspondence*, i, 373.

[114] *Hooke Correspondence*, i, 279: Hamilton to Louis XIV, 22 Aug. 1705 ('*La situation presente de nos affaires est telle par nos jalousies et divisions, mêmes entre les bien intentionnez, que nous ne sommes pas en etat de convenir ensemble pour temoigner conjointement notre reconnoissance à votre Majesté, ni pour prendre les mesures convenables*').

[115] *Hooke Correspondence*, i, 291.

[116] *Hooke Correspondence*, i, 387, 393, 406, 408–9, 415.

This was manifestly not what the duke had intended, but because of various delays and other problems, the jacobites were not able to get an emissary to Paris in a timely manner and missed any chance of a French military intervention in Scotland in 1706.[117] As a consequence the only military response to the overwhelming political power of the court in the session of 1706–7 was a damp squib, in large part owing to Hamilton's intervention to stop it. This does not, however, seem to have stopped the duke from continuing to present himself as a true jacobite, committed to an armed uprising to stop the Union and restore James. And this very nearly got completely out of hand. In sending Straton over to get some money Hamilton, of course, also asked for French military intervention (thus establishing his jacobite bona fides).[118] There was no prospect of this at the time and Straton came away empty-handed. Back in France, though, Hooke and St Germain continued to lobby the *Conseil d'en Haut*, and as news came in of riots and public opposition in Scotland, opinion on the council apparently began to swing towards some kind of ad hoc expedition to Scotland.[119] Hooke accordingly presented a memo to Torcy and Marshal Noailles at the end of November informing them that, according to the latest reports, Hamilton was now fully reunited with the jacobites. Hooke concluded:

That there are grounds to believe that the Scots could be persuaded to commence a war with their own forces.

That this would be greatly to the advantage of the king's [Louis XIV's] service.

That it will take the English many campaigns to subdue the Scots and they may not be able to do so at all.[120]

This was reinforced by a letter sent by Straton at the beginning of November which seems to have arrived at St Germain in mid-December. We do not know the full contents of the letter because only an extract translated into French and passed on to Torcy has survived.[121] The gist is clear, however: Scotland was on the brink of full-scale rebellion. The duke had also indicated, via Carnegy, but probably also through Straton, that he now wanted immediate French military intervention.[122] A crisis meeting was accordingly held at St Germain on 19 December and the exiled court apparently redoubled its efforts to move the *Conseil d'en Haut* to seize the opportunity.[123] And it finally worked. Hooke was instructed to prepare a plan for a surprise attack on Scotland.[124]

[117] Szechi, *Britain's Lost Revolution?*, 76–7, 174.

[118] AECP (A) 221, f. 194: Middleton to Torcy, 24 Aug./4 Sept. 1706.

[119] Blairs Letters, 2/125/13, 16, 20: Carnegy to [Lewis Innes], 12, 26 Oct., 30 Nov. 1706.

[120] *Hooke Correspondence*, ii, 88–93: Hooke's memorandum for Torcy and Noailles, 26 Nov./7 Dec. 1706 ('*Qu'il y a lieu de croire qu'on pourra porter les Ecossois à commencer la guerre avec leurs propres forces./Que le service du Roy entirera des grands avantages./Que les Anglois ne sçauroient reduire les Ecossois qu'apres plusieurs campagnes, et peut-etre point du tout*').

[121] AECP (A) 221, f. 215: extract of a letter from Edinburgh, 8/19 Nov. 1706.

[122] *Hooke Correspondence*, ii, 103.

[123] NLS, MS 14266: Nairne journal, 19/30, 20/31 Dec. 1706.

[124] La Courneuve, Paris, Affaires Étrangères, Mémoires et Documents (Angleterre) 24, ff. 15–17: 'Memoire sur le projet', [Versailles?], Jan. 1707.

The details of the invasion plan need not concern us here. Suffice it to say the first wave would have consisted of Hooke, a handful of expatriate Scots officers in French service and two shiploads of arms, ammunition and money. This was primed and ready to go by the end of January 1707.[125] Hamilton's reaction when he got the news that the French were at last coming is instructive: Carnegy found him 'in a fright' and had to spend an afternoon calming him down.[126] Fortunately for the duke, he was rescued by French cabinet politics. Chamillart, the minister of war, who was pursuing secret peace negotiations with the Grand Alliance, suddenly intervened to postpone the operation pending another fact-finding mission by Hooke. Further news from Scotland then seemed to indicate that the moment had passed and the prospect of a French invasion receded for the rest of the year.[127]

5

We cannot know for sure what would have happened if Hooke and the first wave of invading troops had arrived at Slains castle in early February 1707, but given the febrile political mood in Scotland at the time and the widespread popular anger at the passage of the Union, it seems reasonable to believe that it would have sparked a rising at least by the jacobites and possibly by other opponents of the Union. Potentially at least, Scotland thus came very close to a rising that could easily have slid into a civil war. And that matters came to this pass was in large part because Hamilton was playing utterly irresponsible political games at a time of explosive crisis.

Returning now to our two original questions: what light does the French and jacobite evidence shed on how far the duke's politics were financially driven? He was certainly desperate for money, so desperate that he was willing to take huge political risks to get some from France and – did he ever know it? – from the pope. If his dealings with France had been exposed he would have been politically ruined and had the papal subvention been discovered (even if he did not know where it came from and even if it did not reach him) he would have been personally and politically ruined beyond redemption. On one level the jacobite evidence strongly reinforces the interpretation of Hamilton as primarily driven by his reckless greed/need for money. But on another it does not. Because – whatever amounts actually did reach him from France – he never got the very large sums of money he was demanding (£100,000 sterling by 1705), we have no idea what impact these might have had on his politics. If he had got the money and stayed bought we could reasonably surmise that he was all about the cash. Since he did not, however, the question has to remain open.

Turning to the question of how far his relationship with the Scots jacobites affected his political conduct, the answer has to be nuanced. As far as conventional, legal politics was concerned, the answer would appear to be, 'not much'. The policies and legislation that Hamilton advocated and pushed for in the Scots parliament were supported by a broad range of country politicians, not just the jacobites, and his influence on them in this area

[125] Szechi, *Britain's Lost Revolution?*, 176.
[126] Blairs Letters, 2/151/7: Carnegy to [Lewis Innes?], 9 Feb. 1709.
[127] Szechi, *Britain's Lost Revolution?*, 176–7.

was, if anything, a moderating one. It is highly unlikely that anyone other than Hamilton could have persuaded the jacobites to agree publicly to support the Hanoverian succession in January 1707. And for all that they took it as merely a tactical move in their fight to stop the Union, it was a straw in the wind. Twice more during the next decade the political wing of the Scots jacobite movement showed itself willing to swallow the same bitter pill in order to undo the Union.[128]

To get the jacobites on board in parliament, though, the duke had to endorse their military adventurism. Opinions differ as to the likelihood of the success of a primarily jacobite rising in Scotland around the time of the Union; all may agree that it would have been a terrible and bloody affair. Chris Whatley has, moreover, convincingly demonstrated that Hamilton knew this, and greatly feared another English military conquest of Scotland.[129] Yet despite the fact that a Scots rising against a union with England would certainly have provoked military intervention from England, and quite possibly full-scale war between the two kingdoms, Hamilton still, prima facie, encouraged the jacobites by supporting plans for a French-supported rising. On the other hand, there is strong evidence that he consistently sabotaged every attempt to bring to fruition jacobite/French plotting. It should be added as a rider that he did not do so very effectively after 1705. Hooke's first report mercilessly exposed the duke's prevarications and unreliability, the jacobites ignored him in their further plotting (despite his intermittent endorsement of the need for a military response to the prospect, and then reality, of the Union), and the reasons neither a jacobite rising nor a French invasion transpired before the attempt at both in 1708 were nothing to do with Hamilton. He was out of the loop. The duke did, of course, torpedo the ad hoc attempt by Lockhart, Atholl, and others to use a plebeian march on Edinburgh from Glasgow to begin a national rising, but thereafter slipped back into endorsement mode in order to keep the jacobites sweet. Hence when he was confronted by the imminent onset of Hooke with the officers, arms, and money to set in motion a rising, he simply panicked. If the interpretation advanced here is accepted, that the duke was overtly advocating military action, but covertly (and by January 1707, ineffectively) sabotaging any prospect of this happening, his reversion to Hamilton-the-militant-jacobite in November–January represented a monumental failure of judgment on his part.

So, what do Hamilton's jacobite politics tell us about the duke as a politician and a human being? The man revealed in the preceding argument is in many ways a familiar one. The duke was greedy, reckless, and deceitful. He was also driven by an overweening ambition and convinced of his own cleverness. Contemplating his conduct with respect to the country party and the jacobites one is drawn to wonder if he was ever faithful to anyone or anything other than himself. It may fairly be objected that in displaying such characteristics he was hardly exceptional for his class and his time. The combination in his case, though, was especially powerful in terms of its impact because he was, in a sense, born to the purple. As Scotland's premier nobleman, the impact of the duke's character and conduct was far greater than that of the great majority of his peers, and never more so than during the Union crisis. In terms of conventional politics he directly

---

[128] In 1713 and 1714–15: see my essay, 'The Political Consequences of the Cuckoldy German Turnip Farmer', in *The Hanoverian Succession in Britain and Its Empire: Revolution Reaffirmed*, ed. Allan Macinnes and Brent S. Sorota (Woodbridge, forthcoming).

[129] Whatley, *Scots and the Union*, 249.

and indirectly shaped the outcome of that crisis. What is now clear, however, is that his propensity for playing with political fire quite possibly came far closer to plunging Scotland into civil war than he ever anticipated. This can only be characterised as a blunder of potentially epic proportions (from his point of view) and emphatically demonstrates the sheer depths of his lack of empathy, understanding, and political insight. With Hamilton at their head it is no wonder that the Scots opponents of the Union failed to stop it coming to pass.

''Tis Not in the Power of Words to Tell What My Heart Feels in Favour of You'; or, What the Ossulston Diary Does Not Reveal

CHARLES LITTLETON

Charles Bennet, 2nd Baron Ossulston is largely known through his diary of his daily social encounters, which was first analysed for its political import by Clyve Jones. A further set of documents in the Bennet family papers deepens our understanding of Ossulston's life and his social milieu among the aristocracy under Queen Anne. The love letters sent to him from a Mrs Sarah Sidney throughout 1710 reveal much about life in the aristocratic hothouse of St James's Square. They also show how the 'ministerial revolution' of that year was seen by two politically conversant figures at the margins of the royal court. This relationship was long-lasting and has been a hitherto unknown aspect of Ossulston's life, which may help explain some of his attitudes.

Keywords: aristocratic households; Charles Bennet, 2nd Baron Ossulston; diaries; Elizabeth Gerard, duchess of Hamilton; London parks and pleasure gardens; ministerial changes in 1710; Sarah Sidney; St James's Square

Charles Bennet (1674–1722), 2nd Baron Ossulston, and earl of Tankerville from October 1714, is not a figure whose fame has lasted the three centuries since he lived. In his own time, though, he was a prominent whig and landowner based in the metropolitan region around the English capital. Charles Bennet owed his title and much of his wealth to his father, Sir John Bennet, who, aided by his younger brother, Henry Bennet, earl of Arlington, greatly improved the fortunes of his branch of the Bennets, though not always by the most reputable means.[1] The core of the Bennet estate was the joined Middlesex manors of Harlington and Dawley. Here the family had their principal country seat of Dawley House. By the early 18th century this was a substantial residence with three floors and eight bays, numerous outbuildings, formal gardens, and a double avenue of trees.[2] In addition, the Bennets owned a good deal of property in the English capital itself. Their principal holding was Ossulston House, an opulent townhouse in St James's Square, built by Sir John Bennet in the 1670s after Arlington had acquired the leasehold of the land.[3]

---

[1] *The History of Parliament: The House of Commons, 1660–90*, ed. B.D. Henning (3 vols, 1983), i, 623–4.

[2] *Victoria County History: A History of the County of Middlesex*, iii, ed. Susan Reynolds (Oxford, 1962), 262, 264–5, and plate between pp. 258 and 259.

[3] *The Parish of St James Westminster, Part I*, ed. F.H.W. Sheppard (Survey of London, xxix, 1960), 77–8; Arthur Dasent, *History of St James's Square* (1895), appendix A.

On 24 November 1682, Sir John Bennet was created Baron Ossulston, an honour most likely intended as a favour to Arlington. Ossulston died on 11 February 1695, and his heir, Charles, came into his title and what was reputed to be 'a great estate'.[4] His fortunes improved when in July 1695, only shortly after having come of age, he married Lady Mary Grey, a daughter of Ford Grey, who had just been created earl of Tankerville. Through his wife, Tankerville's sole surviving child, Ossulston eventually came into possession of the additional estates of Chillingham in Northumberland and Uppark in Sussex. By the beginning of the 18th century, Ossulston was riding high, having extended his landed estate well beyond Middlesex and London. He was sufficiently prominent that in October 1714 George I recreated for him the title of earl of Tankerville, which had become extinct on Ford Grey's death in 1701.

We know a good deal about Ossulston because the papers of the Bennet family were deposited with the masters in chancery to assist in a number of legal disputes concerning the estate. There are close to 15 large boxes of miscellaneous papers, largely regarding financial affairs, which were never reclaimed by the family and remain at The National Archives.[5] Buried among them are five small volumes of a diary spanning the period 1703 to 1712. This 'diary' is largely a bald, and illegibly scribbled, daily account of the acquaintances whom the 2nd Baron Ossulston encountered during his meals and other social events.[6] It does not tell us about the inner man, but does reveal the political circles in which he moved, and even provides occasional glimpses of his involvement in the house of lords.

The content of the diary has already been analysed, by Clyve Jones himself. Clyve was able to extract a great deal of data from these terse entries which he presented in three important articles. He used Ossulston's record of the meetings of the junto in their Westminster townhouses for his article on the political organisation of that group and its whig followers, including Ossulston.[7] He also employed the diary to reveal Ossulston's friendship with a number of Scottish parliamentarians, with whom Ossulston formed a 'Westminster Anglo-Scottish dining group'.[8] Perhaps less familiar to political historians is Clyve's paper on 'the London life' of Ossulston. This traced Ossulston's social geography as he frequented parliament, the Temple, the playhouses, and eating and drinking establishments in the English capital.[9] I will take this piece as my basis to investigate some of its themes further. Clyve used not only the entries in the diary but also the voluminous Bennet family papers that were submitted to chancery. But while he mined material beyond the diary, he could

[4] Narcissus Luttrell, *A Brief Historical Relation of State Affairs* (6 vols, Oxford, 1867), iii, 438.

[5] TNA, C 104/81, 82, 83, 113, 114, 116, 147, 148, 149, 150. Some of these catalogue items comprise two or more boxes.

[6] TNA, C 104/116/1: two volumes, covering 12 Nov. 1703 to 13 June 1708; C 104/113/1: three volumes, covering 14 June 1708 to 19 Dec. 1712. Hereafter the entries in these five volumes will be merely referenced in the notes as 'Ossulston diary' and by date. Where the source and date of the entry is explicitly given in the text itself, no further reference in the notes will be provided. I would like to thank Clyve Jones for some early discussions concerning this diary and for passing on to me, so many years ago, his photocopies of its pages. I hope this essay is a partial fulfilment of his wish expressed then that I would continue his initial research on this source.

[7] Clyve Jones, 'The Parliamentary Organization of the Whig Junto in the Reign of Queen Anne: The Evidence of Lord Ossulston's Diary', *Parliamentary History*, x (1991), 164–82.

[8] Clyve Jones, 'A Westminster Anglo-Scottish Dining Group, 1710–12: The Evidence of Lord Ossulston's Diary', *Scottish Historical Review*, lxxi (1992), 110–28.

[9] Clyve Jones, 'The London Life of a Peer in the Reign of Anne: A Case Study from Lord Ossulston's Diary', *London Journal*, xvi (1991), 140–55.

not bring to light everything from this collection relevant to Ossulston's life in London. This essay will supplement Clyve's by re-examining some documents in this family archive which reveal unexpected aspects of Ossulston's life in the capital.

It will concentrate on a period which is important both in national history and in Ossulston's own biography – the year 1710. At the beginning of the year, from 12 January, the house of lords began considering the impeachment articles charging the incendiary high-flying minister, Dr Henry Sacheverell, with high crimes and misdemeanours. Ossulston attended the Lords regularly from 17 January and, as a follower of the junto, even contributed to further the prosecution case against Sacheverell. On 16 March, Ossulston moved that the Commons had made good their first article of impeachment, and was seconded by the earl of Wharton. The ensuing debate lasted close to 12 hours, before the motion was eventually passed. Ossulston, not surprisingly, stood against Sacheverell in the two final votes on 20 and 21 March.[10] The diary reveals that on many occasions in March, Ossulston was so involved in these proceedings that he had his supper brought to him from St James's Square to eat on the parliamentary estate. His close involvement in the trial is the only parliamentary matter that Ossulston recorded consistently in his diary for over a period of more than a week.[11]

Ossulston's wife and five children had also accompanied him on 16 January from Dawley House to Ossulston House so that he could attend parliament. His wife, though, was perpetually bedridden during this period, suffering from severe gout.[12] Her worsening condition runs as a subcurrent in the diary throughout the Sacheverell proceedings. She was brought back to Dawley House on 24 April, after the parliamentary session had ended. On 28 May 1710, Ossulston took a pleasure cruise down the Thames, but on his return to Dawley House found 'my poor wife extremely ill'. The ministrations of celebrated physicians such as Sir Samuel Garth and Sir John Shadwell were to no avail, and she died in the evening of 30 May.

Overcome with grief, Ossulston immediately left Dawley House for London. Perhaps wishing to avoid the memories of happier times, he avoided Ossulston House and within only a few days found lodgings in Poland Street between the Tyburn Road and Broadwick Street. He may have shared this residence with his maternal uncle, Scrope Howe, Viscount Howe, who appears intermittently in the diary entries. On 3 June, Ossulston summoned four of his six children to Poland Street to stay with him while, in their absence, his wife was buried at Harlington parish church. Three weeks later he left Poland Street, on learning that Lord Howe's son had smallpox, and returned to St James's Square.[13] He first visited Dawley House on 23 July, 'not having been there since my poore wife dyed'.

Clyve argued that Lady Ossulston's death 'resulted in a dramatic change in Ossulston's life-style in the short term and a more subtle long-term change'. In the short term, during the summer of 1710, his socialising became more restricted. He often ate alone and 'records seeing very few friends'. He also took frequent 'and unexplained' trips in the evening to

---

[10] *The State Trial of Doctor Henry Sacheverell*, ed. Brian Cowan (Parliamentary History: Texts & Studies, 6, Oxford, 2012), 97, 249, 250; Geoffrey Holmes, *The Trial of Doctor Sacheverell* (1973), 283, 285.

[11] Ossulston diary, 27 Feb., 2, 3, 4, 6, 10, 13, 14 16, 17, 20 Mar. 1710.

[12] Ossulston diary, 1, 6, 13, 16 Jan., 15, 16, 17, 20, 21 Feb., 19, 26, 28 Mar., 16, 18 Apr. 1710.

[13] Ossulston diary, 30 May – 25 [*recte* 24] June; *The Parish of St James Westminster, Part II*, ed. F.H.W. Sheppard (Survey of London, xxxi, 1963), 243–5.

'take the air' in such places as Marylebone, Chelsea, and Hammersmith. Furthermore, 'he also appears to drink more'. Clyve also considered that 'the longer-term changes in his social life are signalled by an increasing tendency to eat out'.[14] In this account, the diary not only provides information on the 'London life' of an early-18th-century aristocrat, but also tells a human story of a young nobleman grieving the death of his wife, the mother of his six children. Tellingly, Ossulston never remarried after her death.

However, documents found in the same box as the volumes of the diary complicate this narrative of Ossulston's grief, withdrawal and eventual re-emergence into public life. For there is a bundle of papers endorsed 'Letters from Mrs Sidney to the late Lord Tankerville etc, about they knew what.' The bundle contains about 107 love letters from a 'Mrs Sidney' to Ossulston. These letters, or more properly notes, are written on small pieces of paper, octavo size if not smaller, usually on one side and many not even filling a whole side. They were dashed off quickly, in a clear hand (much more legible than Ossulston's) and with little or no concern for punctuation, capitalisation, or other formalities. They are, with one exception, undated, and contain no salutations or signatures.

These are a series of love notes – passionate, effusive, full of equal parts love, joy, jealousy, anger, and sadness. Their informal nature and brevity suggest that they came frequently, more than one a day. Extracts from one can give a sense of their content, tone and intensity:

> you order'd me to write and I obey you for possitively nothing can make me find any pleasure in living but when I know I do something to oblige you and I hope obedience may tho' my letters have nothing else to recommend 'em I'm in prodigious good humour to night from the hopes you gave me that you love me to tell you my more than life my soul with what passion I return it wou'd be endless & impossible since 'tis not in the power of words to tell what my heart feels in favour of you my charming Angell … if you will I'l meet you in the walk as we did tonight & bring my sister or if you can't tell me where I may take you up I'l go by my self and stop where you resolve to be and send my servant some message.[15]

This letter was dated merely 'Monday or rather Tuesday morning': all of Mrs Sidney's letters were undated but have indications that they were generally written in the small hours of the morning.

Apparently, then, behind the laconic entries in his diary, Ossulston had a passionate liaison with a Mrs Sarah Sidney; the justification for providing her with this forename will be revealed in the final paragraphs. When was all this going on? Placing it is difficult because, as has been noted, the letters are undated. The first time Ossulston himself mentioned

[14] Jones, 'London Life', 148.

[15] In this, as in all future extracts from Mrs Sidney's notes, standard abbreviations with superscripts have been expanded. Otherwise the original spelling, including her frequent use of contractions and the paucity of capitalisation, has been maintained. Mrs Sidney's letters are single sheets, undated and unfoliated, gathered up miscellaneously in a bundle in TNA, C 104/116/1. Consequently, there is no way to reference individual letters and all subsequent extracts or commentary from the notes in this collection must remain unreferenced. A few indicate the day of the week, and some even the time, when written. Yet as there are several simply marked 'fryday', even referencing the letters by that indication would be insufficiently exact. Readers wishing to follow up individual letters discussed here will, unfortunately, have to call up the entire box and go through the whole bundle.

Mrs Sidney in his diary is his entry for 9 July 1710, for which he noted that, 'about 2 of the clock I take water in my barge, with Mrs Sydney. only she & I went as far as beyound Greenwich I did not go ashore any where but bought 3 dozen of clarett by the way we returned about nine & came ashoar & I came home.'

There is clear evidence, however, that the relationship had started well before that; evidence not from the diary, but from the notes themselves. In one of her lengthier notes Sarah wrote:

> … you'l wonder at the hurry I was in yesterday for by your letter I thought your going out of town was as usuall for a day or two & came with an intention to sitt half an hour but when you told me 'twas a generall remove of your family my heart grew cold & I'm sure you must see my face do quite the contrary I found I had no way left to hide my disorder but going away & to prevent greater confusion coming upon me for by the time I gott to the coach I cou'd hardly speak so much as to tell 'em where I would go … this day I was from ten till eight at night in the city but such a listless creature who is at present a much fitter object for a herse than a coach was never to be ported from place to place … if I do [think] it is of you & that you are out of the reach of my seeing you even at a window …

On 24 April 1710, as we have seen, Ossulston prosecuted such a 'generall remove' of his family from Ossulston House. We can be certain, though, that this is the precise occasion to which Sarah was referring by her addendum to this letter of lament. She ended with the news:

> a Mrs Wharton worth ten thousand pound is going to take up with Ld Alington for a husband so much for the living now for the world's wardrobe it is increas'd by Ld Lumley who died this morning and to prevent people's passion for the footmen's galery going any farther I must tell you a servant of the D: of Marl[borough] was run thro' there last night while I was at the play.

Among the wealth of news and gossip she conveyed here, one item stands out – the death on 24 April 1710 of Henry Lumley, styled Viscount Lumley, heir apparent of Richard Lumley, earl of Scarbrough. She knew that news from 'this morning' and was able to convey it to Ossulston as she lamented his departure to Dawley with his wife.

This is the earliest letter that can be positively dated by the external events it described. It reveals that already in April 1710, Ossulston and Mrs Sidney were conducting an affair, at a time when Ossulston's diary is otherwise preoccupied with his wife's decline. We get from these notes of Mrs Sarah Sidney a sense of the passionate intensity of their relationship (at least on her part), which continued throughout the summer of 1710, well after the death of Lady Ossulston. They complicate the portrayal of Ossulston as a grieving young man who shut himself away over the summer of 1710 before eventually returning to public life just as the Harley ministry took up the government of the realm.

Other sections in this note of 24 April 1710 provide us with important details of Sarah's identity and how she and Ossulston may have met in the first place. She was a courtier of some standing, as she was 'ported' around in a coach in the metropolis for ten hours with (as is revealed in another section of the letter) fashionable company. Most tellingly, she regretted that with Ossulston gone she would no longer be able to see him, 'even at a window'. Sarah was apparently a close neighbour to Ossulston House on St James's Square, whose windows she could see. She started another one of her notes with: 'I'm just come from looking out of the window and have seen Bugg and my next neighbour come home and everybody but my Dear that I watch'd for.' 'Bug', whose arrival she could see from her window, was Henry Grey, duke of Kent, given his unflattering nickname on account of his foul breath. He had his townhouse at 4 St James's Square, only two doors down from Ossulston House (which was located where the modern-day numbers 1 and 2 stand). Sarah evidently had a clear view of the square and her letters often remarked on the comings and goings of its inhabitants at all hours of the night. She lived in a residence from which she could tempt Ossulston with the offer: 'I'm going to dress in sight of your window where I've just now seen that most Dear and charming person that unhappy I admire and positively dote on to distraction.' Ossulston and Mrs Sidney lived close enough to each other on the square that each could see into the other's house.

I argue that Sarah Sidney was connected to the household of James Hamilton, 4th duke of Hamilton, who may well have rented a house which faced Ossulston House across Charles Street (now Charles II Street). There is circumstantial evidence which points to her connection with the duke's household, to Ossulston's acquaintance with the duke and duchess of Hamilton, and to the proximity of their residences. On 2 March 1709, Ossulston recorded dining 'at Duke Hamilton's', and a contemporary list of peers' addresses for the 1708–9 session of parliament indicates that both Ossulston and Hamilton were living on St James's Square at this time. Hamilton, a Scottish representative peer in the first elected British parliament which met in November 1708, was a recent neighbour in the square, and his name does not appear in a similar list for 1706.[16] The rate books providing the names of the occupants of the square are missing for the years 1708–15, but Hamilton's widowed duchess was still in occupation of 'London House' (now 32) in its south-east quadrant when the rate books resumed in 1716. This house's neighbour to the north was 'Derby House' (33) which stood at the south-west corner of Charles Street debouching into the square from the east. Ossulston House was on the north-west corner of that same street. With the absence of the rate books for these years, and the paucity of information which even the *Survey of London* has been able to unearth about numbers 32 and 33, it is impossible to be certain who was renting Derby House, with its windows facing Ossulston House across Charles Street, in 1710.[17] It is not impossible, and highly plausible considering his high status, that Hamilton rented both London House and Derby House while he was trying to make his mark on the political and social scene in London. This, at least, is the likeliest explanation of the proximity of the lodgings of Ossulston and Mrs Sidney, which is so clearly indicated in her notes.

Furthermore, a friendship developed between the Bennet and Hamilton families, probably connected with Ossulston's growing acquaintance with the Scots in the British capital. Hamilton was an occasional presence, though by no means the most frequent, among his

---

[16] Clyve Jones, 'A London "Directory" of Peers and Bishops for 1708–1709: A Note on the Residential Topography of Politicians in the Reign of Anne', *London Journal*, xviii (1993), 27; Clyve Jones, 'The London Topography of the Parliamentary Elite: Addresses for Peers and Bishops for 1706 and 1727–8', *London Topographical Record*, xxix (2006), 55–6.

[17] Dasent, *St James's Square*, appendix A, 220, 248; *St James's Piccadilly, Part 1* (Survey of London, xxix), 202, 206.

Scottish dining companions in the following months when Ossulston was part of the Anglo-Scottish dining group.[18] Ossulston was also one of the few whigs who, on 20 December 1711, voted to allow Hamilton a seat in the house of lords under his British title of duke of Brandon.[19] It may also be significant that the only morsel of 'external' news found in the diary is for 15 November 1712: 'Duke Hamilton and Ld Mohun fought this morn in High Park and they were both killed.'

There may have been an even stronger relation between Ossulston and the duchess of Hamilton, formerly Elizabeth Gerard, daughter of Baron Gerard of Gerard's Bromley. On 8 June 1710, barely a week after his wife's death, when Ossulston and his children were holed up in the lodgings on Poland Street, he recorded that 'Ds. Hamilton came to my daughters'. Was this to comfort them for the loss of their mother? Two days after appears an entry with the first occurrence of an abbreviated 'D: H:' who goes on to appear frequently in the diary throughout the summer of 1710. Coming so soon after the first appearance of the duchess of Hamilton at his lodgings in Poland Street, this abbreviation is most likely the same person. This conjecture would appear to be corroborated by the entry for 11 June, when 'D: H: was here to see the children', repeating the pattern set three days previously when the duchess, with her title fully spelled out, came for the children.

A letter from Sarah, dated 'fryday', made detailed arrangements for an assignation with Ossulston at 7.30 in the evening:

> at which time I shall come from Kensington & shall stop at the end of Holland Walk & alight to agree where our friend & we shall pass the rest of the evening if you think of any better place lett me know 'tis now six a clock fryday morning I've not slept all night.

Ossulston's diary entry for Friday, 23 June (misdated in the diary as 24 June) reads:

> About 6 of the clock I went in a Hackney coach to Hollond walk & walked there about an hour then there came Ann of the Dukes for some reasons we could not stay there so I went to Brompton & then they came after me we walked a little there & then I went into their coach & we rambled about for an hour or two they sett me down att Sommerset house & then I supped at the Temple.

Mrs Sidney's note and Ossulston's entry suggests that a meeting was arranged between them for a Friday evening at Holland Park, which involved Sarah being accompanied by 'our friend'. Ossulston's entry suggests the rendezvous did not work out quite as planned. Could this 'friend' of Sarah's have been 'Ann of the Duke's' from the diary entry? This woman appears regularly, under a number of descriptions. On 3 July, Ossulston also wrote of a meeting with 'Ann of the Duches' on Holland Walk; four days later another entry referred to an encounter with 'Ann of D:' while walking in Brompton Gardens. 'I went to visitt D: H:', Ossulston entered for 19 August, 'and afterwards I went to visit Mrs Masham att

---

[18] Jones, 'Westminster Anglo-Scottish Dining Group', 124.

[19] Clyve Jones, ' "The Scheme Lords, the Necessitous Lords, and the Scots Lords": The Earl of Oxford's Management and the "Party of the Crown" in the House of Lords, 1711–14', in *Party and Management in Parliament, 1660–1784*, ed. Clyve Jones (Leicester, 1984), 152, 157.

Kingsinton and then mett D: H: & L: A: upon the road then we all went to an Indian House in Leicester Fields'. It is highly probable that on this occasion he once again encountered the duchess of Hamilton ('D: H:') and her companion – previously notated as 'Ann of the duchess', 'Ann of the Duke's' – who is here abbreviated as 'L: A:' and who, I argue, is a 'Lady Anne' who appears frequently in Sarah's notes.

To Sarah Sidney, 'Lady Anne' was a person whose movements had to to be taken into account when the two lovers tried to arrange their furtive meetings. In one note she wrote to arrange a rendezvous, suggesting she

> will sett no day for your coming only tell you Lady Ann is engag'd tomorrow I'm order'd not to exceed two a clock & 'tis almost that now so I have not time to say any more than thanking you for letting me know a way to write to you which I'l do this night when I come from Court.

After signing off this note with 'my dear, dear life, adieu', she added as a postscript, 'I'm just now told Ld Sunderland is turn'd out but more of this I'll know by tonight Duke Beaufort has the small pox.' This letter was thus written on or around 14 June 1710, when the junto lord, Charles Spencer, 3rd earl of Sunderland, was dismissed by Queen Anne as secretary of state. Mrs Sidney in the morning was just hearing the first whispers of this dismissal and felt that she would be able to confirm it for Ossulston when she got back that night from her duties at court. She was also accurate about the duke of Beaufort, who did contract smallpox in May, but had rallied by the end of June 1710. Clearly Mrs Sidney held a position which allowed her to frequent the court and to hear, and understand the significance of, the gossip and rumours there. Did she hold this position through this 'Lady Anne' whose schedule she had to obey?

A number of other notes suggest that Sarah was constrained in her ability to see Ossulston through having to be in attendance on Lady Anne. For example, she wrote: 'Lady Anne will be at home so we had better be there to night for I can see you here when we've no other place to see one another at I'l be there about seven do you come at your owne time I know this but just now.' The notes indicate that she was anxious lest Lady Anne suspect that there was an affair going on between her and Ossulston. In one she wrote: 'you'l oblige me so far so 'tis the last favour I shall ask to call at Lady Ann's at 7 night that she may not think I've any way of sending you word'. Everything had to be done with great secrecy:

> if you can be at Lady Annes to night at eight a clock there I'l settle our meeting to morrow & tell you about the glove but don't constrain your self to come if you have any thing else to do for if I don't see you I'l write again to night if you don't like being at Lady Annes I'l call at Collmans before eight, & we'll fix matters.

Other notes making reference to her attendance on Lady Anne provide colourful details of the life of a lady's servant: 'Lady Ann & I have been at White Hall Chappell where I can assure you I was so ill I was ready to dye we shall be at the park at night'; or the intriguing account (which should make the note dateable by its reference to a notable occurrence): 'we had a review to day of the troops to entertain the Indians I went at Lady Ann's desire who had never seen anything of that nature'.

From this wealth of circumstantial evidence I derive my hypothesis that throughout 1710 Ossulston was conducting a liaison with Mrs Sarah Sidney, who was some sort of lady-in-waiting for an, as yet unidentified, 'Lady Anne'. Lady Anne was herself somehow connected to the household of the duchess of Hamilton, whose residence was across Charles Street from Ossulston House. The proximity of these residences can explain the frequency and brevity of the written communications between Ossulston and Sarah Sidney and her many references to seeing him in his house through her own windows.

Mrs Sidney's notes can reveal aspects of the social life of the early-18th-century British aristocracy in St James's Square, an area where they were living cheek by jowl. They show the late hours kept by Sarah herself, and perhaps many of the square's other inhabitants. In one letter she wrote:

> 'tis now not eight a clock & tho' I did not go from looking at the window where I knew you were till two a clock I can't rest till I've told you what you must certainly be convinc'd of, yett must repeat it that I love you more than words can express.

She ends this letter by hoping 'you heard musick at your window this morning between one & two', and then further adding as a postscript, 'This is dated from my bed where I've not slept this night.' These letters provide a glimpse on the life of a courtier in Queen Anne's London, although Sarah Sidney may be exceptional both in the late hours she kept and her lack of sleep. In one she set out her evening schedule:

> 'tis now near eleven a clock and I like to be alone till two or three … for want of [your company] I'm going to read till twelve and so to bed to dream I hope of you lett me know what you do tomorrow for 'tis a pleasure to know where you are I wish you cou'd contrive to drive by these windows or to be somewhere that I might gett a glimps of you.

Some notes are written as late, or as early, as four in the morning. Attentive readers will also have noticed that this is *Mrs* Sarah Sidney, and we are dealing with (until 30 May 1710) two married people carrying on an affair. Strangely, her husband rarely makes an appearance in her communications with Ossulston; Lady Anne is usually more of an impediment to their trysts than her own husband. In one of the few references to her family, she noted that she was hurriedly writing to Ossulston 'when all my family is in their first sleep'.

Some final examples give further instances of the late hours and furtive assignations, the coaches rumbling around the square, the discreet servants and fashionable company that populate these notes:

> You'l think I'm a perfect stroler when I tell you 'tis past twelve & I'm but just come home where at the door I was met by news that rejoic'd & tormented me at the same time I'l tell you why I cou'd not be at home when I'm so happy to see you … a young Lord will waite of you about twelve to morrow he'll tell you how I past part of this day.

> I've been looking this hour in vain out of my window & hope you are a sleep since all seems hush at your Hostelle I'm so little my self when I see you that I forgott to tell you last night a very disobliging thing you said to me on satturday … but more of this to night when I see you which I resolve to do when 'tis dark enough for the Porter to

open the door without being known I can't stay longer than ten a clock & upon the same terms as usual else I retire sooner.

I came home this evening about ten a clock on purpose to have time to answer yours … now I'm forc'd to write almost in my sleep for 'tis two a clock in the morning but the fear I have of company coming in the morning when I wake makes me chuse this time which is the first moment I've had to myself for the minute I came home some Ladies & red coat came to sup with me & are but just gone else I had pleas'd myself sooner by conversing with you & telling you that I drove up & down under your window on Sunday night above an hour.

The principal purpose of these letters was to arrange private meetings between the two lovers. As already indicated, many were conducted furtively in their own houses on St James's Square, but this was evidently dangerous. So elaborate plans were hatched for their trysts. Two other letters provide examples of the complexity of the arrangements, and their delicacy:

I've been at my window & see you are at home & hope I shall have orders before you go out that I may manage my matters accordingly for I wou'd not go to the house you mention'd last night till I've seen you that there may be no blunder made for that wou'd not be of very agreable consequence shou'd there be any mistake so lett me know at what hour & where I shall come to night or when you please sola in my coach & will take you up I owe a visit at Chelsea I'l stop anywhere on that road or go any other to meet you but remember all this I do with the same resolution I took at first … I've a man just come to see me so can say no more.

I'm so impatient to see you again that tho' twenty people has sent to bid me be at home to morrow & I agreed to their desire yett I'l put all things of to see you what day & hour you appoint in the hedged garden … I'l bring my woman with me if you approve for she'll keep at a distance from us & will do better considering your present circumstances than the Lady at the Marble Potts but my Dear life soul Angell & all that's charming I waite your orders in this as in every thing else …

Ossulston's diary, coupled with the notes from Mrs Sidney, could be used to develop a topography of frequent London locations for extramarital assignations in the early 18th century. Hyde Park appears regularly in Ossulston's entries and we have already seen an extract which detailed a failed attempt at a rendezvous in Holland Walk, which was also a favourite for both. Probably Ossulston's preferred area for 'taking the air' and meeting his love was Brompton Gardens.[20]

All did not always run smoothly in this relationship. Mrs Sidney appears to have had a rival in an (as yet) unidentified 'country neighbour' of Ossulston's in Middlesex. There are as many letters expressing jealous rage, sorrowful anguish, and forlorn resignation as there are effusions of love. One issue in particular may have helped to divide the couple – politics. Sarah was clearly politically knowledgeable and a good number of these notes ended by

[20]Ossulston diary, 10, 23, 26 June, 2, 7, 11, 12, 13, 31 July, 16, 17, 30 Aug. 1710.

conveying political news, particularly during the turbulent summer of 1710. It is interesting to note what 'external' news she thought worthy to impart to Ossulston while arranging meetings, complaining of her late hours, and generally telling him how much she loved him. Some of the news she conveyed has already been noted: the death of Viscount Lumley (24 April); the dismissal of Sunderland as secretary of state and the duke of Beaufort's bout of smallpox (14 June). Political news was most prevalent in her notes from September, as she recounted the dissolution of parliament and the 'ministerial revolution' which saw the tories come to power in the Commons and, more ambivalently, in the ministry. Her note of 22 September was unusual in that it primarily dealt with political events. After a few brief sentences trying to arrange an assignation, impeded by the illness of one of her most reliable servants, Sarah proceeded, 'we are very full of news':

> first that her Majesty laid the proclamation upon the council table & said she had considerd & found nesessary the Parliament shou'd be disolv'd & that she was resolv'd upon dissolving it upon which the Chancellor stood up & was going to speak but the Queen imediately rise and went away his Ldsp this morning wou'd have deliver'd up the seales but the Queen wou'd not take 'em but bid him consider of it D: Somersett is gone to Petworth & is soon to go out the D: of Beaufort preses mightily to succeed him I imagine 'tis no news to you that Ld Rochester is President of the Council, D: Buckingham Ld Steward and St Johns Secretary, Mr Aiselby [*recte* Aislabie] Secretary of War, Geo: Granvill to have Sir John Holland's staff Now I'm upon politicks I'll send you this ballad upon some of the Politicians don't loose it for 'tis hard to get another.

Sarah was well informed of the latest confirmed events as well as the rumours doing the rounds at court. As an indication of the frenetic political activity she observed in late summer 1710, she started her section of news in her letter of 26 September with the introduction, 'the changes of this day are …'.

The politics of this febrile partisan world eventually began to divide the couple. Some of the letters suggest that Mrs Sidney was a tory, which would not be surprising if she was somehow connected to the household of the duke of Hamilton. When the whig Ossulston took issue with her political leanings, Sarah first professed ignorance and innocence: 'I'm in the dark as to what you mean about being us'd like a fool & tool of a party … for my politicks that part of your [letter] is soon answer'd for I don't think there's any body in the world meddles so little in that as my self.' But that attitude changed and she taunted him as the whigs were increasingly placed on the back foot: 'I'm mighty glad to know you are so much oblig'd to the whole party & since you stick so close to 'em in their adversity I hope they'l acknowledge it if ever they shou'd chance to have it once more in their power to be insolent in prosperity.' The latest letter in the bundle that can be dated positively from its mention of political news comes from around 16 October 1710, as Sarah gloats at one of the last humiliations of the whigs: 'I have malice enough not [to] be able to end this without telling you with a great deal of pleasure Ld Lincoln has lost his pension & poor Mr Steel his place of Gazzetteer.'

The difference in the lovers' political views is only one aspect of their characters that can be gleaned from these letters. Mrs Sidney's passionate and extravagant character can clearly be seen. Do they, however, tell us anything about the object of her affection, Ossulston himself? A very different Ossulston emerges from these letters than that seen in his own diary. The diary is terse, hurried, and largely concerned with listing those people with whom Ossulston socialised. Through it he does not come across as a particularly arresting individual. However, that he did have such a wide array of acquaintances indicates that he must have had some charm. Mrs Sidney was clearly highly attracted, and her hyperbolic statements regarding the beauty of his character seem at odds with the person who would pen such unreflective and dry entries in his own diary. She suggested that he had intellectual abilities that she could not match. She complained in one letter: 'why do you puzzle your ignorant friends with your terms of art in architecture', and in another: 'you know I want logick to answer the last paragraph of yours about law nature & reason'. She similarly refused to respond to what may well have been a literately refined attempt to end the relationship: 'as to your letter about Platonic Love I shall make no answer'. What is most striking is her frequent references to the beauty of his writing, a feature that one would never suspect from the diary. She despaired of ever

> doing justice to the beauty of your stile for that can never be done but by as good a pen as your owne if such a one is to be found I can impute your conversing with me to nothing but your inclination to improve & delight me & if I guess right at your generous intentions you have success incompassing both for I insensibly find my self wiser by often reading your letters … you bid me attribute your management I complain'd of to your education which I think if there had been any want in it wou'd never have been found out in one to whom nature has been so exstravagantly kind that all art is unessessary & superfluous.

Ossulston even tried his hand at poetry. In one letter Sarah acknowledged receipt of some verse he had sent her: 'I have propagated your stanza you gave me which is very satyrick & much approv'd in my conscience I believe 'tis the product of your own brain.' Unfortunately, only one or two of his letters to her survive, and these are from a later period, so we cannot gauge whether her judgment of his style was justified or she was just engaging in flattery. We know little of Ossulston's education, beyond the fact that he was sent to Eton. That he had some pretensions to learning is suggested by the extensive catalogue of his library at Dawley House, which was comprehensively stocked and whose contents were appraised in 1722 for £115.[21] On the other hand, Sarah Sidney was by far too self-effacing. Her writing is clearly expressive and at times lyrical, with a passionate style. She was cultured enough to make reference in her letters to lines from a play by Dryden and to invoke Cicero as a model of the best literary style. She was a frequenter of the opera and playhouses, often meeting places for her and Ossulston, and she was clearly a courtier conversant with the most fashionable cultural productions of her time.

It appears that the whole bundle of letters and notes can be dated to the summer of 1710, and they can add a human story to that period, which is usually seen as a turning point in British political history, with the fall of the whig ministry and Robert Harley's construction of a tory-based government. Sarah's notes can show the trials of a couple carrying on a clandestine affair while their political world was rebuilt in the heat of party conflict – which may have come close to tearing them apart as well.

[21]TNA, C 104/82: family notebook of Ossulston's mother, Lady Bridget Howe, for his education at Eton; the same box holds the catalogue of Dawley House's library.

All of this raises the question, how long did the relationship last? On several occasions Sarah attempted to call off the affair and demanded, fruitlessly (as this essay itself bears witness), that Ossulston burn her letters. Despite the violent resentments and jealousies which are obvious in so many of Sarah's notes of 1710, they were still together two years later. The last entry in Ossulston's diary concerning 'Mrs Sydney' is from 15 November 1712, when he recorded coming out of London with her to Dawley; the diary itself ends about a month later. The relationship, indeed, lasted until their deaths, both, coincidentally, in 1722. The earl of Tankerville, as Ossulston had become in October 1714, died after a lingering illness in Dawley House on 21 May 1722, having just turned 48 years the previous week. In his will of 31 July 1721, he bequeathed an annuity of £200 to 'Mrs Sarah Sidney, eldest daughter of Thomas Grice, late rector of Alverstoke'.[22] Thus (at long last) we have the evidence by which we know her forename, after so many references in the diary itself merely to 'Mrs Sydney'. Her situation had also changed by this time, as, perhaps through the help of Tankerville, by her death she was a Middlesex property owner herself, and no longer a servant to Lady Anne. Sarah's own will was completed on 14 August 1721, only two weeks after Tankerville's. 'Sarah Sidney of Harlington, Middlesex, widow', bequeathed her property in Charlton and Shepperton, as well as her stock in the African Company, to Tankerville in trust that he provide her sister, Frances Lichere, with an annuity of £40. On Frances's decease the annuity was to go to her daughter, Sarah's niece, Maria Margarita Lichere. The residue of her personal and real estate was to go to Tankerville as well, and after his death to his third son, Grey Bennet. Furthermore, Tankerville was to be her executor. As in the writing of the will, she appears to have died shortly after Tankerville. He died on 21 May 1722 and letters of administration for her estate (now that her named executor was deceased) were taken out on 18 July 1722.[23]

What more do we know of this Sarah Sidney, who played such a prominent role in the last 12 years of Tankerville's life? Her most basic genealogical details are provided by Tankerville's will. A Thomas Grice was ordained on 5 June 1680, started his ministerial career as vicar of Eye in Suffolk in 1681 and later went on to be rector of Alverstoke in Hampshire from 1682 to 1691. Before he moved to his first incumbency in Suffolk, he and his wife, Susanna, had a daughter, christened Sarah on 1 May 1681 in East Grinstead church. A Sarah Grice was recorded marrying a James Sidney in St Sepulchre's church, London, on 16 October 1707.[24] James Sidney is undoubtedly the 'mate' (never 'husband') whom Sarah occasionally mentions in her letters and Sarah further makes two references to her 'family' and one reference to a son's illness. She was a widow at her death and there was no mention in the will of bequests to a child of her own. Her younger sister, Frances, who figures prominently in the will, married a Peter Lichere, as we know from some letters from him to his sister-in-law, found in a different bundle among the Bennet papers.[25] A Susanna Maria Lichere was christened at St Martin's on 3 November 1715, presumably the same girl as the Maria Margarita Lichere featured in Sarah's will.

[22] TNA, PROB 11/585. A clearly legible transcript of the will is in TNA, C 104/147/1, in a bound volume of fair transcripts of relevant documents in the chancery suits.

[23] TNA, C 104/116/1: loose leaf will of Mrs Sarah Sydney; C 104/148/1 (in volume of fair copy transcripts of relevant documents); TNA, PROB 11/586.

[24] Information derived from the websites of the Clergy of the Church of England database (*theclergy-database.org.uk*) and the International Genealogical Index (*https://www.familysearch.org/search/collection/igi*).

[25] TNA, C 104/116/1, bundle endorsed 'Letters to Mrs Sidney': Peter Lichere to Sarah Sydney, 28 Apr. 1716.

It may well be on account of Tankerville's will that we have these letters from Sarah Sidney at all. Clyve Jones posited that the diary and other papers found their way to the chancery section of The National Archives through a suit brought against Tankerville in 1710–11 by a disgruntled tenant of part of Ossulston House, Thomas Brerewood.[26] However, the endorsements on many of the documents clearly come from the heir, Charles Bennet, 2nd earl of Tankerville. More likely, then, their deposit in chancery derives from one of the many suits arising in the years immediately following the first earl's death complaining of the maladministration of his will. The 2nd earl and his three co-executors regularly appeared as defendants in a series of suits brought by Barbara Meres, whose husband, the steward 'Mr Meres', may well be the most frequently named person in the diary. She complained that the annuity of £100 bequeathed her in the will was not being paid and that, when confronted, the executors refused to inform her of the condition of the estate.[27] It is almost certainly from these suits that the Bennet family papers are still available for perusal as they were submitted to the masters in chancery and were, for whatever reason, never returned. This contribution has sought to show that there is still much more to be gleaned from this important and rich collection, to whose existence Clyve Jones first alerted us, and from which he published so many important preliminary findings.

---

[26] Jones, 'London Life', 141.

[27] TNA, C 11/1880/17, 18: *Meres v. Tankerville*, 1723; *Meres v. Cooke*, 1728; C 11/1490/23: *Meres v. Tench, Tankerville and executors*, 1731.

Party and Management in the Irish House of Lords, 1713–15

D. W. HAYTON

The 'constitutional revolution' which occurred in Ireland after 1691 meant that parliamentary management became one of the prime functions of the viceroyalty. Interest focused on the Commons, where supply legislation was drafted. But the upper House, though smaller, less busy, and on the whole more easily managed, could not be ignored, since it could still cause major problems for government. The situation for the incoming ministers in 1714 was problematic, since the Lords had been a tory stronghold, and the 'Church party', buttressed by the bishops, remained powerful. The situation was a mirror image of Westminster in 1710, when Robert Harley's tory ministry had to cope with a whig-dominated house of lords. This essay analyses the means by which Lord Lieutenant Sunderland (1714–15), and his successors, Lords Justices Grafton and Galway, brought the Irish upper House under control, constructing a court party with some of the elements which Clyve Jones has identified as having been crucial to Harley's strategy in 1710–14: moderate or non-party men, pensioners and placemen depending on government largess, new episcopal appointments and a block creation of peerages. In Ireland it was the new peers who played the most important part. The whigs were able to make some inroads into the episcopal bench, previously a stronghold of toryism, until the issue of relief for dissenters rekindled anxiety over the maintenance of the ecclesiastical establishment, prefiguring future problems.

Keywords: bishops; high church; house of lords; Ireland; parliament; patronage; peerage creations; 'test' clause; 3rd earl of Sunderland

1

Following the conclusion of the jacobite war in 1691, Ireland witnessed a 'constitutional revolution'. The Irish parliament became, for the first time, an essential part of the machinery of government. Grants of 'additional' taxes to supplement the royal hereditary revenues were strictly time-limited, to ensure regular sessions. Even when parliaments had to be prorogued or dissolved without adequate votes of supply, as occurred in 1692 and again in 1713, ministers in Whitehall did not seriously contemplate taxing Ireland directly (although this would have been perfectly consistent with the assertion that the Westminster parliament could legislate for Ireland, often enunciated and subsequently enshrined in statute in the British Declaratory Act of 1720). Alongside such traditional concerns as external defence and internal security, the obtaining of a supply was now the prime task of government in Dublin Castle. Successive viceroys focused on the business of parliamentary management, so much so that it became customary for a chief governor, whether a lord lieutenant, lord deputy, or in exceptional cases a commission of lords justices (as was appointed in 1715) to come over to Dublin only for the duration of a parliamentary session.[1]

Given that chief governors were English, rather than Irish, politicians – the exception being the 2nd duke of Ormond, lord lieutenant 1703–7 and 1710–13 – and were not permanently resident in Ireland during their term of office, it was inevitable that even the most capable, experienced, and active among them would need advice and assistance from local power brokers. Within a few years of the Williamite revolution there emerged the so-called 'undertaker system' which prevailed in Ireland for much of the 18th century. Government virtually contracted out the business of parliamentary management to Irish parliamentary factions, who (while careful not to admit as much publicly) in practice 'undertook' to secure the passage of money bills, and the avoidance of parliamentary embarrassment, in return for a privileged influence over policy and patronage.[2]

In this context 'parliamentary management' meant management of the house of commons, for it was in the lower House that the business of supply was decided. The powers of the Irish parliament had been seriously restricted by the imposition of the act known as Poynings' Law (1494), which required that bills be prepared by the Irish privy council and approved by the privy council in England before being returned to Ireland, where the two Houses could either pass or reject them, but could not introduce amendments. By the late 17th century, the strict terms of the statute were customarily circumvented by a procedure known as 'heads of bills': one or other of the two Houses in Dublin would prepare draft bills, known as 'heads', which would be taken to the Irish privy council to be engrossed as bills proper, and thence transmitted to England, where they might still be amended, or suppressed entirely. Most bills originated as 'heads', and the majority began life in the Commons: during the reigns of William and Mary, and Queen Anne, a total of 449 bills originated in the Commons and only 96 in the Lords.[3] In particular, supply legislation, the key to any successful session as far as government was concerned, was always drafted in the Commons, apart from the 'short money bill', a temporary expedient required to begin a parliament, which would be prepared by the Irish privy council before the parliament met. During the 1690s, the lower House developed its functions in regard to supply, establishing a committee of accounts to scrutinise government expenditure, as well as the committees of supply and ways and means, which decided on the quantum to be raised and the form the necessary taxation should take.

Government's attention was, therefore, focused on the Commons, and it was there that 'undertakers' emerged. Management of the house of lords was neither so urgent nor so complex. Contemporary politicians who were reporting on parliamentary proceedings in Ireland usually concentrated on the Commons;[4] indeed, one chief secretary told the English secretary of state in 1705: 'I never trouble you with what the house of lords do, because in

---

[1] On the Irish 'constitutional revolution' of the early 18th century, see C.I. McGrath, *The Making of the Eighteenth-Century Irish Constitution: Government, Parliament and the Revenue, 1692–1714* (Dublin, 2000).

[2] C.I. McGrath, 'English Ministers, Irish Politicians and the Making of a Parliamentary Settlement in Ireland, 1692–5', *English Historical Review*, cxix (2004), 585–613; D.W. Hayton, *Ruling Ireland, 1685–1742: Politics, Politicians and Parties* (Woodbridge, 2004), 106–30.

[3] Information from the 'Irish Legislation Database' hosted by Queen's University, Belfast (*http://www.qub.ac.uk/ild/*).

[4] E.g., BL, Add. MS 38157, f. 33: Sir Richard Cox to Edward Southwell, 15 Dec. 1713.

truth they have very little business before them.[5] To outside observers, like the duke of Leeds in 1698, the principal function of the Lords seemed to be judicial rather than legislative.[6] And attendances were small in proportion to the Commons. At any one time during the period 1690–1750, there were as many as 200 Irish peerages, besides the 22 bishops of the established Church of Ireland, but if we discount catholics, minors, perpetual absentees, and those English politicians with honorific Irish titles, the number of temporal lords who could have attended the House was much smaller. The published *Journal of the House of Lords*, like its English counterpart, recorded attendance, and while we have to assume that the evidence of these published 'presence lists' was subject to similar qualifications as those surrounding the lists produced at Westminster, they are all we have to work with.[7] They show that average daily attendances ranged from about 30 in Anne's reign to 40 under the first two Georges, and also that the bishops formed a substantial element – sometimes as much as half the House.[8] The size of the active membership and the relative strength of the episcopal cohort, many of whom would be looking to the government in Dublin Castle for preferment, should have rendered the business of management less problematic than in the house of commons.

None the less, no viceroy could take the Irish house of lords for granted. The legislative procedure of the parliament meant that the Lords considered all returned bills, whether or not the 'heads' had originated there, and the upper House might occasionally embarrass a ministry by voting down a measure that government, or a majority in the Commons, regarded as important – other than supply bills, that is, which in this respect were sacrosanct. In 1697, the lords justices, Galway and Winchester, only narrowly secured the belated ratification of the articles of Limerick (which had concluded the jacobite war in 1691) in the face of determined opposition in the Lords.[9] But not long afterwards they suffered the embarrassment of losing in the Lords the bill 'for the security of the king's person', whose provisions some members considered too severe on Irish catholics.[10] A decade later an anti-catholic penal law, a popular bill coming from the Commons, was taken to a division in the upper House and passed by only a small majority.[11] From time to time there were also disputes between the two Houses, which might slow down the progress of parliamentary business. Finally, the juridical function of the Lords, while not usually controversial, had the capacity to create political turmoil when dissatisfied parties appealed over the heads of the Irish parliament to the house of lords at Westminster, which claimed a superior jurisdiction.

[5] TNA, SP 63/365, f. 101: Edward Southwell to Sir Charles Hedges, 1 Mar. 1704/5.

[6] Quoted in F.G. James, *Lords of the Ascendancy: The Irish House of Lords and Its Members, 1600–1800* (Blackrock, Co. Dublin, 1995), 73.

[7] Clyve Jones, 'Seating Problems of the House of Lords in the Early Eighteenth Century: The Evidence of the Manuscript Minutes', *Bulletin of the Institute of Historical Research*, li (1978), 132–45; *The History of Parliament: The House of Lords, 1660–1715*, ed. Ruth Paley (5 vols, Cambridge, 2016) [hereafter cited as *HPL, 1660–1714*], i, 41–5.

[8] James, *Lords of the Ascendancy*, 73. One hundred and ninety-seven peers were available to be called to the 1713 parliament (BL, Add. MS 61637A: printed list of the 1713 parliament) but only 47 were recorded in the *Journals of the House of Lords* as attending.

[9] HMC, *Buccleuch MSS*, ii, 557–8.

[10] *Journals of the House of Lords* [of Ireland] (8 vols, Dublin, 1779–80) [hereafter cited as *LJI*], i, 664–5.

[11] *LJI*, ii, 303; *The Letters of Joseph Addison*, ed. Walter Graham (Oxford, 1941), 181–2; BL, Add. MS 34777, f. 68.

The issue arose in the late 1690s, in the case of *The Irish Society of London* v. *the Bishop of Derry*, the first in a serious of conflicts between the two parliaments in 1697–9 which resulted in the indefinite prorogation of King William's last Irish parliament. It threatened to reappear in 1703 over *Ward et al.* v. *Earl of Meath* and eventually erupted volcanically in 1717 over another property dispute, *Annesley* v. *Sherlock*, precipitating a constitutional crisis.[12]

The new whig government installed in Ireland after the Hanoverian succession had every reason to be concerned about the situation in the upper House, for as party conflict had gathered pace in Ireland in the second half of Queen Anne's reign, the Lords had come to be recognized as a bastion of the tory interest. This had been a striking feature of the latter stages of the session of 1711, during the duke of Ormond's second viceroyalty, and the short-lived parliament of 1713, when an aggressive whig faction had taken control of the Commons. Thus the servants of King George's first lord lieutenant, the earl of Sunderland, felt obliged to pay close attention to the probable balance of forces in the Irish house of lords and, in consultation with leading Irish whig politicians, to develop the means of overcoming the previous tory majority. Their situation recalled the way in which Robert Harley, earl of Oxford had coped with an analogous situation at Westminster in 1710–12.

The balance of parties in the British house of lords had presented Harley with a particular problem when he took over the reins of government in 1710. Of course, the crown did enjoy some natural advantages. For one thing bishops were an important element, comprising about a fifth of the total membership, and more reliable in their attendance than many of the peers.[13] There was also a substantial cohort of placemen and pensioners, who, by a combination of temperament and penury, were drawn into the orbit of the court. Some, the so-called 'poor lords', were little more than parliamentary beggars, to use Sir Lewis Namier's phrase.[14] But from the beginning of Queen Anne's reign, at least until the collapse of the Marlborough-Godolphin ministry in 1710, there had seemed to be a natural, almost inbuilt, whig majority, boosted by a phalanx of 'Low Church' bishops appointed under King William. The whig junto had relied on the Lords to frustrate the impeachments orchestrated by the tories in 1701, to defeat the various attempts of high churchmen to outlaw 'occasional conformity' in 1702–4, and to ramp up pressure on Lord Treasurer Godolphin in 1705–8 in order to force their friends into office. After the tory landslide in the 1710 election, the upper House became the principal platform for whig opposition, most notably to the ministers' attempts to secure a peace with France.

In articles and essays, Clyve Jones has studied aspects of Harley's management of the Lords.[15] At one point, in the winter of 1711–12, Harley was reduced to

---

[12] F.G. James, *Ireland in the Empire 1688–1770: A History of Ireland from the Williamite Wars to the Eve of the American Revolution* (Cambridge, MA, 1973), 99–109; Isolde Victory, 'The Making of the 1720 Declaratory Act', in *Parliament, Politics and People: Essays in Eighteenth-Century Irish History*, ed. Gerard O'Brien (Blackrock, Co. Dublin, 1989), 9–29; Hayton, *Ruling Ireland*, 66–84, 222–3.

[13] *HPL, 1660–1714*, i, 33–4, 36; Geoffrey Holmes, *British Politics in the Age of Anne* (1967), 398.

[14] Holmes, *British Politics*, 391–4. One particular example is discussed in Clyve Jones and John Beckett, 'Financial Improvidence and Political Independence in the Early Eighteenth Century: George Booth, 2nd Earl of Warrington (1675–1758)', *Bulletin of the John Rylands Library*, lxv (1982), 8–35; see also *HPL, 1660–1714*, ii, 258–72.

[15] Clyve Jones, ' "The Scheme Lords, the Neccessitous Lords, and the Scots Lords": The Earl of Oxford's Management and the "Party of the Crown" in the House of Lords, 1711–14', in *Party and Management in Parliament, 1660–1784*, ed. Clyve Jones (Leicester, 1984), 123–67.

recommending a block creation of peers in order to prevent his peace policy being sabotaged, but this was an exceptional case and not repeated. Clyve has shown how, across the period of his administration, Harley constructed a court party – a 'party of the crown' – largely through patronage, and, more frequently, promises of patronage. Beginning with a core of loyal tories, Harley exploited the goodwill of moderate men on each side, whose natural bent was to support administration, the so-called 'scheme lords'; and the neediness of supplicants for patronage, the 'necessitous lords', especially Scottish representative peers, whose financial circumstances were often quite spectacularly desperate.

The Irish house of lords resembled its Westminster counterpart in terms of its composition: not only were the spiritual lords over-represented in terms of daily attendance; there was also a significant contingent of 'poor lords', depending on money from government, either as salaries or pensions. However, the Irish episcopate, unlike the English, was, by 1702, predominantly high church rather than low. Even those bishops who might be accounted 'low churchmen' in secular politics took a strong line in defence of the interests of the ecclesiastical establishment. In particular they joined in resisting attempts to ameliorate the position of protestant dissenters by relaxing the provisions of the clause in the 1704 Popery Act that imposed a sacramental test on holders of crown and municipal office. William King, archbishop of Dublin, perhaps the leading 'low churchman' in Ireland, was described as 'a state Whig, and a church Tory'.[16] The situation of the Church of Ireland was infinitely more precarious than that of the Church of England, and Irish bishops could not regard with equanimity the concentration of presbyterians in the north of Ireland, recently reinforced in the 1690s by large-scale immigration from Scotland. A classic example of the mindset of the Church of Ireland clergy is the case of Peter Browne, the provost of Trinity College made bishop of Cork in 1710 as a reward for the support he had given Lord Wharton in the Irish convocation, who soon appeared in parliament in the colours of a high churchman and a tory.[17]

In fact, in terms of party politics the Irish house of lords was a mirror image of the British, and its management posed problems for a whig ministry in the same way as the upper House at Westminster had posed problems for Harley. Not surprisingly, perhaps, the expedients adopted in Ireland in 1714–15, in preparation for George I's first parliament, recalled Harley's methods: concern with 'moderate' opinion; the careful disposal of vacant bishoprics; a strategic distribution of pensions and places; and, above all, the creation of new peerages.[18] It seems likely that Harley's example directly influenced the approach taken by Sunderland and his advisors, just as a decade later Sir Robert Walpole would follow Harley's strategies in managing the British house of lords.[19]

[16] For King's politics, see Philip O'Regan, *Archbishop William King of Dublin (1650–1729) and the Constitution in Church and State* (Dublin, 2000); Christopher Fauske, *A Political Biography of William King* (2011).

[17] A.R. Winnett, *Peter Browne: Provost, Bishop, Metaphysician* (1974), esp. 40–7; and the entry in *ODNB*.

[18] Holmes, *British Politics*, 383–403; Jones, ' "Scheme Lords, Neccessitous Lords, and Scots Lords" '.

[19] Clyve Jones, 'The House of Lords and the Growth of Parliamentary Stability', in *Britain in the First Age of Party, 1680–1750: Essays Presented to Geoffrey Holmes*, ed. Clyve Jones (1987), 93.

2

The Irish parliament presided over by the duke of Shrewsbury as lord lieutenant in December 1713 had been a disaster in terms of political management.[20] The general election in November had taken place in a febrile atmosphere, engendered by the controversial activities of the tory administration in Dublin and especially the behaviour of the lord chancellor, Sir Constantine Phipps. A hot tory and a suspected jacobite, Phipps had exploited his own judicial position and executive authority as a lord justice in a frankly partisan manner, and had persuaded tories on the Irish privy council to follow him. He was accused by Irish whigs of advancing crypto-catholics in local government; of running down the militia in order to weaken the defence of the kingdom; of failing to prosecute jacobites while arresting honest protestants for minor infringements of the law; and of instigating a campaign to 'remodel' borough corporations and 'pack' parliament (as Tyrconnel had attempted to do in 1687–9), by abusing the power of the privy council to approve or disapprove the elections of chief magistrates in particular corporations. By the autumn of 1713, the focus of whig complaints was the privy council's refusal to accept the election of a whig lord mayor of Dublin, resulting in the effective suspension of government in the city. The agitation against Phipps destabilised Ormond's position in the 1711 session, which ended in a flurry of bad temper, confusion, and recrimination. In consequence, Harley determined on a change of viceroy, and replaced Ormond with an ex-whig, Shrewsbury, who was to implement the same kind of 'moderating scheme' that Harley had attempted at Westminster in 1710: to construct a coalition of 'moderate' men, loyal to the queen, and prepared to put aside 'resentments' to work together in a common cause.

Shrewsbury's scheme was doomed, for there were insufficient moderate whigs or moderate tories in Ireland to make it work. Politics was polarised. Crucially, Phipps and his allies on the Irish privy council refused to compromise over the Dublin mayoralty. Chief among this cadre of diehard councillors were the earl of Anglesey (Viscount Valentia in the Irish peerage), a violent high tory who occupied a prominent position in English politics among Harley's tory critics, and the bishop of Raphoe, Thomas Lindsay, the leader of the high church party in the Irish episcopate. On the other side the Irish whigs, led in the Commons by a former lord chief justice, Alan Brodrick, and in the Lords by Archbishop King of Dublin, proved equally intransigent. Brodrick's election to the chair at the start of the session, over Shrewsbury's nominee, was the signal for the whigs in the lower House to launch a full-scale onslaught against Phipps. Inquiries were begun into the proceedings on the Dublin mayoral election, and other grievances against the chancellor, culminating in an address calling for his dismissal. Shrewsbury adjourned the session at Christmas, and having failed to persuade the whig leaders in the Commons to abandon their campaign, prorogued the parliament. With Anne's death in August 1714 it was dissolved.

While the Irish house of commons in 1713 came to be dominated by the whigs, the tories not only maintained, but strengthened, their ascendancy in the upper House. According to the tory chief justice, Sir Richard Cox, two-thirds of the lords attending were tories.[21] At the beginning of the session, whig sympathisers seem to have tried to make a fight of it.

---

[20] For what follows, unless otherwise stated, see Hayton, *Ruling Ireland*, 160–76.

[21] BL, Add. MS 38157, f. 37: Cox to Edward Southwell, 19 Dec. 1713.

Although the Lords ordered addresses of thanks to the queen and lord lieutenant in terms which would have expressed strong support for the peace, and emphasized loyalty to the established church, when these addresses were reported, by Archbishop King and another whig, Lord Mountjoy, approbation of the peace was soft-pedalled and the perceived threat from 'Dissenting teachers' was coupled with that from 'popish priests'.[22] It was not long before whigs were driven firmly on to the back foot. Members of the Lords began their own inquiries into the allegations against Phipps, demanding books and papers in a blatant attempt to obstruct the Commons investigations.[23] They ended by addressing the queen in support of the lord chancellor, and agreed a representation exonerating him from all charges. They also pursued reports of a slanderous attack on Phipps in a Dublin coffee house by an exchequer official, ordering the attorney general to prosecute.[24] Archbishop King and his friends were reduced to entering protests against these various votes, but could muster no more than nine signatories.[25]

One whig pamphleteer was clear that the tory majority in the upper House was essentially a clerical ascendancy. The author of *The Resolutions of the House of Commons in Ireland, Relating to the Lord-Chancellor Phips, Examined* ..., published in London in 1714, set about enlightening English readers as to the true nature of the house of lords in Dublin.[26]

> The mention of a house of lords in Britain, gives the idea of the most august assembly in the world; but if we form our notions of the Irish by the British house of lords, we are vastly wide of the mark. The temporal lords in Ireland that have session, are a very inconsiderable number; for the spiritual ... generally make up the better half of the House ... The bishops then making the most considerable part of the house of lords, it is not much to be wondered at, that the chancellor should gain their voices: I will not say that the three vacant bishoprics could any way influence that venerable order of men; but I dare say this, that a noisy zeal for the church has had a good deal of effect on those reverend prelates.

In terms of the leadership of the tory interest, there was some justice in this analysis: aside from Lords Anglesey and Abercorn (Viscount Strabane in the Irish peerage), the most prominent and active figures on the tory side were bishops. The committee appointed on 18 December 1713 to prepare the address vindicating Phipps, wholly tory in its complexion, comprised three temporal lords – Anglesey, Abercorn, and the earl of Barrymore – and five bishops – Archbishop Vesey, and Bishops Lindsay, Edward Smyth of Down and Connor, Thomas Smyth of Limerick, Thomas Milles of Waterford and Sir Thomas Vesey

---

[22] *LJI*, ii, 422, 424–5.

[23] *LJI*, ii, 430, 432, 434–6, 440–1, 443, 445; *A Long History of a Certain Session of a Certain Parliament, in a Certain Kingdom* ([Dublin], 1714), 61–6, 84–7; *The Conduct of the Purse of Ireland* ... (1714), 36–7; Trinity College Dublin [hereafter cited as TCD], MS 2021, pp. 44–54: Sir John Stanley to Lord Bolingbroke, 19 Dec. 1713; 'An Irish Parliamentary Diary from the Reign of Queen Anne', ed. D.W. Hayton, *Analecta Hibernica*, xxx (1982), 136.

[24] *LJI*, ii, 436–8; Surrey History Centre [hereafter cited as SHC], Brodrick MSS, 1248/3/142–3: Alan Brodrick to Thomas Brodrick, 9 Dec. 1713.

[25] *LJI*, ii, 435, 438; see below, appendix 1.

[26] *The Resolutions of the House of Commons in Ireland, Relating to the Lord-Chancellor Phips, Examined* ... (1714), 28–30.

of Killaloe.[27] The strong involvement of the bishops in general in the proceedings of this parliament can be deduced not just from the emphasis in the loyal addresses on the danger from dissent, but also from the fact that the first two heads of bills produced by the Lords were for the easier recovery of tithes, and the suppression of blasphemy and profaneness.[28] However, not all bishops were high church tories. Even Lord Wharton, whose unsavoury personal reputation and avowed commitment to repeal the test provoked a strong clerical reaction against him, could count in 1709 on the support of six out of 13 bishops in a crucial division.[29] In 1713, King and his friends, St George Ashe of Clogher and John Stearne of Dromore, were among those who protested against the votes in favour of the lord chancellor. And in terms of the weight of numbers, the evidence of the printed 'presence lists' goes against the assertions made by whig propaganda. Temporal lords were in a majority on 19 of the 24 days (79%) in which the Lords sat in this parliament. There was an episcopal majority on only two days, on both of which a tithe bill was under consideration, and the numbers were equal on the remaining three.

Three contemporary analyses of the membership enable us to see more clearly the composition of the tory interest. All are to be found in the Blenheim papers (now in the British Library), and were communicated to Lord Sunderland after his appointment by George I as lord lieutenant: a printed list of the membership of both Houses in the 1713 parliament, with marks against the names of tories, a list of lords divided into whigs and tories, and another marked 'for court' and 'against court'.[30] (Despite Shrewsbury's early preference for a 'moderating scheme' he was obliged to defend Phipps by virtue of the fact that he himself served a tory administration in Whitehall, so that as the 1713 session proceeded the tory side of the House became, *ipso facto*, the court side.) From these lists we can see that the bishops were, indeed, an important element in the court, or tory interest: 15 out of the 18 who attended supported the court. However, they did not form a majority of the court party, being joined in debates and divisions by a larger contingent of temporal lords, even if here the difference between the two parties was not so striking: 18 to nine for the court.

Some of these 'court' peers were committed high church tories: Anglesey and Barrymore, for example, both of whom were active in the tory cause at Westminster;[31] the splenetic and unpredictable Abercorn, who had been perhaps the most irreconcilable opponent in the upper House of the whig Lord Wharton's viceroyalty in 1709–10;[32] and the equally hot-tempered Lord Kerry, who had once challenged a whig lord chancellor, John Methuen, to a duel.[33] Others, whose basic political instincts were tory, were cemented in their allegiance by poverty.[34] The 2nd earl of Granard, sent to the Tower three times by William III

---

[27] *LJI*, ii, 437.

[28] *LJI*, ii, 425–6.

[29] *Addison Letters*, ed. Graham, 179–80, 183.

[30] BL, Add. MS 61637A; 61640, ff. 27–8, 30; see below, appendix 1.

[31] *The History of Parliament: The House of Commons, 1690–1715*, ed. Eveline Cruickshanks, Stuart Handley and D. W. Hayton (5 vols, Cambridge, 2002) [hereafter cited as *HPC, 1690–1715*], iii, 27–34, 145–6.

[32] *Addison Letters*, ed. Graham, 220.

[33] *History of the Irish Parliament 1692–1700*, ed. Edith Mary Johnston-Liik (6 vols, Belfast, 2002), iv, 174; *HPC, 1690–1715*, iv, 802; HMC, *Buccleuch MSS*, ii, 585; National Library of Ireland [hereafter cited as NLI], MS 50,545/2/7: Henry Rose to David Crosbie, [Nov. 1713].

[34] Even Abercorn, who claimed to possess an income of over £4,000 in rents, together with £2,000 in capital and £4,000 in Bank stock, had such expenses, mainly in providing for children, that he was hoping in 1714

as a suspected jacobite, had acquired a pension of £500 on the Irish civil list in 1703, which kept him from bankruptcy: his debts amounted to over £12,000.[35] Other mendicants included Lord Mountcashell, a close friend of Ormond, who had pressed the duke, when lord lieutenant, for various forms of patronage;[36] Lord Athenry, a conforming ex-catholic who had been reduced to a 'very uneasy' state after the loss of the family's lands and depended on a pension of £200 which he hoped the tory ministry would continue;[37] and Athenry's uncle, Theobald Bourke, Viscount Mayo, another convert to protestantism, whose needs were such that he had to be granted the sum of £50 as royal bounty in April 1714.[38] In a similar position was Michael Bourke, Lord Dunkellin, son of the former jacobite loyalist (and now conforming anglican), the earl of Clanricarde. Having been educated at Oxford, Dunkellin had many contacts among English high churchmen, but at the same time was a frequent, and apparently desperate, applicant for jobs, pensions, and honours.[39]

Then there were those, the Irish equivalent of the English and Scottish 'poor lords', whose dire necessities, often dramatised by the peers themselves in terms suggesting destitution, rendered them available for purchase by any ministry. The earl of Inchiquin was a perfect example: under severe financial pressures, through 'ruining himself' by over-spending, he had a record of currying favour with viceroys of every political stripe, in order to obtain relief from his 'unhappy circumstances'.[40] Inchiquin clearly considered the political situation in 1713 too volatile for him to risk exposure, so absented himself from this parliament. Others were not so intimidated. The earl of Cavan, a serving captain of foot, consistently pleaded poverty; having not inherited 'one foot of the estate of the family' he was obliged to subsist on his army pay. He had eventually been granted a pension of £200 in May 1710, as a reward for having supposedly 'managed' for Wharton in the Lords, and the following year was pressing Ormond for promotion in rank, urging the duke to ignore 'the representation that he is a person not in his grace's interest'.[41] The earl of Roscommon also depended on a pension from the crown, in his case £150: he had been 'left quite destitute' by his family's 'ungenerous usage'.[42] Richard Coote, 3rd earl of Bellomont, was another pensioner, this time on the English establishment; a younger son of the spendthrift 1st earl, and described

---

[34] *(continued)* for charity from government to tide him over: Public Record Office of Northern Ireland [hereafter cited as PRONI], D/623/A/3/15: Abercorn to Edward Southwell, 3 Apr. 1714.

[35] Admiral the Hon. John Forbes, *Memoirs of the Earls of Granard*, ed. George-Arthur-Hastings, earl of Granard (1868), 72–80; *Calendar of Treasury Books*, xviii, 226; TCD, MS 2533, p. 245: Archbishop King to Joseph Addison, 2 June 1716.

[36] HMC, *Ormonde MSS*, n.s., viii, 192, 193–4, 216–18, 268, 320; NLI, MS 2483, pp. 441–2: Mountcashell to [Ormond], nd.

[37] Staffordshire Record Office, Dartmouth MSS, D (W) 1778/I.iii/384, 390: Athenry to Lord Dartmouth, 2 June, 7 July 1713.

[38] TNA, T 48/91, p. 56: warrant, 13 Apr. 1714.

[39] NLI, MS 45,308/1: Dunkellin to Sir Donough O'Brien, 24 Nov. 1713; TNA, SP 63/367/74: Ormond to Dartmouth, July 1711; SP 63/367/114: William Wogan to Edward Southwell, 20 July 1711; BL, Add. MS 70294, f. 41: Dunkellin to Lord Treasurer Oxford, 19 Aug. 1712; Bodl., MS Eng. Hist. c. 42, p. 29, Ormond to lords justices, 14 Apr. 1713.

[40] *The Inchiquin Manuscripts*, ed. J.F. Ainsworth (Dublin, 1961), 88, 95, 103, 107; HMC, *Ormonde MSS*, viii, 64, 99, 164, 191, 219; *Addison Letters*, ed. Graham, 152–3; HMC, *Portland MSS*, v, 64; BL, Add. MS 70294, ff. 118–19: Inchiquin to [Oxford], 14 Jan. 1711/12.

[41] Marsh's Library, Dublin, MS Z.1.1.13/26: *The Case of Richard, Earl of Cavan*; HMC, *Ormonde MSS*, n.s., viii, 65–6, 329; TNA, T 14/9, pp. 186–7; HMC, *Portland MSS*, v, 21.

[42] HMC, *Ormonde MSS*, viii, 79; TNA, SP 63/370/105: petition of Roscommon to Queen Anne, [1714].

pithily as 'a beggar'.[43] Not all such 'poor lords' were reliably venal, however. Richard, Lord Bellew, who had conformed to the established church only in 1705, was a difficult man to pigeonhole politically. He was a brother-in-law of the whiggish duke of Richmond, and was returned to the British house of commons on Richmond's interest. On the other hand, he was perceived by contemporaries to harbour tory sympathies, and was granted a pension of £300 in October 1713, which his wife evidently considered insufficient, for after the Irish parliamentary session of 1713, she asked Secretary Bolingbroke if it could be increased. But despite his pension, Bellew opposed the court in the Lords, to the extent of protesting against the address vindicating Phipps.[44]

3

The first step taken by Sunderland in 1714 to tackle the problem of the Irish house of lords was to repeat Harley's stratagem of a block creation of new peers. We cannot be certain that the first batch of 'coronation peerages' – there were to be two sets of creations before the new Irish parliament sat in November 1715 – was entirely motivated by the necessity of safeguarding the ministry's position in the Lords. After all, this was also an exercise in patronage, directed at particular individuals and families, and at the same time a more general public statement. The lord lieutenant was rewarding loyal whigs who had resisted the previous tory government, in what was already being called in whig propaganda 'the worst of times'. Interestingly, early rumours included two names which hinted at a more generous, even eirenic, attitude, perhaps implying an invitation to former tories to put aside party rancour and support the new dynasty, and the new ministry. Sunderland hoped to summon Abercorn's son, Lord Paisley, in his father's barony, and one of the intended recipients of peerages was the young, and very moderate, tory knight of the shire for County Cork in the 1713 parliament, Sir John Perceval.[45] These nominations were not the viceroy's own, but originated with Sunderland's political advisors, who knew the men involved. A lord lieutenant was always obliged to rely on advice from men on the spot, though Sunderland was himself responsible for the decision to implement the scheme.

The decision to create a number of new Irish lords – and working lords rather than the second-rank politicians in England for whom a British peerage would have been inappropriate and who would never come to Dublin – seems to have been taken by late October 1714.[46] William Whitshed, a prominent Irish whig who had recently been appointed lord chief justice of queen's bench in Ireland, returned to Dublin from England with instructions from Sunderland to produce a list of suitable candidates to be raised to the peerage. He consulted the incoming lord chancellor, Alan Brodrick (himself among those to be ennobled) and the lords justices, and was able to come up with eight names, including two eldest sons of peers (Paisley, and Lord Brabazon, the son of the earl of Meath) who could be

[43] BL, Add. MS 61640, f. 32. For the 1st earl, see *HPC, 1690–1715*, iii, 708–10.

[44] *HPC, 1690–1715*, iii, 169–70; *Letters and Correspondence … of … Henry St John, Lord Viscount Bolingbroke …*, ed. Gilbert Parke (4 vols in 2, 1798), iv, 558–9.

[45] SHC, 1248/3/207–8: Alan Brodrick to Thomas Brodrick, 30 Dec. 1714. For Perceval, see *Hist. Ir. Parl.*, ed. Johnston-Liik, vi, 49–50; *The History of Parliament: The House of Commons, 1715–1754*, ed. Romney Sedgwick (2 vols, 1970), ii, 336–8; 'Irish Parliamentary Diary', ed. Hayton, 100–5.

[46] SHC, 1248/3/195–6: Alan Brodrick to Thomas Brodrick, 30 Oct. 1714.

summoned in their fathers' subsidiary titles.[47] Discussions continued throughout December, with potential nominees being canvassed. It was not simply a matter of finding willing lobby fodder. The prospect of leaving the Commons had its drawbacks, given the greater political importance of the lower House, and the potential expense involved in maintaining the dignity of a peer. The annual landed income of prospective nominees was a prime consideration. Eventually a slate was agreed – six including Brodrick, plus Lords Paisley and Brabazon – but one of the six eventually decided he could not accept, and Sunderland, for whatever reason, decided against calling up eldest sons in their fathers' lifetime. Sunderland clearly felt that this number was insufficient, and set Whitshed to work again.[48]

The lord lieutenant's sense of urgency was doubtless increased by the receipt of various calculations of the balance of forces in the Lords. In November 1714, Brodrick had sent his brother, Thomas, a sheet of paper to be shown to the chief secretary, Joseph Addison. It was made up of three columns, the first two consisting of those likely to be for and against the court. 'I will give you liberty to suppose the third column to contain doubtful persons: for I hardly know which way men will go whose principles are very violently one way, and of whom you have no other hold then a small pension: this I say as to some of them.'[49] Then in December, Archbishop King, in his capacity as one of the lord justices also sent a marked list, which Sunderland claimed to find encouraging but did not behave as if he did.[50] Neither of these lists has survived. But Sunderland's papers do contain a third list, which can be dated to April 1715, in a hand strongly resembling that of the earl's under secretary, Charles Delafaye, who had himself been in Ireland in the service of the duke of Shrewsbury and had some personal knowledge of Irishmen and Irish politics, as well as an impressive range of contacts in Dublin.[51]

The April list begins by enumerating the lords present in the 1713 parliament and dividing them into court and opposition: 36 and 12 respectively. Of the 12 oppositionists the earl of Drogheda had since died, while of the court side, four lords were noted to have been in receipt of pensions (Cavan, Granard, Roscommon, and Athenry), two enjoyed places of profit under the crown (Anglesey as vice-treasurer and Barrymore as colonel of a regiment), and three held the prestigious, if unremunerated, office of county governor (Blayney, Charlemont, and Inchiquin). When it came to calculating the disposition of forces in the next parliament, the compiler or compilers counted 28 certain votes 'for gov[ernmen]t' and 24 'certain ag[ain]st'. A further refinement was introduced by noting lords currently resident in Ireland and those who had been absent from the country since October 1714. Removing the absentees left 16 on each side, so everything depended on those considered 'doubtful'. There were two doubtful votes listed for the court side, and 12 against. This was unlikely to provide much comfort to Sunderland, and it is not surprising that even after

---

[47] SHC, 1248/3/199–200: Alan Brodrick to Thomas Brodrick, 4 Nov. 1714; BL, Add. MS 61639, ff. 62–3: Whitshed to Sunderland, 17 Nov. 1714. For Whitshed, see *Hist. Ir. Parl.*, ed. Johnston-Liik, vi, 538–40.

[48] BL, Add. MS 61639, f. 66: William Whitshed to Sunderland, 16 Dec. 1714; ff. 104–5: Whitshed to [Sunderland], 25 Jan. 1714/15; Add. MS 61652, ff. 233–4, 238–40: Sunderland to Alan Brodrick, 22 Dec. 1714, Sunderland to Whitshed, 28 Dec. 1714: SHC, 1248/3/207–8: Alan Brodrick to Thomas Brodrick, 30 Dec. 1714; TCD, MS 1995–2008/1589: Frederick Hamilton to [Archbishop King], 1 Mar. 1714[/15].

[49] SHC, 1248/3/202–2: [Alan Brodrick] to [Thomas Brodrick], 16 Nov. 1714.

[50] BL, Add. MS 61635, ff. 151–2: King to Sunderland, 27 Dec. 1714; 61652, ff. 242–3: Sunderland to King, 13 Jan. 1714/15.

[51] BL, Add. MS 61640, ff. 29–30; see below, appendices 1 and 2.

patents for five new Irish peerages were passed in April (Alan Brodrick, his fellow whigs, Sir Arthur Cole, Richard Fitzpatrick, and Sir George St George, together with the lukewarm tory, Sir John Perceval), followed by another in May (the young whig, George Evans), the lord lieutenant needed further reassurance.

Governmental anxieties were increased by a spate of fatalities in the peerage. Three whig lords, the earls of Meath and Drogheda, and Lord Bellew, had died since December 1713, together with the poverty-stricken earl of Roscommon. The equally vulnerable Lord Mountcashell was reportedly on his deathbed. Only one had left an heir of age, Meath's son Lord Brabazon, whom Sunderland had once intended to summon to the upper House, though the young earl of Roscommon was also said to be close to his majority. Another reliable whig, Mountrath, would probably be unable to attend.[52] In June 1715, Delafaye told Archbishop King that the lord lieutenant was 'sensible of the need of repairing our loss' in the Irish house of lords, and that he intended to move the king for a second set of peerage creations.[53] A figure of ten was talked of.[54] After further canvassing, and some refusals, four more whigs were taken from the Commons and added to the government forces in the upper House (Theophilus Butler, Gustavus Hamilton, John Moore, and Sir Henry Tichborne). All the preparations had been made by September, and the patents were issued a month later.[55]

Meanwhile, Sunderland had been sent another detailed analysis, this time characterising lords as 'good' or 'bad'. Again it was written out in a clerkly hand resembling Delafaye's.[56] This time the results were more encouraging. The 'good lords' who 'will attend' numbered 38 (including the lord chancellor), the 'bad lords that will be present' 20. In addition, there were seven bishops who were 'uncertain' but 'generally go with the court', two other 'good' peers who would vote the right way 'if there' (Burlington) or 'if of age' (Roscommon), and three others (Viscount Lanesborough, the terminally ill Mountcashel, and Bishop Hartstonge of Derry, another martyr to poor health)[57] whose intentions were opaque.

This more optimistic outlook had been brought about not only by the peerage creations in the spring, but also by some significant episcopal appointments, a generally more sanguine appreciation of the likely disposition of the bishops' votes, and by the cultivation of individual 'poor lords'. Three vacant bishoprics had been filled in October 1714. Archbishop King, who always resented the imposition of careerist Englishmen on the Church of Ireland, had pressed for the appointment of clergy who were conscientious as well as politically reliable, men who would attend to their diocesan duties and not absent themselves in Dublin or in England. He was therefore particularly pleased when his protégé, Edward Synge, the chancellor of St Patrick's, Dublin, was nominated to succeed Lindsay at Raphoe, Shrewsbury's former chaplain, Timothy Godwin, was drafted in at Kilmore, and

---

[52]TCD, MS 750/13, p. 42: Archbishop King to Sunderland, 7 Apr. 1715; p. 48: same to Addison, 31 May 1715; BL, Add. MS 61635, f. 121: lords justices to Sunderland, 2 June 1715.

[53]TCD, MS 1995–2008/1659: Delafaye to King, 9 June 1715.

[54]TCD, MS 1995–2008/1688: Frederick Hamilton to King, 2, 8 July 1715.

[55]TCD, MS 750/13, p. 71: Archbishop King to Sunderland, 6 Sept. 1715; MS 1995–2008/1727: Delafaye to King, 20 Sept. 1715.

[56]BL, Add. MS 61640, ff. 31–2; see below, appendix 2.

[57]Royal Irish Academy, MS 3.A.54, pp. 157–8: licences of absence for Hartstonge, 8 Jan., 27 Aug. 1713; TCD, MS 1995–2008/1635: Hartstonge to Archbishop King, 10 May 1715.

Nicholas Forster, a fellow of Trinity College and brother of a former whig Speaker of the Commons, was made bishop of Killaloe. All three appeared on the list of recommendations which King had submitted in advance to Archbishop Tenison of Canterbury.[58] Synge and Forster had the benefit (in King's eyes) of being Irishmen, while Godwin was one of the few English-born colleagues whom he was prepared to tolerate.[59] In addition, Synge was an excellent speaker, and when the parliament met he made an immediate and powerful impression in debate.[60] Several on the government side were also prepared to believe that many of the bishops who had supported the tories in 1713 would prove to be moderate men and would trim their sails under the Hanoverian regime, which probably accounts for the optimism evident in the analysis of parties prepared for Sunderland in the summer of 1715: Sir John Perceval considered Bishop Crowe of Cloyne to be 'no violent churchman or party man', while Milles of Waterford was another whom observers thought had 'turned' in his politics. In neither case would this assessment be borne out by events.[61]

Unlike the creation of new peers, or the filling of vacant bishoprics, the attention paid by government to the 'poor lords' does not appear to have been strategic, but, instead, was a series of responses to recommendations from Ireland relating to individual cases. It is possible that a request made by Sunderland in December 1714 for a copy of the Irish pension list was stimulated, at least in part, by thinking about parliamentary management, but no evidence survives of a systematic examination of the extent to which Irish peers could be pressurised by the withdrawal of funds.[62] However, the Irish politicians and officials who interceded on behalf of indigent peers were well aware of the probable dividend for the court party in the house of lords, and often couched their promptings in these terms. When Archbishop King forwarded to Chief Secretary Addison a request from the earl of Cavan for the colonelcy of a regiment, he drew attention to the fact that Cavan could be as useful to Sunderland in parliament as he had once been to Wharton.[63] Lord Blayney was a rather more problematic case. He had been considered a loyal supporter of the tory ministry, but his only income was an annual pension of £182 10s. on the Irish military list, which had originally been granted to his father.[64] Both King and Lord Chancellor Brodrick considered him a likely catch.[65] Brodrick wrote that:

> He is no friend of mine, so that I do not interpose for him as such, but his condition is low, which forced him to go into measures with the late government here; but I am

---

[58] TCD, MS 2536, pp. 82–5: King to Tenison, 30 Sept. 1714; pp. 109–10: King to Tenison, 12 Nov. 1714.

[59] There are entries on Synge and Godwin in *ODNB*.

[60] Christ Church, Oxford, Wake MSS, Arch. Epist. Wake xii: Bishop Godwin to Archbishop Wake, 20 Dec. [1715].

[61] TNA, SP 63/373/209–10: King to James Stanhope, 5 Nov. 1715; BL, Add. MS 47087, f. 19: 'Bishop of Cloyn's character'; Christ Church, Oxford, Arch. Epist. Wake xii: Godwin to Wake, 22 Oct. 1715.

[62] BL, Add. MS 61652, ff. 238–40: Sunderland to Whitshed, 28 Dec. 1714.

[63] TCD, MS 750/13, p. 63: King to Addison, 4 Aug. 1715. Cavan's previous connection with Lord Galway, one of the lords justices who succeeded Sunderland in Sept. 1715, probably served him well. He was eventually given a lieutenant-colonelcy in Vesey's foot, a regiment raised in Feb. 1716: NLI, MS 2482, pp. 269–70: Galway to [Ormond], nd; Charles Dalton, *George the First's Army 1714–1727* (2 vols, 1910–12), ii, 142; *LJI*, ii, 505.

[64] *Bolingbroke Correspondence*, ed. Parke, iv, 65; TNA, T 48/91, p. 105; *Calendar of Treasury Books*, xvi, 274, 396; xx, 81; xxi, 489–90; xxvi, 256; *Calendar of Treasury Papers, 1708–14*, pp. 133, 379, 429.

[65] TCD, MS 2536, p. 201: King to Shrewsbury, 1 Mar. 1714[/15]; SHC, 1248/3/205–6: [Alan Brodrick] to [Thomas Brodrick], 14 Dec. 1714.

convinced he will act with the greatest duty to the crown and deference to my lord lieutenant: and if his pension be increased he will entirely owe it to my lord, and know he lies under the strictest obligations to do the crown and his excellency all service in his power.

The earl of Granard was similarly problematical. Archbishop King tried several times to get Sunderland to renew Granard's pension or grant him some remunerative office, arguing that despite innate tory sympathies, Granard had always supported what he thought was the interest of the crown and kingdom, and that in the 1713 parliament, not liking 'the then measures … absented himself, which was all that was expected of him'.[66]

Two cases in particular highlight the complex interactions which determined the outcome of solicitations of this kind. During 1714 and 1715, Brodrick spent a great deal of energy and ink in supporting the petitions of Lord Charlemont to retain his place as county governor of Armagh, which was crucial to his standing locally, and of Lord Inchiquin to remain as governor of the fort of Kinsale, which was crucial to his income. Both men were valuable to the ministry not just for their votes in the Lords, but for the electoral interest at their disposal.[67] Brodrick assured Sunderland that, although a tory, Charlemont was not one of the hotter sort, and might be kept in line by retention in his post.[68] Inchiquin, on the other hand, was a natural adherent of any and every government. He had stayed away from parliament in 1713 and therefore had not the same political sins to purge. None the less, his position was under threat from a rival with better whig credentials. Brodrick inquired about both men in a letter to Addison, stating that he was not personally obliged to either but feared the consequences of certain persons persuading the viceroy into making unnecessary dismissals which would imperil the government's position in the Irish house of lords.[69] At the same time Brodrick wrote privately to his brother in London:[70]

By my receiving no letter … in reference to Lord Inchiquin's government of Kinsale and that of Charlemont I give up them also as condemned: I wish those who push and advise things to be carried so far (particularly in the house of peers) may be able to answer for the consequences there. When you have given this hint leave it to their conduct who give such warm advice; one of the lords is in great want, the other really hath that which seems to me to create a very good pretension to his government, unless he hath been greatly faulty.

In the event, both lost their places, Charlemont to the staunch whig, Lord Mountjoy, who would be a stalwart of the court party in the 1715 parliament. However, Inchiquin, thanks to his connection with the earl of Kildare, a colleague of Archbishop King on the commission of lords justices, received another crumb of patronage which kept him loyal to the ministry.[71]

---

[66] TCD, MS 750/13, pp. 54, 58, 67: King to Addison, 7, 25 July, 26 Aug. 1715.

[67] BL, Add. MS 61636, f. 141: Alan Brodrick to Addison, 18 Mar. 1714[/15].

[68] BL, Add. MS 61636, ff. 113–14: Alan Brodrick to [Sunderland], Oct. 1714.

[69] BL, Add. MS 61636, ff. 119–20: Brodrick to Addison, 16 Nov. 1714.

[70] SHC, 1248/3/201–2: [Alan Brodrick] to [Thomas Brodrick], 16 Nov. 1714.

[71] TCD, MS 2536, pp. 121–2: King to Lord Mountjoy, 24 Nov. 1714; BL, Add. MS 61635, f. 207: Lord Kildare to [Sunderland], 24 Nov. 1714.

4

Before the general election of 1715 and the opening of parliament in November, Sunderland had relinquished the lord lieutenancy and been replaced by a pair of lords justices from England, Lord Galway and the duke of Grafton. The preparations that Sunderland had made should have been enough to secure a court majority in the upper House, whether or not these had been devised by the viceroy personally or had emerged from a process of discussion between Sunderland and his Irish advisors. Moreover, unlike the Irish house of commons, where the whig majority was substantial enough to permit factional divisions and the emergence of a body of dissident whigs prepared to ally with the tories in opposition, there was no whig schism in the upper House, and the arrival of the new peers provided a welcome injection of debating talent. This did not mean that the court party would have an easy ride. The tories in the Lords were still formidable in numbers, and had the benefit of experienced and dynamic leadership, especially from Anglesey and Abercorn among the temporal lords, and Lindsay and Bishop Thomas Smyth of Limerick among the bishops. The absence of Archbishop King at the beginning of the session, crippled by gout and confined to his palace, was a serious blow to government.[72] Without guidance, it seems to have taken some time for whig recruits from the Commons to accustom themselves to the different political atmosphere of the upper House. Early on in the session, Lord Moore, supported by Lord Tyrawley, moved for an address denouncing the old ministry, but in terms so intemperate, referring to an 'abandon'd, perjur'd, traitorous set of ministers', that he forfeited the support of several low church bishops, including King's friend, Ashe of Clogher, and lost his motion.[73]

After a slow start to proceedings,[74] the first major clash between the parties occurred on 16 December 1715 over an attempt by the tories, led by Anglesey, to secure the recognition by the House of the validity of the peerage title claimed by Edmund Butler as 6th earl of Mountgarrett. Butler's great-grandfather, the 3rd earl, had been outlawed in 1641 for involvement in the Catholic Confederacy, and although the family considered that the outlawry had since been reversed according to the terms of the Articles of Limerick in 1691, a position upheld by a vote in the Irish house of lords in 1697, there was still an element of uncertainty.[75] Anglesey brought the matter to the notice of the House at the very beginning of the session, raising the issue of a possible breach of privilege against Mountgarrett by JPs in Queen's County who had issued a writ committing him to gaol for failure to take the oath of abjuration. A committee was appointed to inquire into his qualification, with Abercorn in the chair.[76] The whole point of the exercise was probably to enable Anglesey and his friends to test the strength of their party. The loyal addresses prepared by the Lords at the outset of the session had not contained any sentiments to which tories could reasonably object, apart perhaps from a teasing reference in the address to the king to the 'open and secret abettors' of the jacobite pretender, and they could

---

[72] O'Regan, *King*, 223–32.

[73] BL, Add. MS 47028, ff. 100–1: memorandum of debates in Lords, 3 Nov. 1715; f. 129: Charles Dering to Lord Perceval, 9 Feb. 1715/16; Add. MS 61640, ff. 36–8: Moore to [——?], 16 Nov. 1715.

[74] SHC, 1248/3/280–5: [Lord Brodrick] to Thomas Brodrick, 18 Dec. 1715.

[75] *LJI*, i, 675.

[76] *LJI*, ii, 461–3.

scarcely have opposed the bill to recognize George I's title.[77] So they had been reduced to provoking divisions on technical issues, and the results were not encouraging: only four tories entered their dissent on 5 December over a procedural matter, and 11 on another vote two days later, over an otherwise non-partisan privilege complaint.[78] On 16 December, when the committee of inquiry into Mountgarrett's case reported, the tory leaders girded themselves up for a big push. After a long and vigorous debate the question was carried against them by 26 votes to 21.[79] Abercorn and 17 other lords entered protests. Brodrick gleefully reported that 'the mortification which some people showed on this occasion is inexpressible'. Anglesey, in particular, 'was in the utmost confusion, in which rage had a great share'. [80]

The decision over Mountgarrett's right to claim privilege was rightly regarded by supporters of the ministry as 'the major work of that first part of the session'.[81] The tories had suffered a decisive defeat: an attempt to raise morale the following day with a resolution condemning as a breach of privilege any attempt to summon a peer to take to the abjuration was defeated by an even greater margin, 26 to 15.[82] When the House resumed in January, on the news of the rebellion in Scotland, the whigs were able to carry without serious opposition a motion 'to enter into an association, to defend and assist His Most Sacred Majesty King George and the Protestant Succession, in his royal house', which every member signed, as well as preparing an address calling on the lords justices to put the laws into execution against 'papists and other disaffected persons'. Both were framed in the most forthright terms.[83] The Commons' bill to attaint the pretender was then passed without fuss.[84] The upper House seemed to have been brought firmly to heel.[85]

5

How had this transformation occurred? The first thing to be noted about proceedings in the Lords in 1715–16 is that attendances were higher than they had been in 1713, even allowing for the fact that the 1715–16 session lasted much longer. In 1713, 46 lords attended (28 temporal and 18 spiritual); in 1715–16 the figure rose to 61 (40 temporal and 21 spiritual, calculating the latter in terms of episcopal seats held rather than the individuals occupying them). Of the temporal lords attending in 1713, seven were not present in 1715. Three

---

[77] *LJI*, ii, 463–4. A reference in a letter from Lord Chancellor Brodrick suggests, however, that there may have been a contretemps of sorts at the committal of the recognition bill: SHC, 1248/3/280–5: to [Thomas Brodrick], 18 Dec. 1715.

[78] *LJI*, ii, 474 (Abercorn, Altham, Charlemont, and Doneraile), 476 (Altham, Anglesey, Athenry, Bellomont, Charlemont, Kerry, Mayo, Archbishop Lindsay, and Bishops Edward Smyth, Thomas Smyth, and Sir Thomas Vesey).

[79] The division list is tabulated in appendix 2.

[80] *LJI*, ii, 481–7; SHC, 1248/3/280–5: [Lord Brodrick] to [Thomas Brodrick], 18 Dec. 1715.

[81] Christ Church, Oxford, Arch. Epist. Wake xii: Bishop Godwin to Archbishop Wake, 12 Jan. 1715[/16].

[82] *LJI*, ii, 488; SHC, 1248/3/291–3: [Lord Brodrick] to [Thomas Brodrick], 30 Dec. 1715.

[83] *LJI*, ii, 491, 492–4; SHC, 1248/3/300–1: [Lord Brodrick] to [Thomas Brodrick], 20 Jan. 1715[/16].

[84] *LJI*, ii, 498.

[85] Lord Chancellor Brodrick informed his brother that 'our tories in a certain House are so humbled, that as I told you formerly no danger need be apprehended from that quarter' (SHC, 1248/3/300–1: [Lord Brodrick] to [Thomas Brodrick], 20 Jan. 1715[/16]).

of these were whigs: Drogheda, Mountrath, and Bellew. They had all died in the interim. The other four had all voted with the tory ministry in 1713. Of these, Roscommon was dead; Mountcashell was in ill health; and Dunkellin and Lanesborough simply kept away. Of the bishops, only William Moreton of Meath failed to appear in the 1715–16 session: he died a fortnight after the parliament was opened. Moreton had voted with the tories in 1713 and his eventual replacement (in May 1716) was a Welsh whig, John Evans.

As many as 20 of the temporal lords sitting in 1715–16 had not been present in the previous session. Ten of these were newly-created peers, and as was to be expected all sided with the ministry, so far as we can tell from surviving parliamentary lists (tabulated in Appendix 2). Of the other ten, Lord Meath had only recently succeeded his father. The remainder had been absent in 1713 for a variety of personal reasons, but it is worth noting that Lords Shannon and Tyrawley were military men who were now available to take their seats and may have been pressed to do so (indeed Tyrawley had recently been appointed commander-in-chief of the forces on the Irish establishment). Only one newcomer aligned himself against the ministry: Lord Massereene, whom some considered sufficiently extreme in his toryism to label him a jacobite.[86]

Among the spiritual peers there were just three new faces when the session opened, Edward Synge, Timothy Godwin, and Nicholas Forster. The primatial see of Armagh had been vacant in 1713 but Thomas Lindsay had been translated from Raphoe to Armagh in January 1714. In the spring of 1715, Synge was promoted to the archbishopric of Tuam to succeed John Vesey, Forster took his place in Raphoe, and another Irish low churchman, Charles Carr, came in at Killaloe. Then towards the end of the session Evans was nominated to Meath. The cumulative result was a gain of five votes for the whigs.

The government managers thus appeared to be in such a strong position mainly because of the turnover in personnel: newly-created peers and newly-appointed bishops, together with a small phalanx of whig lords in attendance who had not been present two years earlier, and who may have been the subject of some official whipping. However, not all the newcomers were regular attenders. Four barely impinged on proceedings: Perceval, who left for London after a few days, but gave his proxy to the reliably whig Lord Moore;[87] the somewhat doubtful earl of Inchiquin, who only turned up once;[88] Castlecomer, who was needed back at Westminster, where he sat on the whig interest for Ripon; and the earl of Meath. Against these absentees we should set Lords Granard and Howth, both of whom were forecast as likely to oppose the ministry, but did not attend sufficiently to make their votes count, and two members of the bishops' bench, John Vesey, who was in a long-term physical decline,[89] and Simon Digby of Elphin, who may have chosen the path of discretion in staying at home.

The newly-created peers were presumably expected to constitute a powerful cohort of committed whigs, and on the whole they fulfilled expectations. Brodrick did not miss a day; Ferrard (Sir Henry Tichborne), Moore, and Newtownbutler (Theophilus Butler) were almost as regular; while Carbery (George Evans), Ranelagh (Sir Arthur Cole), and Hamilton

[86]BL, Add. MS 61640, ff. 67–8.
[87]*LJI*, ii, 465; BL, Add. MS 47028, f. 115: Perceval to Moore, 3 Jan. [*recte* Feb.] 1715/16.
[88]TCD, MS 2533, pp. 210–1: Archbishop King to Sunderland, 19 Apr. 1716.
[89]Bodl., MS Ballard 36, f. 84: William Perceval to Arthur Charlett, 10 Aug. 1714; Christ Church, Oxford, Arch. Epist. Wake xii: Bishop Godwin to Archbishop Wake, 12 Jan. [1715].

mustered attendance figures that were perfectly respectable. Besides the absentee, Perceval, Lord St George, the former Sir George St George, failed to live up to expectations, arriving to take his seat after the crucial vote on Mountgarrett, and appearing only sporadically thereafter. The most disappointing of the new peers was Richard Fitzpatrick, Lord Gowran, not for his failure to attend, but for his unreliability in divisions. Although he sided with the whigs in one of the procedural divisions that prefigured the final vote on Mountgarrett, he deserted to the tories when it came to the crunch.[90]

In addition, the ministry had been able to win over a few lords who had supported the court in 1713 and who now changed sides, or at least kept away from the House for crucial votes. Two of the 'poor lords' who had voted with the tories in 1713, Cavan and Blayney, came over to the whig government, Cavan now taking a prominent role as a court manager;[91] a third, Granard, while not recorded as voting on the government side, at least did no harm, taking his seat only on 18 November and attending on only ten days thereafter. A whiggishly-inclined pensioner, Lord Mountalexander, who had barely attended in 1713, presumably to save himself embarrassment, now also appeared regularly in the court interest.[92] The bishops' bench also appeared less solidly tory: William Palliser of Cashel, Bartholomew Vigors of Ferns, and William Lloyd of Killala, all of whom had supported Lord Chancellor Phipps in 1713, were absent from the vote on Lord Mountgarrett, while William Fitzgerald of Clonfert sided with the whigs, and Welbore Ellis of Kildare, though voting for Mountgarrett, did not join his episcopal colleagues in protesting, and later in the session divided from tory churchmen.[93]

6

The ministry had secured its position in the Lords by February 1716, primarily through a combination of politically motivated peerage creations, the judicious disposition of ecclesiastical preferments, and changing patterns of attendance, with a handful of tory lords staying away from parliament and whigs being encouraged to take their seats. The part played in ministerial strategy by the continuation of pensions and places to the needy was complicated by the fact that in some cases the lord lieutenant was receiving contradictory advice, especially in the matter of appointments, where some of his advisors might be advocating the retention of potential tory converts, while others urged the claims of aspirant whigs. So although the 'poor lords' were a significant element in the court party in 1713, they provided only a minor addition of strength in 1715.

Patterns of attendance meant that the bishops' remained a significant presence, even though more temporal lords attended in 1715. And here it was not just the advancement of low church clergy recommended by Archbishop King that worked to the advantage of the court, but the waning of high church fervour among bishops who had voted with the tory ministry in 1713. Episcopal votes were much more evenly divided on the Mountgarrett case

---

[90]SHC, 1248/3/291–3: [Lord Brodrick] to [Thomas Brodrick], 30 Dec. 1715.

[91]*LJI*, ii, 468; SHC, 1248/3/280–5: [Lord Brodrick] to [Thomas Brodrick], 18 Dec. 1715.

[92]TNA, T 48/91, p. 105; *Addison Letters*, ed. Graham, 212; BL, Add. MS 38157, f. 133: Sir Richard Cox to Edward Southwell, 9 Oct. 1714; Add. MS 61640, f. 10: Mountalexander to Joseph Addison, 8 Aug. 1715.

[93]Christ Church, Oxford, Arch. Epist. Wake xii: Bishop Godwin to [Archbishop Wake], 9, 19 June 1716.

than they had been two years earlier over tory efforts to vindicate Lord Chancellor Phipps and the tory administration. More bishops voted for Mountgarrett than against, but the margin was only eight to six, and this after Archbishop Lindsay and his friends had strained every sinew to maximise their vote, including, according to Charles Delafaye, dragging into a division a bishop 'who is in a manner bedridden'.[94]

Had the session ended in February the lords justices could have assumed that the problem of managing the upper House had been solved. But the very means by which a majority had been achieved sowed the seeds of future difficulties. The fact that the ministry now relied upon a combination of native-born Irish politicians, with a well-developed sense of their own dignity and importance, and Irish-born or at least Irish-educated prelates, made it likely that, when issues arose which could be presented as outraging 'patriotic' sensibilities, such as a clash between the Irish house of lords and its British counterpart over appellate jurisdiction, the members of the court party might prove difficult to control. Moreover, in the case of the temporal peers, it was harder to find appropriate forms of patronage to satisfy peers who until recently had been among the front rank of their party in the Commons, and enjoyed relatively comfortable incomes, than it had been to manage a crowd of parliamentary beggars whose loyalty could be bought for a pension.

During the second half of the session an issue arose which demonstrated the limitations of the scheme of management which Sunderland had prepared and Galway and Grafton had put into practice, with the aid of the lord chancellor and other principal servants of the crown. It was not a matter of 'patriotic' concern, not a conflict between Irish and British interests, but an issue which touched the sensitivities of bishops, and of staunch churchmen among the laity: the maintenance of the sacramental test. In 1704, when the test had originally been imposed, and again in 1707 and 1709, when viceroys had sought repeal, an overwhelming majority in the Irish house of commons had resisted.[95] It went without saying that the bishops, to a man, were opposed. In 1714, the presbyterian General Synod of Ulster had petitioned Sunderland for relief, and had been fobbed off.[96] Galway and Grafton did not intend to take the initiative, but found themselves bounced into a situation in which the issue was raised again.

The trigger was the jacobite rebellion, which gave the pro-dissenter lobby the opportunity to push for a relaxation of the operation of the test in so far as it related to the armed forces. They managed to get through the lower House 'heads' of a bill for 'the further securing His Majesty's person and government', which indemnified dissenters from having served in the militia in defiance of the test, and to enable them for the future to hold commissions both in the militia and (for a limited period) in the regular army. The Lords responded with a bill of its own, presented by Abercorn, which was identical except that it omitted the clauses relating to the test, thus setting the stage for a confrontation between the two Houses and placing the lords justices in a delicate position.[97]

---

[94] TNA, SP 63/373/336–7: Delafaye to [James Stanhope], 17 Dec. 1715.

[95] Hayton, *Ruling Ireland*, 189.

[96] D.W. Hayton, 'Presbyterians and the Confessional State: The Sacramental Test as an Issue in Irish Politics, 1704–80', *Bulletin of the Presbyterian Historical Society of Ireland*, xxvi (1997), 25–6.

[97] TNA, SP 63/374/99: Grafton to Stanhope, 15 Feb. 1715/16. On this episode, see Neal Garnham, *The Militia in Eighteenth-Century Ireland: In Defence of the Protestant Interest* (Woodbridge, 2012), 26–30.

Tories may have taken the lead in responding to the Commons, but they were receiving strong backing from the low church bishops. King was adamant that there should be no amendment to the test. Racked by gout, he was carried to the chamber to vote. No bishop, he declared, could hope to keep the respect of his flock were he to consent to the Commons' bill.[98] King's friends, Ashe, Stearne, and Synge, were of the same mind, and Bishop Godwin was convinced that there were 'so many Whig lords' determined to oppose the Commons' bill that it had no chance of success.[99] The privy council, which was presented with both sets of heads, did its best to achieve a compromise, merging the two bills into one. The debate there underlined the difficulties the lords justices would face in the upper House. Although the council eventually decided to accept provisions indemnifying dissenters in respect of militia service during the rebellion, and permitting them to serve in the militia in the future, they restricted the relaxation on service in the regular army to the duration of the rebellion. But even this compromise was carried by only one vote, with King, Ashe, and Stearne speaking against, and whigs like Lord Castlecomer joining forces with Abercorn and the few surviving tories on the council.[100]

It was now clear to Galway and Grafton that even the amended bill would not pass on its return to the Lords. It was up to the British privy council to amend the offending clauses, in order to avoid 'breaking the king's friends' in Ireland.[101] To guide ministerial decisions, Charles Delafaye prepared a forecast of how the upper House would divide over the bill if it was returned without amendment. He listed 22 temporal lords for and 12 against, but as he included Castlecomer among those in favour, his calculation must be regarded as optimistic. In any case he was sure that all four archbishops and 17 bishops (the new bishop of Meath, John Evans, had not yet arrived) would vote against, so the likely result was clear: a majority of 33 to 22 against the bill. Even winning over three lords he classed as 'doubtful' (Howth, Inchiquin, and Powerscourt) would make no difference.[102] The British privy council took the only sensible course in these circumstances, and drastically amended the bill. Thus emasculated, it dropped in the house of commons.

Not only did this episode demonstrate that the new court majority in the Lords was vulnerable on particular issues, it also prefigured what would become a long-term problem for government in Ireland, how to restrain the 'patriot' sensibilities of members of the upper House. The issue of the test clause was only a grievance to 'patriot' lords in so far as it represented an attempt by English ministers to impose their will on Ireland regardless of Irish sensibilities. But the leading figures in the Lords' opposition to any attempt to water down the sacramental test, Archbishop King and his fellow low churchmen, would also, in due course, be in the forefront of resistance to claims by the house of lords at Westminster to an appellate jurisdiction over Ireland.

[98] Bodl., MS Ballard 8, f. 43: King to Arthur Charlett, 26 June 1716; Christ Church, Oxford, Arch. Epist. Wake xii: Bishop Godwin to Archbishop Wake, 19 Feb. 1715[/16]; TCD, MS 2533, pp. 133–6: King to Ashe, 8 Feb. 1715[/16]; p. 162: King to Wake, 24 Mar. 1715[/16].

[99] Christ Church, Oxford, Arch. Epist. Wake xii: Synge to [Wake], 2, 14 Feb., 4 Mar. 1715[/16]; Godwin to Wake, 11 Feb. 1715[/16].

[100] TNA, SP 63/374/105–6: Grafton and Galway to Stanhope, 24 Feb. 1715/16; SP 63/374/147: Galway to Stanhope, 16 Mar. 1715/16.

[101] TNA, SP 63/374/147: Galway to Stanhope, 16 Mar. 1715/16; SP 63/374/89: Henry Maxwell to [Stanhope], 16 Mar. 1715/16.

[102] TNA, SP 63/374/94, tabulated in appendix 2, below.

When that issue reached boiling point, in 1719, the Irish-born bishops had a further grievance: the appointment of Englishmen to lucrative Irish dioceses. To some extent this was a product of the imbroglio over the security bills, which prompted some in Ireland to demand the appointment of staunch whigs from England as a means of disciplining the bishops' bench. Evans was the first of these (and would always be the most unpopular).[103] While superficially attractive to ministers as a key element of the management of the Lords, this strategy was counter-productive in the short term, unnecessarily antagonising the 'Irish interest' among the existing bishops. It was also of doubtful value in the long term, since it did not take much time for English bishops transplanted to Ireland to become 'more Irish than the Irish', and like Archbishop Lindsay (who had originally come over from Oxford as chaplain to Lord Deputy Capel in 1695) develop strong attachments to the country in which they resided. It was no wonder that before the Irish parliament met again, under the duke of Bolton in 1717, government had returned to the idea of peerage creations, as a safer, though equally short-term, expedient.

APPENDIX 1: *The House of Lords in the 1713 Parliament 25 Nov.–24 Dec. 1713*

A = Date first attended.
B = Days attended.
C = Marked as a Tory (T) on a printed list of the 1713 Parliament (BL, Add. MS 61637A).
D = Protested (W) against the orders made on 17 December relating to the enquiry into the privy council's involvement in the Dublin mayoral election, and the several resolutions on 18 Dec. 1713 in defence of Sir Constantine Phipps:[104] the number indicates how many of the five protests were signed.
E = List of lords, prepared for Lord Sunderland 1714, divided into Tories (T) and Whigs (W) (BL, Add. MS 61640, ff. 27–8).
F = List of lords present in 1713, prepared for Lord Sunderland 1714/15, divided into those 'for court' (C) and those 'against court' (O) (BL, Add. MS 61640, f. 30).

The names of lords who did not sit in the 1715–16 session are given in italics; indications of whig allegiance in red.

TEMPORAL LORDS

	A	B	C	D	E	F
BARRYMORE	25 Nov.	18	T		T	C
James Barry, 4th earl						
BELLOMONT	25 Nov.	20			T	C
Richard Coote, 3rd earl						
CAVAN	25 Nov.	18			T	C
Richard Lambart, 4th earl						

[103] On this point, see Patrick McNally, ' "Irish and English Interests": National Conflict within the Church of Ireland Episcopate in the Reign of George I', *Irish Historical Studies*, xxix (1994–5), 295–314.
[104] *LJI*, ii, 435, 438.

	Date					
DROGHEDA Charles Moore, 2nd earl (d. 1714)	3 Dec.	5			W	O
GRANARD George Forbes, 4th earl	5 Dec.	11			T	C
KILDARE Robert Fitzgerald, 19th earl	25 Nov.	20		2W	W	O
MOUNTALEXANDER Hugh Montgomery, 2nd earl	8 Dec.	3				
MOUNTRATH Charles Coote, 4th earl (d. Sept. 1715)	25 Nov.	18		5W	W	O
ROSCOMMON Robert Dillon, 6th earl (d. May 1715)	25 Nov.	13			T	C
CHARLEMONT William Caulfeild, 2nd viscount	25 Nov.	16	T		T	C
FITZWILLIAM Richard Fitzwilliam, 5th viscount	25 Nov.	16		5W	W	O
LANESBOROUGH James Lane, 2nd viscount	25 Nov.	16	T		T	C
LOFTUS Arthur Loftus, 3rd viscount	25 Nov.	11			W	O
MAYO Theobald Bourke, 6th viscount	25 Nov.	19			T	C
MOUNTCASHELL Paul Davys, 1st viscount	25 Nov.	17			T	C
MOUNTJOY William Stewart, 2nd viscount	25 Nov.	21		5W	W	O
POWERSCOURT Folliott Wingfield, 1st viscount	25 Nov.	11			T	C
STRABANE James Hamilton, 1st viscount (6th earl of Abercorn [S])	25 Nov.	22			T	C
VALENTIA Arthur Annesley, 6th viscount (5th earl of Anglesey [E])	25 Nov.	19		T	T	C
ALTHAM Arthur Annesley, 4th baron	25 Nov.	19			T	C
ATHENRY Francis Bermingham, 14th baron	25 Nov.	20			T	C
BELLEW Richard, 3rd baron (d. Mar. 1715)	18 Dec.	5		2W	W	O
BLAYNEY Cadwallader Blayney, 7th baron	25 Nov.	16	T		T	C
DUNKELLIN Michael Bourke, 10th baron	25 Nov.	20	T		T	C
HOWTH Thomas St Lawrence, 13th baron	25 Nov.	1			T	C

	A	B	C	D	E	F
KERRY Thomas Fitzmaurice, 21st baron	26 Nov.	16	T		T	C
SANTRY Henry Barry, 3rd baron	25 Nov.	10		3W	W	O
SHELBURNE Henry Petty, 2nd baron	25 Nov.	21			W	O

SPIRITUAL LORDS

	A	B	C	D	E	F
ARCHBISHOPS:						
CASHEL William Palliser	19 Dec.	5	T		T	C
DUBLIN William King	25 Nov.	20		5W	W	O
TUAM John Vesey	25 Nov.	23	T		T	C
BISHOPS:						
CLOGHER St George Ashe	25 Nov.	22		3W	W	O
CLONFERT William Fitzgerald	25 Nov.	22	T		T	C
CLOYNE Charles Crow(e)	25 Nov.	21	T		T	C
CORK Peter Browne	25 Nov.	16	T		T	C
DOWN Edward Smyth	25 Nov.	23	T		T	C
DROMORE John Stearne	25 Nov.	21		1W	W	O
ELPHIN Simon Digby	25 Nov.	16	T		T	C
FERNS Bartholomew Vigors	25 Nov.	16	T		T	C
KILDARE Welbore Ellis	25 Nov.	22	T		T	C
KILLALA William Lloyd	14 Dec.	6			T	C
KILLALOE Sir Thomas Vesey, 1st Bt	25 Nov.	19	T		T	C
LIMERICK Thomas Smyth	25 Nov.	21	T		T	C
MEATH *William Moreton*	*25 Nov.*	*9*	*T*		*T*	*C*
RAPHOE Thomas Lindsay	25 Nov.	22	T		T	C
WATERFORD Thomas Milles	25 Nov.	22	T		T	C

APPENDIX 2: *The House of Lords in the 1715–16 Session 12 Nov. 1715–20 June 1716*

A = Date first attended.

B = Days attended.

C = Government forecast, c. Oct. 1714–Apr. 1715, of whigs (W) and tories (T), distinguishing those 'certain' and those 'doubtful' (?) (BL, Add. MS 61640, ff. 24–5).

D = Government forecast, c. Oct. 1714–Apr. 1715, of those for court (C), for opposition (O), divided in each case into 'certain' (C,O) or 'doubtful'/'uncertain' (C?, O?) (BL, Add. MS 61640, f. 30).

E = Government forecast, c. May 1715, of lords divided into 'good' (C), 'bad' (O) and 'uncertain' (?) (BL, Add. MS 61640, ff. 31–2).

F = Division list on the vote, 16 Dec. 1715, for (pro) and against (con) admitting Lord Mountgarret as a peer (Surrey History Centre, Brodrick MSS, 1248/3/283). The bishops' votes are confirmed in Christ Church, Oxford, Wake MSS, Arch. Epist. Wake xii: Bishop Synge to Bishop Wake, 17 Dec. 1715. Those protesting against the vote (*LJI*, ii, 487) are, in addition, marked with an asterisk.[105]

G = Division list of the minority (pro) in the division of 17 Dec. 1715 on a motion to declare it a breach of privilege for any peer to be summoned to take the oath of abjuration (Surrey History Centre, Brodrick MSS, 1248/3/291–3).

H = Government forecast, c. Mar. 1716, of those who would vote for (pro) and against (con) the bill 'for the security of the king's person and government' with the clauses exempting dissenters in military service from the penalties of the 'test' (TNA, SP 63/374/94). Three lords listed as 'doubtful' (?).

The names of lords who had not sat in 1713 are given in italics and in bold type; indications of support for the Court in red.

TEMPORAL LORDS

	A	B	C	D	E	F	G	H
BARRYMORE	12 Nov.	25	W	C	C	pro★	pro	con
James Barry, 4th earl								
BELLOMONT	12 Nov.	54	T	O	O	pro★	pro	con
Richard Coote, 3rd earl								
CAVAN	12 Nov.	41	W	C	C	con		pro
Richard Lambart, 4th earl								
GRANARD	18 Nov.	10	T?	O?	O			
George Forbes, 4th earl								
INCHIQUIN	*12 Nov.*	*1*	**W**	**C**	**C**			?
William O'Brien, 3rd earl								
KILDARE	12 Nov.	40	W	C	C	con		pro
Robert Fitzgerald, 19th earl								

[105] Lord Massereeene entered a protest but was not recorded on the list as having voted. However, the names of the minority given by Alan Brodrick total only 20, and the accompanying letter gives the figure on the division as 21, so we may safely assume that Massereene's name was omitted in error.

MEATH *Chaworth Brabazon, 6th earl*	**17 Dec.**	**4**		C	W	C	*pro*	
MOUNTALEXANDER Hugh Montgomery, 2nd earl	15 Nov.	55	W	C	C	con		pro
CASTLECOMER *Christopher Wandesford, 2nd viscount*	**22 Nov.**	**5**	W	C	C	*con*		*pro*
CHARLEMONT William Caulfeild, 2nd viscount	14 Nov.	60	T?	O?	C	pro★	pro	con
DONERAILE *Arthur St Leger, 2nd viscount*	**12 Nov.**	**55**	W		C	*con*		*pro*
FITZWILLIAM Richard Fitzwilliam, 5th viscount	12 Nov.	29	W	C	C	pro		pro
LOFTUS Arthur Loftus, 3rd viscount	12 Nov.	54	W	C	C	con		pro
MASSEREENE *Clotworthy Skeffington, 4th viscount*	**2 Dec.**	**28**	**T**	**O**	**O**	**[pro]** ★	**pro**	**con**
MAYO Theobald Bourke, 6th viscount	23 Nov.	9	W?	C?	C	pro★		con
MOUNTJOY William Stewart, 2nd viscount	12 Dec.	32	W	C	C			pro
POWERSCOURT Folliott Wingfield, 1st viscount	12 Nov.	16	W?	C?	C			?
SHANNON *Richard Boyle, 2nd viscount*	**18 Nov.**	**24**	*W*	C	C	*con*		*pro*
STRABANE James Hamilton,1st viscount (6th earl of Abercorn [S])	12 Nov.	64	T	O	O	pro★	pro	con
STRANGFORD *Endymion Smythe, 3rd viscount*	**12 Nov.**	**46**				*con*		*pro*
VALENTIA Arthur Annesley, 6th viscount (5th earl of Anglesey [E])	12 Nov.	21	T	O	O	pro★	pro	con
ALTHAM Arthur Annesley, 4th baron	12 Nov.	36	T	O	O	pro★	pro	con
ATHENRY Francis Bermingham, 14th baron	14 Nov.	28	W	C	C	pro★	pro	
BLAYNEY Cadwallader Blayney, 7th baron	12 Nov.	37	W	C	C	con		pro
BRODRICK *Alan Brodrick, 1st baron* *(Speaker)*	**12 Nov.**	**67**			C	*con*		
CARBERY *George Evans, 1st baron*	14 Nov.	21		C	con			con
FERRARD *Henry Tichborne, 1st baron*	**12 Nov.**	**62**			con			*pro*
GOWRAN	**12 Nov.**	**35**		C	pro			con

	A	B	C	D	E	F	G	H
Richard Fitzpatrick, 1st baron HAMILTON	*12 Nov.*	*41*				*con*		*pro*
Gustavus Hamilton, 1st baron HOWTH	6 Dec.	1	T	O	O			?
Thomas St Lawrence, 13th baron KERRY	12 Nov.	34	T	O	?	pro★	pro	con
Thomas Fitzmaurice, 21st baron KINGSTON	*12 Dec.*	*12*	*T?*	*O?*	*O*	*pro★*	*pro*	*con*
John King, 3rd baron MOORE	*12 Nov.*	*52*				*con*		*pro*
John Moore, 1st baron NEWTOWNBUTLER	*12 Nov.*	*63*				*con*		*pro*
Theophilus Butler, 1st baron PERCEVAL	*12 Nov.*	*7*			C			*pro*
John Perceval, 1st baron RANELAGH	*12 Nov.*	*46*			C	*con*		*pro*
Arthur Cole, 1st baron ST GEORGE	*23 Nov.*	*14*			C	*con*		*pro*
George St George, 1st baron SANTRY	12 Nov.	35	W	C	C	con		pro
Henry Barry, 3rd baron SHELBURNE	12 Nov.	39	W	C	C	con		pro
Henry Petty, 2nd baron *TYRAWLEY*	*12 Nov.*	*38*	*W*	*C*	*C*	*con*		*pro*
Charles O'Hara, 1st baron SPIRITUAL LORDS								
ARCHBISHOPS:	A	B	C	D	E	F	G	H
ARMAGH Thomas Lindsay	12 Nov.	48	T	O	O	pro★	pro	con
CASHEL William Palliser	3 May	10	T?	O?	C?			con
DUBLIN William King	14 Dec.	24	W	C	C			con
TUAM John Vesey (d. 28 Mar. 1716)	12 Nov.	2	T	O	O			con
Edward Synge	*12 June*	*5*						
BISHOPS: CLOGHER St George Ashe	12 Nov.	61	W	C	C	con		con
CLONFERT William Fitzgerald	12 Nov.	39	T?	O?	C?	con		con
CLOYNE Charles Crow(e)	29 Nov.	40	T?	O?	C?	pro★	pro	con
CORK Peter Browne	23 Nov.	33	T?	O?	O	pro★		con
DOWN Edward Smyth	2 Dec.	50	T	O	C?	pro★	pro	con

DROMORE John Stearne	12 Nov.	61	W	C	C	con		con
ELPHIN Simon Digby	12 Dec.	1	T?	O?	O			con
FERNS Bartholomew Vigors	12 Nov.	31	T?	O?	C?			con
KILDARE Welbore Ellis	12 Nov.	59	T	O	C?	pro		con
KILLALA William Lloyd	29 Mar.	9	T?	O?	O			con
KILLALOE *Nicholas Forster* *(until 8 June 1716)*	*12 Nov.*	*42*	*W*	*C*	*C*	*con*		*con*
Charles Carr	*12 June*	*7*						
KILMORE *Timothy Godwin*	*5 Dec.*	*49*	*W*	*C*	*C*	*con*		*con*
LIMERICK Thomas Smyth	14 Nov.	41	T	O	O	pro★	pro	con
MEATH *John Evans*	*3 May*	*16*						
OSSORY Sir Thomas Vesey, 1st bt	12 Nov.	41	T	O	O	pro★	pro	con
RAPHOE *Edward Synge* *(until 8 June 1716)*	*12 Nov.*	*55*	*W*	*C*	*C*	*con*		*con*
Nicholas Forster	*12 June*	*6*						
WATERFORD Thomas Milles	5 Dec.	16	T	O	O	pro★		con

The Members of the House of Lords
and the Hanoverian Succession[*]

STUART HANDLEY

This essay examines what happened in August and September 1714, from the death of Queen Anne on 1 August to the swearing-in of the new privy council on 1 October, specifically from the perspective of the membership of the house of lords. It confirms that most members were present in London during this period and active in parliament, the privy council, the regency, and politics generally. Very few were absent without a good reason.

Keywords: bishops; house of lords; lords justices; parliament; peers; privy council; regency

This essay will attempt to delineate the role of the members of the house of lords during the establishment and stabilisation of the Hanoverian regime, from the death of Queen Anne on 1 August 1714 to the swearing-in of the new privy council on 1 October. On 9 July 1714, parliament had been prorogued until 10 August with the clear expectation that it would be further prorogued until the beginning of the next session in the winter of 1714–15. On 8 July, when politically charged matters were discussed, there had been 14 bishops, ten Scottish representative peers, and 79 English temporal peers in attendance; on the following day, when the queen prorogued parliament, there had been eight bishops, eight Scottish representative peers, and 56 English temporal peers. Many members of the house of lords present during the 1714 session had stopped attending parliament before the beginning of July, including 34 peers,[1] four Scottish representative peers,[2] and ten bishops.[3] Many more were to drift away in the days following the prorogation. By 15 July, James Craggs noted that 'the town grows very thin, and 'tis no easy matter now the parliament's up to learn any sort of news'.[4] The sudden illness of the queen brought many members of the Lords back to London to join those who had not yet departed for their estates.[5]

[*] I wish to thank my colleagues, Robin Eagles and Charles Littleton on the 1715–90 section of the house of lords at the History of Parliament, for providing the intellectual context for this work.

[1] Lexinton, Stamford, Richmond, Chandos, Manchester, St Albans, Thanet, Carlisle, Holdernesse, Schomberg, Warrington, Salisbury, Howard of Effingham, Byron, Berkeley of Stratton, Cornwallis, Barnard, Maynard, Westmorland, Hereford, Exeter, Bridgwater, Leicester, Berkshire, Hatton, Cholmondeley, Herbert of Chirbury, Clarendon, Suffolk, Rutland, Ferrers, Lansdown, Coventry, and Willoughby of Parham.

[2] Breadalbane, Kinnoull, Eglinton, and Atholl. Selkirk had not attended since the prorogation in January 1714.

[3] Crew of Durham (11 June), Blackall of Exeter (11 May), Cumberland of Peterborough (4 May), Fowler of Gloucester (21 June), Hooper of Bath and Wells (15 June), Manningham of Chichester (16 Apr.), Nicolson of Carlisle (11 June), Talbot of Oxford (12 May), Trimnell of Norwich (10 May), and Hough of Lichfield and Coventry (11 May).

[4] BL, Add. MS 32686, ff. 16–17: James Craggs to [Lord Pelham], 15 July 1714.

[5] Those interested in the final days of Queen Anne should consult Edward Gregg, *Queen Anne* (1986), 391–5; H.L. Snyder, 'The Last Days of Queen Anne: The Account of Sir John Evelyn Examined', *Huntington Library*

The membership of the house of lords on 1 August 1714 can be divided into three components:[6] 26 bishops;[7] 16 Scottish representative peers; and 170 English temporal lords.[8] The number of temporal lords able and willing to take their seats was reduced by the fact that 17 were catholics, who were precluded from sitting by virtue of the oaths in place to prevent them,[9] and 19 were minors, disqualified from sitting by age.[10] A further 24 English temporal lords failed to sit in August 1714.[11] A few were nonjurors, who played no part in public life. Lichfield had declined to sit after 11 February 1689; Ailesbury had not sat since 1697 and lived in exile; Winchilsea and Chesterfield succeeded to their titles in August 1712 and January 1714 respectively, but never took their seats.[12] Political scruples may have been partly responsible for Exeter's withdrawal from the Lords after the queen's death, but ill health was also a factor.[13] Mental incapacity ruled out Sandwich.[14] Ill health precluded the attendance of Chandos, who by early September was reported to be dying,[15] and of Leeds, who was confined to his house at Wimbledon.[16]

Several peers were abroad during August, most notably the duke of Cambridge (the future George II), who was yet to arrive in Britain to take his seat;[17] Strafford, who was on diplomatic duties at The Hague;[18] and Clarendon, who was at the Hanoverian court.[19] Richmond was on a mission to the French court to offer the queen's condolences on the death of the duc de Berry. He arrived back on 16 August, but seems to have gone almost immediately to his country residence and did not take his seat until March 1715.[20]

---

5 *(continued)* *Quarterly*, xxxiv (1971), 261–76; Robin Eagles, ' "I have neither Interest nor Eloquence Sufficient to Prevaile": The Duke of Shrewsbury and the Politics of Succession during the Reign of Anne', *Electronic British Library Journal* (2015), 1–14.

[6] I owe an enormous debt to Charles Littleton for his work for the History of Parliament on the composition of the house of lords at various dates.

[7] During the period under review there were only 25 bishops, Bishop Moore of Ely having died on 31 July, a few hours before the queen.

[8] The figure of 170 excludes Baron Crew, who is counted as a bishop on the grounds that he became a bishop in 1671 and succeeded to his barony only in 1697.

[9] Clifford of Chudleigh, Stourton, Stafford, Waldegrave (who took his seat in 1719), Widdrington, Teynham (who took his seat in 1716), Audley, Fauconberg, Norfolk, Langdale, Derwentwater, Gerard of Bromley, Montagu, Arundell of Wardour, Rivers, Dormer, and Petre.

[10] Warwick and Holland, Burlington, Dudley and Ward, Huntingdon, Arundell of Trerice, Lovelace, Gower, Essex, Brooke, Bedford, Craven, Leominster, Shaftesbury, Lonsdale, Gainsborough, Beaufort, Weymouth. Both Dover (Queensberry) and Brandon (Hamilton) are included in this figure.

[11] Cambridge, Lichfield, Ailesbury, Winchilsea, Chesterfield, Exeter, Sandwich, Chandos, Leeds, Richmond, Strafford, Clarendon, Howard of Effingham, Albemarle, Colepeper, Willoughby of Parham, Stawell, Abergavenny, Lindsey, Coventry, Hereford, Leigh, Maynard, Hatton.

[12] Both men died in 1726.

[13] Exeter did take the oaths before the privy council on 6 Sept. 1714 for the lord lieutenancy of Rutland: TNA, PC 2/85/1, p. 67.

[14] Sandwich did attend in 1727.

[15] BL, Add. MS 70236: Edward Harley to Lord Oxford, 3 Sept. 1714; HMC, *Portland MSS*, v, 493. He died on 16 Oct. 1714.

[16] BL, Add. MS 70440: Lord Harley's diary, 17 Aug. 1714. He attended the prorogation on 23 Sept. 1714.

[17] He arrived in England with his father and first attended on 17 Mar. 1715.

[18] Strafford was recalled in Nov. 1714 and first attended the Lords on 17 Mar. 1715.

[19] He took his seat at the prorogation on 23 Sept. 1714.

[20] HMC, *Portland MSS*, v, 489; *The Unpublished Letters of Henry St John, Viscount Bolingbroke*, ed. Adrian Lashmore-Davies (5 vols, 2013), iv, 393.

Howard of Effingham was in Ireland when the queen died,[21] and first sat on 23 September 1714. Albemarle, having abandoned British politics in 1705, was deputed to offer the States General's congratulations to the new monarch on entering Dutch territory on the way to his new kingdom.[22] Subsequently, Albemarle was seen as a possible groom of the stole. He had arrived in England by November 1714, but in the event only sat in the Lords on a few occasions after resuming his seat on 4 April 1715.

It seems likely that some of the missing peers were impoverished 'poor lords',[23] who were awaiting funds to allow them to attend: both Colepeper and Willoughby of Parham were given a bounty until the king made provision for their maintenance.[24] Another, Stawell, did not attend the 1714 parliament at all, although previously in receipt of a pension.[25] Other peers were in no rush to attend, such as Abergavenny, who took his seat on 23 September, and Lindsey, who was in Lincolnshire on 2 August,[26] and did not attend until 17 March 1715, although he was present at the privy council on 30 August.[27] Coventry, Hereford, and Leigh did not take their seats until April, May, and July 1715 respectively.[28]

Many bishops had to travel long distances to attend parliament, and all had significant ecclesiastical duties to perform in their dioceses during the summer. Very few bishops were known to be in London on 1 August. Bishop Robinson of London was attending to his ecclesiastical tasks: he was confirming in the parish of St Stephen Walbrook on 26 July,[29] and was on hand to minister to the spiritual needs of the queen during her final illness.[30] Bishop Atterbury of Rochester was also resident in the capital in his capacity as dean of Westminster. Archbishop Tenison of Canterbury was ensconced in Lambeth Palace, safe-guarding his precarious health. He had not attended the Lords since 27 November 1710, although he would play his part in the events of August 1714, including attending the Lords on 5 August. Bishop Fowler of Gloucester, having taken his seat on 21 June 1714, presum-ably in order to qualify for making a proxy,[31] then retired to his house in Chelsea, where he died on 26 August.[32] Bishop Moore had returned to Ely following the prorogation on 9 July 1714, where he died on 31 July.[33] Neither Bishop Blackall of Exeter (last attended 11 May 1714), nor Bishop Lloyd of Worcester (last attended 6 June 1712) sat after the queen's death.

---

[21] BL, Add. MS 47027, ff. 153–6: Daniel Dering to Sir John Perceval, 14 Aug. 1714.

[22] *The History of Parliament: The House of Lords, 1660–1715*, ed. Ruth Paley (5 vols, Cambridge, 2016) [hereafter cited as *HPL, 1660–1715*], iii, 633.

[23] A concept used in Edward Gregg and Clyve Jones, 'Hanover, Pensions and the "Poor Lords", 1712–13', *Parliamentary History*, i (1982), 173–80.

[24] *Calendar of Treasury Papers*, 1714–19, p. 14.

[25] Gregg and Jones, ' "Poor Lords" ', 173, 176. Stawell attended in March 1715.

[26] BL, Add. MS 32686, ff. 18–19: Lindsey to [Lord Pelham], 2 Aug. 1714.

[27] TNA, PC 2/85/1, p. 61.

[28] Maynard and Hatton did not take their seats until 1716 and 1718 respectively.

[29] BL, Add. MS 70070: newsletter, 29 July 1714.

[30] BL, Add. MS 72501, ff. 156–7: T[homas] B[ateman] to [Sir William Trumbull], 11 Aug. 1714; Add. MS 47027, ff. 146–50: Perceval to Dering, 3 Aug. 1714.

[31] The proxy books indicate a proxy signed on 23 July in favour of Bishop Tyler of Llandaff: *HPL, 1660–1715*, v, 562.

[32] HMC, *Portland MSS*, v, 490–1.

[33] *HPL, 1660–1715*, v, 313.

Many other bishops failed to return to London for the August sitting, although Bishop Gastrell of Chester did make it back for the prorogation of 23 September 1714. He was in Chester on 4 August when the king was proclaimed and left on the 9th.[34] Bishop Nicolson of Carlisle had left London in the Lincoln coach on 14 June.[35] He arrived at Rose Castle, his episcopal palace, on 23 June, gave the charge at Carlisle sessions on 14 July and attended the proclamation of the new king in Carlisle on 4 August.[36] He did not return to London until shortly after the beginning of George I's first parliament in March 1715.[37] Similarly, Bishop Crew was in Durham to proclaim the king on 4 August 1714,[38] but did not attend parliament until March 1715. Manningham of Chichester and Hough of Lichfield and Coventry also did not return until March 1715. Hooper of Bath and Wells did not attend until May 1715, and Cumberland of Peterborough (who had erroneously been reported dead along with Moore and Fowler),[39] did not return until 1 September 1715. Three of the Welsh bishops, Evans of Bangor, Ottley of St Davids, and Fleetwood of St Asaph, had all attended in July 1714, but none of them returned to parliament until March 1715, by which date Fleetwood had been translated to Ely as Moore's successor.

The remaining English bishops returned to the capital as quickly as circumstances allowed. Bishops Trelawney of Winchester and Smalridge of Bristol both attended on 3 August, as did Bisse of Hereford on the 4th, suggesting that all three had remained in or near London after the prorogation. Archbishop Dawes of York attended on 9 August.[40] Burnet of Salisbury and Talbot of Oxford attended on 12 August. The fourth Welsh bishop, Tyler of Llandaff, took his seat on 18 August. Bishop Wake of Lincoln had left London for his diocese on 16 July, and was at his ecclesiastical residence at Buckden on 2 August when he heard of the queen's demise. He returned to London on 18 August and attended parliament on the 20th.[41] Trimnell of Norwich attended on 25 August (the day parliament was prorogued until 23 September).

The 16 Scottish representative peers were in some ways similar to those bishops with distant dioceses. Seven Scottish representative peers were in attendance at the end of the 1714 session (8–9 July), and also on 1 August.[42] Orkney had also attended on 9 July, and was at Ingestre in Staffordshire on 31 July, but, according to his wife, was expected to be in London shortly.[43] He duly attended on 4 August. Kinnoull also sat after the queen's death, on 4 August, having previously attended on 15 March 1714. Balmerino attended

---

[34] *The Diary of Henry Prescott, LL.B., Deputy Registrar of Chester Diocese. Vol. II*, ed. John Addy (Record Society of Lancashire and Cheshire, cxxxii, 1994), 399, 401.

[35] *The London Diaries of William Nicolson, Bishop of Carlisle, 1702–1718*, ed. Clyve Jones and Geoffrey Holmes (Oxford, 1985), 613.

[36] 'Bishop Nicolson's Diaries', *Transactions of the Cumberland and Westmorland Antiquarian and Archaeological Society*, v (1905), 1.

[37] *London Diaries of William Nicolson*, ed. Jones and Holmes, 614–15.

[38] *Post Boy*, 7–10 Aug. 1714.

[39] BL, Add. MS 72501, f. 154: T[homas] B[ateman] to [Trumbull], 2 Aug. 1714.

[40] Dawes will be considered under the regents.

[41] *HPL, 1660–1715*, v, 579.

[42] Findlater, Loudoun, Dundonald, Portmore, Kilsyth, Dunmore, and Mar. The latter had married Francis Pierrepont, daughter of the marquess of Dorchester, on 20 July 1714.

[43] BL, Add. MS 70033, f. 49: Countess of Orkney to [Oxford], 31 July 1714.

on 9 July, but by 14 July it was reported that he was keen to return to Scotland,[44] and he may have done so because he next attended on 16 August. Atholl had last sat on 14 April, before heading for Scotland to preside as commissioner of the general assembly of the Kirk. In August 1714 he was at Blair Castle, before returning to take his seat at the prorogation on 21 November.[45] Five of the Scottish representative peers did not sit again before the dissolution: Breadalbane was in Edinburgh by 4 June;[46] Northesk was also back in Scotland, when he wrote to Montrose on 21 August explaining that he preferred to stay at home;[47] Eglintoun (last sat 15 June 1714); and Rosebery (last sat 7 July 1714). Selkirk, who had taken his seat on the prorogation day of 12 January 1714, spent most of the session in France pursuing claims related to the dukedom of Châtelleherault.[48]

In accordance with the Act of Settlement and the Regency Act, the demise of Queen Anne on 1 August 1714 saw parliament sitting again on that day. In all, the house of lords sat on 15 days during August. The number of peers sitting at some point in that month was 131, comprising 109 English temporal lords, ten Scottish representative peers, and 12 bishops. As one might expect, attendance varied (not least because at the beginning of the month many members were still en route to Westminster). The largest attendance was for the speech given by Lord Chancellor Harcourt on behalf of the lords justices on 5 August, when 89 members were listed as attending (at that date only 102 had been sworn). The 13 missing peers on that day included Dorset, who was on his way to Hanover, North and Grey, who was on military duties as governor of Portsmouth,[49] Bingley, who on the previous day had been badly beaten up when leaving Oxford's residence,[50] Dorchester and Portland (Dorchester having married Portland's sister on 2 August, testimony, perhaps, to the way in which life continued as normal after 1 August). The lowest attendance was 19, on 9 August, although fewer than 40 attended on six other days.[51] Fifty-nine members attended on 13 August, following the return of James Craggs the younger from Hanover; an event which was much anticipated, but which revealed little of the king's intentions. As Charles Ford told Swift, the arrival of Craggs had left the whigs 'dejected' and the tories 'very much pleased', but he conjectured for no other reason than that he brought no orders for 'alterations' with him.[52]

Individual attendance in the house of lords peaked with Harcourt, who was in the chair for all 15 sitting days in August. Harcourt apart, only 16 members of the House attended on ten or more occasions in August 1714.[53] None of them were lords justices. Fourteen

[44] HMC, *Portland MSS*, x, 322 (as were Northesk and Kilsyth).

[45] *HPL, 1660–1715*, v, 753.

[46] BL, Add. MS 70032, f. 287: Breadalbane to Oxford, 5 June 1714.

[47] *HPL, 1660–1715*, v, 651.

[48] *HPL, 1660–1715*, v, 662. He was returned again as a Scottish representative peer in 1722.

[49] HMC, *Portland MSS*, v, 484.

[50] *The Correspondence of Jonathan Swift DD*, ed. David Woolley (5 vols, Frankfurt am Main, 1999–2014), ii, 49. Bingley registered a proxy signed on 5 Aug. 1714: *HPL, 1660–1715*, v, 153–4. He was also missing from the privy council until 14 August.

[51] 12, 16–20 August.

[52] *Swift Correspondence*, ed. Woolley, ii, 73–4.

[53] 14: Lincoln; 13: Poulett and Rochester; 12: Guilford, De la War, Rockingham, Scarsdale, Dundonald, and Bishops Robinson and Smalridge; 11: Masham and Findlater; 10: Northampton, St Albans, Guernsey, and Mountjoy.

members attended for only a single day. These included Torrington on 2 August (his last ever sitting); Ferrers (9 August), who had significant family matters to attend to following the death of his heir, Viscount Tamworth, on 5 July;[54] and Peterborough (18 August).[55] Peterborough had previously attended on 16 July 1713, and then been encouraged to take his mercurial temper abroad. As he was in France when he heard of the queen's death he took the opportunity of an audience with Louis XIV,[56] before returning to London on 7/8 August 1714,[57] to offer his insight into the attitude of the French monarch to the Hanoverian succession. By December he was on his way to Italy.[58]

The poor attendances of members of the Lords in general, and of lords justices in particular, attests to the perception that power was not located in the house of lords in August 1714, but in two other institutions dominated by members of the upper House: the privy council and the regency. Following the queen's death at Kensington Palace between 7.00 am and 7.30 am, six members of the privy council met and adjourned to St James's for the formal opening of the regency.[59] This was probably to facilitate the arrival of Archbishop Tenison from Lambeth with his copy of the list of those nominated by the new king to govern the realm in his absence, which had to be compared with those in the possession of the Hanoverian resident, Kreienberg, and Lord Chancellor Harcourt. Forty-one privy councillors met at St James's, 33 of them members of the house of lords.[60] After the three copies of the instrument naming the regents had been validated,[61] the proclamation of the new king was issued with 128 signatories (57 members of the Lords).[62] The Lords met, with two bishops and 47 temporal peers in attendance, including Thomas, Baron Pelham (the future duke of Newcastle) who sat for the first time on that day, having come of age on 1 July.[63] A total of 68 members participated in either the signing the proclamation or attending the House. Forty peers did both, nine attended the Lords, but did not sign the proclamation,[64] and 19 signed the proclamation, but did not attend.[65]

---

[54] HMC, *Townshend MSS*, 223–9. Ferrers attended the privy council on 1 August.

[55] The others were Godolphin, Carlisle, Warrington, Byron, Bridgwater, Marlborough, Dorset, Wharton, Dorchester, and Cleveland.

[56] Philip, earl of Hardwicke, *Miscellaneous State Papers: From 1501 to 1726* (2 vols, 1778), ii, 528.

[57] HMC, *Portland MSS*, v, 485–6; Abel Boyer, *The Political State of Great Britain* (60 vols, 1718–40), viii, 173.

[58] HMC, *Stuart MSS*, i, 339; *Portland MSS*, v, 502–3.

[59] Shrewsbury, Buckingham, Rochester, Bingley, Bromley, and Wyndham: TNA, PC 2/85/1, p. 5.

[60] Boyer, *Political State*, viii, 113–14, lists Tenison, Harcourt, Shrewsbury, Buckingham, Dartmouth, Somerset, Ormond, Northumberland, Argyll, Roxburghe, Kent, Poulett, Northampton, Sunderland, Radnor, Rochester, Orford, Mar, Loudoun, Ferrers, Oxford, Portmore, Bolingbroke, Bishop Robinson, Lexinton, Berkeley of Stratton, Guilford, Somers, Guernsey, Cowper, Mansell, Lansdown, Bingley, William Bromley, Henry Boyle, Thomas Coke, Sir William Wyndham, Sir John Trevor, John Hill, Sir Richard Onslow, and John Smith.

[61] Boyer, *Political State*, viii, 114–15.

[62] *London Gazette*, 31 July–3 Aug. 1714. Roxburghe and Stair, former representative peers, also signed.

[63] Thirty peers who had attended on 9 July also attended on 1 August: Bishops Robinson of London and Atterbury of Rochester; Lord Chancellor Harcourt; the dukes of Somerset and Grafton; Lord Steward Poulett; the earls of Lincoln, Dorset, Scarsdale, Cardigan, Berkeley, Rochester, Abingdon, Rochford, Greenwich [Argyll], Mar, Loudoun, Findlater, Dundonald, and Dunmore; Viscount Bolingbroke; and Barons Willoughby de Broke, Paget, Hunsdon, Rockingham, Guilford, Weston [Arran], Halifax, Hervey, and Cowper. Weymouth, who also attended on 9 July, had died on the 28th of that month.

[64] Bishop Atterbury, Manchester, Abingdon, Portland, Rochford, Godolphin, Howard of Escrick, Weston [Arran], and Hervey.

[65] Archbishop Tenison, Buckingham, Shrewsbury, Dartmouth, Orford, Ferrers, Northumberland, Ormond, Roxburghe, Northampton, Oxford, Mansell, Lexinton, Somers, Bingley, Guernsey, Cowper, Bruce, and Carteret.

The unveiling of the regents on 1 August caused a few surprises. The regents had changed upon the death of Princess Sophia, a few weeks previously on 28 May,[66] with a new document arriving in London with Bothmer on 8 June.[67] Those appointed by virtue of being great officers of state were Archbishop Tenison of Canterbury, Lord Chancellor Harcourt, Lord President Buckingham, Lord Treasurer Shrewsbury, Lord Privy Seal Dartmouth, First Lord of the Admiralty Strafford, and the lord chief justice of king's bench, Sir Thomas Parker.[68] The 19 selected by the elector were Archbishop Dawes of York, the dukes of Shrewsbury,[69] Somerset, Bolton, Devonshire, Kent, Argyll, Montrose, and Roxburghe;[70] the earls of Pembroke, Anglesey, Carlisle, Nottingham, Abingdon, Scarbrough, and Orford; Viscount Townshend; and Barons Halifax and Cowper. Many contemporaries believed King George had made a very astute choice of men, intending to reassure the tories by excluding the more partisan whigs such as Sunderland, Wharton, and Somers,[71] while including the most prominent Hanoverian tories, such as Abingdon and Anglesey, or, as Lady Mary Wortley Montagu phrased it, excluding 'any man grossly infamous in either party'.[72] Not all observers took the same view. Jonathan Swift thought them 'all the rankest Whigs', except for the four or five 'proselytes', who had 'quarrelled about the peace and treaties and danger to the succession'.[73] Marlborough, too, was missing from the list, but this was due to his absence abroad when the list was drawn up and the likelihood that his exile would continue for some time.[74]

The sudden nature of the queen's demise meant that only 11 lords justices were present at the privy council meetings on 1 August,[75] and only one further regent was available to sign the proclamation of George I later in the day, namely, Halifax.[76] In addition, Abingdon was one of seven lords justices to attend the house of lords that day.[77] Messengers, both official and private, were dispatched to the remainder to hasten them to London.[78] Warrants signed by the lords justices on 3 August demonstrate that three of those

[66] Compare with BL, Add. MS 70278: 'the Electorice's Regents copied by Earl Rivers at Hanover'. This is undated, but refers to Baron Wharton, who was promoted to an earldom in December 1706. It names the archbishop of York in being; the dukes of Somerset, Ormond, Bolton, Marlborough, Montagu; the earls of Bridgwater, Manchester, Peterborough, Rivers, Sunderland, Radnor, Orford; Barons Wharton, Mohun, Raby, Lexinton, and Somers.

[67] R. Pauli, 'Actenstücke zur Thronbesteigung des Welfenhauses in England', *Zeitschrift des Historischen Vereins für Niedersachsen* (1883), 54.

[68] Parker, although not a member of the Lords at this point, was an assistant to the House in his capacity as a judge.

[69] Shrewsbury had become an *ex officio* regent by being named lord treasurer a few days previously.

[70] Neither Montrose nor Roxburghe were members of the Lords at this point, although they had served as representative peers, and were elected again in 1715.

[71] BL, Add. MS 47027, ff. 146–50: Perceval to Dering, 3 Aug. 1714; *The Wentworth Papers 1705–39* …, ed. J.J. Cartwright (1883), 409.

[72] *The Complete Letters of Lady Mary Wortley Montagu*, ed. Robert Halsband (3 vols, Oxford, 1965–7), i, 213–14.

[73] *Swift Correspondence*, ed. Woolley, ii, 60–2.

[74] Marlborough had been in exile since the end of November 1712: *HPL, 1660–1715*, ii, 607.

[75] Tenison, Harcourt, Buckingham, Shrewsbury, Dartmouth, Somerset, Kent, Argyll, Roxburghe, Orford, and Cowper: TNA, PC 2/85/1, pp. 5, 18.

[76] Halifax was not sworn a member of the privy council during Anne's reign, but attended on 6, 8, and 15 September.

[77] Harcourt, Somerset, Kent, Argyll (Greenwich), Halifax, Cowper, and Abingdon.

[78] *Calendar of Treasury Books*, xxix, 81.

summoned by name, Bolton ('in the west'), Townshend (Norwich), and Lord Chief Justice Parker (Staffordshire) had already returned to the capital, as had Devonshire, who may have been closer. Nottingham (Rutland) and Scarbrough (Nottinghamshire) were also back by the time the lords justices paraded before parliament to support Harcourt's speech to both Houses on 5 August.[79] Indeed, Nottingham had been summoned back before any official message, in a letter penned by Sunderland, while at Bothmer's London residence on 30 July.[80] Parker, it seems, had also been summoned back on the 30th.[81] Thus, an impressive 16 lords justices signed an order relating to the royal mint on 3 August,[82] and 17 an order on 5 August requiring officeholders to return to their posts.[83] Seventeen lords justices also attended the Lords on 5 August.[84]

The other six lords justices were further afield on 1 August. By the time an express reached Archbishop Dawes, he had arrived at his palace at Bishopthorpe.[85] He stayed long enough in York to grace the proclamation of George I on 3 August, and arrived in London on 9 August. He may have travelled to London with the earl of Carlisle, who had left a proxy on 21 June and was in the north to enjoy the horse racing at York when the queen died. News of the queen's death produced a short-term security headache in that city as many catholics were among the crowds attending the race meeting when orders arrived for the king's proclamation. Fortunately, Carlisle was on hand to advise the lord mayor, together with three MPs or former MPs.[86] Having overseen the proclamation of the king at York, he travelled to London. He was sworn a lord justice on the evening of 9 August and first attended parliament on the 13th.[87] Montrose was in Edinburgh and attended the proclamation of the king there on 5 August; he then left the following day for London, arriving on the 9th and being sworn in as a regent the next day.[88] On 26 July, Anglesey had set out from London for Ireland,[89] and efforts to reach him before he embarked failed.[90] In response to the summons, he set sail from Dublin on the morning of 7 August,[91] and Henry Prescott in Chester reported on the 8th that Anglesey had left there at about 5 pm post-haste.[92] Anglesey made it to London on 10 August,[93] was sworn into the privy

[79] Privy council records indicate that Bolton and Townshend were sworn on 2 August, Parker and Devonshire on the 3rd and Nottingham and Scarbrough on the 4th: TNA, PC PC2/85/1, pp. 23, 24, 28.

[80] *HPL, 1660–1715*, ii, 1015.

[81] *Swift Correspondence*, ed. Woolley, ii, 40.

[82] *The Correspondence of Isaac Newton*, ed. H.W. Turnbull, J.F. Scott, A. Rupert Hall and Laura Tilling (7 vols, Cambridge, 1959–77), vi, 168.

[83] *London Gazette*, 3–7 Aug. 1714. Buckingham signed the first order, but not the second; Nottingham and Scarbrough the second order, but not the first; Tenison did not sign any, having retreated to Lambeth.

[84] Neither Parker nor Roxburghe were members of the house of lords.

[85] BL, Add. MS 72501, f. 155: T[homas] B[ateman] to [Trumbull], 4 Aug. 1714.

[86] *Post Man and Historical Account*, 12–14 Aug. 1714.

[87] Very efficiently, Oxford's memorandum of 10 August has Carlisle's name erased from the column of absentees.

[88] *Daily Courant*, 14 Aug. 1714; HMC, *Mar and Kellie MSS*, 506.

[89] BL, Add. MS 70070: newsletter, 29 July 1714.

[90] BL, Add. MS 72501, f. 155: T[homas] B[ateman] to [Trumbull], 4 Aug. 1714.

[91] BL, Add. MS 47027, ff. 151–3: Dering to Perceval, 7 Aug. 1714.

[92] *Prescott Diary II*, ed. Addy, 399–400.

[93] *Swift Correspondence*, ed. Woolley, ii, 68.

council on the following day, and first sat in the Lords on 13 August.[94] Pembroke was noted by Charles Ford as still being absent on 12 August,[95] but on that day he attended and took the oaths in both parliament and privy council.[96] Of the lords justices, only Strafford, who was still in The Hague, failed to sign the proclamation of 15 September offering a reward of £100,000 for the capture of the pretender should he land in the king's dominions.[97]

The lords justices undertook their duties diligently, sitting from nine in the morning on most days, and dealing with matters of security, the army and navy, papists and the embargo, the queen's funeral, and Irish matters, especially the affairs of Dublin corporation. They deputed the earl of Berkeley to command the fleet in the channel,[98] and Dorset was sent after James Craggs junior, who had already been dispatched to Hanover.[99] They also had to deal with the delicate matter of the queen's secret papers, found when a search was conducted for her will. According to Bothmer, a sealed packet was found in the queen's closet at Kensington, with clear instructions that the contents should be burnt after her death. The regents consulted Bothmer, who agreed that her wishes should be respected, whereupon Somerset threw the packet into the fire. This action broke open the cover to reveal letters written in French-style characters, the supposition being that they were the pretender's letters to his half-sister.[100]

The lords justices also dealt with most of the important decisions regarding parliamentary proceedings. The absence of the Speaker of the Commons, Sir Thomas Hanmer, for the first three days of the parliamentary session, delayed matters slightly. He had been sent for on 30 July,[101] and arrived on the evening of 3 August. The key meeting of parliament was set for 5 August, and there is evidence that this was arranged to accommodate the lords justices, with Shrewsbury writing to Hanmer on 4 August:

> I have this morning spoke with several of the lords justices and they are all of opinion the session should be opened with a speech (which they intend tomorrow). I am therefore directed to acquaint you that it would be agreeable to them if the house of Commons after taking the oaths did adjourn themselves till tomorrow morning.[102]

This is exactly what occurred.[103]

The lords justices also filled up several posts which were vacant. Bolton was named lord lieutenant of Hampshire, the previous incumbent, Beaufort, having died on 24 May. The politically sensitive lord lieutenancy of Lancashire, vacant since the death of the duke of

---

[94] TNA, PC 2/85/1, p. 46.

[95] *Swift Correspondence*, ed. Woolley, ii, 68.

[96] TNA, PC 2/85/1, p. 47.

[97] *London Gazette*, 14–18 Sept. 1714.

[98] HMC, *Portland MSS*, v, 483.

[99] *Swift Correspondence*, ed. Woolley, ii, 44.

[100] Wolfgang Michael, *England under George I: The Beginnings of the Hanoverian Dynasty* (1936), 62–3; BL, Add. MS 17677 HHH, ff. 333–7: L'Hermitage's despatch, 6/17 Aug. 1714; *Wentworth Papers*, ed. Cartwright, 413–14.

[101] *Swift Correspondence*, ed. Woolley, ii, 39–40.

[102] National Library of Wales, Bettisfield MSS, 73: Shrewsbury, to Hanmer, 4 July [*recte* Aug.] 1714 (History of Parliament transcript).

[103] *CJ*, xviii, 3.

Hamilton in 1712, was given to the whig soldier and former incumbent, the earl of Derby.[104] Otherwise everything depended upon the decisions of the new king on his arrival. It seems that Somers, Cowper, and Parker were in agreement as to the powers of the lords justices; the chief officers of the realm (lord treasurer, lord president, lord privy seal, lord chancellor, and first lord of the admiralty) had to remain in the hands of the incumbents until the arrival of the new monarch.[105] This left ample scope for politicians to plot and manoeuvre for advantage. Letters were written to the king and his ministers, and detailed memoranda written to advise the king on the proper course to take after his arrival.[106]

If the king's choice of regents gave more than an inkling of those expected to be favoured in the new reign, the *ex officio* regents were in a more uncertain position. Shrewsbury, having been named as a lord justice by George, was seen (not least by himself) as a stopgap at the treasury.[107] Halifax had long coveted the post as lord treasurer and was now in a strong position to claim it. It seems that many whigs encouraged his ambitions, while working behind the scenes to prevent it. The Prussian resident, Bonet, later believed that Halifax had been promised the staff in the same manner as Marlborough had been assured of the post of captain general, and expected to be appointed lord treasurer soon after the king landed at Greenwich.[108] Lady Cowper thought that Marlborough, Townshend, and Sunderland had all encouraged Halifax's pretensions, while being opposed to the appointment of a lord treasurer (as was the king).[109] The duchess of Marlborough later recalled hosting a dinner party at Marlborough House, where Halifax 'hardly spoke a word the whole dinner time, looked full of rage, and as if he could have killed everybody at table', because he had been thwarted in his ambition.[110]

Archbishop Tenison and Lord Chief Justice Parker were special cases. Tenison held his office for life and continued in post until his death in December 1715. Parker, a whig appointed just prior to the assumption of power by the tories in 1710, was a protégé of Cowper.[111] He held his office during good behaviour and in 1714 his prospects were good. He retained his office under George I and was reappointed to the privy council, eventually succeeding Cowper as lord chancellor in 1718.

Harcourt was expected to relinquish the great seal to Cowper. In the interim he had many official duties to fulfil, and seems to have prevaricated over whether to approach George I. When he did so he hoped that his large share in current business would excuse his tardiness in writing.[112] When he solicited the advice of Bishop Atterbury as to the manner of his

[104] TNA, SP 35/1, f. 18. The warrant was ordered on 9 August.

[105] Edward Gregg, *The Protestant Succession in International Politics, 1710–1716* (New York, 1986), 216.

[106] Perhaps the most famous was Cowper's, 'An Impartial History of Parties', printed in John, Baron Campbell, *Lives of the Lord Chancellors and Keepers of the Great Seal of England* ... (8 vols, 1845–69), iv, 421–9, although his scheme for the judges on pp. 349–50 was perhaps even more pertinent.

[107] James Macpherson, *Original Papers; Containing the Secret History of Great Britain, from the Restoration to the Accession of the House of Hanover* ... (2nd edn, 2 vols, 1776), ii, 639–40.

[108] Geheimes Staatsarchiv Preussische Kulturbesitz Abteilung Berlin-Dahlem: Bonet despatch, 20 May 1715.

[109] *The Private Diary of William, First Earl Cowper*, ed. E.C. Hawtrey (Roxburghe Club, xlix, 1833), 57–8.

[110] Frances Harris, *A Passion for Government: The Life of Sarah Duchess of Marlborough* (Oxford, 1991), 206.

[111] David Lemmings, 'Lord Chancellor Cowper and the Whigs, 1714–16', *Parliamentary History*, ix (1990), 169–74, where Cowper described him as 'the man I raised'.

[112] *The Epistolary Correspondence of the Right Reverend Francis Atterbury, D.D., Lord Bishop of Rochester*, ed. John Nichols (5 vols, 1783–90), ii, 42–3.

approach, he met with a sarcastic rebuttal and a suggestion for an alternative missive, in which Harcourt placed himself at the head of the tories and attempted to project a position of political strength.[113] Harcourt was replaced by Cowper on 21 September and thereby missed out on the windfall profits from the fees generated by the creation of a prince of Wales.

Buckingham played an important role as lord president in the handover of power to the regents.[114] Thereafter, he chaired almost every meeting of the privy council between 1 August and 17 September. Following George I's arrival, he 'entertained the king a great while with telling him, that he was misinformed and that he had yet heard but one side, and he could make it plain to him that the Whigs was but a handful of people in respect to the Church party'. The king listened politely but within the hour sent Townshend to Buckingham to inform him of his dismissal.[115] The replacement was Nottingham, a man also not afraid to give the new king the benefit of his advice, albeit from a much stronger position than his predecessor.[116]

Dartmouth, who had been in office throughout Anne's reign, might have expected to be re-employed, but his association with the Oxford regime was too strong and he was replaced as lord privy seal by Wharton. Strafford had been a peculiar choice as first lord of the admiralty and it was widely expected that Orford would resume his place, which he did in October as part of an enlarged admiralty board. However, when Orford had been appointed in 1709 there had been disputes over the choice of his fellow commissioners and there was always the possibility that he would storm off back into retirement. Strafford in any case would have preferred a diplomatic posting or some other recognition from the new monarch. He would have liked to have come home following the queen's death, but was unsure of his legal position, and only Shrewsbury seems to have argued for his return.[117] The king wanted him to stay in The Hague, and Strafford did at least have the opportunity of meeting George several times as the new king awaited a fair wind for England.

The two secretaries of state, William Bromley and Viscount Bolingbroke, were not included in the regency but played an important part issuing orders under the direction of the lords justices. Bromley was offered a lucrative sinecure by the new regime, but declined. Bolingbroke's position was more precarious. In the last years of Anne's reign he had advocated a strategy of consolidating tory power by entrenching the party in office and thus ensuring that the new dynasty could not dislodge them. As he told Strafford, the suddenness of the queen's death had been 'a very great surprise; for though I did not imagine she could hold out long, yet I hoped she would have got over the summer'.[118] This meant that the restructuring of the ministry and the armed forces had barely started. Marlborough was on his way back, but not now as a confederate, and his meetings with whig commoners such as James Stanhope, James Craggs, William Pulteney, and Robert Walpole, were of

[113] *Atterbury Epistolary Correspondence*, ed. Nichols, ii, 43–4.

[114] Michael, *England under Geo. I*, 54; *Wentworth Papers*, ed. Cartwright, 409.

[115] *Wentworth Papers*, ed. Cartwright, 423–4.

[116] Henry Horwitz, *Revolution Politicks: The Career of Daniel Finch Second Earl of Nottingham, 1647–1730* (Cambridge, 1968), 247–8.

[117] *Wentworth Papers*, ed. Cartwright, 413–14.

[118] *Letters and Correspondence … of … Henry St John, Lord Viscount Bolingbroke …*, ed. Gilbert Parke (4 vols in 2, 1798), iv, 582–4, where it is misdated 1713.

little consequence.[119] When the queen died, one of the schemes upon which the ministry was embarked was a diplomatic alliance with France, Spain, and Sweden.[120] The discovery of this scheme was made the pretext for Bolingbroke's removal.[121] On the evening of 30 August, instructions arrived ordering the lords justices to dismiss him. Three lords justices, Shrewsbury, Cowper, and Somerset, were deputed to demand his seals of office and secure his papers.[122] Bolingbroke's response was to prepare to retire into the country,[123] although he retained his equanimity sufficiently to write Cowper a letter thanking him for the manner in which he had been treated.[124] Bolingbroke's successor was Townshend, who was well known to the Hanoverian court by virtue of his previous diplomatic roles,[125] but who was not sworn into office until 17 September.[126]

Those omitted from the regency had more time to ponder their futures. Oxford was still in London when the queen died. The appointment of Shrewsbury as lord treasurer on 30 July was perceived by many as a manœuvre to prevent Oxford from exploiting the lack of a successor to reclaim a role at the centre of affairs, although as Harcourt pointed out it was also essential to keep flowing the funds upon which government depended.[127] As it was, Oxford returned to the privy council on 31 July,[128] signed the proclamation on 1 August, and took part in the accompanying procession.[129] He wrote to the king on 6 August,[130] and continued to manœuvre for advantage. Swift thought that Oxford 'intends to strike in with the new world; by his treating with Kings [regents]. He thinks he has a kind of merit by his ill usage.'[131]

Oxford, for one, thought the lord justices important. He devoted a memorandum to them on 10 August, which made plain his intention to visit each one of them. By that date he had already visited 11 regents,[132] which left six to visit,[133] with five absent.[134] He

---

[119] *Swift Correspondence*, ed. Woolley, ii, 33–4.

[120] BL, Add. MS 47027, ff. 150–1: Perceval to Dering, 7 Aug. 1714.

[121] Gregg, *Protestant Succession*, 258.

[122] Michael, *England under Geo. I*, 66–7; *Wentworth Papers*, ed. Cartwright, 417–18; BL, Add. MS17677 HHH, ff. 370–1: L'Hermitage's despatch, 31 Aug./11 Sept. 1714.

[123] TNA, SP 35/1, f. 117: Bolingbroke to Atterbury, 'Friday one o'clock' [3 Sept. 1714]; this copy is dated more exactly than BL, Stowe MS 242, ff. 177–8, or Macpherson, *Original Papers*, ii, 651.

[124] Hertfordshire Archives and Local Studies, Cowper (Panshanger) MSS, DE/P/F56: Bolingbroke to Cowper, 4 Sept. 1714 (History of Parliament transcript).

[125] J.M. Rosenheim, *The Townshends of Raynham: Nobility in Transition in Restoration and Early Hanoverian England* (Middletown, CT, 1989), 230–1.

[126] J.C. Sainty, *Officials of the Secretaries of State 1660–1782* (Office-holders in Modern Britain, ii, 1973) 24.

[127] BL, Add. MS 78514A: John Evelyn diary, 30 July 1714.

[128] *Swift Correspondence*, ed. Woolley, ii, 38–9.

[129] BL, Add. MS 47027, ff. 146–50: Perceval to Dering, 3 Aug. 1714. However, Oxford only attended the privy council on 1, 2, and 22 August.

[130] HMC, *Portland MSS*, v, 484.

[131] *Swift Correspondence*, ed. Woolley, ii, 66–7.

[132] Archbishop of York, Shrewsbury, Dartmouth, Bolton, Devonshire, Kent, Abingdon, Scarbrough, Orford, Townshend, and Cowper.

[133] But Cowper was listed again, along with Archbishop Tenison, Buckingham, Somerset, Nottingham, and Halifax.

[134] Pembroke, Anglesey, Strafford. Carlisle and Montrose were crossed through, denoting their arrival. Argyll, Roxburghe, and Parker were not assigned in any of the columns.

wished to act in concert with Dartmouth, Shrewsbury, and Ormond, referring in a letter to Dartmouth of having 'free discourse' with Shrewsbury.[135] On 18 August, Oxford, his son, Lord Harley, his cousin, Thomas Harley, and Dartmouth, had dinner with Bothmer and Kreienberg.[136] Two days later Oxford penned a long memorandum to Dartmouth on the way forward, which he hoped to discuss with Dartmouth and Bromley on the following day.[137] However, such was Oxford's reputation that even the 'entertainment' held to celebrate the settlement of the outstanding issues relating to the Cavendish inheritance, which was shared between Lord Harley and Lord Pelham, provoked suspicions, because both Townshend and Cowper attended.[138] By the end of August, Oxford had achieved little, but he was adept at turning events to his advantage. As Bothmer reported on 3 September, Bolingbroke's dismissal was claimed by Oxford as testimony to his own influence. This 'pretence' of having power was then used to press Devonshire to put in for the post of lord president (and so thwart Nottingham), so that Oxford's ally, Poulett, could keep the lord stewardship.[139] Oxford remained in London, awaiting the arrival of the king, but his cold reception at Greenwich and inability to secure a private audience with the monarch, demonstrated his lack of influence at court.[140] He duly attended the privy council on 22 September,[141] but was omitted from the new one sworn in on 1 October.[142]

It was always assumed that Marlborough would resume command of the army. There were rumours, or 'flying reports', of Ormond's replacement by Marlborough around 20/21 August, and again on 31 August.[143] These rumours were well founded because Bothmer had in his possession a commission for Marlborough to act as general, but with strict instructions to employ it only in extreme circumstances.[144] Meanwhile, after attending the Lords on 5 August, Marlborough embarked on an extensive tour, taking in Windsor, Bath (where his daughter, the countess of Sunderland, was convalescing), Blenheim, and St Albans.[145] There seems little doubt that Marlborough was keen to reassert his power, although at this stage he promised Townshend 'to desire no more than to be declared general again'.[146]

The omission of Somers from the regency was probably because of the perceived decline in his powers. His recent parliamentary performances had sometimes been embarrassing as

[135] HMC, *Dartmouth MSS*, i, 320.

[136] BL, Add. MS 70440: Lord Harley's diary, 18 Aug. 1714; Add. MS 70299: D[artmouth] to [Oxford], 'Wednesday morning 9' [18 Aug. 1714]; HMC, *Dartmouth MSS*, i, 321.

[137] HMC, *Dartmouth MSS*, i, 321.

[138] *Swift Correspondence*, ed. Woolley, 73–4.

[139] Macpherson, *Original Papers*, ii, 650.

[140] Nicolas Tindal, *The Continuation of Mr. Rapin de Thoyras's History of England from the Revolution to the Accession of George II* (2 vols, 1751), ii, 401–2; BL, Add. MS 72502, ff. 6–7: T[homas] B[ateman] to [Trumbull], 20 Sept. 1714; Geheimes Staatsarchiv Preussische Kulturbesitz Abteilung Berlin-Dahlem: Bonet despatch, 21 Sept. 1714; Godfrey Davies, 'Letters from James Brydges, Created Duke of Chandos, to Henry St. John, Created Viscount Bolingbroke', *Huntington Library Bulletin*, ix (1936), 135–6.

[141] *London Gazette*, 21–25 Sept. 1714.

[142] *London Gazette*, 28 Sept.–2 Oct. 1714.

[143] *Prescott Diary II*, ed. Addy, 402; BL, Add. MS 47027, ff. 161–2: Ph[ilip] P[erceval] to Sir John Perceval, 21 Aug. 1714; *Wentworth Papers*, ed. Cartwright, 417–18.

[144] Macpherson, *Original Papers*, ii, 653.

[145] *Letters of Sarah, Duchess of Marlborough Now First Published from the Original Manuscripts at Madresfield Court* (1875), 112–13, gives the intended movements of the duchess; see also Harris, *Passion for Government*, 204.

[146] HMC, *Portland MSS*, vii, 206.

he fell prey to the ravages of age and forgot his train of thought in mid-speech.[147] However, his incapacity can be overemphasized, as he remained capable of considerable vigour for the next year, as evinced by his attendance at the privy council during the 1715 rebellion.[148] Sunderland was a divisive figure, and was probably left out for that reason. He reputedly went pale when the names of the lords justices were read out on 1 August.[149] He attended four of the opening five days of the parliamentary session, and on 5 August reported from committee the Lords' address of condolence and congratulations to George I. His omission enabled him to visit his ailing wife at Bath, although he cannot have been too pleased with the speculation linking his name with the lord lieutenancy of Ireland, a prestigious post but outside the main channels of power. His aim was rather to be reappointed secretary of state.[150]

Wharton was horse racing in Yorkshire on 1 August,[151] and, as he was not named to the regency, did not hasten back to London, arriving on the 9th,[152] being sworn into the privy council on the 10th,[153] and attending the Lords only on the 13th. He switched his attentions between London and Buckinghamshire, hosting a dinner on 21 August at his country house at Winchendon for the peripatetic Marlborough.[154] He was soon distracted by the forthcoming elections (due by law to be held within six months of the queen's demise), particularly in his native Buckinghamshire, where his attempts to entice Richard Hampden to stand on a joint ticket with Richard Grenville were rebuffed, and he turned his attentions to effecting a compromise with the tories. When this was achieved, the resultant carefully crafted agreement between Grenville and John Fleetwood (signed by 21 people, including five peers)[155] was challenged by Hampden, causing Wharton further trouble.[156]

Ormond remained commander-in-chief until the king's arrival. He was a poor attender of both parliament and privy council, probably because his main preoccupation was with military matters. Thus, he was instrumental in ordering the earl of Northampton back to his post in the Tower on 30 July.[157] He was much in Bothmer's thoughts, being briefly seen as a potential lord lieutenant of Ireland and then as a household official for the prince of Wales.[158] He was seen by some, such as Sir Richard Cox, the former lord chancellor of Ireland, as a potential protector of the tory interest in the new reign.[159]

Bishop Atterbury's hopes of becoming lord privy seal were dashed by the queen's death. What precisely Atterbury was doing, particularly on 1 August, has been a matter of

[147] *HPL, 1660–1715*, iv, 480.

[148] William L. Sachse, *Lord Somers: A Political Portrait* (Manchester, 1975), 314.

[149] *Wentworth Papers*, ed. Cartwright, 409.

[150] Macpherson, *Original Papers*, ii, 650.

[151] *Lady Mary Wortley Montagu Letters*, ed. Halsband, i, 210–11.

[152] BL, Add. MS 70292: Wharton diary, 9 Aug. 1714.

[153] TNA, PC 2/85/1, p. 42.

[154] HMC, *Portland MSS*, vii, 201–2.

[155] *Verney Letters of the Eighteenth Century from the MSS at Claydon House*, ed. Margaret Maria, Lady Verney (2 vols, 1930), i, 317.

[156] BL, Add. MS 70292: Wharton diary entries for August and September, demonstrate Wharton's problems in Buckinghamshire.

[157] HMC, *Townshend MSS*, 220.

[158] Macpherson, *Original Papers*, ii, 639–40.

[159] BL, Add. MS 38157, ff. 108–9: Sir Richard Cox to Edward Southwell, 14 Aug. 1714.

controversy, with some accounts suggesting that he urged the proclamation of the pretender as James III,[160] but generally these suggestions have been dismissed by historians. However, it should be noted that Atterbury did not sign the proclamation of the king, and that one of the stories told against him revealed a meeting held at Harcourt's at nine that morning between Atterbury, Ormond, Bolingbroke, Bathurst, and Sir William Wyndham,[161] making it plausible that a meeting was held to at least discuss the options available. More certainty concerns his efforts to rally the tories in the weeks following the succession, which eventually resulted in his polemic, *English Advice to the Freeholders of England*.[162]

The tories, in general, were still raw from the struggle which had seen Bolingbroke oust Oxford, but fail to implement his planned reorganisation of the ministry. Oxford's partisans crowed somewhat at their predicament, especially when Atterbury began to preach tory unity. Both sides sought to blame the other. Oxford posed as the man who had thwarted Bolingbroke's designs to bring in the pretender, aided and abetted by Atterbury and Harcourt. An indication of the depth of tory ill feeling was provided by Erasmus Lewis, writing to Swift on 10 August 1714, who conjectured that 'the earth has not produced such monsters' as Bolingbroke, Harcourt, and Atterbury.[163] Dr Stratford, another of Oxford's supporters, thought that this cabal would 'endeavour to draw the church party into an open breach with the present powers in hopes of heading them and being protected by them'.[164] On the other side, Swift was the recipient of Bolingbroke's criticism of Oxford, who had 'an air of such familiar friendship, and a heart so void of all tenderness, to such a temper of engrossing business and power, and so perfect an incapacity to manage one with such a tyrannical disposition to abuse the other'.[165]

The battle for places in the new regime may perhaps be best illuminated by an examination of the jockeying for position over the one post which everyone knew was up for grabs: the vacant and valuable bishopric of Ely. Lobbying began immediately, and reflected the divisions within the church. On 6 August, Bothmer in London recommended Dr John Hill to Bernstorff,[166] while on the following day William Bishop told Arthur Charlett that Bishop Talbot of Oxford was talked of for the vacancy.[167] White Kennett, the dean of Peterborough, explained the sequence of events. First in the field had been Lord Treasurer Shrewsbury on behalf of his kinsman, Bishop Talbot, followed swiftly by Nottingham in favour of his brother, Henry Finch, the dean of York. There was also support among the regents for the translation of Robinson from London, for Ely was a richer see and would

[160] See *Anecdotes, Observations, and Characters, of Books and Men … By Rev. Joseph Spence* (2nd edn, 1858), 55; BL, Add. MS 35837, f. 509: Col. Stanhope to Carteret, 29 Aug. 1722. G.V. Bennett, *The Tory Crisis in Church and State 1688–1730: The Career of Francis Atterbury, Bishop of Rochester* (Oxford, 1975), 182, is sceptical of these claims.

[161] BL, Add. MS 35837, f. 509: Col. Stanhope to Carteret, 29 Aug. 1722.

[162] Bennett, *Tory Crisis*, 185–95.

[163] *Swift Correspondence*, ed. Woolley, ii, 63–5.

[164] HMC, *Portland MSS*, vii, 199–200.

[165] *Swift Correspondence*, ed. Woolley, ii, 65–6.

[166] Macpherson, *Original Papers*, ii, 640. Hill can be identified by the references to him as a layman and to him resigning his admiralty position, where he had been a member of Prince George's council, 1702–8, and registrar of the admiralty court, 1712–14, when he resigned it to Samuel Hill, as he did the post of Latin Secretary. See J.C. Sainty, *Admiralty Officials 1660–1870* (Office-holders in Modern Britain, iv, 1975), 13; Sainty, *Officials of Secretaries of State*, 82.

[167] Bodl., Ballard MS 31, f. 128: William Bishop to Arthur Charlett, 7 Aug. 1714.

allow Robinson to be replaced by a man more congenial to the new regime. Kennett also noted that many supported Hill, despite him being 'in the habit and life of a layman for about 30 years past'. Kennett blamed Tenison for not declaring his opinion sooner, which would have forestalled lobbying: 'if he had pleased to tell the other Justices at first that he intended to recommend the bishop of St Asaph [Fleetwood] I believe nobody would have set up any thoughts of competition'.[168] Kennett was correct both in noting Tenison's role in recommending to the vacancy and in his assessment of tory support for Hill, which included the backing of Archbishop Dawes and Sir Thomas Hanmer.[169] The tory view was summed up by the Reverend Ralph Bridges, who wrote to Sir William Trumbull: 'I don't know any more pleasing step our gracious King George can do to ingratiate himself with the clergy of his Church.'[170] Even Kennett, however, missed other supplicants. Francis Hare, Marlborough's former army chaplain (soon to be made dean of Worcester), put himself forward on the grounds that Ely was seen as the province of Cambridge University, and that that being the case the only current bishop to fit that requirement was Fleetwood of St Asaph.[171] As no decision was made before the king's arrival, speculation did not cease. In September and October Finch and Hill were each variously reported to have secured the prize,[172] before the matter was settled when a *congé d'élire* for Fleetwood's election was issued on 18 November and the 'public papers' confirmed Fleetwood's translation on 19 November.[173]

Meanwhile, the king was delayed by contrary winds. He landed at Greenwich at six in the evening on 18 September,[174] where the first appointments were set in motion. Once in London, a meeting of the privy council was convened on 22 September. This was attended by 59 members, of whom 43 were current members of the Lords.[175] Three more councillors were sworn that day, Archbishop Dawes, Nottingham, and Halifax.[176] A clear indication of the shape of the new regime can be gleaned by comparing the attendance at the last privy council meeting, on 22 September, with that of 1 October. No fewer than 20 of those in attendance on 22 September were left out of the new body. These included Oxford and his allies, Mansell and Bingley, together with tories like Lansdown, Secretary Bromley,

---

[168] BL, Lansdowne MS 1013, f. 199: White Kennett to Rev. Samuel Blackwell, 21 Aug. 1714.

[169] Macpherson, *Original Papers*, ii, 641–2.

[170] BL, Add. MS 72496, ff. 153–4: Ralph Bridges to Sir William Trumbull, 3 Sept. 1714.

[171] BL, Add. MS 61303, ff. 33–4: Francis Hare to Marlborough, 3 Sept. 1714. Another candidate was Bishop Tyler of Llandaff: Bodl., Ballard MS 19, f. 62.

[172] HMC, *Portland MSS*, v, 493; Lambeth Palace Library, MS 930 (Tenison papers), no. 196: Tenison to Townshend, 5 Oct. 1714; BL, Add. MS 72502, ff. 13, 16–17: T[homas] B[ateman] to [Trumbull], 22 Oct., 1 Nov. 1714; *Prescott Diary II*, ed. Addy, 410.

[173] *Fasti Ecclesiae Anglicanae 1541–1857*, comp. Joyce M. Horn, vii: *Ely, Norwich, Westminster and Worcester Diocese* (1992), 9; *Prescott Diary II*, ed. Addy, 415.

[174] HMC, *Portland MSS*, v, 495.

[175] Four were former Scottish representative peers: Annandale, Ilay, Montrose, and Roxburghe. Annandale had been abroad since April 1712 (*HPL, 1660–1715*, v, 714), but was sworn into the privy council on 30 August.

[176] *London Gazette*, 21–25 Sept. 1714. Interestingly, Halifax attended the privy council on 6, 8, and 15 September, but appears never to have been sworn under the old council.

and Chancellor of the Exchequer Wyndham.[177] In all, 34 members of Queen Anne's privy council were not reappointed by her successor in the first year of the new reign.[178]

The old privy council was dismissed on 29 September and a new one constituted, with 33 named members to be sworn on 1 October.[179] All of George I's choices as regents were retained in the new privy council, and it was dominated by members of the Lords: 26 were members of the upper House (Montrose and Roxburghe would soon be again), and only five were commoners, Lord Chief Justice Parker, Vice-Chamberlain Thomas Coke, Paymaster Robert Walpole, Secretary James Stanhope, and the lieutenant-general of the ordnance, Thomas Erle.[180] The privy council was then expanded, so that by the end of October, there were 40 members.[181] By the end of the year a whole host of peers had been added and sworn in, including Bradford, Carleton (the former Henry Boyle), Derby, Dorchester, Ilay, Loudoun, Manchester, Northampton, Orrery, and Uxbridge.[182]

In the two months following the death of Queen Anne, the members of the house of lords played a significant role in ensuring that an orderly succession took place from the Stuarts to the Hanoverians. Apart from those disabled by reason of age or religion, very few failed to appear in London at some point during this period, and some of them had very good reasons for absence, such as diplomatic duties. Members were active in preparing for the king's arrival as well as manœuvring for position under the new regime.

[177] The full list is Northumberland, Stamford, Clarendon, Rochester, Mar, Findlater, Orkney, Oxford, Portmore, Guilford, Mansell, Trevor, Lansdown, Bingley, Secretary Bromley, Sir William Wyndham, Sir John Holland, John Smith, James Vernon, and John Hill. Findlater and Portmore returned in the 1720s.

[178] However, four prominent councillors were reappointed later in the reign: Portmore (1721), Harcourt (1722), Findlater (1723), and Trevor (1726).

[179] TNA, PC 2/85/1, pp. 86–7, shows that 26 were sworn, the exceptions being Archbishop Dawes, Wharton, Halifax, Pembroke, Anglesey, Abingdon, and Carlisle.

[180] TNA, PC 2/85/1, pp. 86–7.

[181] TNA, PC 1/2/262: list of the council October 1714. Annandale, Cholmondeley, Guernsey (soon to be Aylesford), Boscawen, Onslow, and Paul Methuen had been added by the end of October (probably by virtue of their appointment to offices). Also appointed was Stair, a Scottish representative peer in 1707–8 and again in 1715.

[182] TNA, PC 2/85/1, pp. 115, 118.

'A Reward for so Meritorious an Action'? Lord Hervey's Summons to the House of Lords and Walpole's Management of the Upper Chamber (1727–42)

ROBIN EAGLES

In 1733 Lord Hervey was summoned to the house of lords early. The move has traditionally been seen as part of an effort by Walpole to increase his ministry's strength in the upper chamber in spite of objections voiced by allies such as the duke of Newcastle. This essay seeks to reconsider the circumstances of the move and question more broadly the management of the Lords during the 'Robinocracy'.

Keywords: duels; excise crisis; house of lords; peerage; Sir Robert Walpole

1

On 14 February 1734, Lord Hervey wrote to his long-term friend, Henry Fox, detailing the happenings in parliament the previous day:

> We had yesterday a great debate in both Houses on the same Questions. The first was a Bill to make all commissions in the Army for life, which was moved in the House of Lords by your friend the Duke of Marlborough, who was extremely frightened, said but little, and what he did say was neither remarkably well or ill. He was seconded by Lord Winchilsea, who did better than usual; his words flowing easier, though his matter did not at all strengthen the stream … Lord Chesterfield spoke much the best on that side, and much the longest. He answered your humble servant, who, though not the best, spoke longest of any body on our side.[1]

Hervey's intervention in the debate on the Army Officers' Bill was his second major outing in the Lords since being called up early by a mechanism known as a writ in (or of) acceleration on 11 June 1733.[2] The conventional wisdom was that Hervey's summons at

---

[1] *Lord Hervey and His Friends 1726–38: Based on Letters from Holland House, Melbury, and Ickworth*, ed. earl of Ilchester (1950), 193–4.

[2] Hervey was introduced formally into the chamber on 12 June between Lords Walpole and De la Warr: *LJ*, xxiv, 307. H.T. Dickinson suggested inaccurately that Hervey, along with Lords Talbot, Hardwicke, and Hinton were all summoned to the Lords in 1734 'when Walpole's hold on the Lords seemed to be slipping': H.T. Dickinson, *Walpole and the Whig Supremacy* (1973), 79. Of these four, only Hinton was called up in 1734; Hervey, Hardwicke, and Talbot all received their summons the previous year, though it was not until 17 Jan. 1734 that Hinton, Hardwicke, and Talbot assumed their seats: *LJ*, xxiv, 320–1. It is also not, strictly speaking, accurate to describe all of these as new creations. Both Hervey and Hinton were heirs to earldoms, summoned by writs of acceleration at

that point had been intended to help bolster the court's presence in the upper chamber as a response to the threat to Walpole's administration which had been rocked first by the excise crisis[3] and then by the Lords' defeat of the ministry over the projected enquiries into the South Sea Company.[4] Hervey himself viewed his promotion to the Lords more as a means of increasing the ministry's cohort of capable speakers rather than simply increasing its voting bloc.[5] This interpretation was endorsed warmly by J.H. Plumb when considering Walpole's management of the Lords. Plumb viewed the handful of additions to the Lords of 1733 as evidence of Walpole's masterly handling of the chamber, supplementing the ministry's cohort of capable speakers with the addition of the contrasting talents of Hervey and the less flippant, but more rigorous, Lord Hardwicke.[6] This view was developed by Paul Langford, arguing that Hervey's admission to the Lords was one element in a two-part response by Walpole to improve his management of the upper chamber, 'partly by exerting more rigorous discipline over his followers there, partly by creating new peers who would add to the government's debating power'.[7] The ministry's problem in this regard appears to be borne out by a letter written in late May 1733 describing a debate of a few days previously when the court was 'overmatched in good speakers, the battle being chiefly maintained by the duke of Newcastle and Lord Islay', who were faced by the impressive talents of the dukes of Argyll and Montrose, the marquess of Tweeddale, and several others, including the earl of Chesterfield and Lord Carteret.[8] In this situation the prospect of offering Newcastle and his lieutenants some assistance certainly seems to make good sense.

There are, however, additional factors that need to be considered alongside the traditional explanations put forward for Hervey's elevation at this juncture. If it was intended simply as a way of bolstering the ministry's numbers in the Lords, the addition of Hervey at this point made little real difference, his summons being granted when the session was all but concluded. Ministries under pressure had previously responded to problems in the Lords with the addition of several new lords at once, but this was not Walpole's response now.[9] Besides, Walpole faced dissent in both houses of parliament, and although he could be

---

[3] On 29 March 1733, Lord Bathurst had warned Jonathan Swift: 'Now I must tell yu I want exceedingly to see yu here, & I wou'd have yu come just abt midsum[m]er, if yu come a moment before that time, yu will find the Parlt sitting, all in a flame abt Excises, & go into wt Company yu will, yu can hear of nothing else ...': *The Correspondence of Jonathan Swift DD*, ed. David Woolley (5 vols, Frankfurt am Main, 1999–2014), iii, 612.

[4] The best account of the excise crisis remains Paul Langford, *The Excise Crisis: Society and Politics in the Age of Walpole* (Oxford, 1975). According to Shin Matsuzono, the session of 1732–3 was 'a watershed in the long premiership of Sir Robert Walpole', most notably seen over the opposition to the Excise Bill: Shin Matsuzono, ' "Attaque and Break Through a Phalanx of Corruption ... the Court Party!" The Scottish Representative Peers' Election and the Opposition, 1733–5: Three New Division Lists of the House of Lords of 1735', *Parliamentary History*, xxxi (2012), 333.

[5] 'Just before the Parliament rose Lord Hervey was called up by writ to the House of Peers, where there was so great a want of speakers that the Court determined to make a recruit by next winter and began with this': *Some Materials towards Memoirs of the Reign of King George II, by John, Lord Hervey*, ed. Romney Sedgwick (3 vols, 1931), i, 204.

[6] J.H. Plumb, *Sir Robert Walpole: The King's Minister* (1960), 281.

[7] Paul Langford, *A Polite and Commercial People: England 1727–1783* (Oxford, 1989), 34.

[8] HMC, *Carlisle MSS*, 117–18.

[9] Walpole may well have been reluctant to fall foul of the same criticism which he himself had directed at his predecessor, Robert Harley, earl of Oxford, who had overseen the addition of 12 new peers at a stroke in the winter of 1711–12.

entirely confident that Hervey would be replaced with a complacent member of his family in the seat he was vacating,[10] he was losing a valuable supporter in the Commons.

Adding to the ministry's speaking strength in the upper chamber would, on the face of it, seem a plausible reason for recruiting Hervey to the Lords at this point. He had a reputation as an effective speaker in the Commons and such talents were in relatively short supply in the upper House.[11] In February 1730, he had spoken in support of the ministry in the debate on the Hessians:[12] a dramatic occasion that saw one former ministry MP, George Heathcote, abandon the administration after making 'a flaming speech against the Court, which he had collected from a common-place book on tyranny and arbitrary power'.[13] Thomas Winnington, in his report of the proceedings, noted that Hervey 'spoke for them very well', though what was perhaps most noteworthy was that he did so without notes.[14] Newcastle, on the other hand, was considered a ponderous orator and few others on the government benches in the Lords were much more enlivening. Despite this, Hervey claimed that Newcastle opposed admitting him to the Lords, as did Walpole's son-in-law, Lord Cholmondeley.[15] Newcastle was said later to have been similarly vehement in his opposition to Hervey being made lord privy seal.[16] If this was so, Walpole's sponsoring of Hervey's peerage was presumably key, though according to a memoir compiled by Arthur Onslow, Walpole paid little heed to the Lords. According to Onslow the Commons was:

where the chief scene of business lay, and if he [Walpole] got his affairs through that place he was not very solicitous as to what might happen in the House of Lords, where

[10] Hervey had represented Bury St Edmunds since April 1725. The seat was dominated by his father as high steward and almost invariably returned either a member of the Hervey family or a close associate. The exception was in 1722, when Hervey's elder brother, Carr Hervey, had lost his seat, having failed to make any effort to maintain his interest in the borough: see *The History of Parliament: The House of Commons, 1715–1754*, ed. Romney Sedgwick (2 vols, 1970) [hereafter cited as *HPC, 1715–54*], ii, 132–5.

[11] Michael McCahill has pointed out for the period after 1760 that: 'If few peers attended the house of lords on a regular basis, fewer still spoke during its debates'. At the time of Hervey's summons, the levels of attendance were not quite so low as in the period with which McCahill is concerned, but there does seem some correlation with a corps of ministerial and anti-ministerial speakers dominating interventions in the chamber: M.W. McCahill, *The House of Lords in the Age of George III (1760–1811)* (Oxford, 2009), 114.

[12] By coincidence, 13 years later one of Hervey's final interventions, just six months before his premature death, was on the similar subject of the Hanover troops. According to John Campbell, on this latter occasion (1 Feb. 1743) Hervey 'spoke long and handsomely against the measures of forming an army in our pay in Flanders', while mentioning the Hanover troops in particular: *The Correspondence of John Campbell MP, with His Family, Henry Fox, Sir Robert Walpole and the Duke of Newcastle, 1734–71*, ed. J.E. Davies (Oxford, 2014), 132.

[13] As Jeremy Black has pointed out: 'In the first half of the eighteenth century some of the bitterest parliamentary debates over foreign policy centred on the issue of the payment of subsidies to the Landgraves of Hesse-Cassel': Jeremy Black, 'Parliament and Foreign Policy in the Age of Walpole: The Case of the Hessians', in *Knights Errant and True Englishmen: British Foreign Policy, 1660–1800*, ed. Jeremy Black (Edinburgh, 1989), 42, 49.

[14] Speaking without recourse to papers seems to have been highly prized. A manuscript account of the debates surrounding Viscount Limerick's motion to have a secret committee established to investigate Walpole following his fall from power in the spring of 1742 made particular mention of the contribution by Pitt the Elder, 'who always speaks well and as he answered all that had been said, it cou'd not be a set speech': Kent History and Library Centre, Sackville MSS, U269/O303: proceedings in the Commons, 23 Mar. 1742. Hervey seems to have had the same talent for speaking without any need for prompts.

[15] *Hervey Memoirs*, ed. Sedgwick, i, 204.

[16] Hannah Smith and Stephen Taylor, 'Hephaestion and Alexander: Lord Hervey, Frederick, Prince of Wales, and the Royal Favourite in England in the 1730s', *English Historical Review*, cxxiv (2009), 301.

the party against him was very small, and a speech or two from Lord Carteret and from two or three more, was all he had to fear.[17]

Why, then, was Hervey projected into the upper chamber at this point? This essay will seek to revisit the political conditions that may have contributed to the move and Hervey's own apparent desire to quit the Commons and seek a more suitable home for himself in the house of lords. It will also reflect more broadly on the state of the peerage in the early years of George II and how the king's famously parsimonious attitude towards new creations and keen interest in the personnel of his own household may help explain the promotion of a man like Hervey to the upper chamber in the 1730s.[18]

2

From the restoration of the monarchy (and house of lords) in 1660 to the accession of George I, the overall size of the English (later British) peerage capable of taking their seats in the Lords remained remarkably stable. At the close of 1660 some 132 men were eligible to sit in the House, and by the close of 1715 this number had risen to just 140. This relatively small increase, however, fails to reflect the number of new creations made by Charles II, James II, William III and Mary II, and finally by Queen Anne.[19] Although there had been years when Charles II admitted few new members to the upper House, overall his reign saw a substantial rise in the numbers of those admitted to peerages. The rate of creations in James II's brief reign was not dissimilar to that under his brother, while William and Mary rewarded many for their support during the 'Glorious Revolution' with 14 receiving new honours in 1689 alone. The situation had become more dramatic still under Queen Anne, when, on two occasions, 'mass creations' had been used for clear political ends. First, in March 1703 there were seven peerages handed out in the space of a few days: five of them new baronies, and the other two promotions in the peerage for the marquess of Normanby[20] and earl of Rutland.[21] More controversially, in the winter of 1711–12 was the creation of 'Harley's dozen': an almost unprecedented mass creation of new peers with the purpose of stabilising the regime of Queen Anne's lord treasurer, Robert Harley, earl of Oxford (himself only recently the recipient of a new peerage). Outrage at the 1712 mass creation would later lead to the whigs including it within the articles of impeachment brought against Oxford following Queen Anne's death,[22] but this did not stop George I

---

[17] HMC, *14th Report*, ix, 471.

[18] According to Hervey's biographer, Robert Halsband, the intervention of the king and queen was at the heart of Hervey's promotion to the Lords, though in arguing this, Halsband follows closely, and relatively uncritically, Hervey's own interpretation of events: Robert Halsband, *Lord Hervey: Eighteenth-Century Courtier* (Oxford, 1973), 147–8.

[19] *The History of Parliament: The House of Lords, 1660–1715*, ed. Ruth Paley (5 vols, Cambridge, 2016), i, 17.

[20] John Sheffield, marquess of Normanby, created duke of Buckingham and Normanby.

[21] John Manners, 9th earl of Rutland, created duke of Rutland.

[22] Oxford's flooding of the Lords caused resentment for a number of reasons, one of which was alluded to in a notice in the newspapers at the time of Thomas Parker's creation as Baron Parker: ''Tis observable, that as his Lordship's Merits set forth in the Preamble to his Patent, are bright and unquestionable, so the style is truly Noble and Roman, and without any Blunders, which were common in a Dozen Patents made all together not many years ago': *Flying Post*, 13–15 Mar. 1716.

from making use of his privilege of creating significant numbers of new members of the Lords on occasion as well. There were 14 coronation peerages created in 1714, and in June 1716 six more leading figures were rewarded with British titles (five of them new baronies and one a promotion from baron to viscount) to help add to the administration's numbers in the upper House.[23]

If the overall numbers remained relatively static, this is explicable through the loss of a number of catholic peers, who surrendered their right to sit in the Lords by refusing to take the appropriate oaths, by the succession of a number of peers under age,[24] and by the significant numbers of peers who failed to produce heirs to carry on their titles. Between the Restoration and the Hanoverian succession several prominent dynasties became extinct.[25] The picture remained fairly similar during the early years of the new dynasty. The dukedom of Shrewsbury became extinct on the death of the first duke in 1718,[26] and the barony of Torrington, awarded to Thomas Newport in 1716, failed on his death a few years later allowing the title to be recreated (as a viscountcy) in 1721 for Sir George Byng. Similarly, the rate of creations matched closely what had gone before. In his reign of just over a dozen years (1714–27) George I awarded 66 new peerages at a rate of just over five a year. Some of these amounted to additional titles for the same person (for example Thomas Coningsby, the recipient of both a barony and an earldom), while there were also awards to women, unable to sit in the House, and several titles granted to members of the royal family.[27] Under his son, however, there was a dramatic reversal. Promotions to the house of lords under George II were markedly less frequent than they had been under any monarch post-Restoration. It is especially striking that no new peers were created in 1727, the year the king came to the throne, with the majority of those anticipating new honours being made to wait until the early summer of the following year.[28] Even his eldest son, the prince of

[23] Baron Coningsby, Baron Onslow, Baron Torrington, Baron Cadogan, Baron Romney, and Viscount Castleton.

[24] E.g., on the death of John Sheffield, duke of Buckingham, in 1721, he was succeeded as 2nd duke by his underage son, Edmund, who died 14 years later, just short of his 21st birthday, and thus never attended the Lords.

[25] The Villiers title of duke of Buckingham failed with the death of the 2nd duke in 1685, though a cadet branch endured with the earls of Jersey. The Lennard Lords Dacre (briefly earls of Sussex) barely made it into the Hanoverian period before the barony fell into abeyance between the sisters of the last earl and was only revived finally in the 1750s. Some new creations, such as the earldom of Romney, created for Henry Sydney, failed on the death of the first holder of the title, as did the barony of Somers created for the junto leader, John Somers, shortly after the accession of George I.

[26] The earldom was inherited by the duke's catholic cousin, Gilbert Talbot, who, as a jesuit priest, declined to adopt the title.

[27] Andrew Hanham points out that between 1714 and George I's death there were 22 additions to the Lords (excluding grants to immediate members of the royal family), underlining the extent to which a large proportion of new grants were additions to those already sitting in the upper chamber. If one includes the title earl of Graham granted to the marquess of Graham, heir to the dukedom of Montrose, and that of earl of Ker granted to the marquess of Bowmont, heir to the dukedom of Roxburghe, both of them Scots peerages and thus excluded from the Lords except through election as one of the 16 representative peers of Scotland, the figure increases to 24: Andrew Hanham, 'The Politics of Chivalry: Sir Robert Walpole, the Duke of Montagu and the Order of the Bath', *Parliamentary History*, xxxv (2016), 271.

[28] The one exception to this was the Commons' Speaker, Sir Spencer Compton, who was promoted Baron Wilmington in January 1728. The remaining creations of that year were all handed out on 28 May, with their warrants timed to avoid confusion about their respective precedencies: see J.C. Sainty, *Peerage Creations: Chronological Lists of Creations in the Peerages of England and Great Britain 1649–1800 and of Ireland 1603–1898* (Oxford, 2008), 35–6.

Wales, was made to wait until January 1729 – some 18 months after his father had acceded to the throne – to be confirmed as such, being left in the intervening period technically as duke of Edinburgh.[29] In the course of that year there was just one more creation – an earldom for Baron Waldegrave. In 1730 one new man was admitted to the house of lords, with three others being promoted.[30] In 1731 there was, again, one addition (and one promotion).[31] No peerages were handed out between 1735 and 1740 and between 1756 and 1759 there was another desert period during which anyone hoping for elevation to the Lords was left disappointed. Indeed, in the whole of George II's reign of 33 years just 74 peerages were doled out (a rate of just over two a year) and (as above) some of these were promotions in the peerage to existing peers, while another three were peerages granted to women who could not sit in the house of lords. This appears to bear out the popular (if not entirely warranted) conception that George II was not a generous man.[32] Under him there was a demonstrable reduction in the rate of adding men (and women) to the highest accolade in society: membership of the titled peerage.[33]

George II may have been chary of creating new peers, but that did not prevent the usual speculation emerging in the press at regular intervals about prominent individuals who were expected to be awarded with membership of the Lords. In June 1727, one paper predicted confidently that Sir Robert Sutton, Sir Thomas Watson Wentworth, Sir John Hobart, Sir Thomas Coke, and Sir William Morgan of Tredegar were all to be made peers, pointing out that they were all knights of the recently restored order of the Bath.[34] Two months later, there were reports of the promotion of Admiral Sir John Norris, which failed to come to pass.[35] However, this does not mean to say that the king (with the advice of his ministers) was unwilling to make use of his prerogative when it was politically expedient. This is the

---

[29] Frederick Lewis, prince of Wales, was inaccurately referred to as duke of Gloucester for much of his grandfather's reign, prior to his creation as duke of Edinburgh in 1726 (shortly after turning 21 years). It was, in part, the determination of the house of lords to send him a writ of summons that eventually compelled George II to bring him over from Hanover in 1728.

[30] The new peer was William Stanhope, created Baron Harrington; the other three creations were all earldoms for respectively Lord Ashburnham, Lord Fitzwalter, and Lord Wilmington. According to the newspapers there ought to have been at least two more with reports circulating in April of a peerage for Sir Charles Hotham and in July of one for Henry Pelham, Newcastle's younger brother: _London Evening Post_, 7–9 Apr., 23–5 July 1730.

[31] The addition was Robert Raymond, lord chief justice of king's bench, created Baron Raymond; the promotion was Lord Howard of Effingham, advanced to an earldom.

[32] The king's frugality was a byword during his lifetime. In the summer of 1733, Viscount Perceval recorded a conversation with Horatio Walpole in which the latter stated: 'that nothing ever did the King so much hurt as asking for the £115,000 some years ago; that it is not forgot yet, it being known that his Majesty, when even Prince, was a frugal manager of his revenue and had saved': HMC, _Egmont Diary_, i, 375.

[33] Andrew Thompson has gone some way to addressing the assumption that George II was mean: 'Accusations of parsimony need to be balanced by the king's unostentatious use of his own funds in support of worthy causes': A.C. Thompson, _George II: King and Elector_ (2011), 7. Hannah Smith makes the point that in one regard George II did demonstrate a degree of liberality by increasing the numbers of officeholders at court, but she concedes 'beyond this he proved chary': Hannah Smith, _Georgian Monarchy: Politics and Culture, 1714–1760_ (Cambridge, 2006), 70. In addition, Andrew Hanham has argued persuasively that it was not so much George II as Walpole who was to blame for the dearth of peerages, pointing out that: 'the number of peerage creations was noticeably more plentiful during the years when Walpole was not in power': Hanham, 'Politics of Chivalry', 271.

[34] _Daily Journal_, 10 June 1727. Of the men listed, Watson, Wentworth, Hobart, and Coke were created peers in 1728. The others were unsuccessful.

[35] _Parker's Penny Post_, 11 Aug. 1727. Norris was married to the daughter of an Irish peer, Lord Aylmer, and had thus far been a dependable ministry supporter as MP for Rye and Portsmouth. He rebelled in 1730 and was removed from office the following year, remaining in opposition until 1734: see _HPC, 1715–54_, ii, 298.

clear implication of the creations of May 1728, all of which were handed out to men who had been mentioned in the press some time before as likely to receive such an accolade and who appear to have been made to wait while the new administration settled in.[36] It also helps underscore the fact that the king remained a central figure in the granting of certain key distinctions closely associated with the prerogative. Appointments to his household were one; the granting of peerages another.[37]

Walpole's attitude (as suggested above) was also telling. He had stood out against the proposed Peerage Bill in 1719, regaling his listeners with details of a conversation he claimed to have heard from another MP, who had expostulated, 'What, shall I consent to the shutting the door upon my family ever coming into the House of Lords?'[38] Some contemporaries (and many later historians) may have viewed the period of 'Robinocracy' as one during which the Commons became more significant than the Lords,[39] but this did not mean that a peerage was a mere bauble. Walpole certainly understood the value of the honour. This was true both of those seeking promotion to the British house of lords, as well as those seeking additional honours in, for example, the peerage of Ireland.[40] Besides, if Walpole preferred for the majority of his career to remain in the Commons, eschewing elevation to the Lords in the early 1720s, he was not unwilling to see his family ennobled. Thus, rather than accepting a peerage for himself[41] one was granted instead to his heir, another Robert, as Baron Walpole.[42]

In one regard, though, the situation under George II mirrored exactly that under George I, during whose reign four heirs to peerages were summoned to the Lords by writs of acceleration.[43] Under George II the device was employed on four occasions, in favour of Baron Hinton (heir to Earl Poulett), Baron Hyde (heir to the 4th earl of Clarendon and 2nd earl of Rochester), Baron Cavendish (heir to the 3rd duke of Devonshire) and Lord Hervey.[44] Summoning by writ of acceleration was a device that was used sparingly but

[36] The recipients were Sir John Hobart, created Baron Hobart; Sir John Monson, created Baron Monson; Sir Thomas Wentworth, created Baron Malton; and Sir Thomas Coke, created Baron Lovel.

[37] A well-known example of the king asserting his rights over a household position was when the duke of Newcastle attempted to foist on him the superannuated duke of Dorset as the king's new groom of the stole. The king had none of it, and Dorset was, instead, appointed master of the horse.

[38] HMC, 14th Report, ix, 459.

[39] W.B. Pemberton's study of Lord Carteret emphasizes that Carteret's greatest 'misfortune' was to have inherited a peerage: 'At the date of his majority the Lords was the nerve-centre of the body politic, and a seat in the Upper House was the goal of every member of the Commons … But within a space of twenty years Walpole had reversed the importance of the two Houses': W.B. Pemberton, *Carteret: The Brilliant Failure of the Eighteenth Century* (1936), 123.

[40] At the same time as Lord Hervey was granted his peerage, Viscount Perceval was lobbying hard to secure his own advancement to an Irish earldom: HMC, *Egmont Diary*, i, 384.

[41] The title offered was said to have been the earldom of Walsingham.

[42] It is also worth noting that by no means all of those elevated to peerages during the period of Walpole's ascendancy were superannuated politicians seeking retirement. In May 1728, Sir Hobart, Sir John Monson, and Sir Thomas Coke were among those elevated to peerage. Hobart was aged 34 years, Monson around 35 years, and Coke just short of 31 years. Monson and Coke, besides, had been in the Commons only since 1722, so in neither case could these be considered 'long service awards'.

[43] Baron Willoughby d'Eresby, Baron Lumley, Baron Lucas, and Baron Townshend.

[44] Hervey's father, John Hervey, earl of Bristol, had been one of those first ennobled during the 'mass creation' of March 1703 as Baron Hervey. He was subsequently promoted to the earldom among the 1714 coronation honours.

was a helpful means of adding to the numbers in the house of lords without technically increasing the size of the peerage as the recipients were expected to inherit their peerages in due course, thereby cancelling out the additional grant. Summoning Hervey to the Lords in this way seems to underscore the fact that this was an elevation reflecting political necessity. Why else would the king (advised by Walpole) seek to remove a loyal member from the house of commons and send him 'upstairs'?

Certainly, the timing is suggestive that Hervey's acceleration reflected political necessity. As has been suggested above, the years 1732–3 were particularly fraught for Walpole, with the divisions over the excise coming close to terminating his premiership.[45] Even the normally pliable house of lords, easily manipulated through the election of reliable Scots peers[46] and nomination of dependable bishops, threatened to upset his programme. Hervey's *Memoirs* noted:

> It was hoped by Sir Robert Walpole's enemies, more than feared by his friends, that the defection among the Lords on this point of the excises would be very considerable, and that several who had long wished him ill in secret, though in public they had abetted all his measures, would take this opportunity to strike at him.[47]

Most worrying for Walpole was the desertion of men like the earl of Chesterfield to the ranks of the opposition, but there was also a minor downturn in the numbers of government supporters as a result of the death of a small number of British peers during the period. In the course of 1733, the house of lords saw the loss of seven peers – one of them a Scots representative.[48] Another, Philip Gerard, Lord Gerard, was a catholic (indeed he was a jesuit priest) so had never taken his seat in the Lords, and his death constituted no loss to the government. Charles Howard, 9th earl of Suffolk, had been an opponent of Walpole and was succeeded by another anti-Walpole member, Henry Howard, 10th earl of Suffolk, thereby retaining the balance. However, the death of Lord Raymond did result in a slight decrease in the government's voting strength, as Raymond's heir was underage and unable to take his seat. Combined with the loss to the opposition of men like Chesterfield, this constituted a small but potentially worrying diminution in the government's voting strength and helps to explain the promotion of three men to the Lords to help make up for these losses. Thus, the addition to the house of lords in the course of the year of Hervey, along

---

[45] Opposition to the scheme for introducing an excise on wine and tobacco inspired widespread popular protests as well as divisions at court. According to James Ralph: 'Never, in the Memory of Man, was the Nation so alarm'd at the Design of a Minister, as in the Case of the projected Excise': quoted in Langford, *Excise Crisis*, 1.

[46] The Act of Union of 1707 had provided for the election of 16 representative peers from among the Scottish peerage. In theory, this was an open election, but in reality, ministries had become adept at ensuring that only men from their approved lists tended to be returned. This, of course, did not mean that the men returned remained pliant, and there had been several occasions when the Scots peers acting en bloc had caused administrations considerable difficulties. For more, see Clyve Jones, 'The Division that Never Was: New Evidence on the Aborted Vote in the Lords on 8 December 1711 on "No Peace Without Spain" ', *Parliamentary History*, ii (1983), 191–202; and Clyve Jones, ' "Venice Preserv'd; or A Plot Discovered": The Political and Social Context of the Peerage Bill of 1719', in *A Pillar of the Constitution: The House of Lords in British Politics, 1640–1784*, ed. Clyve Jones (1989), 84–5.

[47] *Hervey Memoirs*, ed. Sedgwick, i, 135–6.

[48] George Byng, Viscount Torrington; George Cholmondeley, 2nd earl of Cholmondeley; Philip Gerard, Lord Gerard; Thomas Herbert, 8th earl of Pembroke; Charles Howard, 9th earl of Suffolk; Robert Raymond, Lord Raymond.

with Sir Philip Yorke, created Baron Hardwicke, and Charles Talbot, created Baron Talbot, offset the loss of Raymond and even added to the administration's forces by two.

And yet is this enough to explain Hervey's promotion? Hervey's summons came just days before a prorogation, so his elevation is more suggestive of an administration planning for the session ahead – and perhaps anticipating a need to strengthen its future debating talent, as Hervey himself suggested – rather than an immediate requirement to bolster numbers. Other factors also need to be considered. Hervey had proved a vital conduit between parliament and the court during the excise crisis, and in May 1733 the Lords had witnessed spirited debates about the use of the sinking fund to help supply £80,000 towards the princess royal's wedding portion. Did this close assault on the court prompt George II (and perhaps also Queen Caroline) to suggest the addition of a reliable courtier to the Lords to attend to such matters, rather than the administration merely seeking to make up for the defection of a highly-talented speaker, Chesterfield, to the opposition? Hervey, after all, had been appointed vice-chamberlain of the household in 1730 and since then had proved a loyal adherent of the royal family.[49] He was particularly attached to the queen, uniting with her against the prince of Wales, with whom Hervey had once been closely associated.[50] Certainly there is evidence elsewhere for the king taking a close interest in the disposition of places in his household, most notably in 1755 when the duke of Newcastle and Lord Hardwicke agitated for a place in the bedchamber for George, 3rd earl of Orford, and to foist the ageing duke of Dorset on him as groom of the stole. George II refused both, preferring the earl of Essex to Orford and putting his foot down over Dorset, whom he considered too old to undertake the duties of a groom of the stole.[51] The role of the queen, too, needs to be borne in mind.[52] Hervey claimed to spend much of his time reporting back to Queen Caroline the proceedings in either House, and it may as much have been his role as a go-between for the queen's household to parliament as a loyal ministry supporter that helped ensure his progression to the upper House.[53]

3

Hervey's elevation had been long anticipated. Towards the end of January 1731 he and his erstwhile friend, William Pulteney, member of parliament and political journalist, had faced off for a duel over a piece written by Pulteney in the form of a letter to the *Craftsman*. Pulteney's piece was composed in answer to a pamphlet, *Sedition and Defamation Display'd*,

---

[49] It is perhaps significant, also, that Hervey's brother, Thomas, was appointed vice-chamberlain of the queen's household in 1733.

[50] Smith and Taylor, 'Hephaestion and Alexander', 293–4. Hervey himself casts some doubt on just how crucial the role of the king and queen may have been in initiating his elevation. Rather, he suggested that the idea was Walpole's, who recommended it to Queen Caroline, by whom it was passed to the king and thence back to Walpole again: P.C. Yorke, *The Life and Correspondence of Philip Yorke, Earl of Hardwicke* (3 vols, Cambridge, 1913), i, 118.

[51] Thompson, *George II*, 230–1.

[52] Some have pointed to the joint interventions of Walpole and the queen as crucial at this point: 'With the Commons docile again, Walpole tackled the mutinous clique in the House of Lords. The Queen agreed that discipline was as necessary in an administration as in an army': R.L. Arkell, *Caroline of Anspach: George the Second's Queen* (Oxford, 1939), 205.

[53] *Hervey Memoirs*, ed. Sedgwick, i, 143.

the preface to which had in all probability been penned by Hervey (though Hervey denied its authorship). Pulteney's response, accusing Hervey (among other things) of homosexuality, had been viewed widely as provocative. It had left Hervey little room for manœuvre[54] and a challenge had been the result. On 25 January both men, accompanied by their seconds, Henry Fox for Hervey, and Sir John Rushout for Pulteney, made their way to St James's Park and proceeded to settle the matter at sword point. The affair was not protracted and resulted in Hervey sustaining minor injuries to his neck and arm,[55] while Pulteney seems to have got off with a grazed hand.[56] One report suggested that Hervey had been disarmed, but this was soon retracted.[57] Another reported that Pulteney had almost succeeded in running his opponent through, but that his foot had slipped on the frosty ground and the respective seconds had intervened.[58]

The story surrounding the duel, such as it was, has been studied in detail elsewhere.[59] However, one aspect of the duel's aftermath is less well known: shortly afterwards reports circulated that Hervey and Viscount Malpas (heir to the earldom of Cholmondeley and Walpole's son-in-law) were both to be called up to the Lords by writ.[60] The first suggestion of this appears to have been a report in the *Daily Post* of 29 January, which was repeated in other papers and in private correspondence.[61] In a letter to his father, James Cheape, laird of Rossie, a significant Fife and Perthshire landowner, Harry Cheape, wrote that Hervey's promotion was intended specifically 'as a reward for so meritorious an action' in his recent duel with Pulteney.[62] While this reflected the court's unsurprising hostility to Pulteney, it also presented an attitude at odds with the usual reaction to duelling. While it was an accepted part of the honour code of the period, duelling was frowned upon by the authorities. Parliament took a close interest in its members engaging in such quarrels and on numerous occasions took action to prevent duels taking place. Duellists were not protected by the law in any way and anyone killing his opponent was deemed guilty of either murder or manslaughter in the eyes of the law, depending on the circumstances of the affair.

The rumour that Hervey was to be rewarded so publicly is thus of interest in itself. One correspondent writing to the earl of Carlisle in the aftermath of the duel reckoned 'the whole will turn to Lord Hervey's service, he knowing well how to make a merit of this at Court', though she did not mention any rumour of him being summoned to the

---

[54]In his diary entry for 25 Jan. 1731, Hervey's father, the earl of Bristol, recorded: 'Monday, my son Lord Hervey upon the justest provocations sent a challenge to his till then suppos'd friend, Mr William Pulteney, & fought a duel with him in St James's Park': *The Diary of John Hervey, First Earl of Bristol* … (Wells, 1894), 81.

[55]*London Evening Post*, 26–8 Jan. 1731.

[56]*Daily Journal*, 29 Jan. 1731.

[57]*Daily Post*, 30 Jan. 1731. The account was repeated in the *London Journal* for 30 Jan. 1731, presumably borrowing the story from the *Daily Post*.

[58]Lucy Moore, *Amphibious Thing: The Life of Lord Hervey* (2000), 120.

[59]Robert Halsband, 'The Duel', *History Today*, xxii (1972), 346–54; Halsband, *Hervey*, 113–19.

[60]George Cholmondeley, Viscount Malpas, had married Walpole's daughter in 1723. At the time of the reports of his likely summons to the Lords he was MP for New Windsor, having previously represented East Looe from 1724 to 1727.

[61]*Country Journal or the Craftsman*, 30 Jan. 1731; *Universal Spectator and Weekly Journal*, 30 Jan. 1731.

[62]St Andrews University Library, Cheape papers, MS 36929, box 7/627: Harry Cheape to James Cheape of Rossie, 6 Feb. 1733.

Lords.[63] None the less, in the days following the duel there appeared to be every reason to believe that (whatever the justification) the rumours of new peerages being granted were well founded. On 4 February, one paper reported that the previous Tuesday (2 February) both Malpas and Hervey had presented themselves at the court of exchequer and taken the oaths 'in order to qualify themselves to sit in the House of Peers; but no writs having been served as yet for that purpose, they have not yet taken their seats in that House, as has been reported in several newspapers'.[64] A delay in issuing the anticipated writs may have been because Walpole was simply not in need of additions to the Lords at this point and thereafter the story appears to have disappeared from the press.[65] A brief overview of the business before the Lords during that period underscores this lack of need for additions at this juncture. On 21 January an opposition effort to move an address in reply to the king's speech was easily defeated by 84 votes to 23. The following month, on 19 February, the Pension Bill was batted away with little difficulty, with the administration carrying the day by 48 votes to 16, and the following day a second division on the bill resulted in another government victory, by 81 votes to 30. On 2 March the ministry was able to prevent the Pension Bill being committed by 93 votes to 48, and on 1 May carried the division on the Hessians by 73 votes to 22. None of these votes suggests that the ministry was ever in serious difficulty during the session, which may help to explain the failure to award Hervey a peerage, whatever the rumours of likely rewards for his gallantry may have suggested.

4

By 1733, the situation for the government had altered substantially. Walpole's travails over the excise had come perilously close to toppling him and he was by then in very definite need of additional resources in both houses of parliament. Towards the end of the year, two dependable government supporters were advanced to the Lords: Yorke and Talbot, the former a firm adherent of Newcastle's, who had represented Lewes and then Seaford on the duke's interest. According to Reed Browning: 'the two men founded what would become the most powerful friendship of eighteenth-century politics', with Hardwicke acting as Newcastle's 'sheet-anchor'.[66]

Prior to these creations, the ministry's numbers in the Lords had been further strengthened with Hervey's summons. There are indications that word of Hervey's likely promotion (and perhaps those of others) had been circulating for some time before he was eventually called to the Lords. In March at least one newspaper reported that his brother, Thomas, was to stand for Bury St Edmunds at the next election (in 1734).[67] There was nothing to suggest that Hervey's partner in the seat, Thomas Newton, was likely to step down, which suggests

[63] HMC, *Carlisle MSS*, 80.

[64] *Daily Courant*, 4 Feb. 1731.

[65] On 15 January, Sir Robert Raymond had been summoned to the Lords as Baron Raymond. There were no other creations that year until December when Francis Howard, Lord Howard of Effingham, was granted a promotion to an earldom: see Sainty, *Creations*, 36.

[66] Reed Browning, *The Duke of Newcastle* (New Haven, CT, 1975), 18.

[67] *London Evening Post*, 15–17 Mar. 1733. The story was repeated in the *Daily Courant* on 19 Mar. 1733. This report followed on from another of a few days before it, recording that Thomas Hervey was to be appointed the queen's vice-chamberlain: *London Evening Post*, 8–10 Mar. 1733.

that Hervey's retirement from the Commons (or relocation to another seat) was already anticipated. At the same time that Hervey was finally granted his writ of summons, reports suggested that Arthur Onslow would also join him in the upper House.[68] Onslow was far from so straightforward a ministerial vote as Hervey. A nephew of Sir Richard Onslow, he had been a supporter of Walpole, but in 1731 had fallen from favour and in 1732 had voted with the opposition on the army estimates. He had returned to the court fold over the excise, which may have helped fuel rumours of his being rewarded with ennoblement.

In spite of the numerous rumours circulating of Hervey's likely summons, his elevation appears to have taken his father by surprise:

> As I am a stranger to ye many secret motives which must have influenced your choice so suddenly to exchange ye important House you was a member of for so insignificant an one as your friend and you have endeavoured to make that you are to be translated to, I will not take upon me to determine whether upon the whole it was well judged or not.[69]

(As had been trailed some months before) Hervey's advancement left open his seat at Bury St Edmunds, but on 18 June, Hervey was able to assure the king that his brother was unopposed there, and that his only reason for making the journey to Bury himself was 'to obey the commands of your Majesty's Speech to your Parliament, and as far as my capacity will assist my zeal, to undeceive the deluded, and point out the force of Truth with regard to every misrepresented measure of this last winter'.[70]

Hervey's relief at being freed from attendance of the Commons was palpable and offers a further explanation for his removal to the Lords. In December 1731, in a letter to his intimate friend, Stephen Fox, he complained: 'I look with more horror on the meeting of the Parliament, than my little son does on Monday sennight, when the holidays determine and he is to go to school again.'[71] He expressed similar sentiments soon after his elevation to the Lords in a letter to his 'cousin', Charlotte Digby.[72]

5

Hervey may have been glad to leave off his duties in Bury St Edmunds, but he was soon propelled into similar prominence in the Lords. His first significant contribution was when he was required to speak in answer to the address in January 1734, for which he claimed only to have been given 48 hours' notice.[73] Describing this experience to Henry Fox at the end of the month, he emphasized his lack of concern for the session ahead, characterised as it had been thus far with poor debating and with little of real moment to disquiet the ministry:

[68] *London Evening Post*, 9–12 June 1733.

[69] *Letter-books of John Hervey, First Earl of Bristol* … (3 vols, Wells, 1894), iii, 92.

[70] *Hervey and His Friends*, ed. Ilchester, 163.

[71] *Hervey and His Friends*, ed. Ilchester, 128.

[72] *Hervey and His Friends*, ed. Ilchester, 164.

[73] Hervey was nominated to the committee for the address on 17 Jan. 1734, from which he reported the same day: *LJ*, xxiv, 322–3.

The debates hitherto in both Houses have been very bad; and, notwithstanding all the menaces thrown out before the Parliament met, I believe it will prove a short and easy session. The Triennial Bill, the Debt of the Navy, the Pension Bill, the new modelling the Army, and a Domestic-family proposal which I dare not mention plainer, are the things at present talked of as the bones of Parliamentary contention for this year …

Hervey also insisted that the only division thus far in the Lords, moved by Lord Bathurst, for the king to lay an account before the House of the good offices he had used for re-solving recent disputes, was firmly rejected, and the only significant ministerial rebel, Lord Willoughby, explained his actions as having been on account of Walpole rewarding 'that rascal, his brother, Varny' in spite of Willoughby warning him not to do so.[74]

Hervey's assessment is, of course, partial and as so often with his writings to be taken with a substantial degree of scepticism. He makes no reference, for example, to the devel-oping alliance between disgruntled Scots representative peers and opposition peers such as Chesterfield, who met at the beginning of 1734 and undertook to collaborate.[75]

The situation was undoubtedly more sensitive than Hervey cared to suggest and, for all his braggadocio about his unwillingness to exert himself, his early career in the Lords was clearly more significant than he was willing to let on. The accounts recorded in Ebenezer Timberland's *History of the Lords* underline the extent of Hervey's contribution.[76] And yet contemporary commentators appear to have paid less attention to him than one might ex-pect. In March 1734, he was noted as speaking in favour of the address of thanks, but as he was one of eight prominent peers to back the motion there is little indication that his contribution on this occasion was especially necessary and the ministry carried the division comfortably by 78 to 39.[77] The following February he, again, spoke for the ministry against the Scots petition, joined by Hardwicke, the lord chancellor, Newcastle, and Cholmondeley. Sir Thomas Robinson, reporting on the debate, noted several of the key speakers, but Her-vey was relegated to a brief afterthought in which Robinson detailed: 'The new lords who have spoke today, which did not in the former debate', comprising Hervey, Lord Gower, and the bishop of Salisbury.[78] Indeed, it was not until April 1736 that Robinson remarked on Hervey making a particularly noteworthy contribution, when he 'made several very judicious calculations' in the debate on the Mortmain Bill.[79] In May 1738, Francis Hare, bishop of Chichester, reporting to his son the debates in the House on the bill for restrain-ing privilege of parliament, chose to highlight the contribution of the earl of Scarbrough, who 'spoke incomparably well for it', rather than any other peer. The following June (1739) when reporting the debate on the state of the nation, Bishop Hare, again, picked out the principal speakers, noting those for the ministry as having been Newcastle, Cholmonde-ley, Hervey, the lord chancellor, and Scarbrough. Scarbrough's contribution was called to

---

[74] *Hervey and His Friends*, ed. Ilchester, 190–1.

[75] Matsuzono, ' "Attaque and Break Through …" ', 337.

[76] Ebenezer Timberland, *History and Proceedings of the House of Lords* (7 vols, 1742), iv, 187, 219, 229, 245, 283, 375, 410, 448, 460, 514; v, 14, 92, 94, 134, 165, 179, 202, 361, 473; vi, 26, 134, 194, 236, 290; vii. 398, 476, 517, 591, 620.

[77] HMC, *Carlisle MSS*, 135.

[78] HMC, *Carlisle MSS*, 153, 155.

[79] HMC, *Carlisle MSS*, 169.

attention once more as having been 'very strong', but no further mention was made of Hervey's role in the debate, which was completed in around three hours, when the Lords had expected to be kept at it for at least twice that time.[80]

Of course, it is quite possible that Hervey believed – or had been flattered to believe – that it was his talent as a speaker that was most in need, but that he was soon eclipsed by others such as Scarbrough. This, once again, raises the question of why Hervey was moved to the Lords in the summer of 1733. Might it be possible that the real reason for Hervey's advancement to the Lords owed as much to his own desire to retreat to a chamber which he believed would be more conducive to his talents and disposition, than to any urgent need to boost numbers or speaking strength? Hervey had, after all, spent relatively little time in the Commons. First elected in 1725, he had been absent abroad throughout 1728 and 1729 seeking a cure for his famously poor health. The first rumours of his removal to the Lords, then, came just over a year after his return to attendance of the Commons and not long after he had suffered a well-documented breakdown in health at court at the beginning of 1731.[81] Did Hervey hope, perhaps, for a quieter regime in the upper House, which he expected to find more conducive? Certainly, by the close of 1731 he was still complaining of his regime at court, commenting to Stephen Fox how 'The Duke of Newcastle's and the Prince's balls have almost demolished me.'[82]

Two further possibilities suggest themselves, one hinted at in the *Memoirs*. Having emphasized the ministry's need to recruit more speakers, Hervey proceeded to note a significant feature of his elevation. Admitting his personal 'pride and vanity' in accepting the promotion, he remarked that: 'he had a mind to strengthen the interest of his family in Parliament'. By vacating his own seat, he allowed his brother to come into the Commons, while adding to the Hervey bloc in the Lords, where his father already sat as earl of Bristol. It is an admission that echoes part of the speech delivered by the then earl (later duke) of Dorset in favour of the repeal of the Triennial Act and its replacement with the Septennial Bill. Triennial parliaments, Dorset had insisted, destroyed family interest – and as the Sackvilles were in the position to provide for a number of kinsmen in several boroughs this was a significant consideration.[83] The Herveys by comparison were able to wield only very modest 'family' interest, but Hervey's ambition appears all the more plausible when considered in the light of Dorset's argument.

The second point harks back to the original rumours of Hervey's likely elevation in the early months of 1731. At that time both he and Viscount Malpas were expected to receive writs, and were recorded as having qualified themselves to take their seats, only to be disappointed. On 7 May 1733, just a month before Hervey was finally summoned to the Lords, Malpas succeeded his father as 3rd earl of Cholmondeley. Was this a further factor in the decision to summon Hervey? Might it have been considered only reasonable once Malpas had achieved his seat in the Lords that Hervey should also join him there?

[80]HMC, *14th Report*, ix, 247.
[81]Suffolk RO, Bury St Edmunds, Hervey of Ickworth MSS, 941/47/25: Hervey to Stephen Fox, 11 Jan. 1731.
[82]Suffolk RO, Bury St Edmunds, Hervey of Ickworth MSS, 941/47/25: Hervey to Stephen Fox, 27 Nov. 1731.
[83]Timberland, *Hist. and Proceedings*, iii, 29–30.

6

Hervey's career continued to develop during the remainder of Walpole's ascendancy. He proved committed to the administration, teasing Walpole at one point in October 1735 at the opening of an account of political developments at home and abroad, 'if you are not sincere when you tell me you like to hear from me often, you are a very good Courtier, but a very bad Politician'.[84] His progress culminated in his appointment as lord privy seal in the spring of 1740. It was a promotion welcomed warmly by John Campbell, a regular correspondent of Henry Fox's and firm supporter of Walpole. In a letter of 29 March, he conveyed the news to his son, Pryse Campbell, expressing his satisfaction and commenting: 'He has great abilitys, and great knowledge and I believe him a very honest man.'[85] More to the point, Hervey was well liked both by Walpole and at court. He survived in post for just six months after Walpole's fall and died the following year. Walpole, meanwhile, who had first been associated with a peerage in 1722 when it was rumoured that he was to be created earl of Walsingham,[86] finally accepted promotion to the Lords as part of the package securing his personal safety following his resignation and took his place in the upper chamber as earl of Orford, a nod to his old junto mentor, Edward Russell, former holder of the title.

Negotiating promotions to the peerage was always a sensitive affair. Viscount Perceval, seeking promotion to an earldom in the summer of 1733, was at pains to ensure that his efforts were conducted by a third party, Lord Grantham, rather than sully himself with asking directly.[87] Hervey, too, emphasized that as his peerage had first been suggested to him by Walpole himself, 'without being solicited by him, it was impossible for Sir Robert … to go back'.[88] A later episode also helps underscore the careful manner in which such matters needed to be handled. In the late summer of 1766, the marchioness of Tweeddale sought to secure a British barony for herself, that could be passed on to her son. Writing to the newly created earl of Chatham on 26 September, she acknowledged that she understood she was far from the only person to be requesting such a distinction, noting: 'I can easily imagine many of the Scotch nobility are applying to get English peerages in their familys', but insisting, nevertheless, that her case was a particular one. As the daughter of Earl Granville,[89] all of whose titles were to be rendered extinct by his death without male heirs, she hoped that the king would look favourably on her plea insisting: 'it wou'd be hard that not one Peerage of so many shou'd revive in his Grandson'. However, rather than arguing for a special remainder conveying one of Granville's titles, she suggested, instead, the creation of a new barony of Chilton, reflecting her inheritance of estates in Hampshire from her grandfather, Sir Robert Worsley. This, she hoped, might be favoured as she conceived there was 'no case similar to mine' and she was sure of Chatham's assistance, he being 'as much superior to ye rest of mankind in distinterestedness & benevolence of mind as you are in

[84] Cambridge University Library, Cholmondeley (Houghton) MSS, CH(H) corresp. 2482: Hervey to Walpole, 26 Sept./7 Oct. 1735.

[85] Campbell Corresp., ed. Davies, 58.

[86] Daily Journal, 12–14 Apr. 1722.

[87] HMC, Egmont Diary, i, 384.

[88] Hervey Memoirs, ed. Sedgwick, i, 204.

[89] Formerly Lord Carteret.

abilitys' contrasting with Lord Shelburne (who had ignored her petition), who she dismissed as 'so perfect a courtier & so imperfect a friend'.[90]

In spite of these efforts, and her apparently persuasive case for securing a British peerage, Lady Tweeddale was not successful. Her failure underscores the importance of appropriate interest at court in securing such awards, but also the caution with which monarchs after 1715 viewed augmenting the membership of the house of lords. With the exception of coronation honours, creations of more than a handful of individuals in any one year were rarities. This, then, perhaps helps explain the identification of Lord Hervey as a useful recipient of a peerage in 1733. As the heir to an earldom his early summons made no overall change to the membership of the chamber and as a man with close connections at court – as well as with the dominant power in the ministry – he was an ideal candidate. For Hervey himself, removal to the Lords offered the possibility (not to be realized) of a retreat from the busyness of the Commons. As he commented in his letter to Charlotte Digby, by quitting the Commons he was able 'to take leave (for my father's life at least) of all Corporation solicitation, hypocrisy, flattery and nonsense' and in answer to her anticipated suggestion that there would be more of the same in the Lords he concluded:

> you must allow the difference of actors makes a great difference in every farce, and that the same drama and characters that entertain and keep up one's spirits in Drury Lane might lay one to sleep acted by strollers in a country fair.[91]

[90]TNA, PRO 30/8/64, ff. 248–50.

[91] *Hervey and His Friends*, ed. Ilchester, 164.

'Hereditary Guardians of the Nation': The House of Lords and the East India Company in the Age of the American Revolution

RICHARD CONNORS AND BEN GILDING

The reform of the East India Company following its acquisition of vast territories in Bengal in the mid 1760s raised hopes that it could provide Britain with a fund to alleviate the burdens of the national debt in the wake of the failure of American taxation. Concomitantly, it elicited genuine fears that the acquisition of such revenues and patronage by the state would radically augment the already overgrown 'influence of the crown'. Studies of the parliamentary debates surrounding East India reform have consistently emphasized the house of commons as the principal scene of action. Inspired by the work of Clyve Jones in reasserting the centrality of the house of lords as a 'pillar' of the 18th-century constitution, this essay seeks to redress the balance, arguing that the Lords was a key arena through which co-ordinated parliamentary and extra-parliamentary activities and press campaigns altered the trajectory of the regulation and reform of the East India Company. Through the use of its distinct privileges, such as the right of opposition lords to protest any vote of the House and the right of peers to an audience with the monarch, as well as its determination to uphold its status as a mediator between the powers of the crown and the Commons, the upper chamber played a crucial role in shaping debates in the 1770s and 1780s over the future of the East India Company and its place in a burgeoning British Empire.

Keywords: constitution; East India Company; Fox–North coalition; house of lords; King George III; parliament; politics; protests; reform

1

On 25 November 1783, James Sayer produced his striking print, *A Transfer of East India Stock* (Figure 1).[1] The caricature, which did not sell as well as his more famous, and even more caustic, *Carlo Khan's Triumphant Entry into Leadenhall Street*, none the less effectively lampooned the Fox–North ministry at the outset of a tempestuous parliamentary session, which would ultimately seal the fate of that seemingly most unholy of political alliances.[2]

Simple, though hardly elegant, the print mocked and satirised the Fox–North coalition's attempts to bring the East India Company under the control of parliament. It depicted a colossal Charles James Fox carrying the company's London headquarters, the East India

[1] [James Sayer], *A Transfer of East India Stock*, 25 Nov. 1783; British Museum, Satires 6271. For a discussion of these prints, see N.B. Robinson, *Edmund Burke: A Life in Caricature* (New Haven, CT, 1996), 53–78; P.D.G. Thomas, *The American Revolution: The English Satirical Print 1660–1832* (Cambridge, 1986), 25–30; Thomas Wright, *Caricature History of the Georges* (1876), 370–6.

[2] John Cannon, *The Fox-North Coalition: Crisis in the Constitution* (Cambridge, 1969).

Figure 1: [James Sayer], *A Transfer of East India Stock*, 25 November 1783; BM Satires 6271. © Trustees of the British Museum.

House, to St James's. It is an excellent pictorial distillation of the opposition's main arguments against the bill – namely that it sought either to appropriate the patronage of the company to increase the influence of the crown, by which Fox would be seen as entirely hypocritical and unprincipled, or that Fox was attempting to accrue the influence to himself and thereby overpower the crown.[3] Nathaniel Wraxall later wrote that the two Sayer prints: 'both conceived with admirable humour, were circulated throughout the metropolis … it is difficult to conceive the moral operation and wide diffusion of these caricatures through every part of the country'.[4] Fox would later observe that these prints did much to sway public opinion against the bill and that: 'Sayer's caricatures had done him more

[3] The print is, therefore, an example of the close relationship between graphic satires and the ideas and rhetoric of parliamentary debates as well as those aired in the newspaper and pamphlet press: see H.M. Atherton, *Political Prints in the Age of Hogarth* (Oxford, 1974), 260.

[4] *The Historical and Posthumous Memoirs of Sir Nathaniel William Wraxall 1772–1784*, ed. H.B. Wheatley (5 vols, 1884), iii, 254. Sir Richard Hill commented upon Sayer's 'A Transfer of East India Stock', in his speech in the Commons on the East India Bill on 27 Nov. 1783 when he noted: 'He [Fox] looked as if he really could carry

mischief than the debates in Parliament or the works of the press.[5] Fox's view is vindicated by the fact that William Pitt the Younger, when prime minister, rewarded Sayer with the sinecure office of marshal of the court of exchequer, a testament to the power of his pen.[6]

Within days of the print's publication, and in the wake of an audience with George III, Earl Temple offered up to his fellow peers the famous message proclaiming that those who supported the bill in the Lords would no longer enjoy the king's friendship.[7] Within weeks, the coalition had been swept from power and replaced by the so-called 'mince-pie' administration led by William Pitt.[8] Aspects of the protracted constitutional crisis of 1783–4 are well known to historians of the period.[9] Yet, equally important and less well understood and studied is the central place of the East India Company in the British constitution and how that relationship was perceived in the house of lords, not only during this crisis but throughout the tumultuous decades following the accession of George III. Rather than being merely coincidental in late 1783, as some have suggested, a crisis over the relationship between the East India Company and the British state had been brewing since the early 1760s. In what follows, we wish to reconsider the house of lords, the East India Company, and the events of 1783 to illustrate that issues of state, the constitution and the company were not only inextricably interconnected in the minds of contemporaries, but occupied considerable time, energy, and thought in the house of lords long before the memorable events of December 1783.

2

Before turning to the particular involvement of the Lords in East India Company reform, it is necessary to examine briefly how the affairs of the company became a major issue for politicians and for parliament. Before 1756, the company's territories in India were more or less confined to coastal enclaves, burgeoning towns organised around the lucrative trade which the company brought. These towns, most prominently the 'presidencies' of Calcutta, Bombay, and Madras, had developed from the 'factories' which the company had established, with the permission of local rulers, in the 17th century. It has recently been argued that such territories, and the political powers they exercised, constituted what has been termed a company-state.[10] While it is certainly true that the territories held by the company on

---

[4] (continued) the India House on his back, as a print just published humorously represented him to be doing': see *Cobbett's Parliamentary History of England* (36 vols, 1806–20), xxiii, 1289.

[5] Horace Twiss, *The Public and Private Life of Lord Eldon* (3 vols, 1844), i, 162.

[6] M.D. George, *English Political Caricature to 1792: A Study of Opinion and Propaganda* (Oxford, 1959), 169.

[7] M.W. McCahill, *The House of Lords in the Age of George III (1760–1811)* (Oxford, 2009), 184–7; M.W. McCahill, *Order and Equipoise: The Peerage and the House of Lords, 1783–1806* (1978), 24–7; A.S. Turberville, *The House of Lords in the XVIIIth Century* (Oxford, 1927), 410–12.

[8] L.G. Mitchell, *Charles James Fox* (Oxford, 1992), 67; D.F. Taylor, *The Politics of Parody: A Literary History of Caricature* (New Haven, CT, 2018), 145; see also Matthew Kilburn, 'Mince-Pie Administration (act. 1783–84)', *ODNB*.

[9] Paul Kelly, 'British Politics, 1783–4: The Emergence and Triumph of the Younger Pitt's Administration', *Bulletin of the Institute of Historical Research*, liv (1981), 62–78; Paul Langford, *A Polite and Commercial People: England 1727–1783* (Oxford, 1989), 559–64; Jeremy Black, *George III: America's Last King* (New Haven, CT, 2006), 252–63.

[10] P.J. Stern, *The Company-State: Corporate Sovereignty and the Early Modern Foundations of the British Empire in India* (Oxford, 2011); see also Philip Stern, 'Company, State, and Empire: Governance and Regulatory Frameworks

the Indian subcontinent possessed municipal political and judicial institutions, consistent with the powers granted to town, borough, and city corporations in Britain, it was clear to contemporaries, both in Britain and India, that their political and constitutional nature had undergone a dramatic alteration between 1757 and 1765. The company's conquest and acquisition of vast territories in Bengal in those years was nothing short of what it was called at the time, in both British and Persian sources: a 'revolution' or '*inquilab*'.[11] It can be described more accurately, however, as a series of political 'revolutions' in Bengal that led to a complete 'revolution' of the company's situation as a chartered monopoly trading corporation.[12] Moreover, it fundamentally altered the nature of the company's trade, devolving upon them the responsibility for governing the provinces of Bengal, Bihar, and Orissa, and granting them the right to collect taxes. It was this state of affairs that attracted attention and jealousy from politicians and the public in Britain. The company's affairs, which had been kept outside of the purview of parliament for much of the 18th century, suddenly emerged as essential objects of political attention and became crucially entangled with the prevailing domestic political arguments.[13]

As early as 1758, shortly after the company had initiated the process of acquiring large territories in Bengal, Colonel Robert Clive wrote to William Pitt the elder, then secretary of state, reporting his concerns that 'so large a sovereignty may possibly be an object too extensive for a mercantile company; and it is feared they are not of themselves able, without the nation's assistance, to maintain so wide a dominion'.[14] In the midst of war, this suggestion fell on deaf ears. However, Pitt did not forget Clive's implicit proposal. Following the conclusion of the war in 1763, the burden of the national debt and public expenditure became something of a 'national obsession'.[15] The government initially looked to America as a means to relieve some of the immense expenditure occasioned by the conquest and retention of a vastly expanded global empire. George Grenville's now infamous molasses and stamp duties must be understood within the context of this domestic obsession with economy in the nation's finances.[16] These measures, of course, backfired with disastrous results for the British *imperium* in North America. In the immediate term, however, the failure of the Sugar or Stamp Acts to deliver any significant yield, or even to provide relief for the costs of permanently stationing an army in America, led politicians to search for alternative sources of revenue.[17]

---

[10] (continued) in Asia', in *Britain's Oceanic Empire: Atlantic and Indian Ocean Worlds, c. 1550–1850*, ed. H.V. Bowen, Elizabeth Mancke and J.G. Reid (Cambridge, 2012), 130–1, 145.

[11] David Armitage and Sanjay Subrahmanyam, 'The Age of Revolutions, c.1760–1840 – Global Causation, Connection, and Comparison', in *The Age of Revolutions in Global Context*, ed. David Armitage and Sanjay Subrahmanyam (Basingstoke, 2010), xii–xvi.

[12] Robert Travers, *Ideology and Empire in Eighteenth-Century India: The British in Bengal* (Cambridge, 2007), 1–66; P.J. Marshall, *The Making and Unmaking of Empires: Britain, India and America, 1750–1783* (Oxford, 2005), 119–272.

[13] Philip Lawson, *The East India Company: A History* (Harlow, 1993), 86–96.

[14] *The Correspondence of William Pitt, Earl of Chatham*, ed. W.S. Taylor and J.H. Pringle (4 vols, 1838), i, 390.

[15] Philip Lawson, *George Grenville: A Political Life* (Oxford, 1984), 181.

[16] John L. Bullion, *A Great and Necessary Measure: George Grenville and the Genesis of the Stamp Act, 1763–1765* (Columbia, MO, 1982).

[17] P.D.G. Thomas, 'The Cost of the British Army in North America, 1763–1775', *William and Mary Quarterly*, xlv (1988), 510–16.

To their good fortune (or so they thought), an opportunity appeared to arise in the east. Just as the Rockingham ministry was awaiting the thanks of the Americans for repealing the Stamp Act, news arrived in Britain of further military victories and territorial acquisitions on the part of the East India Company. Robert, now Lord, Clive had sent word to his friends and attorneys in Britain that the company had acquired a vast new source of wealth through the *diwani* or revenue-collection rights of Bengal. As Huw Bowen has uncovered, Clive accompanied this news with advice to make large purchases of East India stock before the news became widely known, in an early example of what we would now call insider trading.[18] Lord Rockingham and William Pitt, by then earl of Chatham, each received word that the company would produce a revenue from this source of over £2,000,000 annually. To put this into perspective, the crown in 1763 could only count upon total revenues of approximately £8,000,000, and £5,000,000 of this was paid towards the interest on the debt.[19] Such a large sum, evidently deemed too great to be divided merely among the stockholders of the East India Company, was seen by Chatham, when he became first lord of the treasury in 1766, as 'a kind of gift from heaven', which could result in 'the *redemption* of a nation'.[20] Almost immediately upon taking office, Chatham resolved to bring the East India Company's affairs before parliament to determine whether the company was competent to govern its newly-acquired territories and whether, by law, these territories belonged to the crown rather than to the company.[21] While bringing the business before the Commons, William Beckford, Chatham's deputy, called upon MPs to 'Look to the rising sun ... your Treasury coffers are to be filled from the East, not from the West.'[22] Such sentiments were echoed by many inside and outside parliament, but of course clashed violently with the views of the company's stockholders, who believed that their rights and property were being invaded.[23] However, Clive had truly let the cat out of the bag: even the king reiterated the view held by Chatham and Beckford, arguing that 'the real glory of the Nation depends' upon the outcome of obtaining, in some manner, a portion of the company's revenues, 'the only safe method of extracting this Country out of its lamentable situation owing to the load of Debt it labours under'.[24]

The company waged a successful opposition to the Chatham administration's plans to seize its territories and revenues. A compromise was reached by which the company paid

[18] H.V. Bowen, 'Lord Clive and Speculation in East India Company Stock, 1766', *Historical Journal*, xxx (1987), 909–10.

[19] R.J. Chaffin, 'The Townshend Acts of 1767', *William and Mary Quarterly*, xxvii (1970), 91. For the notices received by Chatham and Rockingham, see TNA, Chatham MSS, PRO 30/8/99, part iii, f. 178; Sheffield Archives [hereafter cited as SA], Wentworth Woodhouse Muniments, WWM/R/66. For analysis of the information given to Chatham, see *Chatham Correspondence*, ed. Taylor and Pringle, iii, 61–4.

[20] *Autobiography and Political Correspondence of Augustus Henry, Third Duke of Grafton*, ed. Sir W.R. Anson (1898), 110–11.

[21] H.V. Bowen, 'A Question of Sovereignty? The Bengal Land Revenue Issue, 1765–67', *Journal of Imperial and Commonwealth History*, xvi (1988), 155–76.

[22] Sir George Colebrooke, *Retrospection: or Reminiscences Addressed to My Son Henry Thomas Colebrooke* (2 vols, 1898–9), i, 108. For Beckford and his relationship with the company, see Perry Gauci, *William Beckford: First Prime Minister of the London Empire* (New Haven, CT, 2013), 126, 255–6.

[23] See, e.g., the second reason in the Lords' protest of 8 Feb. 1768, in *LJ*, xxxii, 68–69; see also BL, Add. MS 32988, f. 50: Newcastle to James West, 19 Jan. 1768.

[24] Royal Archives, Windsor Castle, official papers of George III, GEO/MAIN/549: George III to Grafton, 9 Dec. 1766.

£400,000 annually to the treasury for the recognition of its right to maintain its territorial possessions in Bengal. Ultimately, however, the company's revenues failed to live up to the speculations of Clive and the hopes of ministers. The difficulties of transferring the revenues via a purchase of goods to send to London for sale and the dramatic increase of military and administrative expenditure meant that by late 1772 the company was closer to bankruptcy than opulence.[25] By this stage, however, the issue of corruption in its various forms had become almost indelibly connected with the company's reputation both at home and abroad. The parliamentary inquiry in 1767 brought the affairs of the company to widespread public notice for the first time, and soon afterwards reports of stock-jobbing among proprietors of India stock and maladministration, peculation, and oppression by the company's servants abroad became ubiquitous in the newspaper and pamphlet press. Secret and select committees of the house of commons were formed to investigate the company's accounts and determine the extent of corruption, as opinion coalesced around the belief that the territories and revenues of the company were a national or public concern rather than simply the property of merchants.[26]

An important shift took place in the decades following the first inquiry in 1767, during which the East India Company's business, revenues, and territories were increasingly brought within the ideological, if not the administrative, structure of the British Empire. In 1773, this can be observed through the prevalent concern that corruption within the company was squandering the opportunity of the British state to fund its national debt.[27] To make matters worse, for those who felt the company was harming rather than helping Britain's finances, Lord North's plans of reform in 1773 involved a £1,400,000 loan to the company, in addition to temporarily forgoing the yearly £400,000 that was due to the state. Clearly North's hope was that such a manœuvre would be temporary and would allow the company to regain financial stability and continue to contribute towards the necessities of government. In exchange for such a bail-out, however, North imposed crucial reforms on the company. North's reforms, however hesitantly they may have asserted state control over the company's affairs, and however short they may have fallen from the hopes of speculative philosophers of empire who had spent vast quantities of ink in developing schemes by which the company could be brought more formally within the fold of British *imperium*, none the less set a crucial precedent by restructuring the executive offices of the Bengal government and vesting their appointment in the crown and ministry in Britain. The erection of a supreme court composed of crown-appointed justices only added to this effect. Suddenly the employees of the East India Company served two masters, adding complexity and confusion to an already byzantine institution. The division of loyalties between the company's stockholders, the court of directors, and now the British ministry – not to mention personal ambitions of acquiring a fortune in the east – led to a confusion of the power structures in India and in many ways broadened the scope of corruption abroad. North's reforms had further blurred the lines between the British state and the East India

[25] H.V. Bowen, *The Business of Empire: The East India Company and Imperial Britain, 1756–1833* (Cambridge, 2006), 38.

[26] On these themes, see Lawson, *East India Company*, 116–25; Philip Lawson, 'Parliament and the First East India Inquiry, 1767', *Parliamentary History*, i (1982), 99–114.

[27] For instance, the letter signed '*An Enemy to East-India Oppression*', in *Gazetteer and New Daily Advertiser*, 26 Mar. 1772.

Company and helped to solidify the belief that the company's overseas possessions formed an increasingly important part of the British Empire.[28]

If the East India Company was to play its role as a redeemer of British fortunes in the wake of costly and destructive wars, it was necessary to devise a method of incorporating it safely within the British state. One of the most sacred and widely-held constitutional tenets in 18th-century Britain was the concept of a mixed and balanced constitution, whereby the two branches of parliament shared power with the crown within a broadly outlined legal framework.[29] Since the accession of George III in 1760, the most significant fear concerning the constitution was that the powers of the crown had disproportionately increased at the expense of parliament. This, it was argued, had upset the desired balance established at the revolution of 1688 and tipped the scales in favour of the monarchy. These fears gained significant traction during the 1770s and 1780s through the movement for 'economical' reform which reached its apogee in parliament with the passage of John Dunning's famous motion in 1780 that 'the influence of the crown has increased, is increasing, and ought to be diminished'.[30] Less well understood and recognized is the reciprocal relationship between these debates on the nature of the constitution and the regulation of the East India Company. Fears concerning the company's impact on the constitution were largely responsible for the haphazard and ambivalent attempts to reform the company in the 1770s and 1780s; conversely, in 1783–4 the company became a flashpoint in the debates concerning the relationship between the respective powers of parliament and the crown.

Each time the East India Company's affairs had been brought before parliament since the company acquired the *diwani* rights in Bengal, concerns were raised about its potential to increase the influence of the crown. Fears that the crown would claim both sovereignty over, and possession of, the company's newly-acquired territories, raised the prospect that the crown would also obtain a valuable source of patronage.[31] This involved the right to appoint the new civil and military servants sent to the East Indies as well as the opportunity to fill the positions of the company's executive officers such as governors and councillors. The company's patronage, it was claimed, would prove to be so large an addition to the influence of the crown that the foundations of the constitution would be severely damaged if not destroyed.[32] Edmund Burke, arguing that the 'places and pensions … furnished by the British establishment' were already too great, implored the Commons to imagine what would 'become of us, if Bengal, if the Ganges pour in a new tide of corruption'?[33]

[28] H.V. Bowen, *Revenue and Reform: The Indian Problem in British Politics, 1757–1773* (Cambridge, 1991), 119–89; Marshall, *Making and Unmaking of Empires*, 207–72; P.J. Marshall, *The Impeachment of Warren Hastings* (Oxford, 1965), xvi–xix, 1–21.

[29] E.A. Reitan, 'From Revenue to Civil List, 1689–1702: The Revolution Settlement and the "Mixed and Balanced" Constitution', *Historical Journal*, xiii (1970), 571–88.

[30] On this theme, see I.R. Christie, *Wars and Revolutions: Britain, 1760–1815* (Cambridge, MA, 1982), 135–8; I.R. Christie, 'Economical Reform and "The Influence of the Crown", 1780', *Cambridge Historical Journal*, xii (1956), 144–54; Langford, *Polite and Commercial People*, 547–9; E.A. Reitan, *Politics, Finance and the People: Economical Reform in England in the Age of the American Revolution, 1770–1792* (2007); and most recently Julian Hoppit, 'Economical Reform and the Mint, 1780–1816', *British Numismatic Journal*, lxxxiv (2014), 177–90.

[31] *The Correspondence of Edmund Burke*, ed. L.S. Sutherland (10 vols, Cambridge, 1958–78), ii, 351, 399; SA, WWM/R/1/1402: Rockingham to Charles Turner, [c.7 Apr. 1773]; BL, Add. MS 88906/1/4, f. 56: Isaac Barré to Shelburne, 12 Aug. 1773.

[32] *Cobbett's Parl. Hist.*, xvii, 671.

[33] *Cobbett's Parl. Hist.*, xvii, 668.

Each time the government proposed to reform the institutions of the East India Company, and the relationship between the company and the state grew increasingly intertwined, opposition politicians claimed that the reform was dangerous to the constitution because it would grant the crown an inordinate increase in patronage which would enable it to purchase stronger support in the house of commons. The opposition argued in this manner against the attempt of the Chatham administration to gain control of the company's territories and revenues in 1767 and again against North's Regulating Act of 1773, which was described as a 'robbery' despite not vesting any permanent or direct patronage in the crown.[34]

3

Scholarly attention on the parliamentary debates and political opposition to the ministry's efforts between 1767 and 1784 to reform the East India Company has focused on the house of commons. There are several reasons why the Commons has been prioritised over the Lords on this thorny and protracted issue. First, George III proved unwilling to grant English peerages to returned servants of the East India Company: both Robert Clive and Sir George Pigot received only Irish peerages, which did not entitle them to a seat in the English house of lords. This prevented many experienced and potentially well-informed individuals from contributing their knowledge of East India affairs to the debates of the upper House.[35] Clive, in particular, proved one of the most prolific and controversial contributors to Commons debates on East India affairs between 1768 and 1774.[36] Deprived of crucial first-hand experience in the governance of the company in India, the Lords was similarly lacking in acquaintance with the company's affairs at home. No sitting peer served as chairman or deputy chairman of the company during this period, nor were any elected to the company's executive body, the court of directors.[37] Aristocratic investment in East India stock was relatively low, mirroring the nobility's lack of interest in other aspects of City business and finance.[38] What Clyve Jones has revealed of the 'negligible' aristocratic investment in the Old and New Companies in 1700 was broadly true throughout the century.[39]

[34]See the speech of John Wilkes in London's Guildhall in a debate over whether the City should send a petition to the house of commons in solidarity with the East India Company: *Annual Register* (1773), 104.

[35]G.M. Ditchfield remarks on the lack of 'nabobs' in 'The House of Lords in the Age of the American Revolution', in *A Pillar of the Constitution: The House of Lords in British Politics, 1640–1784*, ed. Clyve Jones (1989), 204.

[36]Clive spoke over 30 times on Indian affairs in the Commons during this period: Bowen, *Revenue and Reform*, 33. Several of his speeches were widely published: *Lord Clive's Speech in the House of Commons, 30th March 1772 on the Motion made for Leave to bring in a Bill* ... (1772); *Lord Clive's Speech in the House of Commons, on the Motion made for an Inquiry into the Nature, State, and Condition of the East India Company* ... (1772). Pigot, too, gave his only recorded speeches during these debates: BL, Egerton MS 248, pp. 84–7, 204–6; Egerton MS 249, pp. 198–200; see also *The History of Parliament: The House of Commons, 1754–1790*, ed. Sir Lewis Namier and John Brooke (3 vols, 1964) [hereafter cited as *HPC, 1754–90*], iii, 279–81.

[37]J.G. Parker, 'The Directors of the East India Company, 1754–1790', University of Edinburgh PhD, 1977, esp. appendix I.

[38]J.V. Beckett, *The Aristocracy in England, 1660–1914* (Oxford, 1986), 84–6.

[39]Clyve Jones, ' "A Fresh Division Lately Grown Up Amongst Us": Party Strife, Aristocratic Investment in the Old and New East India Companies and the Vote in the House of Lords on 23 February 1700', *Historical Research*, lxviii (1995), 306.

As Huw Bowen has shown, peers as a percentage of East India Company stockholders rose to a peak of just over 8% in 1783 but for much of the period accounted for only around 6%. The aristocracy, he concluded, left only a faint imprint upon the company.[40] This absence of expertise and financial interest in the company has helped ensure that the role of the house of lords in the company's reform has been neglected by historians.[41] Lucy Sutherland focused almost exclusively upon the interplay between the Commons and East India House and John Cannon gave little credit to the active role of the Lords in the constitutional crisis of 1783–4 which he analysed almost entirely in domestic terms.[42] Indeed, Cannon charac-terised the Lords as 'an adjunct of the crown' where officeholders provided 'an automatic majority for the government of the day'.[43] In attempting to discern the extent of the var-ious East India Company interests in parliament, C.H. Philips listed only members of the lower House.[44] The focus of scholarly attention upon the state regulation of the East India Company, therefore, has rested heavily on the activities of the Commons and its members, and largely ignored the contribution of the Lords.

While compromised by numerous disadvantages of expertise and experience on com-pany matters, the Lords was, nevertheless, a 'pillar of the constitution', and its unique priv-ileges rendered it an important nexus of political activity concerning the reform of the East India Company. Through the use of its distinct privileges, such as the right of opposi-tion lords to protest any vote of the House and the right of peers to an audience with the monarch, as well as its determination to uphold its status as a mediator between crown and Commons, the upper chamber played a crucial role, alongside debates in the Commons, press campaigns, and co-ordinated political activities in East India House, in shaping de-bates in the 1770s and 1780s over the future of the East India Company and its place in the empire.[45]

The most important procedural contribution of the Lords to debates on the East India Company was the ability of its members to enter a dissent or protest against any vote. These dissents were entered into the journals as a permanent record of the opposition of peers to a particular vote, and in the case of protests, included a numbered list of reasons.[46] Both dissents and protests were considered to be 'ancient' privileges of peers. However, the

[40] Bowen, *Business of Empire*, 103; see also H.V. Bowen, 'Investment and Empire in the Later Eighteenth Cen-tury: East India Stockholding, 1756–1791', *Economic History Review*, xlii (1989), 195.

[41] It must be noted, however, that the general lack of experience and interest on Indian issues was replicated to a considerable extent among members of the Commons. Wraxall notes that: 'We may indeed safely assume that only a small proportion of the 558 members who then composed the Lower House possessed ability, industry, and leisure sufficient, in addition to local knowledge, for enabling them to weigh in their own scales the East India Bill [of 1783] – a measure of so complex and comprehensive a nature in itself, and at that time not at all generally understood throughout the kingdom': *Wraxall Memoirs*, ed. Wheatley, iii, 195. Bowen echoes these sentiments in *Business of Empire*, 19; and *Revenue and Reform*, 31.

[42] L.S. Sutherland, *The East India Company in Eighteenth Century Politics* (Oxford, 1952); Cannon, *Fox-North Coalition*; and McCahill's criticism in *House of Lords*, 186.

[43] Cannon, *Fox-North Coalition*, 125.

[44] C.H. Philips, *The East India Company 1784–1834* (Manchester, 1968), 340–7.

[45] On this theme, see C.A. Bayly, *Imperial Meridian: The British Empire and the World, 1780–1830* (1989), 100–63; Lawson, *East India Company*, 126–43.

[46] Clyve Jones, 'Dissent and Protest in the House of Lords, 1641–1998: An Attempt to Reconstruct the Pro-cedures Involved in Entering a Protest into the Journals of the House of Lords', *Parliamentary History*, xxvii (2008), 309–10.

first dissent was only recorded in 1549 and the practice of protesting emerged in 1641.[47] Shortly after their introduction, the practices of dissenting and protesting were standardised through a standing order of 5 March 1642, which required them to be submitted on the next sitting day.[48] Following the introduction of this standard procedure, entering protests became a frequent opposition tactic, until an explosion in their use in the early 1720s. Between 1721 and 1723, 60 protests were entered by opposition peers, who began, for the first time, publishing and disseminating them as a means by which to consolidate their political and ideological principles and popularise their opposition to the ministry.[49] In an attempt to avoid such protests being entered in the first instance, the ministry restricted them to being submitted before two o'clock on the next sitting day, which was formalised as standing order 114.[50] Neither the additional time constraints, nor repeated attempts to expunge protests from the journals, succeeded in stopping the practice. However, with some notable exceptions, such as those surrounding the fall of Walpole in 1741–2, protests in larger numbers and signed by more than a single peer only began to re-emerge following the accession of George III.[51]

The resurgence of the practice of Lords' protests in the early years of George III's reign can be traced, as W.C. Lowe has argued, to the emergence of an organised and principled opposition under the leadership of the marquess of Rockingham.[52] This kind of opposition coalesced in the context of differing responses to the emergence of the new challenges facing British parliamentarians in the wake of the Seven Years' War.[53] domestically, the issue of John Wilkes and general warrants galvanised and divided political opinion; overseas, the desire to extract revenue from the American colonies and the constitutional confusion about the status of the East India Company's territories within the structures of the empire proved equally contentious. Although numerous protests were entered in the Lords on Wilkes's later tribulations concerning his expulsion from the Commons and the coercive measures imposed upon the American colonies in the wake of the Boston Tea Party, it was on the issue of the regulation of the East India Company that the Rockingham whigs developed and refined their use of protests as both a procedural tool of parliamentary opposition and a uniquely powerful facet of propaganda.

According to Lowe, the Rockinghamite protest of 8 February 1768 proved a defining moment, both for the development of Lords' protests as an opposition strategy in parliament and for their use as a tool to solidify and publicise the guiding principles of party ideology.[54] This protest, against what was essentially an extension of an act passed the previous year to restrict the East India Company from declaring a dividend to its stockholders of over 10%,

---

[47] Jones, 'Dissent and Protest', 310.

[48] *LJ*, iv, 628; see also *A Complete Collection of the Protests of the Lords with Historical Introductions* …, ed. J.E. Thorold Rogers (3 vols, Oxford, 1875), i, p. xxi.

[49] Jones, 'Dissent and Protest', 315–16; see also Turberville, *House of Lords*, 28–9.

[50] For the text of standing order 114, see *LJ*, xxi, 704–5.

[51] W.C. Lowe, 'The House of Lords, Party, and Public Opinion: Opposition Use of the Protest, 1760–1782', *Albion*, xi (1979), 144.

[52] Lowe, 'Use of Protest', 146. For the ideological and organisational development of the Rockingham whigs, see Frank O'Gorman, *The Rise of Party in England: The Rockingham Whigs, 1760–82* (1975).

[53] Ben Gilding, 'Imperial Crises and British Political Ideology in the Age of the American Revolution, 1763–1773', University of Ottawa MA, 2014.

[54] Lowe, 'Use of Protest', 146.

was unique in so far as it drew together into a set of coherent and consistent principles, various strands of Rockinghamite policy on American taxation, on the increasing influence of the crown, and on the Grafton administration's treatment of the East India Company.[55] However, by emphasizing the protest of 8 February 1768, rather than its precursor on 26 June 1767, Lowe privileges the development of Rockinghamite ideology and propaganda, instead of tracing the increased use of Lords' protests as an opposition strategy co-ordinated alongside political manœuvres outside parliament.

The protest of 26 June 1767 was entered following the passage of the acts by which the East India Company's dividend was restricted and it was required to pay to the state the annual sum of £400,000 in recognition of its rights to its territorial possessions on the subcontinent. This protest is important for several reasons. It was among the first official statements of parliamentary opposition to the government's measures against the company. The fact that accounts of parliamentary debates were not yet widely published in the newspaper press only accentuates its importance in this regard.[56] While Lowe is correct in arguing that the 1767 protest focused its opposition to the provisions of the bill itself rather than stating the general Rockinghamite opposition to the measures of government, several sections of the protest clearly anticipated the major lines of opposition to the ministry's policy towards the company. For example, the ninth reason for the protest argued that

> legislative interposition controuling the dividend of a trading Company legally voted and declared by those to whom the power of doing it is entrusted … tends to lessen the idea of that security and independence … which have induced all Europe to deposit their money in the funds of Great Britain, the precedent may be attended with the most fatal consequences to public credit.[57]

Furthermore, the 13th reason complained that the bill, by restraining the dividends, had already anticipated what ought to be a judicial decision: 'that the right to the territorial acquisitions of the Company, in the East Indies, is not in the Company, but in the public', a measure which the protestors argued was 'highly dangerous to the property of the subject, and extremely unbecoming the justice and dignity of this House'.[58] These two aspects of the protest would become major elements in the Rockinghamite opposition to the India legislation of the Grafton and North ministries.

The account in *Cobbett's Parliamentary History*, describes, in a rare preamble, the protest of 1767 as 'strong and nervous', and there are several good reasons for this. Not only was it among the first attempts to articulate an opposition to the Chatham ministry's East India policy, it was also drafted in the context of continued attempts to form an opposition coalition between the Bedford, Grenville, and Rockingham factions.[59] Furthermore, the

---

[55] *Cobbett's Parl. Hist.*, xvi, 404–5.

[56] P.D.G. Thomas, 'John Wilkes and Freedom of the Press (1771)', *Bulletin of the Institute of Historical Research*, xxxiii (1960), 86–98; W.C. Lowe, 'Peers and Printers: The Beginnings of Sustained Press Coverage of the House of Lords in the 1770s', *Parliamentary History*, vii (1988), 241–56.

[57] *Cobbett's Parl. Hist.*, xvi, 356.

[58] *Cobbett's Parl. Hist.*, xvi, 358.

[59] SA, WWM/R/1/774,797: Newcastle to Rockingham, 4 Apr. 1767, Richmond to Rockingham, 12 June 1767. On the controversy surrounding these negotiations, see Gilding, 'Imperial Crises and British Political Ideology', 143–4.

secretary of state, Henry Seymour Conway, and the chancellor of the exchequer, Charles Townshend, had both publicly opposed the government's India policy and the opposition was seeking to gain their support in a unified opposition.[60] Given the lack of precedent for the principles by which it attempted to defend the company from the encroachments of government, and the conciliation necessary for three groups from the parliamentary opposition to collaborate, it is hardly surprising that the protest of 1767 was not a shining example of pure Rockinghamite ideology. More importantly, however, it is indicative of the ways in which opposition would, in the coming years, harness Lords' protests as one part of a wider repertoire of parliamentary and extra-parliamentary strategies against government policy.[61]

The protest of 1767, while not specifically co-ordinated with the company, closely followed the lines of the company's defence of its charter privileges. On 29 May, the company petitioned the Lords to offer its own defence against the restriction of its dividends, arguing in very similar terms to the later protest.[62] The company had identified the Lords as a body which could offer protection from the encroachments of the house of commons, a testament to contemporary perceptions of the continuing importance of the upper chamber within the constitution. Not only was this a strategy that would be repeated in future attempts to defend the rights of the company, but in 1767 it almost succeeded, with a fairly close-run vote in the Lords (59 to 44) against a ministry that possessed strong support from the crown. The later publication of the protest in the newspaper press can be interpreted as a message of solidarity with the company, despite the defeat in the Lords, setting the stage for closer co-operation between parliamentary and extra-parliamentary opposition to the government's East India legislation.[63]

Rather than being a novelty in the use of Lords' protests, the protest of 1768 followed a similar trajectory to that of the previous year. The company first petitioned the Commons,[64] then the Lords,[65] and opposition peers protested following the passage of the bill.[66] In a crucial development, however, the protest of 1768 referred back to its predecessor, in what would become a commonality in Rockinghamite protests concerning the East India Company. Protests were intended as statements of principle, and, as statements of principle, it was important for a party to be able to display consistency over time.[67] Just as the protest

---

[60]Sutherland, *East India Company*, 151–76; L.B. Namier and John Brooke, *Charles Townshend* (1964), 169–72.

[61]The third reading of the bill to restrain the company's dividends was hard fought, passing by only 59 to 44. Ultimately, 19 lords signed the protest, including representatives from the Bedford, Grenville, and Rockingham groups. The protesting lords were: Winchilsea and Nottingham, Scarborough, Trevor, Fortescue, Richmond, Dudley and Ward, King, Weymouth, Gower, Temple, Portland, Sondes, Dorset, Rockingham, Albemarle, Eglinton, Abergavenny, Ponsonby, and the bishop of Exeter.

[62]BL, IOR/B/257, pp. 108–9: general court minutes, 29 May 1767.

[63]*St James's Chronicle or the British Evening Post*, 7 July 1767.

[64]BL, IOR/B/257, pp. 153–4, 160–1: general court minutes, 23 Dec. 1767, 13 Jan. 1768.

[65]BL, IOR/B/257, pp. 166–67: general court minutes, 27 Jan. 1768.

[66]This protest, unlike its predecessor, was not printed in newspapers, but it appeared later in *Annual Register* (1768), 219–21.

[67]Edmund Burke pointed out in 1772 that neither he nor the party ought to feel 'tied down to a servile adherence to the Maxims which we supported in 1767 … we might be allowd, without any suspicion of deserting our principles, to alter an opinion upon six years experience, if six years experience had given us reason to change it': *Burke Correspondence*, ed. Sutherland, ii, 384–5. William Dowdeswell saw protests as a means of 'assert[ing] & publish[ing] your … principles': SA, WWM/R/1/1482: Dowdeswell to Rockingham, 8 Apr. 1774.

of 1768 harked back to an earlier protest, the widely publicised protest of 23 December 1772 specifically stated that the dissenting peers 'think ourselves obliged to oppose' the bill to restrain the East India Company from sending supervisors to manage and reform its affairs in India because of their continued 'adher[ence] to the principles of the Protest of the 9th of February 1768'.[68] In the intervening period between protests, however, the political landscape outside parliament had changed dramatically, despite the relative stability of the ministry now headed by Lord North. The protests of 1767 and 1768 against the government's East India legislation, though not widely printed, had established a crucial precedent for using Lords' protests as yet another means of publicising opposition to the ministry. Protests lodged against the power of the Commons during the Middlesex election case were extensively published in the press and several peers had even taken steps in early 1770 to secure the arrest of the offending printers.[69] By 1772, however, printers had largely won their battle against parliament over the publication of its proceedings. Even if the Lords shut out 'strangers' (including members of the house of commons) from their debates between 1771 and 1775, they could no longer seriously oppose the publication of protests from their journals.[70] The immediate result was that the protests of 23 December 1772[71] and of 11 and 19 June 1773[72] were almost universally published throughout the country, each of which was directed against the government's attempts to restrict and impose reforms upon the East India Company.[73] News of these protests spread across the Atlantic[74] and newspaper writers drew upon their authority while offering their own critiques of North's Indian reforms.[75] Protests from the Lords had emerged as a means of publicising the principles of the political opposition in the popular press in a way that suited the aristocratic tendencies of the Rockingham party.[76]

The Lords' protests of 1773 were characterised by the indefatigable efforts of the duke of Richmond, who attempted to defeat, or at least frustrate, the government's attempts at East India reform through a direct collaboration between the parliamentary opposition and the company's independent stockholders. Initially Richmond was hesitant to participate in the opposition to the government's measures against the company but once in London he

---

[68] LJ, xxxiii, 490–2.

[69] Cobbett's Parl. Hist., xvi, 829–30, 978; see also McCahill, House of Lords, 172. This was not the first time ministerial peers had attempted to prevent the distribution of printed copies of protests. In 1722, the earl of Sunderland had complained that protests were 'printed, handed about in coffee-houses, and sent all over the kingdom, to inflame the minds of the people against the administration; and therefore he thought it high time to have the method of Protesting regulated': Cobbett's Parl. Hist., vii, 969.

[70] Lowe, 'Peers and Printers', 246–7.

[71] Printed in London Evening Post, 26 Dec. 1772; Morning Chronicle, 26 Dec. 1772; Public Ledger, 26 Dec. 1772; Middlesex Journal, 26 Dec. 1772; Hibernian Magazine …, Feb. 1773, pp. 57–9. It was further reported, but without the reasons, in Public Advertiser, 28 Dec. 1772, and Morning Chronicle, 30 Dec. 1772.

[72] For the text of the protest of 11 June 1773, see LJ, xxxiii, 670–1; for the text of the protest of 19 June 1773, see LJ, xxxiii, 681–2.

[73] The protest of 11 June 1773 was printed in Middlesex Journal, 15 June 1773; Morning Chronicle, 15 June 1773; Public Advertiser, 15 June 1773. That of 19 June was printed in London Chronicle, 22 June 1773; Middlesex Journal, 22 June 1773; Morning Chronicle, 22 June 1773; Lloyd's Evening Post, 23 June 1773; Town and Country Magazine …, July 1773, pp. 373–4. An extract was even printed in Morning Chronicle, 24 Nov. 1783, in response to the re-emergence of the regulation of the East India Company as the dominant issue in British politics.

[74] SA, WWM/R/1/1457: James De Lancey to Rockingham, 26 Oct. 1773.

[75] E.g., Public Advertiser, 14 Oct. 1773.

[76] Lowe, 'Use of Protest', 155.

led their efforts with vigour.[77] He purchased enough East India stock to obtain the right to speak and vote in the general courts of the company and urged his Rockinghamite colleagues to do the same.[78] Richmond partnered Governor Johnstone and several Rockinghamite allies in the company's general court and helped to draw up several petitions to the Commons in May 1773 against North's proposed regulations.[79]

Following the passage of North's regulating bill in the Commons, Richmond was not only responsible for drawing up and presenting the company's petition to the Lords,[80] but also led opposition debates against the bill, and signed both protests against it. The first of these protests, it is important to note, called into question the way in which the house of lords was being treated by the Commons during the legislative progress of the bill. Richmond was pushing for a conference with the Commons and for the upper House to be given copies of the reports of the secret committee, which had supposedly provided the evidence on which the Commons had voted for the bill. Both measures were delaying tactics, but Richmond argued that the legislation was being rushed through the Lords in such a way as affected its dignity, an argument he would reiterate in his opposition to Fox's India Bill in 1783.[81] The house of lords had, he argued, 'exerted the greatest diligence through the whole of a very long session' in the case of the South Sea Company in 1720, and engaged in 'a strict parliamentary inquisition into facts, before they thought themselves authorized to resort to an extraordinary use of the legislative powers'.[82] Richmond was not alone in calling on peers to uphold the dignity of their House. One writer, purporting to be '*An Injured Proprietor*' from Salisbury, considered the Lords to be the 'only hope' of preventing a bill 'so pregnant with injustice, tyranny, and oppression' from passing into law. 'That august House', he declared, 'has often stood forth in defence of the liberties of the people; for when the madness of party rage, or venality of former House of Commons, have brought us to the brink of ruin, then their generous interpositions have saved this country from it.[83] As rhetorically powerful as the Lords' protests of June 1773 were in attacking the 'manifest contradiction and absurdity' of North's legislation, they were, as a matter of course, a signal of the opposition's defeat in parliament. The dissenting peers declared that

> after struggling vainly against these evils, we have nothing left but the satisfaction of recording our names to posterity, as those who resisted the whole of this iniquitous

[77] SA, WWM/R/1/1411: Richmond to Rockingham, 2 Nov. 1772; *Burke Correspondence*, ed. Sutherland, ii, 387. Richmond's initial unwillingness to participate in the opposition arose more from his love of country life and fox hunting than lack of zeal regarding the East India Company, for whose independence from government he was among the most consistent advocates, even into 1783–4. Furthermore, in late 1772 the Rockingham whigs were caught up in a debate on whether to secede temporarily from parliament as a general protest against the North administration's policy towards American duties, which certainly encouraged Richmond to remain at Goodwood: *Burke Correspondence*, ed. Sutherland, ii, 362.

[78] For details concerning voting qualifications see H.V. Bowen, ' "The Little Parliament": The General Court of the East India Company', *Historical Journal*, xxxiv (1991), 859.

[79] BL, IOR/B/89, pp. 114–16, 175–80; see also Bowen, *Revenue and Reform*, 174.

[80] BL, IOR/B/89, pp. 242–4.

[81] *An Authentic Account of the Debates in the House of Lords, on Tuesday, December 9, Monday, December 15, and Wednesday, December 17, 1783 …* (1783), 28.

[82] *LJ*, xxxiii, 670–1.

[83] *Morning Chronicle*, 14 June 1773.

system, as men who had no share in betraying to blind prejudices or sordid interest everything that has hitherto been held sacred in this country.[84]

The Lords' protests of 1773 were not simply a 'defiant act from a thoroughly dispirited and downhearted opposition'.[85] Richmond's dual tactics in the house of lords and East India House forced North to concede on several key aspects of his Regulating Act.[86] The Lords' protests may have signified the cessation of legislative opposition, but, with their strong statement of principles and wide publication, they marked the beginning of a year-long attempt by Richmond and his erstwhile supporters among the proprietors of India stock to frustrate the implementation of North's reforms. Richmond, at the head of a committee of proprietors, drafted a set of alternative instructions to the governor general and supreme council of Bengal, intended to subvert key aspects of the Regulating Act.[87] Ultimately, Richmond's opposition was halted by a series of defeats at East India House which followed the Regulating Act's disenfranchisement of over a thousand stockholders holding less than £1,000 of India stock.[88] Utilising one of the central corporate institutions of the City as the locus for opposition activity was unorthodox for a peer, particularly one of his rank, and many of Richmond's aristocratic colleagues in the Rockingham party were far less inclined to participate.[89] The defeat of Richmond's opposition, in the election of 24 new directors of the company in April 1774, marked the high point of the Rockinghamite opposition to the reform of the company for nearly a decade, as it was overshadowed by the American war.[90] When the East India Company re-emerged as a major issue in British politics following the introduction of Charles James Fox's famous India Bill in 1783, the shadow of the previous protests loomed large.

4

By March 1783, the remnants of the Rockingham whigs, led by Charles James Fox after Rockingham's death in July 1782, had formed a coalition government with North and his followers. The coalition was deeply unpopular among the public, and parliamentarians viewed their alliance with suspicion.[91] Either Fox, or North, or both, were accused of gross inconsistency, considering their near decade-long opposition, with innumerable pernicious

---

[84] *LJ*, xxxiii, 681–2.

[85] Bowen, *Revenue and Reform*, 186.

[86] Sutherland, *East India Company*, 264–5.

[87] The directors' original instructions can be found in BL, IOR/B/258, pp. 303–15. Richmond's alternate instructions, delivered on 15 Dec. 1773, are in BL, IOR/B/258, pp. 321–38.

[88] Bowen, ' "Little Parliament" ', 868.

[89] SA, WWM/R/1/1428: Admiral Augustus Keppel to Rockingham, 15 Mar. 1773; *Burke Correspondence*, ed. Sutherland, ii, 497.

[90] Horace Walpole wrote: 'there ended the Duke of Richmond's Indian Campaign, in which his spirit, address, insinuation and application had greatly distinguished him and acquired a large number of adherents, by whom he had so long balanced the power of Government at a moment when Opposition had in a manner given up the contest in Parliament': *Journal of the Reign of King George the Third, from the Year 1771 to 1783* (2 vols, 1859), i, 301.

[91] See, among innumerable newspaper paragraphs, *The Coalition, or an Essay on the Present State of Parties* (1783); Francis Dobbs, *A Letter to Lord North and Mr Fox* (1784); Nathaniel Buckington, *Serious Considerations on the Political Conduct of Lord North* (1783).

epithets traded between the two leaders and their friends.[92] As Richmond claimed in the house of lords later that year: 'one of three things must be true; either Lord North had given up his principles to the Duke of Portland [the nominal first lord of the treasury in the coalition ministry], the Duke of Portland to Lord North, or that the Cabinet was divided on every principle, and therefore no good could possibly be expected from either'.[93] Others attempted to defend the coalition by arguing that the major bone of contention between Fox and North during this period, the American war, had ended, and thus it was at least possible that they could work together toward future policies.[94] Richmond disagreed, and justified his decision to resign from the government by arguing that 'he could not see his own name standing to so many protests against Lord North, and consent to act with him'.[95] He had already refused to resign from Shelburne's ministry alongside Fox, following diplomatic disputes and the death of Rockingham, but for Richmond this was the final straw and completed his 'gradual defection' from the Rockinghamites that had begun following the failure of his opposition to North's Regulating Act in 1773–4.[96] For Richmond, the contest with North went deeper than the single issue of North America.

The Rockingham whigs continued the practice of issuing Lords' protests against the progression of the American conflict.[97] But they had perfected the strategy of protesting over issues such as East India Company reform and the Middlesex election disputes, when Fox was either supporting the ministry, or was only a very recent convert to opposition.[98] As a member of the Commons, such protests could not bind Fox, but the same cannot be said for several of his noble colleagues, such as the dukes of Devonshire and Portland, and Earl Fitzwilliam, who had each signed protests against the North administration's East India legislation.[99] When Fox's India Bill was introduced in late 1783, the consistency of the protesting lords formed a leading argument from the opposition benches.

Fox's India Bill sought to go further than North's Regulating Act. Based on the cumulative experience of the decade-long experiment of North's Indian system and the reports of select and secret committees which had been sitting for over two years, it consciously sought to initiate a thorough reform of the company's affairs by changing both men and measures.[100] Although the committee reports were heavily criticized in the press and in

[92] *The Beauties and Deformities of Fox, North, and Burke, Selected from their Speeches from the Year 1770, down to the Present Time* (1783–4); this pamphlet went through at least five editions in year following its publication.

[93] *A Full and Accurate Account of the Debates on the East-India Bill in the House of Lords on Tuesday the 9th, on Monday the 15th, Tuesday the 16th, and Wednesday the 17th of December, 1783* (1784), 18.

[94] William Godwin, *A Defence of the Rockingham Party in their Late Coalition with Lord North* (1783).

[95] Walpole, *Journal*, ii, 589.

[96] Alison Olson, *The Radical Duke: The Career and Correspondence of Charles Lennox Third Duke of Richmond* (Oxford, 1961), 31–47; McCahill, *House of Lords*, 177.

[97] The opposition protested at least 11 times between 1774 and 1781 against the North ministry's handling of the American war: *Protests*, ed. Rogers, ii, 142–211. The number of protests reached such a height that Lord Camden rightly cautioned that 'protesting in my opinion will become a very feeble weapon & lose its edge if too often used': SA, WWM/R/1/1616a: Camden to Rockingham, 28 Oct. 1775.

[98] Loren Reid, *Charles James Fox: A Man of the People* (1969), 25–6.

[99] Portland had signed all five protests against the Grafton/North Administration's East India legislation; Devonshire signed three in 1772–3; Fitzwilliam signed only the two protests in 1773, but was ineligible to sign in 1767 and 1768 because he was not yet of age to take up his seat.

[100] The select committee, headed by Edmund Burke and General Richard Smith, had been sitting since February 1781 and had produced 11 reports. Dundas's secret committee had been sitting from April 1781 to 1782 and had produced a further six reports.

the house of commons, there remained a pervasive belief that the miserable state of the company's affairs required comprehensive reformation.[101] Before Fox introduced his measure into parliament, Pitt had warned him not to bring in anything 'merely palliative' and was evidently prepared to attack him for not doing enough to regulate the company.[102] In the event, however, such encouragement was unnecessary. Fox's reforms had already been drafted, and they went far beyond anything that Pitt and his followers were willing to support. The proposed measures generated a hail of controversy and ultimately proved fatal for an unpopular coalition ministry which had come into office by 'storming the closet' and limiting the king's ability to choose his own ministers. Fox's India Bill involved vesting control over the company's affairs at home and abroad in a group of seven parliamentary commissioners who would be named in the act. The company's commercial activities would have been nominally left to a group of nine assistant commissioners, many of whom were former or current directors. The direction of the company's political, military, and diplomatic affairs in South Asia, then, was vested in a London-based parliamentary commission and even measures on the commercial side required their approval. The only caveat was that the measure was supposedly temporary, being limited to four years. It was, as Lucy Sutherland described, 'a more sweeping attack on the independence of the Company than anyone had ever suggested since Beckford had blustered in the House of Commons in 1767'.[103]

Every time the East India Company's affairs came before parliament, they carried with them the spectre of augmenting the influence of the crown. Fox's bill, coming as it did from the coalition ministry, which was already widely seen as being unprincipled and self-interested, seemed to confirm the fears of opposition. Opponents of the act weaved their criticism of the proposed legislation and of the Fox–North ministry itself into a plausible narrative, that by vesting the patronage of the company in the hands of seven parliamentary commissioners, handpicked by the coalition, the India Bill would lead to the erection of what they described as a 'fourth estate' in British politics.[104] This fourth estate, independent of crown and parliament, would enable Fox's party to remain in power indefinitely, it was argued, by allowing them to purchase a strong and permanent support in parliament to an extent hitherto unknown to the constitution. Not only would it eradicate all the benefits produced by the economical reforms of the Rockingham–Shelburne ministry, it would also overshadow the influence of the crown, whose supposed augmentation in the new reign Fox and Edmund Burke, in particular, had spent much of their careers fighting against.[105] The opposition to Fox's India Bill appeared to reveal an attempt by the coalition to sustain

---

[101] See criticism of the committees in [N.B. Halhed], *The Letters of Detector, on the Seventh and Eighth Reports of the Select Committee and on the India Regulating Bill* (1783); [N.B. Halhed], *A Letter to the Rt. Hon. Edmund Burke, on the Subject of his Late Charges against the Governor-General of Bengal* (1783); John Scott, *A Letter to the Right Honourable Edmund Burke* (1783); Joseph Price, *A Letter to Edmund Burke, Esq; on the Latter Part of the Late Report of the Select Committee on the State of Justice in Bengal* (1782).

[102] *Cobbett's Parl. Hist.*, xxiii, 1141, 1156.

[103] Sutherland, *East India Company*, 398.

[104] *Cobbett's Parl. Hist.*, xxiv, 1327; William Pulteney, *Effects to be Expected from the East India Bill upon the Constitution of Great Britain* (1784); *A Warning Voice; or An Answer to the Speech of the Right Honourable Mr. Secretary Fox, upon East-India Affairs* ... (1783); *Morning Chronicle*, 25 Feb. 1784.

[105] *Cobbett's Parl. Hist.*, xxiii, 1253–4, 1310, 1395.

their power indefinitely without the support of the king and to undermine the ability of independent MPs and Lords to preserve the desired balance of the constitution.

Such criticisms hurt the remnants of the Rockingham party all the more for their much-vaunted ideological consistency. Throughout their existence as a distinct parliamentary faction and since the emergence of the East India Company as a major issue in British parliamentary politics in 1767, the Rockingham whigs had taken a clear position against the intervention of the British state into the affairs of the company. While Burke argued as early as 1773 that they ought not feel bound to their previous position in light of new evidence and new circumstances, they had in fact opposed North's reforms in 1773 upon much the same ground as they had Chatham's 'predatory raid' upon the company in 1767.[106] The Lords' protests, as we have seen, were a crucial element in the articulation of these principles. They offered a means of presenting views to the public unaccompanied and unopposed by competing arguments.[107] Moreover, each protest referred specifically to earlier instances of dissent on similar issues, forming a distinct chain of principled Rockinghamite opposition to government measures. This consistency, often viewed as a strength by historians and contemporaries alike, could also prove to be a source of weakness, as became clear during the introduction and subsequent defence of Fox's India Bill in parliament.[108]

The precise details of Fox's Indian reforms were a closely guarded secret in the weeks and months leading up to the bill's introduction on 18 November 1783.[109] Several days prior to its introduction, however, Fitzwilliam expressed reservations about several crucial aspects of the bill. He had been approached by Portland to accept a role at the head of the new parliamentary commission but expressed sincere misgivings about his fitness for the role, how much of his time it would occupy, and whether or not he would be in charge of the '*political* affairs of the Company *only*, leaving to a Comm[itt]ee of Directors the management of the detail of Commerce'.[110] Revealingly, however, he called upon the duke to 'read our protest in 1773'. Fitzwilliam pointed to the third reason in the protest of 19 June 1773 which argued that the 'election of executive officers in parliament is plainly unconstitutional' because it was 'calculated for extending a corrupt influence in the crown' and 'frees ministers from responsibility, whilst it leaves them all the effect of patronage'. These measures, it was then argued, would 'defeat the wise Design of the Constitution'.[111] In his letter to Portland, Fitzwilliam maintained that these points were 'argued upon such general principles that I do not see the possibility of getting over it. No circumstances, no situation, can make any change in so general a principle.'[112] As a signatory to the protests

---

[106] *Burke Correspondence*, ed. Sutherland, ii, 384–5; P.J. Marshall, *Problems of Empire: Britain and India 1757–1813* (1968), 30.

[107] Lowe has shown that some later protests against the American war were combatted in the press by counter-protests and articles denouncing them which reduced their effectiveness. The only instance of this in the case of a Lords' protest against East India Company reform was in 1784 when five lords protested against the passage of Pitt's India Act: *Morning Post*, 14 Aug. 1784.

[108] O'Gorman, *Rise of Party*; Warren Elofson, *The Rockingham Connection and the Second Founding of the Whig Party, 1768–1773* (Montreal and Kingston, ON, 1996).

[109] HMC, *8th Report*, pt 3, 132–3.

[110] University of Nottingham Library, Portland (Welbeck) MSS, PwF 3757: Fitzwilliam to Portland, 16 Nov. 1783.

[111] *LJ*, xxxiii, 681–2.

[112] University of Nottingham Library, PwF 3757: Fitzwilliam to Portland, 16 Nov. 1783.

of 1773, Fitzwilliam felt very uncomfortable participating in a policy so evidently contrary to the principles they had then laid down for posterity. What is more, the remnants of the Rockingham party were now partners in a coalition with many of those against whom they had protested in 1773. North could hardly be accused of inconsistency in attacking the rights of the East India Company and their stockholders. But the Rockingham whigs had publicly pledged themselves in defence of the company over the course of the preceding two decades and were now accused of attempting to appropriate its patronage in precisely the manner in which they had previously attacked North. Fitzwilliam even argued that 'it will be ten times better to meet the thing boldly, & give the King the appointment for the purpose of creating *Responsibility* in *those, who advise him to appoint*'.[113] Fitzwilliam's last suggestion is particularly interesting because, although it is clear that Pitt and others were prepared to attack Fox for inconsistency and for attempting to augment the influence of the Crown, if this advice was followed the king would not have had the excuse he eventually found to oust the coalition. Perhaps Fox's bill would still have been defeated in the Lords, but it would have raised significantly different constitutional issues in the process.

Fitzwilliam was not the only person to raise the question of consistency in the days following the bill's introduction. When William Grenville, Sir Richard Hill, and others dredged up the protests for the benefit of the house of commons, and when these same concerns of inconsistency were aired in the newspaper press, it was a charge to which the framers and proponents of Fox's bill felt obliged to respond. In support of his arguments against the bill in the Commons, Grenville ironically drew upon the authority of the protests in the Lords in 1773 in which 'the same sentiments would be found, but expressed with infinitely more dignity, more ability, and more authority, than he could ever pretend to lay claim to'.[114] He also remarked on the difference, laid bare by Fox's India Bill, between the marquess of Rockingham, known for his 'uniform and consistent adherence to fixed principles' and the remnants of his party 'who had chosen to proceed on opposite principles'.[115] Grenville then proceeded to read the protests to the Commons in support of his own arguments that Fox's measure would increase the influence of the crown. Sir Richard Hill also made reference to the protests during the debate on the second reading, when it was becoming increasingly clear that the bill would pass the Commons with a large majority. He affected to be reassured that the company had such 'a powerful friend in the other House to plead their cause, and to support their rights; he meant the noble duke [of Portland] at the head of the Treasury board, who, when the East India regulating bill was brought in, just ten years ago (which bill did not go near so far as the present), testified his hearty dissent from it'.[116] He hoped that Portland would be 'as steady in his principles till death, as the much lamented marquis [of Rockingham], who joined with him in the protest' and therefore throw out the bill.[117]

The fact that members of both Houses frequently pointed towards Lords' protests when discussing issues of consistency and political integrity as proof of their claims, is a testament to the importance of the protests in the eyes of contemporaries as authoritative statements of

---

[113] University of Nottingham Library, PwF 3757: Fitzwilliam to Portland, 16 Nov. 1783.

[114] *Cobbett's Parl. Hist.*, xxiii, 1228.

[115] *Cobbett's Parl. Hist.*, xxiii, 1228.

[116] *Cobbett's Parl. Hist.*, xxiii, 1290.

[117] *Cobbett's Parl. Hist.*, xxiii, 1290; xxiv, 43.

principle. When expressing similar sentiments concerning the consistency of the protesting peers on the issue of reforming the East India Company, James Townsend was called to order for referring to the upper House as 'superior' and told by the Speaker that 'it was extremely disorderly for any member of that House to state either of the three branches of the legislature as superior to the others'. Townsend resumed his argument, stating that he 'only meant to speak his opinion of the privileges enjoyed by the other House, of recording their sentiments upon any measure to posterity; and declared, that calling the protests of the Lords on the bill of 1773, political libels, was, in his mind, a very indecent presumption'.[118] When William Grenville read the 1773 protests it was observed that their language was 'remarkably spirited and warm', which must have drawn suggestions from members that such language was libellous. By defending the protests as a unique privilege of a 'superior' house, Townsend was, in a similar manner to Grenville, ironically defending the language of those who proposed Fox's India Bill, against which he was a 'very strenuous' opponent.[119]

Supporters of Fox's bill in the Commons handled criticisms of their principles and consistency with marked awkwardness. Lord John Cavendish, chancellor of the exchequer, and uncle of the duke of Devonshire, who had signed both protests in 1773, said that 'had he been a peer, he would have set his name to the protest', and argued that circumstances had changed in the intervening period which justified a measure in 1783 that he had opposed in 1773. The justification, he argued, was that of necessity; that without Fox's bill, the East India Company would neither be able to support itself nor preserve its territorial possessions, possessions contemporaries increasingly saw as a crucial part of the empire.[120]

Discussion of the Lords' protests of 1773 only increased when Fox's bill passed from the Commons to the Lords on 9 December 1783. Richmond, who had signed almost every protest against measures to reform the company since 1767, was among the foremost speakers in opposition to the bill and vehemently attacked his former colleagues for what he regarded as their inconsistency and hypocrisy over the issue.[121] Richmond confronted Portland with charges that by promoting Fox's bill he was violating principles to which they were both signatories in the two protests of 1773. First, he argued, Portland was refusing to bring before the Lords the company's papers and accounts that had been submitted to the Commons during the passage of the bill through the lower House. This was a direct violation, he argued, of the protest they had both signed on 11 June 1773 against the precipitation with which North had been attempting to push through his Indian legislation.[122] Second, Richmond pointed out that Portland had signed the protest of 19 June 1773 against the principle of 'a measure of a very inferior degree of atrocity' to Fox's bill. 'How was it possible', he asked, to 'support such a measure without a sacrifice of every principle he had formerly professed?'[123]

---

[118] *Cobbett's Parl. Hist.*, xxiv, 54–5.

[119] See *HPC, 1754–90*, iii, 537–8.

[120] *Cobbett's Parl. Hist.*, xxiii, 1231.

[121] The only protests concerning the East India Company that Richmond did not sign between 1767 and 1784 were against the Bengal Judicature Act, 13 July 1781, and against Pitt's India Act, 9 Aug. 1784: *LJ*, xxxvi, 357; xxxvii, 149.

[122] *Full and Accurate Account* …, 17.

[123] *Authentic Account* …, 26.

Richmond laid his most destructive trap, however, when he presented the petition of the City of London against the India Bill. The petition condemned the bill as 'not only a high and dangerous violation of the charters of the Company, but a total subversion of all the principles of the law and constitution of this country'. It argued that 'the election of executive officers in parliament is plainly unconstitutional, productive of intrigue and faction, and calculated for extending a corrupt influence in the crown;' and 'that it frees ministers from responsibility, while it leaves them all the effect of patronage'.[124] When the clerk finished reading the petition, the duke of Manchester, a prominent supporter of the coalition, walked straight into the snare by denouncing the unparliamentary language of the petitioners.[125] Richmond then informed the House that the City's petition had been 'drawn up in the very language of a famous protest, signed by the late marquis of Rockingham, and many other noble lords'.[126] Through another collaboration between extraparliamentary opposition and Lords' protests, Richmond had exposed the inconsistency of his former colleagues.

To press home his point, Richmond flaunted his own consistency, observing that 'he gloried in having signed that protest [of 19 June 1773]'.[127] He stood by the principles he had always held; that 'it was entirely owing to the interference of Government that the East India Company had been ruined'.[128] For Richmond, a protest was a pledge of principles and if a peer 'altered his opinion, posterity would judge of the motives for such a conduct'.[129] Portland could only deny that he had changed his principles. He 'still adhered to them, and subscribed most heartily to the sentiments of the protests which he had signed in 1773'. Like Lord John Cavendish in the Commons, Portland claimed that the circumstances had changed over the decade and justified Fox's bill on the basis of necessity. Without regulation, he argued, both company and nation would be ruined.[130]

The records of debates on Fox's India Bill reveal that the coalition ministry was rhetorically defeated in the house of lords, a fact that largely matched expectations, even those of Fox himself.[131] He had admitted to being afraid that Portland would be overwhelmed by opposition to the bill.[132] Feeling assured of his majority in the lower House, Fox claimed that the Lords would become the true 'scene of action' and, due to the 'vigorous and hazardous' nature of his India Bill, he believed Portland would 'find less support upon this question than upon others'.[133] Indeed, Fox had long recognized that the 'delicate nature' of parliamentary interventions into the affairs of the East India Company meant that 'if ever Opposition is likely to be formidable' it would be upon such a question.[134] Particularly in

---

[124] *Cobbett's Parl. Hist.*, xxiv, 144.

[125] *Cobbett's Parl. Hist.*, xxiv, 145.

[126] *Cobbett's Parl. Hist.*, xxiv, 145 (there is an alternate version of Richmond's speech in *Full and Accurate Account* …, 56).

[127] *Authentic Account* …, 29.

[128] *Full and Accurate Account* …, 17.

[129] *Authentic Account* …, 28–9.

[130] *Authentic Account* …, 27; see *Full and Accurate Account* …, 18.

[131] *Gazetteer and New Daily Advertiser*, 25 Nov. 1783; *Public Advertiser*, 3 Dec. 1783; *Morning Herald*, 5 Dec. 1783.

[132] HMC, *8th Report*, pt 3, 137.

[133] BL, Add. MS 47567, f. 4: Charles James Fox to earl of Northington, 7 Nov. 1783; HMC, *8th Report*, pt 3, 137–8.

[134] BL, Add. MS 47567, ff. 11–13: Fox to Northington, 17 July 1783.

the case of an India Bill 'the variety of private interests that will militate against us can not fail of making it a most tempting opportunity to opposition'.[135] However, while admitting that 'the majority of debaters is against us', in early December Fox still believed that 'in point of numbers … there is no cause to fear'.[136]

It is difficult to obtain a clear picture of the coalition ministry's strength in the Lords and, as McCahill has shown, it is uncertain whether even the coalition themselves were aware of the precise numbers.[137] In fairness to the coalition's parliamentary managers, the uniquely bold nature of the India Bill meant that some of its traditional supporters in both Houses voted against it.[138] Furthermore, the ministry's storming of the closet, and the widespread rumours of the king's hostility towards them, placed a number of officeholders in the Lords in an equivocal position before the views of the king became known. Each of these factors militated against an accurate prediction of numbers for and against the measure. Despite the general unpopularity of the coalition upon its formation in April 1783, Fox felt confident of the coalition's strength in the Lords, where it successfully saw through the controversial Irish Appeals Act.[139] By the time the India Bill came before the Commons in November 1783, he was hoping for crushing majorities in the lower House which he believed would help to persuade the Lords to accept it.[140] This reflected his view, confirmed by his opposition to Pitt's ministry in early 1784, that the Lords was the inferior chamber, likely to capitulate in the face of large Commons majorities.[141]

The outcome of debates in the Lords and the numerical calculations in the months before the bill's introduction in the upper House were entirely overshadowed, however, by the unprecedented actions of the king in December 1783. On 11 December, between the first and second readings of the India Bill in the Lords, Temple had a conference with the king during which they finalised the plan to defeat the bill in the upper House. In the course of the meeting, George III provided Temple with a note that empowered him to say on behalf of the king 'that whoever voted for the India Bill was not only not his friend, but would be considered by him as an enemy'. As a signal of the depth of George's opposition to the India Bill, he further authorised Temple to 'use whatever words he might deem stronger and more to the purpose'.[142] Following this meeting, Temple and others industriously propagated the

---

[135] BL, Add. MS 47568, ff. 205–6: Fox to John Burgoyne, 7 Nov. 1783.

[136] HMC, *8th Report*, pt 3, 138.

[137] McCahill, *House of Lords*, 184.

[138] E.g., *Anecdotes of the Life of Richard Watson, Bishop of Llandaff* (1817), 124–5.

[139] BL, Add. MS 47579, ff. 21–2: Fox to earl of Upper Ossory, 18 Apr. 1783. On the Irish Appeals Act (23 Geo. III, c. 28), see M.J. Powell, *Britain and Ireland in the Eighteenth-Century Crisis of Empire* (Basingstoke, 2003), 225–6. The Shelburne ministry's previous commitment to that legislation, however, suggests that it could have given a false impression of the coalition's strength in the upper chamber.

[140] BL, Add. MS 47579, f. 35: Fox to Upper Ossory, 21 Nov. 1783.

[141] This view was also ascribed to Fox and the coalition in *Whitehall Evening Post*, 6 Jan. 1784, and in a letter 'To the Real Electors of Westminster', signed 'A Brother Elector', in *Public Advertiser*, 25 June 1784.

[142] *Memoirs of the Court and Cabinets of George the Third from Original Family Documents*, ed. duke of Buckingham (2nd edn, 2 vols, 1853), i, 285. An alternative and stronger version of the king's message is provided by John Burgoyne, who claimed to be relating 'the precise Expressions used in the Conference' from a source he refuses to reveal in correspondence: 'I think this Bill unprecedented, unparliamentary, and subversive of the Constitution, as in producing a fourth Power which does not belong to it. If this Bill passes, I am no more a King. I shall look upon those, who support the Bill, not only as not my friends, but as my absolute Enemies. My Lord, if you can find terms stronger to express my Disapprobation, you have my authority to use them': BL, Add. MS 38716, ff. 142–3: Burgoyne to Northington, 15 Dec. 1783.

news of the king's vehement opposition in the hopes that it would persuade enough peers to defeat the bill.[143] In the event, the king's personal intervention was the crucial factor that rendered the India Bill fatal to the ministry. As McCahill has argued, George III's message did not necessarily induce a decisive swing of the so-called 'party of the crown' away from the coalition,[144] but it did persuade enough peers of diverse complexions to reject the bill on 17 December 1783.[145] As late as 11 December, however, the earl of Clarendon, who at this time was negotiating with Pitt on behalf of the king, reported that: 'it is apprehended that the contested bill will pass the H. of Lords if Power remains where it is'.[146] This echoed the expectations of those close to the coalition ministry, who continued to believe that the bill would pass, despite vocal opposition to it in the Lords.[147]

There was, however, a mounting belief in the press that the Lords could, and even that it *ought* to, defeat the bill, reflecting its role as the 'Refuge of the People of this Country … unmoved by *those Motives* which sway inferior Orders of Men.'[148] Even the earl of Northington wrote to Fox from Dublin that 'it is supposed here, that it is likely you will be turned out by the failure of the East India Bill in the House of Lords'.[149] When rumours began to circulate that the king had authorised Temple to deliver a message to peers outlining his opposition to the bill, it was treated with derision and ridicule by many in coalition circles. William Eden regarded it as a trick by Temple to 'gain five or six recruits'. For the king to act in such a way, he believed, 'would be madness'.[150] None the less, Portland, who

---

[143] Wraxall recalled that 'Lord Temple, though one of the first individuals thus authorised, formed by no means the sole or exclusive medium through which the royal pleasure was so signified and circulated': *Wraxall Memoirs*, ed. Wheatley, iii, 187. The duke of Rutland approached the bishop of Llandaff (*Anecdotes of the Life of Richard Watson*, 125); William Pitt contacted Lord Grantham ('Lord Grantham and William Pitt, 12 December 1783: A Side-Light on the Fall of the Fox–North Coalition', ed. I.R. Christie, *Historical Journal*, xxxiv (1991), 143–5). The king himself called on Lord Weymouth to come to town (Eridge Park, Abergavenny MSS, 526: Atkinson to John Robinson, 12 Dec. 1783), while John Robinson was charged with obtaining the votes of Lord Abergavenny, the duke of Beaufort, and Lord Montagu (Eridge Park, Abergavenny MSS, 523: Charles Jenkinson to Robinson, 5 Dec. 1783), and Lord Sydney attempted to persuade Lord Onslow to withdraw his proxy (Cannon, *Fox-North Coalition*, 134; BL, Add. MS 47568, f. 218: Charles Townshend to Fox, 14 Dec. 1783).

[144] The bishops, Scottish representative peers, and officeholders: David Large, 'The Decline of the "Party of the Crown" and the Rise of Parties in the House of Lords, 1783–1837', *English Historical Review*, lxxviii (1963), 669–95. The contrary opinion was expressed in the *Morning Chronicle*, 8 Dec. 1783: 'Many people imagine that Mr. Fox's Bill will be very close run in the Upper Assembly; but a man, may make a good shrewd guess, if he knows how wag my Lords the Bishops.' Richard Fitzpatrick, remarking on the same phenomenon, claimed that: 'The Bishops waver & *The Thanes fly from us*': BL, Add. MS 47579, f. 123: Fitzpatrick to Upper Ossory, 15 Dec. 1783.

[145] McCahill, *House of Lords*, 186–9.

[146] Bodl., MS Clarendon dep. c. 347, pp. 618: Clarendon to Pitt, 11 Dec. 1783.

[147] Eridge Park, Abergavenny MSS, 527: Richard Rigby to John Robinson, 12 Dec. 1783; see also BL, Add. MS 33100, ff. 450, 473–4: Burgoyne to Northington, 9 Dec. 1783, William Windham to Northington, 18 Dec. 1783; *Gazetteer and New Daily Advertiser*, 25 Nov. 1783; *Morning Herald*, 5 Dec. 1783; *Whitehall Evening Post*, 11 Dec. 1783.

[148] *Public Advertiser*, 3 Dec. 1783. The following newspapers predicted that the Lords would reject the India Bill: *Whitehall Evening Post*, 27 Nov. 1783; *Public Advertiser*, 28 Nov. 1783; *London Chronicle*, 27 Nov. 1783; *General Evening Post*, 29 Nov. 1783; *Felix Farley's Bristol Journal*, 6 Dec. 1783; *Public Advertiser*, 11 Dec. 1783; *Public Advertiser*, 12 Dec. 1783; *General Evening Post*, 13 Dec. 1783.

[149] BL, Add. MS 47567, f. 72: Northington to Fox, 30 Nov. 1783.

[150] BL, Add. MS 47567, f. 456: William Eden to Northington, 12 Dec. 1783; see also BL, Add. MS 47567, f. 522: Windham to Northington, 12 Dec. 1783.

had previously dismissed the rumours of Temple's audience with the king as false, raised the issue in the Lords along with accusation that, if true, the behaviour was unconstitutional.[151]

Almost simultaneously, a similar line of opposition against the king's message to Temple was adopted in the Commons. When introducing his motions against Temple's actions, William Baker called for the resolutions of 12 November 1640 and 16 December 1641 to be read, both of which, he argued, were instances when the Commons had defended itself against external attempts to bias its deliberations.[152] In his first motion, he argued that

> it is now necessary to declare that, to report any opinion, or pretended opinion, of his Majesty, upon any bill, or other proceeding, depending in either House of Parliament, with a view to influence the votes of the members, is a high crime and misdemeanour, derogatory to the honour of the crown, a breach of the fundamental privileges of parliament, and subversive of the constitution of this country.[153]

By this motion, the Fox-North coalition was implicitly engaging in an attack on what was seen to be another of the unique prerogatives of the house of lords, the right of peers to demand an audience and to advise the king.[154] It is, therefore, incorrect to argue that 'neither Fox nor his allies in the Commons responded to their defeat by attacking the prerogatives of the House of Lords'.[155] Foxites were less concerned with the *fact* that they were defeated in the Lords, than the *means* by which the votes were obtained to reject the bill. Rather than directly challenging the king's actions – for the 18th-century monarch 'could do no wrong' – they targeted the fact that Temple had deliberately circulated the message in order to disrupt the legislative agenda of the government.[156]

In the Lords, Temple met the issue head on, as did his allies in the Commons. They explicitly argued on the basis that Temple was simply exercising his legitimate prerogative as a peer of the realm. The coalition had introduced the question in both Houses without specifically referring to Temple. However, in attempting to defend Temple against the rumours of his conference with the king, Richmond inadvertently let slip his name while relating to the House the contents of a newspaper article and forced Temple to confront the issue directly.[157] He did so, it was reported, 'upon his highest horse', avowing that he had an audience with the king in which he gave advice 'unfriendly to the principle and object of the [India] Bill'.[158] By doing so he argued that he had 'acted a dutiful part towards his sovereign, and one worthy the approbation of their lordship[s]'.[159] In the lower House, Temple's allies argued along similar lines. Their focus, too, was in defence of the preroga-

---

[151]BL, Add. MS 47567, ff. 468–9: Burgoyne to Thomas Pelham, 16 Dec. 1783; see also *Cobbett's Parl. Hist.*, xxiv, 154–5.

[152]*Cobbett's Parl. Hist.*, xxiv, 198.

[153]*Cobbett's Parl. Hist.*, xxiv, 199.

[154]Ditchfield, 'House of Lords', 203, notes that Temple's was not the only instance of a peer exercising his right to an audience with the monarch in this period, but it 'was the most spectacular' and the most controversial.

[155]McCahill, *House of Lords*, 190.

[156]The sanctity of the king's person was repeatedly reaffirmed in the debates concerning Temple's actions: *Cobbett's Parl. Hist.*, xxiv, 158, 159, 197, 199, 218.

[157]*Cobbett's Parl. Hist.*, xxiv, 153.

[158]BL, Add. MS 33100, ff. 468–9: Burgoyne to Pelham, 16 Dec. 1783.

[159]*Cobbett's Parl. Hist.*, xxiv, 154.

tive of peers to give advice to the sovereign and in the process they accused the coalition of attempting to circumscribe the independence of the upper chamber.[160] Unsurprisingly, the Pitt administration defended the prerogatives of the house of lords, the arena within which the India Bill had been defeated, thereby also ensuring the dismissal of the coalition ministry.

5

When Portland initially dismissed the rumours of Temple's audience with the king, he did so because he reported that 'His Majesty had never expressed to him the slightest disinclination to give the Bill his full support & even on the Friday when the Duke was with him, did not give him the least hint of what had passed with Lord Temple.'[161] Reeling from the defeat of his bill in the Lords, Fox wrote to his lover that: 'We are beat in the H. of Lds by such treachery on the part of the King, & such meanness on the part of his *friends* in the H. of Lds as one could not expect even from him or them.'[162] Fox and Portland evidently felt all the more betrayed by the king as he had apparently acquiesced in the Indian reforms at every previous stage.[163] Sir Gilbert Elliot, a close supporter of the coalition and one of those responsible for drafting the India Bill, reported that: 'the King had seen it in all its stages, and encouraged his ministers to proceed, without, however, any express or explicit approbation of it'.[164] Two major questions, then, remain to be answered: when did the king first begin to oppose the bill? And, perhaps more important, at what stage did Fox's India Bill reach a level of maturity that could have enabled him to form such a judgment against it?

It is well known that, from its inception in April 1783, the king wanted to be rid of the coalition ministry. Ever since Thomas Pitt had submitted his crucial memorandum, advising the king not to abdicate and to 'give Fox and North rope enough to hang themselves', George III was awaiting an opportunity to dismiss the ministers who had forced themselves upon him.[165] Writing to Temple, the king described the coalition as 'the most unprincipled … the annals of this or any other nation can equal', which 'cannot be supposed to have either my favour or confidence'. He called upon Temple to

> join other honest men in watching the conduct of this unnatural combination, and I hope many months will not elapse before the Grenvilles, the Pitts, and other men of abilities and character will relieve me from a situation that nothing could have compelled me to submit to, but the supposition that no other means remained of preventing the public finances from being materially affected.[166]

[160] *Cobbett's Parl. Hist.*, xxiv, 199–202.

[161] BL, Add. MS 33100, ff. 471–2: George Augustus North to Thomas Pelham, 16 Dec. 1783.

[162] BL, Add. MS 47570, f. 156: Fox to Elizabeth Armistead, [17 Dec. 1783].

[163] George III had supported the previous attempts to reform the East India Company in 1767 and 1773: Royal Archives, GEO/MAIN/548: George III to Henry Seymour Conway, 6 Dec. 1766, to Grafton, 9 Dec. 1766; GEO/MAIN/549; George III to Grafton, 17 Jan. 1767; *The Correspondence of King George the Third from 1760 to December 1783* …, ed. Sir John Fortescue (6 vols, 1927–8), ii, 458–9, 480.

[164] *Life and Letters of Sir Gilbert Elliot First Earl of Minto from 1751 to 1806*, ed. countess of Minto (3 vols, 1874), i, 89–90.

[165] *Correspondence*, ed. Fortescue, vi, pp. xi, 318–19.

[166] *Memoirs*, ed. Buckingham, i, 218–19.

The king's refusal to create new peerages and his general attitude towards ministers became something of an obsessive preoccupation in coalition circles in the spring and summer of 1783.[167] That George III detested the coalition is hardly in doubt. He was simply awaiting the right moment to dismiss them.

As early as the closing speech at the end of the first parliamentary session of 1783 in July, the king let it be known that: 'The consideration of the affairs of the East Indies will require to be resumed as early as possible, and to be pursued with a serious and unremitting attention.'[168] In such circumstances, it can only be assumed that members of the Fox-North ministry were working on aspects of the bill over the summer months. The first record of this process, however, is a letter from Sir Gilbert Elliot on 20 August 1783. He reported that: 'Burke is to draw out on paper some sort of plan which Fox is to consider as soon as possible.' Everything, at that stage, however, was still 'very much afloat'.[169] By 20 September the main contours of the bill had been drafted. Portland informed the duke of Manchester that the proposed Indian reforms

> had been already confidentially discussed, not generally in the Cabinet but with Lord North, who concurs in it, and with some of our principal and most active friends both in the Lords and Commons, and also with such of the Directors and Proprietors [of the East India Company] as it could be opened to with safety, and, I think, it is so far advanced as that it may be considered as a measure upon which the existence of the present Administration will be fairly staked.[170]

The correspondence of Lord Thurlow, still a confidant of the king despite being dismissed as lord chancellor by the coalition, reveals that at this stage the king had little knowledge of the bill beyond the rumour that its chief idea was to appoint 'the Directors by Parliament'.[171] Thurlow did not however believe these rumours, feeling it 'so unprincipled, irregular, and rash, that I do not impute to them so much want of common sense'.[172] According to Lord Stormont, lord president of the council in the coalition ministry, the cabinet 'had not yet thought of India Matters' as late as 19 October.[173] This, however, probably reflected the fact that Stormont was not included in the inner circle of confidential friends to whom Fox and Portland had shared their ideas on India.[174] Stormont probably knew as little as the king or Thurlow. We know from Lord Loughborough that aspects of the India Bill were still being finalised in the weeks prior to its introduction to parliament in November.[175] By

[167] BL, Add. MS 47579, ff. 23–4: Fox to Upper Ossory, 12 Aug. 1783.

[168] *Cobbett's Parl. Hist.*, xxiii, 1420.

[169] Cannon, *Fox-North Coalition*, 107; see also *Elliot*, ed. Minto, i, 86.

[170] HMC, *8th Report*, pt 3, 132–3.

[171] John Brooke argued that Fox made a strategic blunder in forcing the king to dismiss Thurlow as lord chancellor in April 1783: 'In office Thurlow would have tried to reconcile Fox to the King; out of office, he intrigued for Fox's dismissal': Brooke, *King George III* (1972), 252.

[172] HMC, *5th Report*, pt 1, 210.

[173] BL, Add. MS 29161, f. 31: John Scott to Warren Hastings, 21 Oct. 1783.

[174] Suspicion of Stormont turned out to be well-placed. He defied the cabinet and voted against the India Bill in its second reading in the Lords: *The New Annual Register … 1784* (1785), 128–9.

[175] BL, Add. MS 47568, f. 230: Loughborough to Fox, [nd]; Add. MS 47568, f. 234: Loughborough to Fox, [23 Nov. 1783].

this time, however, it is clear that the bill had been approved by cabinet and that the king had seen it and at the very least had not given any indication of hostility.

It was probably unfair of John Brooke, in his biography of George III, to argue that the king 'never bothered with the details of legislation' and simply acquiesced in the 'principle' of the India Bill because he believed in the 'principle' of East India Company reform.[176] It is certainly going too far to say that 'Fox's India Bill was a measure after the King's own heart'.[177] While we have no indication of the king's early views on Fox's specific proposals for reform, Thurlow's thorough opposition to even their general tendency suggests that if he conferred with any of his close associates, he was unlikely to gain a positive impression. Furthermore, when Fox's measures were presented to parliament for the first time, indications began to emerge that those closest to the king were substantially in opposition to it. When the bill came before the Commons, Charles Jenkinson, a long-time confidant of the king, raised serious concerns about the intended effect on royal power. He argued that the bill established 'within the realm a species of executive government, independent of the check or controul of the crown' and that it threatened 'ruinous consequences to British liberty'.[178] While contemporaries were probably not aware of the precise extent of his relationship to the king, it was commonly believed that Jenkinson was the leader of the so-called 'king's friends', a group of parliamentarians and officeholders who were said to form a strong body of support for the crown.[179] Jenkinson's speech caused some in coalition circles to fear that it was indicative, or could be perceived by others to be indicative, of the king's own views, a belief echoed in the press.[180] Fox, reporting on the parliamentary debates, felt that Jenkinson's 'appearance will have some bad effects', but consoled himself with the thought that among his supporters it may actually have 'had some good'.[181] Richard Fitzpatrick felt that it went deeper than mere appearances. He argued that Jenkinson's speech was a 'strong symptom of the opinion of the Closet'.[182] The fact that all indications pointed to Lord Mansfield and his nephew Stormont also opposing Fox's bill only added to the belief that the king looked upon it unfavourably.[183] Since the king had not told them directly, however, Fox and the other ministers were inclined to assume either that he would remain silent or that rumours about his opposition to the bill were false.

The first clear indication of George III's disapproval of the India Bill comes from a memorandum penned by Temple and Thurlow and delivered to the king on 1 December.[184]

---

[176] G.M. Ditchfield, *George III: An Essay in Monarchy* (Basingstoke, 2002), 115–18, argues, on the contrary, that George III paid close attention to details of policy and particularly in policies concerning the East India Company.

[177] Brooke, *George III*, 251.

[178] *Cobbett's Parl. Hist.*, xxiii, 1238–9.

[179] For more on the 'King's Friends' see Richard Pares, *King George III and the Politicians* (Oxford, 1953), 107–8; *The Jenkinson Papers 1760–1766*, ed. N.S. Jucker (1949), xxiv–xxviii.

[180] *Gazetteer and New Daily Advertiser*, 26 Nov. 1783; *General Evening Post*, 13 Dec. 1783; National Library of Scotland, MS 11196, ff. 17–18: Sir George Cornewall to Sir Gilbert Elliot, [Dec. 1783].

[181] BL, Add. MS 47579, f. 35: Fox to Upper Ossory, 21 Nov. 1783.

[182] BL, Add. MS 47579, f. 121: Richard Fitzpatrick to Upper Ossory, 21 Nov. 1783.

[183] John Scott reported the opposition of Lords Mansfield and Stormont to Warren Hastings in India: BL, Add. MS 29161, f. 36: Scott to Hastings, 10 Nov. 1783. This had also become a common rumour in the newspapers: *Gazetteer and New Daily Advertiser*, 26 Nov. 1783; *Whitehall Evening Post*, 27 Nov. 1783; *General Evening Post*, 29 Nov. 1783; *Public Advertiser*, 3 Dec. 1783.

[184] There is evidence that Temple was meeting the king before December 'upon particular business', but at that stage there was 'no idea of change [in ministers]': *Memoirs*, ed. Buckingham, i, 281.

In the memorandum, Temple and Thurlow desired to know whether the king agreed with them that Fox's bill was 'a plan to take more than half the royal power, and by that means disable [the Crown] for the rest of the reign'. In order to defeat the bill, however, they argued that it must be opposed in the Lords, and the only means of success would be for the king to acquaint peers 'with his wishes, and that in a manner which would make it impossible to pretend a doubt of it'.[185] This memorandum established both the goal of defeating the bill in the Lords *and* the means by which this was to be accomplished. It is important to note, however, that the memorandum argued that a change of ministers was the only way to avoid the India Bill; not that the bill was a perfect opportunity to dismiss the king's ministers, as it has been commonly viewed.[186] The fact that Pitt only consented to forming a ministry at the last moment suggests that, from the perspective of the crown and those who supported its prerogatives, this was a direct response to a unique and particularly dangerous piece of legislation.[187] That a question concerning the East India Company could have provoked so severe a reaction is also one that should not be surprising. From 1765 it was clear that any question of genuine reform of the company would require the establishment of some means by which its revenues and patronage could be incorporated safely within the British state without unbalancing the constitution. Presaged by the rhetoric of Lords' protests from 1767 onwards, the furore over Fox's India Bill, was, in many respects, long overdue. The debates it raised over the respective powers of crown and parliament serve to highlight the role of the house of lords in upholding constitutional equipoise.

However, an important feature of Temple and Thurlow's memorandum, which provides further evidence of the crucial place of the upper chamber in the Hanoverian constitution, has been overlooked. The argument that the house of lords was the best location to defeat the bill emerged from two presuppositions. First, that it was virtually impossible to break Fox's Commons' majority in time enough to defeat the bill, which ruled out the lower House. More important, however, the memorandum argued that 'the refusing the Bill, if it passes the Houses is a violent means'.[188] In other words, the legislative power of the monarch to refuse the royal assent to legislation was considered too violent a step. It was a crucial part of the constitution but it had fallen out of use under the Hanoverians to such an extent that it had become questionable, even to the conservative mind of Thurlow, whether its continued use was either legitimate or advisable.

The last recorded use of the royal veto occurred in 1708 when Queen Anne withheld her assent to a bill settling the Scottish militia.[189] When the question was raised in 1783 over Fox's India Bill, opinions were sharply divided over whether British monarchs still had the power to overrule their parliaments. The majority of opinion in the press suggests that, at least in the extreme case of the India Bill, the king *could* and *should* exercise his right to

---

[185] *Memoirs*, ed. Buckingham, i, 289.

[186] Marshall, *Impeachment*, 22.

[187] See Lord Clarendon's reports on negotiations with Pitt to form a new ministry on 9 and 12 Dec. 1783, in Bodl., MS Clarendon dep. c. 347, pp. 604–7.

[188] *Memoirs*, ed. Buckingham, i, 289.

[189] *The History of Parliament: The House of Commons, 1690–1715*, ed. Eveline Cruickshanks, Stuart Handley and D.W. Hayton (5 vols, Cambridge, 2002), i, 383. Geoffrey Holmes noted that the use of the veto in 1708 'produced not even a ripple of political excitement at the time, let alone a sense of constitutional "occasion" ': Geoffrey Holmes, *British Politics in the Age of Anne* (rev. edn, 1987), 186.

withhold the royal assent.[190] Of the opinions in favour of the king exercising his veto, many saw it as the culmination of a legislative process in which they, too, could participate. For example, the *Gazetteer and New Daily Advertiser* of 11 December 1783 argued that further opposition was intended against the India Bill after its passage in the Lords 'as follows: The protesting Peers, dissenting Commons, Corporation of London, present Directors of the India Company, and all the Proprietors that oppose it, are to wait on the King with a petition, requesting that his Majesty would with-hold his Royal Assent.'[191] This writer was not alone in proposing petitions to persuade the king to take such an action.[192] The very idea of petitioning the king to promote the use of his veto foreshadows the campaign of loyal addresses to the throne in support of his actions in dismissing the coalition ministry and defeating the India Bill in early 1784.[193] The opposite view, though far less prominent, argued that the royal prerogative of vetoing legislation had been lost to the constitution through lack of usage.[194] Even Wraxall, an opponent of the India Bill, admitted that the veto had become 'scarcely known to the British constitution' and that 'all past experience' suggested that 'no British sovereign could venture to oppose himself personally against the representatives of the people sustained by the peers'.[195]

While few went so far as to argue that the king no longer possessed this right, the consideration, none the less, weighed heavy even with the king's staunchest supporters. Temple and Thurlow felt it would be a 'violent' measure. Clarendon argued that 'nobody who prefers a calm to a storm' would advise such a policy.[196] For the same reason, Fox and John Burgoyne agreed that 'there is not Boldness enough to, give the Negative of the Crown' to the India Bill.[197] Wraxall reported, however, that George III had taken the resolution that, if the bill passed the Lords, 'to have nevertheless refused to give it the royal assent'. Whether or not this was true, Wraxall was evidently relieved that 'the middle line which he adopted prevented the necessity of recurring to such painful extremities'.[198] Yet, by relying upon the Lords to kill the legislation, George III and his advisors amplified the importance of the upper chamber in the constitution while avoiding sole responsibility for defeating the bill and dismissing the ministry. If the royal negative was still, strictly speaking, constitutionally valid in 1783, it was, none the less, considered a 'violent' and 'painful' measure.

While the veto had become a scarcely viable option in the eyes of some, particularly in the wake of the tumultuous early decades of George III's reign, which were characterised by accusations that the power and influence of the crown had been augmented to an alarming degree, it becomes easier to understand why the king behaved so controversially in

---

[190] *Gazetteer and New Daily Advertiser*, 11 Dec. 1783; *Whitehall Evening Post*, 11, 13, 16, 25 Dec. 1783; *Morning Herald*, 13 Dec. 1783.

[191] *Gazetteer and New Daily Advertiser*, 11 Dec. 1783.

[192] *Gazetteer and New Daily Advertiser*, 12 Dec. 1783; *Morning Herald*, 13 Dec. 1783.

[193] D.R. McAdams, 'Addresses to the King and the Fox-North Coalition', *Huntington Library Quarterly*, xxxv (1972), 381–5.

[194] *General Evening Post*, 13 Dec. 1783.

[195] *Wraxall Memoirs*, ed. Wheatley, iii, 164.

[196] Bodl., MS Clarendon dep. c. 347, f. 603: Clarendon to baron d'Alvensleben, 4 Dec. 1783.

[197] BL, Add. MS 38716, f. 143: Burgoyne to Northington, 15 Dec. 1783.

[198] *Wraxall Memoirs*, ed. Wheatley, iii, 192.

Figure 2: Thomas Rowlandson, *The Times – or a View of the Old House in Little Brittain – with Nobody going to Hannover*, 23 January 1784; Royal Collection Trust, RCIN 810028. © Her Majesty Queen Elizabeth II 2019.

attempting to persuade peers to reject the India Bill.[199] The reluctance to exercise the veto throws into sharp relief and helps to accentuate the precise contours of the crucial place of the house of lords as a 'pillar of the constitution'. Indeed, just as in its protests against the government's attempts to reform the East India Company, the upper chamber is revealed in Blackstone's words, as 'a body of nobility … more peculiarly necessary in our mixed and compounded constitution, in order to support the rights of both the crown and the people, by forming a barrier to withstand the encroachments of both'.[200]

6

In the wake of the crisis surrounding Fox's India Bill, the essence of the events and their political and constitutional consequences were astutely captured by the artist and caricaturist Thomas Rowlandson in a famous print published on 23 January 1784 (see Figure 2).

The print depicts a dilapidated public house, 'Magna Carta', whose lower floor labelled 'Public Credit' with its entrance 'Funds' is padlocked and guarded by a Fox chained to a crooked pillar titled 'coalition'. Beside Fox, and on a turnstile, sits Lord North, saying: 'Give me my Ease and do as you please.' Providence gazes down upon the scene suggesting it is

[199] Christie, 'Economical Reform', 144–54; Langford, *Polite and Commercial People*, 521–64.
[200] Sir William Blackstone, *Commentaries on the Laws of England* (4 vols, Oxford 1765–9), i, 153.

time to 'turn out the Robbers and repair the House'. Meanwhile, a trumpeter (Edmund Burke) calls for Richard Sheridan who entertains rogues and revellers as two lawyers, one of whom is Attorney General John Lee (ridiculed for his speech in the Commons on the East India Company's charter), chop down a support titled 'prerogative of the Crown', while the crown itself sits on a box waiting to be sold. Weighed down by the burden of taxes from the American War, George III abandons poor Britons as he departs for Hanover. Significantly, all that is left holding up the public house, 'Magna Carta', and Britain itself is a single sturdy pillar labelled 'The Lords'. Rowlandson's caricature astutely reflected popular perceptions of the political atmosphere and constitutional climate within which the East India crisis played out.[201]

Indeed, echoing Blackstone and the imagery embodied in Rowlandson's 'The Times', in the case of Fox's India Bill, it was argued, the conduct of the Lords was 'altogether becoming the hereditary Guardians of the Nation; to preserve a due equilibrium between the different branches of Government, which must have been destroyed had the proposed Bill been carried into a law'.[202] The events of the autumn of 1783 clearly illustrate that there were those in parliament, in public, and in the palace who readily agreed with such an analysis of the power of the house of lords. Their voices and protests help us appreciate why the Lords was so central to deciding the protracted and problematic issues of regulating and reforming the East India Company in the age of the American revolution.

---

[201] Thomas Rowlandson, *The Times – or a View of the Old House in Little Brittain – with Nobody going to Hannover*, 23 January 1784; Royal Collection Trust, RCIN 810028. © Her Majesty Queen Elizabeth II. Attorney General John Lee had observed that 'a charter is nothing more than a piece of parchment with a bit of wax dangling from it': Paul Langford, *Public Life and the Propertied Englishman, 1689–1798* (Oxford, 1991), 214; Diana Donald, *The Age of Caricature: Satirical Prints in the Reign of George III* (New Haven, CT, 1996), 130–9; H.T. Dickinson, *Caricatures and the Constitution, 1760–1832: The English Satirical Print 1660–1832* (Cambridge, 1986), 11–41.

[202] *Whitehall Evening Post*, 20 Dec. 1783.

A Great Electioneer and His Motives Reconsidered: The 4th Duke of Newcastle*

RICHARD A. GAUNT

The 4th duke of Newcastle (1785–1851) is recognized as one of the most prominent peers with electoral influence in early-19th-century Britain. This essay considers the way in which he deployed that influence and the purposes to which it was turned. The essay explains why Newcastle became a leading symbol of the campaign for parliamentary reform and details the nature of his opposition to the bill which eventually became the 'Great' Reform Act of 1832. In some respects, Newcastle was an atypical electioneer, because he was less overtly concerned with the desire for office, patronage, or income. On the other hand, the methods by which that influence was deployed, and the anti-reform purposes to which it was turned, meant that he was inevitably numbered among the reactionary forces opposing political change in this period.

Keywords: Aldborough; Boroughbridge; duke of Newcastle; Earl Grey; East Retford; elections; house of lords; Newark; parliamentary reform; Reform Act

1

On Stanton moor in Derbyshire stands a stone tower, 150-feet tall. It does not mark the site of an ancient battle, nor does it signify the location of a deserted medieval village. Rather, standing majestically over the landscape in which it sits, the tower provides one of the more unusual forms of commemoration celebrating the passage of the Great Reform Act of 1832. It was founded by William Pole Thornhill (1807–76), the last member of the Thornhill family which owned estates at Stanton Hall in Derbyshire. Thornhill served as high sheriff of Derbyshire in 1836 and as MP for North Derbyshire from 1853 to 1865. His strong dedication to reform resulted in the creation of the Earl Grey tower on the eastern edge of Stanton moor.[1]

To contemporaries like Thornhill, the passage of the piece of legislation formally known as the Representation of the People Act (2 & 3 Will. IV, c. 45) was a matter for widespread celebration, when it received the royal assent on 7 June 1832. Commercialisation went hand-in-hand with commemoration, as manufacturers rushed to meet the seemingly insatiable demand for celebratory wares, be it hundreds of prints and caricatures, transfer-printed pottery, cordial flasks shaped to look like leading politicians involved in the passing of the bill, and specially-minted coins and tokens. While *McLean's Monthly Sheet of Caricatures* had

*This essay was originally delivered as a lecture at the exhibition 'A Selection of Elections', held at the Weston Gallery, University of Nottingham, during autumn 2018. I am grateful to all those who commented on the paper then and subsequently.
[1]For Thornhill, see Edward Walford, *The County Families of the United Kingdom* (1860), 952.

the prime minister, Earl Grey, doubting whether his name would long be associated with the measure of reform, and worrying about his posthumous fame – 'Now the giddy multitude have got their toy, they seem to cast it aside, no general rejoicings, no triumph, no idolising, as I was led to expect' – generations since have come to know the name of 'Lord Grey of the Reform Bill'. Grey also lived long enough to see the erection of a splendid monument in the centre of Newcastle-upon-Tyne, honouring his role in the passage of the Reform Act in a manner whose purpose and significance required little interpretation.[2]

The Great Reform Act of 1832 provides one of the anchor points of English history, comparable with the Battle of Hastings in 1066, Magna Carta in 1215, and the Glorious Revolution of 1688. The perceived defects of the electoral system before 1832 have become familiar to us, in different ways, through literature, drama, and long-forgotten lessons from our schooldays. Parliamentary reformers argued that the electoral system had failed to keep pace with population changes and with internal migration patterns which were leading people away from the countryside towards the burgeoning industrial towns of northern England. So it was that the infamous rotten boroughs continued to enjoy the right of representation, returning two MPs to the house of commons, in spite of their declining, or wholly decayed, populations.[3]

Pocket boroughs, by contrast, were characterised by their biddable constituents. Their dependence on powerful local landowners or the borough corporation made them particularly susceptible to being influenced – by the promise to bestow, or withhold, patronage, employment, a tenancy, or other forms of benefit. Some election practices walked a fine line between the legitimate 'treating' of electors with food, drink, and transport to the poll, and illegitimate corruption, in the form of bribery and venality. The latter had been immortalised on canvas by William Hogarth in his famous series of paintings illustrating the notorious Oxfordshire election of 1754. The financial sums involved in fighting an election and the potential for abuse meant that contests, stretching over weeks rather than (until 1918) a single day, could quickly descend into drink-sodden punch-ups and all-out violence.[4]

However, contrary to some of the claims later made by the act's memorialists, it was not the intention of the authors of the Reform Act to eradicate all these practices or to legislate for a democratic political system of the sort which we enjoy today. In their famous satirical history book, *1066 and All That*, first published in 1930, Walter Sellar and Robert Yeatman summarized the terms of the Great Reform Act as follows:

This Bill had two important clauses, which said:

(1) that some of the Burrows [*sic*] were rotten and that the people who lived in them should not be allowed either to stand [for parliament] or to have seats.
(2) that 'householders leaseholders and copyholders who had £10 in the towns or freeholders who paid 40/- in the county for 10 years or lease-holders (in the country)

---

[2] *McLean's Monthly Sheet of Caricatures*, 1 July 1832; George M. Trevelyan, *Lord Grey of the Reform Bill* (1920).

[3] Cornwall was a particularly egregious example for reformers. See Edwin Jaggard, *Cornwall Politics in the Age of Reform, 1790–1885* (Woodbridge, 1999).

[4] Robert J. Robson, *The Oxfordshire Election of 1754: A Study in the Interplay of City, County and University Politics* (Oxford, 1949).

and copyholders for 21 years in the towns (paying a rent of £50) should in some cases (in the towns) have a vote (for 1 year) but in others for 41 years (in the country) paying a leasehold or copyhold of £10 should not'.

When this unforgettable Law was made known there was great rejoicing and bonfires were lit all over the country.[5]

In satirising the convoluted terms of the legislation, Sellar and Yeatman were drawing attention to the fact that, even after 1832, the right to vote was still largely a matter of wealth; a privilege which was confined to the respectable propertied classes, whose property signified their responsibility and 'soundness'. Men – and for the first time in history the Reform Act defined the franchise as male – were thus trustees for the whole population, electors and non-electors alike, and their vote, being a trust, was exercised publicly, rather than through the secret ballot. Only in this way could the large majority of non-electors see, and hold the electors accountable, for the exercise of that trust.[6]

As a result of the 1832 Reform Act, approximately 800,000 adult males qualified for the vote across the United Kingdom. However, this figure masked major internal variations. In England and Wales, one in five adult men enjoyed the franchise, and in Scotland it was one in eight, but, due to much poorer economic conditions in Ireland, only one in 20 qualified. However, over the course of the next 30 years, while the population of England and Wales increased by 50%, the electorate did so by 60%, as property came within the reach of much larger numbers of the industrious working classes.[7]

2

The Great Reform Act is today regarded as a long overdue reform of a corrupt and outdated electoral system and the first step on the long road to the modern system of democratic political representation. That it was incomplete and insufficient was quickly recognized by contemporaries, not least by the speedy emergence of the Chartist movement in the late 1830s and 1840s. The 'six points' of the People's Charter provided a rallying point for those working men who felt that, having campaigned for the Reform Act, they had been 'betrayed', by their continuing exclusion from the franchise.[8]

But what of those individuals who felt, not that the Reform Act had not gone far enough, but that it had gone too far? These are voices which tend to have been drowned out in the history books, on the not unreasonable grounds that many of them were out of touch and self-interested in their opposition to change. Of these voices, perhaps one of the more notable examples is Henry Pelham Fiennes Pelham-Clinton, 4th duke of Newcastle-under-Lyne (1785–1851).

---

[5] Walter C. Sellar and Robert J. Yeatman, *1066 and All That* (1990 edn), 97–8.

[6] See *Defining the Victorian Nation: Class, Race, Gender and the British Reform Act of 1867*, ed. Catherine Hall, Keith McClelland and Jane Rendall (Cambridge, 2000).

[7] Philip Salmon, 'The English Reform Legislation, 1831–32', in *The History of Parliament: The House of Commons, 1820–1832*, ed. D.R. Fisher (7 vols, Cambridge, 2009) [hereafter cited as *HPC, 1820–32*], i, 374–412.

[8] Malcolm Chase, *Chartism: A New History* (Manchester, 2007).

Newcastle's prominence as an electioneer and a 'borough monger' needs little introduction to readers of *Parliamentary History*. Under the careful eye of Clyve Jones, an edition of his diaries was published in 2006, with a further volume to follow.[9] Newcastle was the representative of a family who had risen to wealth, title, and prominence over the course of the preceding century. His grandfather, the 2nd duke, had been notable for the extensive reach of his property interests and electoral influence in parliament. The so-called 'Newcastle Ninepins' was a memorable shorthand quantifying the extent of his influence in the house of commons. As a peer of the realm, he was excluded from exercising the franchise in his own right, in parliamentary elections, but his ability to return MPs, through the weight of his property influence and his patronage network, made him someone whom governments of the day could ill-afford to ignore. In an era before organised political parties, when the power of the crown and the reach of the executive over the electorate was greater than we might recognize today, influential magnates like Newcastle were essential allies in building and sustaining a political following in the house of commons. Lewis Namier famously wrote about pre-Reform electoral politics largely in terms of the machinations of men like Newcastle and his successors. In Namier's classic works, these men were devoid of, or not seriously motivated by, ideas or principles, but wished to extend their personal influence, power and standing, usually at the expense of their fellow magnates.[10]

Since Namier's time, a great deal of research has been devoted to the pre-Reform electorate: historians have explored the operation of the electoral system in 'open' boroughs, emphasizing the 'participatory' element, while, in relation to the electioneering of aristocratic magnates, there has been a strong challenge to the assumption that these 'borough mongers' were motivated solely by personal self-interest and the desire to 'do down' their fellow peers. In 1965, John Golby argued that: 'As a peer of the realm', the 4th duke of Newcastle 'believed that he was one of God's "instruments" chosen to safeguard the constitution and uphold the principles of the Church and State'. This was at variance with the usual insinuation that electioneers were motivated by the desire for political office, preferment, patronage, or income.[11]

The 4th duke of Newcastle inherited his estates and title in 1806. The preceding decade had seen a steady erosion in the family's electoral power. The deaths, in quick succession, of the 2nd and 3rd dukes, in 1794 and 1795, meant that the 4th duke inherited as a minor, and the estates were under the control of trustees, until he reached his legal majority at the age of 21 years. During this period, some element of 'borough mongering' took place, in order to raise much-needed capital for the family's depleted finances, but the degree of personal involvement by Newcastle was probably minimal. The most famous example of such activity was the sale of one of the family's parliamentary seats at Boroughbridge,

---

[9] *Unrepentant Tory: Political Selections from the Diaries of the Fourth Duke of Newcastle-under-Lyne, 1827–38*, ed. Richard A. Gaunt (Parliamentary History Record Series, 3, Woodbridge, 2006); '*The Last of the Tories': Political Selections from the Diaries of the Fourth Duke of Newcastle-under-Lyne, 1839–50*, ed. Richard A. Gaunt (Parliamentary History: Texts & Studies, forthcoming).

[10] For Namier and his critics, see D. W. Hayton, *Conservative Revolutionary: The Lives of Lewis Namier* (Manchester, 2019).

[11] Frank O'Gorman, *Voters, Patrons and Parties: The Unreformed Electoral System of Hanoverian England, 1734–1832* (Oxford, 1989); John A. Phillips, *The Great Reform Bill in the Boroughs: English Electoral Behaviour 1818–1841* (Oxford, 1992); John Golby, 'A Great Electioneer and His Motives: The Fourth Duke of Newcastle', *Historical Journal*, viii (1965), 204.

Yorkshire, to Sir Francis Burdett, in May 1796, for £4,000. Burdett's father-in-law, Thomas Coutts, was the Newcastle family banker, and in the straitened circumstances of a minority, the trustees of the 4th duke (John Gally Knight and George Mason) thought the transaction prudent in more than one respect. The terms of the agreement included a provision for returning Burdett again, should the parliament not last six years, and for Burdett to pay expenses not exceeding £300, in the event of his re-election upon accepting office. Even so, it still proved necessary for Burdett to subscribe to the usual round of local patronage expected of the MP, including subscription to the local races.[12]

On attaining his majority in 1806, the 4th duke quickly sought to re-establish what he saw as his family's rightful place in the electoral affairs of Nottinghamshire. He moved to install blood relations within the constituencies where he exercised influence, both in Nottinghamshire and Yorkshire, and swiftly curtailed the ambitions of his stepfather, Sir Charles Gregan Craufurd. Craufurd had married the duke's widowed mother in 1800 and proceeded to flex his muscles, telling Henry Dundas that:

> In consequence of [my marriage] the management of all the duke's affairs and interests of course devolves upon me, jointly, during his minority. It would certainly be superfluous to enter into any detail with you upon the extent of the very great and preponderating parliamentary influence of the family …

Craufurd had been trying to build his own family interest, by proxy. Newcastle reasserted the influence of the legitimate family line, the Clintons, and their satellites, but overreached himself when he challenged the 3rd duke of Portland for a right to be consulted about the representation of Nottinghamshire, at the general election of 1806. Portland sent Newcastle away with a flea in his ear.[13]

For the first 20 years of his ducal life, Newcastle appeared to fit the standard definition of a powerful aristocratic magnate motivated by a policy of self-aggrandisement for his family and personal interests. Things might have been different, had the governments of the day not been defenders of the existing constitution in church and state. On many occasions, Newcastle risked provocation in order to gratify his ambitions. In 1812, he observed:

> I have a right to be consulted upon [the representation of the County], as the greatest freeholder in the county, and those who think clandestinely and surreptitiously to step in a representative without consulting me on the subject act unwisely for themselves and unjustly towards me.

When a candidate was recommended to Newcastle with the honest admission that he was 'not qualified to shine in the Senate and I apprehend not in the least likely ever to open his lips in the house of commons', Newcastle responded that the character given was

---

[12] University of Nottingham Manuscripts and Special Collections [hereafter cited as UNMASC], Ne 6 E 4/12: memorandum dated 3 May 1796; receipts at Ne E 432, Ne E 441, Ne A 751/23/1, Ne A 751/24, Ne A 751/44/1.

[13] National Library of Scotland, MS 15, 77/81–3: Charles Gregan Craufurd to Henry Dundas, 5 Mar. 1800; UNMASC, Pw H 334: Portland to Titchfield, 15 July 1806, reprinted in Peter Jupp, *British and Irish Elections, 1784–1831* (Newton Abbot, 1973), 23.

'most engaging' and supplied 'the place of a mine of talent'.[14] Given the need to conciliate constituents, whether they enjoyed the franchise or not, these attitudes exposed the duke's candidates to ridicule and opposition at election time.[15]

Matters began to change markedly from the mid 1820s. Newcastle became increasingly politicised, attending debates in the house of lords more frequently and turning his thoughts to how he could use his electoral influence in the Commons to shore up the defence of the status quo. The great issue of the day was the campaign for catholic emancipation. This was intimately connected with parliamentary reform because catholics had been excluded from election to the house of commons by the Test and Corporation Acts. In the face of a vigorous campaign for emancipation, Newcastle turned his political patronage towards ensuring that he not only had sound protestant defenders of the establishment in parliament but that they would defend that establishment to the hilt. When the duke of Wellington's government introduced a Catholic Relief Bill, granting emancipation, in 1829, in an attempt to head off the threat of civil unrest in Ireland, Newcastle responded in kind. When his cousin, William Henry Clinton, the MP for Newark, decided to support the bill, there was a painful parting of the ways. As Clinton observed:

> From that moment his tone & manner changed. He was very civil but he was a different man from what I had ever seen him & plainly shewed that to differ with him in politics was a thing he could not endure.[16]

Lady Louisa Stuart told Clinton's daughter, Louisa, that she had 'apprehended mischief, the moment I found in what key his Chieftain was disposed to play'. Thus, Newcastle was more than prepared to disclaim blood ties in the service of a political cause. This was the more significant because, as Lady Stuart observed: 'if the Duke of Newcastle had no son, your father would succeed him as Earl of Lincoln', as his nearest living male heir. Newcastle secured the services of Michael Thomas Sadler, a talented opponent of emancipation, as Clinton's successor. This raised a good deal of local hostility at Newark, partly because Sadler was a 'stranger' to the borough, but, perhaps as significantly, because he lacked any sort of family connection to the duke.[17]

Catholic emancipation passed into law and Newcastle subsequently supported those who brought down the Wellington government in November 1830. The passage of emancipation encouraged demands for parliamentary reform, because some commentators argued

[14] Nottinghamshire Archives [hereafter cited as NA], C/QACP/5/2/56: Newcastle to Edward Smith Godfrey, 3 Oct. 1812; John Rylands University Library Manchester [hereafter cited as JRULM], Clinton papers (uncatalogued): Newcastle to W.H. Clinton, 20 May 1817; Newcastle to W.H. Clinton, 5, 12 Feb. 1820; W.H. Clinton to Newcastle, 9 Feb. 1820.

[15] Marmaduke Lawson, *Substance of a Speech Delivered at the Boroughbridge Election, Previous to the Poll; on Saturday, June the 20th, 1818* (2nd edn, 1818); Jon Lawrence, *Electing Our Masters: The Hustings in British Politics from Hogarth to Blair* (Oxford, 2009), 25–7.

[16] JRULM, Clinton papers: W.H. Clinton diary, 9 Feb. 1829; Richard A. Gaunt, 'William Henry Clinton and the Perils of the Soldier-Politician', in *Politics and Political Culture in Britain and Ireland, 1750–1850: Essays in Tribute to Peter Jupp*, ed. Allan Blackstock and Eoin Magennis (Belfast, 2007), 176–93.

[17] *Letters of Lady Louisa Stuart to Miss Louisa Clinton*, ed. James A. Home (2nd ser., Edinburgh, 1903), 145–6; *Letters of Lady Louisa Stuart to Miss Louisa Clinton*, ed. James A. Home (Edinburgh, 1901), 226; Richard A. Gaunt, 'On the Campaign Trail, Georgian Style: The Newark By-Election of 1829', *The Nottinghamshire Historian*, No. 84 (2010), 10–13.

that the country was much more hostile to the measure than those who had passed it through parliament. Newcastle shared these views, although he did not prescribe parliamentary reform as a solution for them. Nevertheless, he welcomed the appointment of Lord Grey as prime minister in November 1830 and was willing to give a cautious support to the new government. This situation was not to last for long.[18]

3

It is no surprise to find that Newcastle was in the vanguard of those who opposed the whigs' Parliamentary Reform Bill, when it was introduced into the house of commons on 1 March 1831. Such was the sweeping nature of its proposals to disenfranchise rotten boroughs and revise the terms upon which people qualified for the franchise that opponents quickly likened it to 'Pride's Purge' – the moment, in December 1648, when troops of the New Model Army under the command of Colonel Thomas Pride forcibly removed all those from the Long Parliament who were not its supporters.[19]

Newcastle quickly assumed prominence in the 15-month conflict over the Reform Bill, not only as a leading opponent of the measure in the house of lords, but as someone who was frequently cited in the arguments of reformers themselves. Given that the duke was one of about 200 peers exercising influence in the house of commons, at this time, what explains this prominence?[20]

In the first place, Newcastle quickly came to personify all the manifold abuses of the unreformed electoral system. Parliamentary sketch writers, such as James Grant, noted that the usual reaction to Newcastle's short, vituperative speeches in the house of lords was the observation: 'What a passion he is in!' The duke was a proud, shy, man, in private, whose personal life had been blighted by the death of his wife in childbirth in 1822. However, his public face was as an uncompromising martinet, utterly unyielding and uncompromising in his political views. It is hardly surprising that reformers fastened upon him as the arch-representative of an exclusive system of privilege which they were trying to dismantle.[21]

Second, Newcastle's portfolio of constituencies covered the whole spectrum of borough types among the unreformed electorate, typifying the vagaries by which individuals qualified for the vote in different areas of the country. By 1832, the duke theoretically enjoyed influence in five parliamentary constituencies – the Nottinghamshire boroughs of East Retford and Newark, the county seats for Nottinghamshire, and the Yorkshire boroughs of Aldborough and Boroughbridge. Though Newcastle remained a substantial property owner in Nottingham, the expanding influence of the town's corporation had seen off any interference by the duke, and other local magnates, long ago; a fact which explains the

---

[18] On developments during this period, see B.T. Bradfield, 'Sir Richard Vyvyan and the Fall of Wellington's Government', *University of Birmingham Historical Journal*, xi (1968), 141–56.

[19] The best study remains Michael Brock, *The Great Reform Act* (1973).

[20] James J. Sack, 'The House of Lords and Parliamentary Patronage in Great Britain, 1802–1832', reprinted in *Peers, Politics and Power: The House of Lords, 1603–1911*, ed. Clyve Jones and David Lewis Jones (1986), 369.

[21] James Grant, *Random Recollections of the House of Lords: From the Year 1830 to 1836, Including Personal Sketches of the Leading Members* (1836), 96.

difficult relationship which existed between Newcastle and the Nottingham authorities, throughout his lifetime.[22]

The highest degree of ducal dominance was exercised in Aldborough and Boroughbridge, which returned four MPs between them. At Aldborough, the electoral qualification resided in those who paid scot and lot. Eighty people were qualified to vote in 1831 out of a population of nearly 600. In Boroughbridge, by contrast, 65 individuals out of a population approaching 1,000 qualified as 'occupiers of burgage properties who had been admitted at the court of the lord of the manor of Aldborough'. The lord of the manor was the duke of Newcastle. In this capacity, he appointed the bailiffs who acted as returning officers at elections in the boroughs, and these were usually his tenants. After 1818, this level of control was challenged by a local, resident family, the Lawsons, who contested the right of nomination at every opportunity. It was local influence, rather than alternative politics, which motivated these battles, for the Lawsons were, like Newcastle, essentially tories.[23]

At East Retford, the duke came up against a different sort of challenge. Here, the franchise was vested in the freemen of the borough, who could qualify by birth, apprenticeship, and redemption, so long as they were resident at the time of their admission. Outright bribery and payment for votes was endemic among the electorate. Though Newcastle attempted to assert the family's traditional right of nomination in one of Retford's two seats, at the general election of 1812, he did not press the point, having been faced with the insatiable demands of a small electorate well used to extracting a high price for their services. As Newcastle pithily remarked to a correspondent, at the time: 'I would not pay and they would not vote.'[24]

In Nottinghamshire, Newcastle pressed his claims to be treated with respect, from an early date, not only as a major property owner in the county, but, after the death of the 3rd duke of Portland in 1809, as its lord lieutenant (1809–39). Newcastle finally achieved success in 1814, when his preferred candidate, Admiral Frank Sotheron of Kirklington, became one of the county's two MPs. Sotheron was still representing the county at the time of the Reform Bill debates in 1831.[25]

Newark was the seat which has perhaps attracted most attention from historians but, even here, describing it as a pocket borough does an injustice to its political complexion. The franchise rested in those who paid scot and lot, but, as so many of these individuals were in a dependent relationship with the major property ownerships in the borough – Newcastle first among them – a prudent electoral compromise, 'the united interest', was thought essential to keep electoral harmony between them, at least until it broke down, amid mutual recrimination, in 1830. Newcastle's tenants were pacified, between elections, with an annual Christmas gift of coal.[26]

---

[22] John V. Beckett, 'Aristocrats and Electoral Control in the East Midlands, 1660–1914', *Midland History*, xviii (1993), 65–86.

[23] Sir Thomas Lawson-Tancred, *Records of a Yorkshire Manor* (1937); Boroughbridge Historical Society, *A History of Boroughbridge, A Historic Yorkshire Town* (Boroughbridge, 2019), 19–30; also see above, note 15.

[24] JRULM, Clinton papers: Newcastle to Henry Clinton, 26 Oct. 1812.

[25] *The History of Parliament: The House of Commons, 1790–1820*, ed. R.G. Thorne (5 vols, 1986), iii, 828–9.

[26] For the origins of 'the united interest', see UNMASC, MS 71/3: dowager duchess of Newcastle to J.C. Brough, 26 Mar. 1803; for its dissolution, see *Unhappy Reactionary: The Diaries of the Fourth Duke of Newcastle-under-Lyne 1822–50*, ed. Richard A. Gaunt (Thoroton Society Record Series, Nottingham, 2003), 73–4.

During the 1820s, a vigorous campaign for 'independence' grew in Newark, finding its ablest champion in Serjeant Thomas Wilde, a lawyer with a growing reputation and a winning style of oratory. Having unsuccessfully fought Sadler, in the by-election provoked by W.H. Clinton's resignation in 1829, Wilde continued to contest Newark, at successive elections, with the duke's interest firmly in his sights. Louisa Stuart, still smarting from Clinton's abrupt removal, had to 'check' herself 'from wishing Sergeant Wilde success', during the 1830 contest, 'for fear he should be *fool enough* to feel hurt at it, otherwise, if ever [a] man deserved being fairly ousted, it is his Grace (of Newcastle)'.[27]

It was not just that Newcastle's parliamentary influence seemed to typify the irrationality of the existing electoral system, but managing that influence gave rise to the abuses which reformers were at pains to condemn. Newcastle was encouraged to throw his influence behind one of the candidates at East Retford in the 1826 general election, but the contest descended into wholesale violence. As Lord Fitzwilliam's local agent, John Parker, observed:

> The Riot Act has been twice read already and the civil power is quite set at defiance … Some men have been nearly killed, not by freemen but by a hired mob of the scum of the neighbourhood … The principals in these riots are the most abandoned characters about Retford … encouraged privately by party zeal …[28]

After a parliamentary enquiry, the franchise at Retford was altered in 1830, by enlarging the boundaries of the constituency through incorporating it with the neighbouring hundred of Bassetlaw. Critics complained that this actually served to increase Newcastle's influence, given the extent of his property interests there.[29]

More direct and serious were Newcastle's acts of retribution against those who defied his wishes at Newark. Trouble had begun in 1826, when a 'third man' contested the constituency as an 'Independent'. Newcastle told his agent, W.E. Tallents, that 'On full consideration I am sure that the straightforward course will be best and that no song no supper, or no votes no houses, shall be the distinguishing rule.' Three years later, some three dozen tenants were evicted from tenancies under the duke's control for having failed to support Sadler. This action assured maximum national publicity against Newcastle, because some of the tenants were evicted from land which the duke leased from the crown. It initiated a long-running battle with the forces of 'Independence' in the borough, and led Newcastle into an infamous public defence of his rights of nomination:

> Is it presumed, then, that I am not to do what I will with my own, or that I am to surrender my property and the inherent rights belonging to it into the hands of those who desire to deprive me of it? This is the simple question – to which I answer, that whilst the laws of England exist and are respected, I shall permit neither clamour nor threats nor even force itself to deter me from doing as I may think fit with my property …

[27] *Stuart to Clinton*, ed. Home, 221.

[28] *HPC, 1820–32*, ii, 803.

[29] For local whig positioning in advance of the change, see UNMASC, Pw H 987: Earl Manvers to the duke of Portland, 20 July 1830.

Gladstone later reflected that Newcastle's 'own kindly nature would recoil much more strongly' from these views 'than those of many who revile him'. However, at the time, Louisa Stuart correctly foresaw that they would produce no good outcome, telling Louisa Clinton: 'the Duke is in for it, and will as surely lose the borough as I sit here. I am sorry, because I know it will vex your father.'[30]

4

In some respects, Newcastle had good reason to fear the effects of the Reform Bill, for, under its terms, he was to lose the right of representation at Aldborough and Boroughbridge completely. He regarded this as an uncompensated loss to his property worth £200,000. By contrast, in 1833, the whig government compensated the owners of former slaves, to the sum of £20 million, in the legislation which abolished slavery in the British Empire. Likewise, in 1785, William Pitt the Younger's unsuccessful Reform Bill included the purchase of 36 small boroughs, with the electors' consent, and compensation of £1 million for borough 'owners', in consideration of their loss of influence. However, as Julian Hoppit has argued, in so far as compensation for compulsory dispossession is concerned, the definition of property was 'not a fixed unchanging given', in this period, but 'the outcome of debate and disagreement, fed by different ideals and assumptions in which the outcome was not at all predictable'. While the possessors of Irish boroughs were compensated under the Act of Union with Great Britain in 1801, 'those in Britain were not at reform in 1832'. Nor does anyone seem to have made a serious case for such compensation.[31]

In other respects, however, Newcastle had less cause for concern. Not only was the redistribution of seats proposed by the bill strongly directed towards the counties, which were traditionally seen as the most prestigious constituencies and the ones most susceptible to landed influence, but, even in Newark, there was cause for optimism. Though the voting rights of the scot and lot electors would only be retained for their lifetime, eventually reducing the electorate of Newark from approximately 1,600 to 600, William Tallents calculated that it would still leave the duke's interest with a majority of about 140 over their opponents.[32]

However, for Newcastle, the fact remained that the Reform Bill was a 'revolutionary' measure, which he must exert every nerve to oppose, by every means in his power. As he memorably put it, on one occasion:

> [The Reform Bill] is the arrantest counterfeit, the most barefaced cheat, the most tangled mass of incongruities, impracticabilities, injustice, and nonsense that ever emanated from

---

[30] Newcastle to Samuel Ellis Bristowe, 28 Sept. 1829, reprinted in *The Times*, 7 Oct. 1829; *The Prime Ministers' Papers: W.E. Gladstone*, ed. John Brooke and Mary Sorensen (4 vols, 1971–81), ii, 14; *Stuart to Clinton*, ed. Home, 178.

[31] Julian Hoppit, 'Compulsion, Compensation and Property Rights in Britain, 1688–1833', *Past & Present*, No. 210 (2011), 123; John Cannon, *Parliamentary Reform, 1640–1832* (Cambridge, 1972), 81, 92, 102, 131, 160, 209–10.

[32] NA, DD/TL/1/1/195: W.E. Tallents to Newcastle, 11 Mar. 1831; DD/TL/1/1/233: Newcastle to Tallents, 29 Sept. 1831; DD/TL/1/1/234: Tallents to Newcastle, 30 Sept. 1831; DD/TL/1/1/236: Tallents to Newcastle, 2 Oct. 1831.

the brains of rational men, or ever was ushered in under the auspices of a talented Cabinet.[33]

How was Newcastle to resist the measure? Three options were open to him: to influence the house of commons, to influence the house of lords, and to influence the king, William IV. Each of these options corresponded with the different stages through which the bill would have to pass before becoming law, and each of them corresponded with the different parts of the British political system necessary to enact legislation. Each of them raised different forms of resistance from Newcastle.

Between the introduction of the Reform Bill into the house of commons in March 1831 and its defeat there, six weeks later, Newcastle deployed his parliamentary nominees against it. Though he had known that some reform was coming, he had been 'hopeful that some practical and unobjectionable meliorations only were thought of'. When the bill was defeated in the Commons, by one vote, in April 1831, the government dissolved parliament and called a general election. The battle thus moved to the constituencies, where Newcastle tried to secure a solid phalanx of anti-reform MPs. He was particularly keen to have Nottinghamshire send opponents of the bill back to the Commons.[34]

Newcastle was to be disappointed. Admiral Sotheron, the long-serving county member, retired from parliament, while Sadler decided to move from Newark to Aldborough. Sadler's successor, Sir Roger Gresley, had been accused of electoral bribery in an earlier stage of his parliamentary career, and, after a long and bruising contest, the Newcastle interest was convincingly beaten into third place by Thomas Wilde. The duke was no more successful in the county seats, where moderate opinion swung decisively behind reform. As Newcastle bitterly concluded, when the final results came in: 'It is melancholy to think that of the 8 members returned from this County all are reformers.' Later, he publicly condemned the government for the frequency with which it had deployed the king's name to gain electoral support: 'You have complained of the interference of Peers in elections [he observed] if this be an evil, how much greater must that be.'[35]

The government, having ensured a majority for its measure among MPs, introduced a revised Reform Bill, which passed through the house of commons and was sent up to the house of lords in the autumn of 1831. In the early hours of Saturday, 8 October, it was defeated, by a majority of 41 votes. Newcastle featured prominently among their number. As is well known, the bill's defeat provoked a number of reactions, including the Reform Bill riots in Bristol, Derby, and Nottingham. Newcastle's unoccupied mansion house, Nottingham Castle, was set on fire, and military preparations were instituted for the defence of his family home at Clumber.[36]

The violent confrontation between authority and popular pressure, as manifested in the riots, only served to reinforce Newcastle's prejudices against the bill. To the duke, the government had wantonly and unreasonably encouraged those whom he described as

[33]Duke of Newcastle, *An Address to all Classes and Conditions of Englishmen* (1832), 119.

[34]Newcastle, *Address*, 109.

[35]*Unhappy Reactionary*, ed. Gaunt, 77–82; Newcastle, *Address*, 113.

[36]John Beckett, 'The Nottingham Reform Bill Riots of 1831', in *Partisan Politics, Principle and Reform in Parliament and the Constituencies, 1689–1880: Essays in Memory of John A. Phillips*, ed. Clyve Jones, Philip Salmon and Richard W. Davis (Edinburgh, 2005), 114–38.

'revolutionary harpies'. The results were obvious: 'We see [political] unions, associations, and other unlawful assemblies usurping the power of the Executive; mob law substituted for the law of the land.'[37]

Attention now turned to the constitutional deadlock between the two houses of parliament. With a favourable Commons and an unfavourable Lords, attention focused on the attitude of the king. Historically, the precedent for breaking a constitutional impasse between the two Houses was for the monarch to use his or her prerogative powers and create new peers, in order to bolster the government's support in the upper chamber. This was a tactic which Newcastle thought to be particularly objectionable. He now turned all his efforts towards preventing its realization.[38]

In the spring of 1832, Newcastle issued his 153-page *Address to all Classes and Conditions of Englishmen*. This reviewed the events of the preceding year in detail but was principally concerned with two objectives: detailing the duke's objections to the Reform Bill and attempting to stop William IV from carrying through the threat of peerage creation.[39]

In respect of the Reform Bill, which was once more in the process of passing through the house of commons on its way to the Lords, Newcastle remained unrepentant:

The Bill remedies none of the evils which it professes to cure.

Does it make the constituency more pure? No ...

Does it destroy the influence of the Peers? No ...

Does it equalize the representation? No ...

Though Newcastle was opposed to what he called 'the theoretical notion that it is the birth-right of every man to possess a vote', he saw real danger in promising people a sham reform on a false prospectus. Not only was the 'patronage of boroughs still ... extensively retained', but 'the same arbitrary power which disfranchises a borough for no delinquency, and violates the house of lords because it is honest, will deprive you, when it pleases, of your valued rights, laws and liberties!'.[40]

Newcastle then moved to his second objective, offering his readers a lesson on the English political system and, by extension, defending the constitutional position of the house of lords. Having expressed his hopes that 'William IV will never betray his duty, nor outrage the lawful independence of any class of his subjects', he reminded the king, rather pointedly, that James II had been removed from the throne, at the time of the Glorious Revolution, for 'having endeavoured to *subvert the Constitution*'. The matter of peerage creation was particularly objectionable to Newcastle, because it interfered with the delicate, mixed system of government which had operated in this country since that time:

---

[37] Newcastle, *Address*, 98, 115.

[38] For 18th-century antecedents, see *A Pillar of the Constitution: The House of Lords in British Politics, 1640–1784*, ed. Clyve Jones (1989), 79–112.

[39] *Unrepentant Tory*, ed. Gaunt, 178, 181. The *Address* was noticed in: *The Times*, 20 Mar., 31 Oct. 1832; *Fraser's Magazine for Town and Country*, v (1832), 351–60; and *Quarterly Review*, xlvii (1832), 587–9.

[40] Newcastle, *Address*, 119–20, 122, 150.

> If the Constitution of England acknowledges the house of lords as an essential constituent part of parliament … and that the purpose for which parliament is created is to consult and deliberate freely and without control, how could it be endured that all deliberation should be rendered nugatory by a previously *created* majority?

The monarch should play no role in the legislative process until a bill had passed through both houses of parliament and he was asked to give it his consent, or else refuse it. 'The King acts unconstitutionally, if he seeks unlawfully, through his Ministers or others, to control a debate', Newcastle argued. If he does more, 'he does what he does not possess the right to do, and he acts unconstitutionally'.[41] The issue at hand, parliamentary reform, had become part of a wider debate about the relative weight and influence of different parts of the British political system – notably the house of lords – and the legitimacy which they claimed for affecting the legislative process.[42]

In spite of Newcastle's best efforts, the Reform Bill did pass through the house of lords, without the mass creation of peers, because the Conservative front bench, led by the duke of Wellington, recognized that William IV had committed himself to create the necessary peers to pass the legislation and wished to protect the house of lords, and the monarchy, from further embarrassment. In the later stages of the bill's passage through the house of lords, Newcastle specifically raised the issue of peerage creation, referencing a letter published in the *Morning Chronicle*, 'which purported to be … from his Majesty, pledging himself to the Minister to create as many peers as might be necessary to carry the Reform Bill'. Grey denied the letter's authenticity, but when Newcastle enquired of the lord chancellor whether the government would institute criminal proceedings against the *Morning Chronicle* for publishing it, Lord Brougham 'begged leave to remind the noble Duke, that he was not the public prosecutor'. Newcastle followed up this intervention with a proposal for a motion 'that would test the opinion of the House as to the prerogative of creating peers'. However, finding little appetite for this, or for a motion on the state of the nation, Newcastle abandoned the effort on 1 June. Three days later, he was one of only 22 peers who voted against the third reading of the bill and, three days after that, when William IV gave it the royal assent, Newcastle pointedly refused to illuminate the windows of his London home.[43]

5

The Reform Bill had passed but revolution did not come. Newcastle's parliamentary influence in the house of commons continued, not least in Newark, where the young William Ewart Gladstone was returned as a Conservative MP, alongside Thomas Wilde, in December 1832. Perhaps as significantly, Newcastle's son and heir, Lord Lincoln, was encouraged to stand for the newly-created southern division of Nottinghamshire. There was less success elsewhere. In spite of its incorporation with the hundred of Bassetlaw, East Retford failed to return one of Newcastle's younger sons to parliament, in the general election of 1835.

---

[41] Newcastle, *Address*, 132–6.

[42] See, e.g., Corinne Comstock Weston, *The House of Lords and Ideological Politics: Lord Salisbury's Referendal Theory and the Conservative Party, 1846–1922* (Philadelphia, PA, 1995).

[43] *Unrepentant Tory*, ed. Gaunt, 192–7; Hansard, *Lords Debates*, 3rd ser., xii, cols 1096–8.

Nevertheless, on balance, it would be easy to conclude that Newcastle continued to operate as if the Reform Act had never been passed.[44]

Though the duke was clearly trying to continue the sort of family interest which he had nurtured before the Reform Act, his actions continued to demonstrate quite clearly that, while blood might be thicker than water, it was not stronger than his own unyielding political ideals. In 1846, when Sir Robert Peel's government decided to repeal the corn laws, Newcastle succeeded in removing both Gladstone and Lincoln from their seats. In the case of Lincoln, he went so far as to issue a public address, urging the voters of south Nottinghamshire to reject his son. This was not just a simple case of compliant voters following the duke's bidding. In an agricultural constituency, the practical impact of repeal as an issue provided as strong a motivation as any electoral influence at Newcastle's command.[45]

Today, the idea that anyone should influence parliamentary elections, or interfere with our democratic choice, strikes us as a violation of our basic civil rights. But, as it is sometimes observed, the British system of parliamentary representation is a work in progress and any advances made are hard-fought and vulnerable to assault. The role of the peerage in modern politics remains a contentious issue, although the monarch's right to create peers has largely been supplanted by the ability of political parties and the prime minister to swell the ranks of the house of lords with their own nominees. It would, perhaps, be hard to think of any resonance between the events of the 1830s and those of today.[46]

However, in 2013, the well-respected Labour peer, Lord Dubs, introduced a private members bill into the house of lords which, had it been successful, would have provided members of the Lords with the right to vote at parliamentary elections. Of 189 countries in the Inter-Parliamentary Union, the United Kingdom is the only country where members of the second chamber are disqualified, by virtue of that membership, from voting in elections to the lower chamber. As Lord Dubs observed:

I think we are the only Members of a second chamber in any democratic country in the world who do not have the right to vote in general elections. It seems to me that there is a point of principle here. Many of us campaign in elections. I have window bills up in my house, and yet I am not allowed to vote for reasons that have disappeared in the mists of history and which make no logical sense today … the point of voting is to choose or influence the Government of this country. That is the right that we do not have as Members of this legislature, unless we are given the right to vote.

It has been the resolution of the house of commons since 1699 that peers could not vote in parliamentary elections and, where this has been challenged, the veto has been reinforced in case law.[47]

[44]Richard A. Gaunt, 'A Stern Unbending Tory and the Rising Young Hope: Gladstone, Newark and the Fourth Duke of Newcastle, 1832–46', in *The Gladstone Umbrella*, ed. Peter Francis (Hawarden, 2001), 14–35.

[45]James B. Conacher, 'Mr. Gladstone Seeks a Seat', *Report of the Annual Meeting/Rapports Annuels de la Société Historique du Canada*, xli (1962), 55–67; John R. Fisher, 'Issues and Influence: Two By-Elections in South Nottinghamshire in the Mid-Nineteenth Century', *Historical Journal*, xxiv (1981), 155–65.

[46]The persistent refrain may be summed up in the title of a recent survey: Peter Dorey and Alexandra Kelso, *House of Lords Reform since 1911: Must the Lords Go?* (2011).

[47]House of Lords Library and Matthew Purvis, *Extension of Franchise (House of Lords) Bill [HL] (HL Bill 6 of 2013–14)* (House of Lords Library Note, LLN 2013/016, 2013), 1–2, 4, available at *https://researchbriefings.parliament.uk/ResearchBriefing/Summary/LLN-2013-016#fullreport* (accessed 3 Sept. 2019).

Not even the 4th duke of Newcastle argued that, as a peer of the realm, he should exercise an individual right to vote in elections. Rather, he saw his rights as being safeguarded through his ability to influence the choice of MPs in constituencies where he enjoyed a 'natural influence' resulting from his status and property ownership. It was this, in essence, which motivated his opposition to the Reform Bill. As a substantial property owner with (what he regarded as) 'legitimate influence', he was defending himself from being disenfranchised.[48] As a senior member of the nobility, he was defending himself from what he regarded as the degradation of the peerage, through the government's threatened new creations. It was Newcastle's continuing sense of the threat to the nobility as a body and the house of lords as an institution which helps to explain his political interventions after the Reform Act had passed.[49]

In the context of 21st-century Britain, Lord Dubs's sentiments might be dismissed as easily as those of the duke of Newcastle were dismissed in the context of the early 19th century. But they might also give us pause for thought. Not for the first time in our history, a matter of parliamentary and electoral reform has raised fundamental issues about the nature of the representative system under which we operate and the purposes to which it is turned. Given our current political preoccupations, it is unlikely to be the last.

---

[48]On influence, see Alan Heesom, ' "Legitimate" versus "Illegitimate" Influences: Aristocratic Electioneering in Mid-Victorian Britain', *Parliamentary History*, vii (1988), 282–305. Gladstone thought seriously about this issue during his canvass of Newark in 1832: *Prime Ministers' Papers*, ed. Brooke and Sorensen, ii, 12–15.

[49]See, e.g., *Unrepentant Tory*, ed. Gaunt, 219–20. This theme is developed in *'The Last of the Tories'*, ed. Gaunt.

Fixing the Membership of the Lords and Commons: The Case of Sir John Cam Hobhouse and the Nottingham By-Election, 1834

JOHN BECKETT

When Melbourne replaced Grey in 1834 he looked to recruit men with experience to join his government. He enlisted Sir John Cam Hobhouse, but Hobhouse needed a seat in the Commons. This was achieved by a writ of acceleration, whereby Viscount Duncannon, one of the sitting MPs for Nottingham, was called into the Lords in his father's lifetime to release a seat in the Commons. Writs had normally been used to strengthen the power of the government in the Lords, and the resentment in Nottingham at this political fix was expressed in a full-scale contest with accusations that the town was being turned into a government nomination borough. Hobhouse might have hoped for a free run as he had already been appointed to the cabinet. Rather, he was forced to fight for the seat, and to go through most of the activities more frequently associated with general elections.

Keywords: Duncannon; elections; Hobhouse; house of commons; hustings; Melbourne; newspapers; Nottingham; writs of acceleration

On 16 July 1834, Viscount Melbourne was summoned by King William IV and asked to form a government. Melbourne accepted the commission and set about assembling a cabinet. Among those he identified for a place around the table was Sir John Cam Hobhouse, widely known as one of Lord Byron's friends, and formerly MP for Westminster 1820–33. Thirteen days later, Hobhouse had been nominated for Nottingham, he had been to the town for the election, had returned to London, and had taken his seat in the house of commons. The story behind this by-election enables us to examine some of the ways in which electoral politics worked in the wake of the Great Reform Act of 1832, and also one particular link between the lower and upper Houses at Westminster.

Earl Grey resigned as prime minister on 9 July 1834. For a week there was a hiatus at Westminster, and after much discussion the king invited Melbourne to try to form a government. Melbourne, home secretary in Grey's government, had many reservations, not the least of which was his concern about experience in government among potential ministers. To this end he wanted Hobhouse in his cabinet. On 16 July, the same day that Melbourne accepted the challenge of forming a cabinet, Hobhouse was summoned to a meeting with Lord Althorp, leader of the whigs in the Commons, and informed that Melbourne had him earmarked for the position of first commissioner of woods and forests. The postholder was responsible for the crown estates, and the position carried with it a seat in the cabinet.[1] Once he had kissed hands, Melbourne wrote directly to Hobhouse 'in very handsome terms' inviting him to join the cabinet, 'and all those likely to be members of the government concurred in it'.[2]

Hobhouse was a political ally of Melbourne and had no qualms about accepting the post.[3] The problem was that he was not an MP. Having resigned his seat for Westminster in 1833 he had resisted offers of alternative constituencies. Now the situation was different: 'we talked of a seat in Parliament for me and Althorp recommended Nottingham … Sudbury was also talked of, a vacancy having been made there by the death of Michael Angelo Taylor.'[4] A means had to be found of insinuating Hobhouse into the Commons, and Nottingham became the chosen route. Hobhouse spoke with General Ferguson, the other MP for Nottingham, 'of which place he gave me some useful information'.[5]

How was this to be done? First, a sitting MP had to agree to give up his seat. A by-election would then be called, at which Hobhouse could be nominated and – hopefully – elected with, or for preference without, a contest. The practice of requiring MPs appointed to certain ministerial and legal offices to seek re-election on taking up office was introduced in 1707 and not abolished until 1919. However, contested re-elections peaked in 1833–5, and the circumstances surrounding the Nottingham by-election of 1834 were unconventional because Hobhouse was not actually in the Commons when appointed to office.[6] It was rumoured, as well, that Hobhouse's election expenses were being guaranteed by the government.[7] The *Standard* had heard that 'it is generally understood that Sir J.C. Hobhouse's expenses will be guaranteed to him by the government'.[8]

Since Hobhouse was not the sitting member, a behind-the-scenes deal had to be done. Both before and after 1832, Nottingham returned two members to parliament. The 1832 legislation preserved the voting rights of the burgesses, and this arrangement was popular, as it meant that anyone who had served an apprenticeship in the town had the vote. The electorate was, as a result, socially a broadly based franchise composed of both property owners

---

[1] The commissioners were charged with the management of crown lands, and the first commissioner was either an MP or a member of the house of lords. The main sources used for this essay are contemporary newspapers including the *Nottingham Review* and the *Nottingham Journal*, together with Hobhouse's own writings. Hobhouse kept a diary for most of his life. Many of the volumes were deposited in the British Museum (now the British Library) with a proviso that they should not be opened until 1900 or later. Meantime, in his sixties, he reflected on his life and wrote a five-volume memoir which was printed but never published: *Some Account of a Long Life* [1865]. A copy is held in the British Library. After 1900 Hobhouse's daughter, Lady Dorchester, edited his writings in *Recollections of a Long Life: With Additional Extracts from his Private Diaries* (6 vols, 1909–11). I have used *Some Account*, and *Recollections*, but there are no diaries for 1834–6. Lady Dorchester assembled material from the diary, *Some Account*, and in a few instances his published works. She used the printed memoir when the diary is missing. So, in 1834, when Hobhouse stood for Nottingham, she had no diary to work from and so had to use the printed memoir. She edited the material vigorously. To show how she edited sections, where I quote *Some Account* below I indicate through the words in italics the wording she reproduced in *Recollections*. The non-italicised words were omitted by Dorchester.

[2] *Some Account*, iii, 21.

[3] *London Gazette*, 22 July 1834.

[4] *Some Account*, iii, 20–1; Hobhouse kept Sudbury as first reserve, possibly because he wanted to avoid accusations that he had accepted a nomination borough rather than one which would need contesting.

[5] *Bury and Norwich Post*, 23 July 1834.

[6] Angus Hawkins, 'Government Appointment By-Elections 1832–86', in *By-Elections in British Politics, 1832–1914*, ed. T.G. Otte and P.A. Readman (Woodbridge, 2013), 51–76.

[7] *Standard*, 24 July 1834.

[8] *Standard*, 24 July 1834.

and manufacturing workers.[9] In 1832, 5,220 electors were registered from a population of 50,000 or so – about one in five males. These numbers did not change greatly because the population of the town was essentially static until the 1850s.[10]

Nottingham had been well known for its radicalism since the 1790s, and was at the forefront of protest during the 1831 Reform Bill riots when the duke of Newcastle's castle was burnt down.[11] At the first post-Reform election in 1832, two whigs were elected: General Sir Ronald Craufurd Ferguson (who had been MP for Nottingham since 1830 and was a consistent supporter of reform) and Viscount Duncannon, a government whip and the first commissioner of woods and forests. Duncannon had been instrumental in drafting the Reform Bill. Both men were well-known reformers and were nominated by Nottingham's whig-Liberal corporation at the election. The tories were so weak in Nottingham that they struggled to find candidates, let alone men with any real hope of winning one of the seats.

Now, in 1834, a deal had to be done, but the mechanism deployed was one which had not been invented for this purpose at all. It was a writ of acceleration. These writs had first been used by Charles II to summon an heir to an English peerage into the upper House in his father's lifetime. Writs of acceleration were used also by William III, partly to try to boost the size of the Lords. At the time, there were 164 male members of the peerage, but this apparently healthy figure was reduced to 116 when minors (21), and Roman catholics and nonjurors (27) were omitted.[12] The advantage of a writ of acceleration was that it temporarily, rather than permanently, increased the size of the Lords. It avoided offering a peerage to a family which might then have membership of the Lords, in theory, for ever. When a writ of acceleration was deployed, the young man involved was expected eventually to succeed his father to the family title (and estates) so that the additional peerage created by calling a son into the Lords while his father was already a member would last only until his father died.[13] Two of those summoned in the winter of 1711 were among the earl of Oxford's 'dozen' new peers. Oxford needed to increase tory numbers in order to be able to conduct business effectively.[14] By raising younger sons in their father's lifetime, he was able to boost the ministry's position in the upper House in the short term, without potentially creating a permanent party advantage.[15] Between the Restoration and the dissolution of Queen Anne's last parliament on 5 January 1715, 13 eldest sons of peers were summoned to the Lords by way of writs of acceleration.[16]

---

[9] M.I. Thomis, *Politics and Society in Nottingham, 1785–1835* (Oxford, 1969), 143.

[10] John Beckett, 'An Industrial Town in the Making', in *A Centenary History of Nottingham History*, ed. Beckett *et al.* (Manchester, 1997), 189–219.

[11] John Beckett, 'The Nottingham Reform Bill Riots of 1831', in *Partisan Politics, Principle and Reform in Parliament and the Constituencies, 1689–1880: Essays in Memory of John A. Phillips*, ed. Clyve Jones, Philip Salmon and Richard W. Davis (Edinburgh, 2005), 114–38; John Beckett, 'Radical Nottingham', in *Centenary History*, ed. Beckett *et al.*, 284–316.

[12] *The History of Parliament: The House of Lords, 1660–1715*, ed. Ruth Paley (5 vols, Cambridge, 2016) [hereafter cited as *HPL, 1660–1715*], i, 26–7, 334–6.

[13] G.E. Cokayne, *The Complete Peerage of England, Scotland, Ireland, Great Britain and the United Kingdom*, ed. Vicary Gibbs *et al.* (12 vols, 1910–59) [hereafter cited as GEC, *Complete Peerage*, i, 489, appendix G].

[14] *HPL, 1660–1715*, i, 18.

[15] *HPL, 1660–1715*, i, 67, 330; Robin Eagles, 'Geoffrey Holmes and the House of Lords Reconsidered', in *British Politics in the Age of Holmes*, ed. Clyve Jones (Oxford, 2009), 25–6.

[16] We should learn more about the use of writs of acceleration when post-1715 volumes of the house of lords sets are issued by the History of Parliament Trust.

The power to make writs of acceleration was affirmed in the 1832 Reform Bill. The intention was to give the king powers, which he might or might not need to exercise, to create sufficient peers to pass the legislation. William IV was not keen on mass creations, and to keep him on board, the cabinet considered requesting him to create a preliminary batch of eight to ten peers, and to prevent any permanent increase in the size of the house by promoting the eldest sons of existing peers or the heirs collateral.[17] This was, in effect, a reuse of writs of acceleration with the intention of strengthening the hand of the government in the upper House by increasing (temporarily) the number of peers eligible to participate in its affairs. By promoting heirs to titles *vita patris* there was less danger of swamping the Lords with newcomers considered to be of inferior merit by the existing members.[18] In the end it came to nothing because the tories gave way and mass peerage creations were unnecessary to pass the Reform Bill through the upper House.

Writs of acceleration remained on the statute book and were used in 1834 to make possible Hobhouse's election to parliament for Nottingham. In this case it was not to strengthen the Lords, but to free up a space in the Commons. Viscount Duncannon had sat for various constituencies since 1805. He held a courtesy title as he was the eldest son of the earl of Bessborough, an Irish peer with a seat in the house of lords. Duncannon would not normally have expected to go to the Lords until he succeeded his father in the earldom, but he was evidently open to offers. Melbourne invited him to become home secretary, the post which the new prime minister was vacating – and in return he was created Baron Duncannon of Bessborough, county Kilkenny *vita patris* – literally, 'in his father's lifetime'. In other words a United Kingdom title was created for him personally, and it was time-limited to the day on which he succeeded his father as earl of Bessborough.[19] The idea was not primarily to boost the government in the Lords, but to create a vacancy in the Commons, which would require a by-election. The candidate recommended by both Duncannon, as the outgoing MP for Nottingham, and also by his fellow Nottingham MP, Ferguson, was Hobhouse.

The political fixer was probably Henry Richard Fox, Lord Holland, nephew of the great radical, Charles James Fox, and leader of the Holland House set, which included Hobhouse's running mate in Westminster elections during the 1820s, Sir Francis Burdett. Since 1809, Holland had been honorary recorder of Nottingham. He had been a friend and political mentor of Byron – who was always a welcome visitor to Holland House – and he knew Hobhouse well. He also knew all about Nottingham politics.[20]

In Lady Dorchester's published version of her father's diary, Hobhouse is quoted as noting merely that on 18 July 1834: 'I accepted an invitation to stand for Nottingham, and went there the same evening.'[21] His own version of events is more revealing. He spoke with

[17] John Cannon, *Parliamentary Reform, 1640–1832* (Cambridge, 1972), 230–1.

[18] *HPL, 1660–1715*, i, 23, 26–7, 67, 330.

[19] GEC, *Complete Peerage*, ii, 172; R.E. Zegger, *John Cam Hobhouse: A Political Life, 1819–52* (Columbia, MO, 1973), 210; Henry Field, *The Date-Book of Remarkable and Memorable Events Connected with Nottingham and its Neighbourhood, 1750–1879* ... (Nottingham, 1884), 416.

[20] John Beckett, 'Politician or Poet? The 6th Lord Byron in the House of Lords, 1809–13', *Parliamentary History*, xxxiv (2015), 201–17; A.D. Kriegel, *The Holland House Diaries, 1831-40* (1977), 120–1; C.J. Wright, 'Holland House set', *ODNB*.

[21] *Recollections*, iv, 357: 18 July 1834. Overnight carriage travel was popular from the 1770s. It was regarded as less dangerous than day journeys, and quicker: Dorian Gerhold, *Bristol's Stage Coaches* (2012), 56, 80, 306.

© 2020 The Author. Parliamentary History *published by John Wiley & Sons Ltd. on behalf of Parliamentary History Yearbook Trust.*

Althorp and Duncannon, and 'both advised my going immediately to Nottingham'. In those days, before the railway, it took just over 12 hours to complete the journey – we know that when Hobhouse travelled to Nottingham for the 1837 election he 'Left London at 4 a.m. and arrived Nottingham at 5.30 p.m'.[22] Hobhouse set out for Nottingham on the evening of 18 July 1834, probably on the overnight London mail, but rather than travelling all night, he broke his journey:

> and slept at Newport Pagnell. The next day I went to Bunny Park, and, dining with Lord Rancliffe, got to Nottingham in time to have some talk with Mr Wakefield and Mr Hurst, the principal supporters of the Liberal interest. *I refused to canvass the electors, or to give any pledges; and in my address merely referred to my past life, and my resolution to do my duty, as I had always done.* I told them that I feared there might be an objection made to transferring the seat from one Chief Commissioner of Woods and Forests to another. They owned the charge might be made, but that I should carry the election easily notwithstanding.[23]

In itself, this was not a particular surprise. It was normal for a candidate, whether or not he was opposed, to go to the constituency for which he was intending to stand even if it was only to spend a few minutes going through the formal business in the event of no opposition being mounted. Few by-elections were contested; for the period 1790–1832 just 14% of by elections resulted in a poll.[24] Ministerial by-elections, or by-elections of the type held when Hobhouse was appointed to office, were usually uncontested: 432 out of 504 between 1832 and 1886 (86%). Most constituencies dutifully returned unopposed their sitting member when ministerial or legal office required re-election, and this would later be the case with Hobhouse.

Given the habitual weakness of the tories in Nottingham, Hobhouse had no real reason to anticipate a contest in 1834. He was, after all, a well-known supporter of the 1832 Reform Act, and he was running for election in a borough constituency which was radical in its political sympathies.[25] Unfortunately for Hobhouse, others saw the situation rather differently, particularly those who resented the assumption that this Westminster deal could be brought about with the tacit support of the Nottingham electorate simply because of its radical credentials. As the *Nottingham Journal*, the town's leading tory newspaper, put it: 'it is settled in Downing Street that, as our town may now fairly be considered a close Ministerial borough, the said Sir John Cam is to be the member for Nottingham'. On receipt of this news in the town, a handbill was printed and circulated, claiming that the newly appointed ministry 'have resolved to complete your political degradation, by making your once

---

[22] BL, Add. MS 61828, f. 76: 20 July 1837.

[23] *Some Account*, iii, 22–3. From this quotation only the section in italics can be found in Lady Dorchester's edited version of her father's memoir and is an indication of her editing technique. Bunny Park is between Nottingham and Loughborough on the (modern) A60.

[24] Philip Salmon, ' "Plumping Contests": The Impact of By–Elections on English Voting Behaviour, 1790–1868', in *By-Elections in British Politics*, ed. Otte and Readman, 26.

[25] Cannon, *Parliamentary Reform*, 216; John Beckett, 'Parliament and the Localities: The Borough of Nottingham', in *Parliament and Locality, 1660–1939*, ed. David Dean and Clyve Jones (Edinburgh, 1998), 60–1; Beckett, 'Radical Nottingham', 289–301.

high-minded and independent borough a substitute for Old Sarum, a refuge for the destitute!' This, the handbill concluded, needed to be resisted.[26]

Even as Hobhouse was on the road to Nottingham, 'a meeting of electors convened by
hand bill, was held at the Durham Ox room, at which nearly 200 voters were present'. Those
present were unhappy with what they saw as a political fix in which the constituency was
being treated simply as a pawn on behalf of the government, 'and there were not wanting
those who expressed a desire for some person connected with the town or trade of Nottingham to be put in nomination'. This was not unreasonable, but since the dissidents had
no obvious local candidate to propose they were forced to back the nomination of William
Eagle, a relatively well-known radical and a would-be parliamentarian. Eagle claimed to be
in favour of the ballot, triennial parliaments, the abolition of the corn laws, and the reform
of town corporations, but he had no local roots and his candidature was certainly divisive
since he and Hobhouse were – in theory – on the same 'Liberal' side.[27]

Hobhouse had only a few days to mount an effective campaign. His first move, on the
morning of Saturday 19 July, was to publish his address – similar to a modern manifesto
– and to have it distributed through the town.[28] Hobhouse knew how elections worked
from his days as MP for Westminster and he was prepared for the hurly-burly which was
likely to occur whether or not a contest took place. He was soon out and about among the
electors:

> In the evening of Saturday, Sir John met a numerous party of those who have been
> in the habit of taking the most active part in elections and they agreed to support his
> pretensions to the representation of Nottingham; at a later period of the evening, he
> paid a visit to some of the political houses, where we understand he gave a satisfactory
> explanation of his conduct in regard to military flogging.[29]

William Eagle arrived in Nottingham only on the evening of Sunday, 20 June, and he met
with his supporters on the Monday morning in order to explain to them his position on
key political issues. Next came the modern equivalent of a television debate between the
candidates, as reported in the *Nottingham Review*:

> On Monday evening [21st] a meeting in the Exchange Hall was called for the purpose of
> hearing Sir John Hobhouse, but such was the tumult created by some of his opponents,
> that it was scarcely possible to hear a word. We have reason to believe that this conduct,
> and the similar course pursued on Wednesday at the nomination, disgusted many of
> those who were favourably inclined to Mr Eagle and either prevented them from voting
> or induced them to support Sir John Hobhouse.

[26] *Morning Post*, 21 July 1834, quoting the *Nottingham Journal*.

[27] *Morning Post*, 23 July 1834, carried an editorial condemning the decision to put up a candidate against
Hobhouse (History of Parliament, draft constituency article on Nottingham 1832–68).

[28] *Some Account*, iii, 23.

[29] *Nottingham Review*, 25 July 1834. The flogging issue was frequently raised. Hobhouse had wished to abolish
flogging before he held the position of secretary at war but once in power he was prepared to sponsor legislation
limiting, but not abolishing, flogging.

'Candidates', Jon Lawrence has written, were 'expected to put up with a good deal of derisive and boorish behaviour in the name of accountability and letting people have their say'.[30] Canvassing continued through Tuesday, 22 July, and then, after all this political foreplay, the candidates prepared for the hustings on 23 July.

Hustings were often held on specially-constructed platforms in open spaces, but the tradition in Nottingham was to use the Exchange Hall, which sat on the same site as the modern Council House until it was demolished in 1926. The hall was described by a contemporary as a

> noble spacious room, which is 75 feet long, 30 feet wide, and 30 feet high, with an arched ceiling; there are two smaller rooms on the same line, communicating with the large one by folding doors, and when these are thrown open they form a room of 123 feet long, and in it we have seen more than 400 persons sit down to dinner. Here public meetings are held, and here also the last election was carried on; and sometimes it is used for exhibitions, amusements, balls, &c.[31]

On 23 July the room was full by the time the nomination proceedings commenced at noon; indeed, according to one of the town's newspapers it was

> crowded to excess for some time before the nomination; the usual noise and tumult, the accompaniments of political contests, prevailed to a considerable degree, with the addition of several excellent imitations of cock crowing.[32]

Hobhouse, somewhat less charitably, attributed the turnout to the fact that 'a murderer was executed in the morning, and the crowd that attended that spectacle adjourned afterwards to our exhibition'.[33] Initially, as the clock struck midday the undersheriff read aloud the acts of parliament prescribed by statute to be recited at the nomination, and Thomas Roberts and Thomas Bishop, sheriffs, took the oath as returning officers.[34] Then William Reader, the assessor [returning officer], 'read to them the names of the candidates about to be proposed for their selection; they were William Eagle, Esq., of Leighton Hall, Suffolk, and the Right Honourable Sir John Cam Hobhouse, Bart, of Berkley Square, Middlesex'.[35]

Next, the candidates, in alphabetical order, Eagle first, Hobhouse second, and their sponsors, were invited, in the traditional manner, to address the meeting. George Gill, a lace commission agent in Nottingham, nominated William Eagle. Gill castigated Hobhouse as a corporation stooge, and suggested that by putting Eagle forward, the Radicals were teaching the corporation a lesson: 'that they could no longer usurp the right of electing members,

---

[30] Jon Lawrence, *Electing Our Masters: The Hustings in British Politics from Hogarth to Blair* (Oxford, 2009), 7.

[31] [R. Sutton], *The Strangers' Guide through the Town of Nottingham, Being a Description of the Principal Buildings, and Objects of Curiosity in that Ancient Town* (1827), 11.

[32] Field, *Date-Book*, 417.

[33] Field, *Date-Book*, 417.

[34] *Nottingham Review*, 25 July 1834; *Records of the Borough of Nottingham* …, ed. W.H. Stevenson *et al.* (9 vols, 1882–1956), viii, 386, 387, for evidence of a stage being erected.

[35] *Nottingham Review*, 25 July 1834.

trampling on their rights, and of converting this ancient seat of freedom into a nomination borough'.[36]

Gill was followed on to the podium by Benjamin Boothby, an iron founder, who '*made the most insolent attack that ever had been made even upon me, who had heard so much of that sort of eloquence. He accused me of every political crime – apostasy, baseness, love of place, love of money, cruelty, and what not besides telling the meeting that my wife's sisters, were pensioners on the public. All this I bore patiently, because obliged to hear it; only once or twice I said, "That is false". The fellow went on reading charges against me from the True Sun, and treating me as the worst of political delinquents.*'[37] The *Review* recorded Boothby's comments a little differently:

> We have before us the Right Honourable the First Commissioner for Woods and Forests (hisses, groans and loud cheers) – who, in his address assures us that he comes forward at the request of a body of our brother electors, – (Shouts of 'a lie') … whether it be decent, that in the selection of a suitable man to represent your interests in Parliament, we should be satisfied to submit to the Right Honourable Gentleman being sent from Downing Street, by and through their agents, who reside amongst us … Is Nottingham to become the Old Sarum for the Whigs? (Cries of 'no, no').

Boothby went on in this manner for some time, suggesting that Hobhouse had moved across the political spectrum from his days as a Radical reformer, to his present position as 'a thoroughgoing Whig', which was true. Hobhouse, despite his years of experience in Westminster, was clearly shocked by the claims.[38] Having been nominated, and having accepted the nomination, Eagle was now invited to speak, and his first and most powerful point was that he was not a stooge of the government:

> I have not been sent down in a band box from Downing-street, labelled at the Treasury, ticketed to the Corporation of Nottingham, and addressed especially to the Whig dictator who presides over it. (Tremendous cheers and some hisses.) I am not sent down here, but put up by yourselves. I am not come here because I desire a seat in Parliament, and from a necessity to patch up an administration, but I am come to fight your battles against Whig dictation, and to give new impulse to reform.[39]

Hobhouse noted that he was obliged to listen to these speeches because this was what was to be expected at an election, but the quid pro quo, as far as he was concerned with more than a decade of experience of Westminster behind him, was that he and his sponsors were afforded the same conditions when they came to speak. Tradition dictated that just as Eagle's sponsors had been heard, so Hobhouse and his sponsors should also have been listened to as part of the ritual of the occasion. According to the *Nottingham Review* the way in which Hobhouse and his sponsors were drowned out was 'to say the least, disrespectful'[40].

[36] *Nottingham Review*, 25 July 1834.

[37] *Some Account*, ii, 25. The *True Sun* was a London evening newspaper published 1832–7. It was pro-whig.

[38] *Recollections*, iv, 357–8.

[39] *Nottingham Review*, 25 July 1834. A band box is a circular cardboard box for carrying hats to prevent them from being damaged on a journey.

[40] *Nottingham Review*, 24 July 1834.

George, Lord Rancliffe went first. A contemporary of both Hobhouse and Byron, Rancliffe had been educated, like Byron, at Harrow. He succeeded his father in 1800, while still under age, and in 1806 inherited from his grandfather, Sir Thomas Parkyns, the family estates, which included Bunny Park. In 1812 he became involved in Nottingham electoral politics, canvassing vigorously on a radical platform of peace, parliamentary reform, and liberty of conscience. He was returned to the house of commons in 1812 and again in 1817, but stood down in 1820. He was returned again in 1826, and overlapped with Hobhouse, who was by then one of the members for Westminster. Rancliffe stood down in 1830, but continued to play a role in Nottingham that was at least semi-active, in that he appeared from time to time at nomination day to propose a candidate, or to speak in his favour. He supported the Reform Bill in 1831. Now, in the Exchange Hall he stood up to speak 'amidst partial hisses, which were speedily drowned out amidst the most tremendous cheers, interrupted with some groans … After attempting for some time to speak, without obtaining silence, Rancliffe concluded "I will not detain you longer, further than to propose the Right Hon Sir John Cam Hobhouse, Baronet, as a proper person to represent you in Parliament." '[41]

The seconder was Thomas Wakefield, a successful local businessman, described in the 1832 trade directory as a cotton spinner, who lived at 12 Low Pavement. Wakefield was a member of the corporation, and leader of the whigs: 'The real master of the borough', wrote Hobhouse many years later, 'at that time was Thomas Wakefield, a nephew of Wakefield, the editor of Lucretius, and the correspondent of Charles Fox. He was a manufacturer with a flourishing business, very much respected and esteemed. I am talking of 1834.'[42] A year after the events described here he would be mayor, and among his many other achievements he was a founder member and active participant in the activities of Bromley House Library. Wakefield stood up to speak but he got no further than saying 'Gentlemen' before hooting and groaning, mixed with shouts and cheers, made it impossible for him to go on:

> Hobhouse now stood up, and presented himself amidst the tumult of hisses, groans and some cheers and was very imperfectly heard; he said he would not refrain from complaining of the manner in which he had been attacked; he did not wish to impute falsehood to anyone, but he did think that the honourable seconder of his opponent [Boothby] might have spared some of the epithets he had made use of. The honourable candidate had said that if he were conscious of the political offences charged upon him (Sir John) he should desire the earth to open and swallow him up; he (Sir John) would only say, so should he, if he felt guilty of what he had been charged with. The tumult increased so much that he concluded his address by saying he should meet them again on Saturday.[43]

As Hobhouse later recalled: 'neither Lord Rancliffe nor Mr T[homas] Wakefield was heard at all. I experienced the same treatment. I pulled out my watch and said I would give

---

[41] BL, Add. MS 56,549: Hobhouse diary, 16 July 1824, available at *https://petercochran.wordpress.com/hobhouses-diary/* (accessed 18 Nov. 2019).

[42] *Some Account*, iii, 24.

[43] *Nottingham Review*, 24 July 1834.

them five minutes to become silent; this had no effect.[44] The failure to control the crowd was subsequently noted by the *Morning Post*: 'it would be quite impossible to describe the rough manner in which [Hobhouse] was received … The confusion and uproar became so great that Sir J Hobhouse was obliged to desist addressing the meeting. He asked them if they would hear him, but they cried aloud, "No, no, no" and yelled horribly.'[45]

Hobhouse resented this treatment but it could not have been entirely unexpected, given Nottingham's track record in elections. In any case he had no intention of withdrawing his candidature. The second traditional event at the hustings was the 'show of hands' among those attending the nomination. Since voters and non-voters alike were entitled to 'vote', it was only a rough guide to the different candidates as to whether they should continue with their candidacy, but this was the last point at which a man could chose to withdraw and save the potential expense of a contest. The losing candidate or candidates in the show of hands, if they judged success at the poll as at least possible, would still be expected to call for a contest, but if they interpreted the show of hands as foretelling defeat they were expected to pull out on the grounds that they had no real hope of success and no need to commit to funding an expensive contest. Hobhouse recognized that: 'the great majority in the body of the hall was certainly for Eagle; on the hustings about 200 hands were held up for me, and away we came'. Judging that the majority of those held up their hands for Eagle did not have the vote, and furious at the way he had been treated, Hobhouse 'said, "very well then the poll shall decide it" '.[46] Did Hobhouse expect to win? He does not say, but he added a significant caveat: 'I was the object of this blind hatred at Nottingham. A good deal, however, of the opposition was directed against the Corporation, who were my friends, and the friends of the Whig party.'[47]

Once an election had been called, the contest usually took place immediately, or, to allow time for the rival parties to complete their arrangements in larger boroughs, on the following day or two. Meanwhile the candidates continued to attempt to persuade and influence the electors, by delivering speeches and even venturing into public spaces to meet potential voters. The candidates might also march to their inn or tavern in full party regalia and colours, with a band and the inevitable crowd of supporters (whether qualified voters or not). This might also be the point at which largesse was distributed to potential voters, although Hobouse claimed that in 1834 he neither canvassed nor bribed.[48]

With more than 5,000 potential voters, the main delay in Nottingham between the nomination and the poll was the time needed for the election booths to be set up. From 1832 the authorities were obliged to provide multiple polling stations where there were more than 600 registered voters: these could be scattered around the constituency or, as in Nottingham, linked to the hustings but with several temporary booths.[49]

[44] *Recollections*, iv, 358.

[45] *Morning Post*, 25 July 1834.

[46] *Morning Post*, 25 July 1834.

[47] *Recollections*, iv, 358; Frank O'Gorman, 'Campaign Rituals and Ceremonies: The Social Meaning of Elections in England, 1780–1860', *Past & Present*, No. 135 (1992), 79–115.

[48] *Recollections*, iv, 357: 18 July 1834.

[49] Lawrence, *Electing Our Masters*, 33.

Edward Staveley was the corporation employee entrusted with this task. His first task was to set up the 'nomination stage' in the Exchange Hall.[50] In 1830, we know that he was responsible for putting up the election booths, and then 'for removing the same which included labour, carriage, waste and injury of timber and deals, and making good the pavement'.[51] For the 1834 by-election four booths were set up in the market place, one each for the electors of St Peter's, and St Nicholas's parishes, each with two compartments. The country voters, men with the franchise who lived beyond the town boundaries, also voted at these booths. The other two booths were for the north and south divisions of St Mary's parish – the biggest by far of Nottingham's three parishes – and each of these had four compartments, meaning that in total there were twelve 'polling bars'.[52]

Polling was scheduled to take place over two days, 24 and 25 July, between 8 am and 4 pm. The restriction to two consecutive days was introduced in 1832.[53] Canvassing continued throughout the two days, and at the end of the first day Hobhouse went to his committee room at the Exchange, and from the window addressed the assembled multitude. For a considerable period he was completely inaudible, from the noise created by hooting, groaning, and shouting, in one part of the crowd. He noted that:

> his situation in the poll fully justified his expectation, and the calumnies that had been spread against him, without the opportunity of answering them, had not influenced the great majority of the electors. He thanked them sincerely for the pre-eminent station he occupied, but begged they would not relax their exertions … Lord Rancliffe was loudly cheered, and said that though Hooted yesterday, he again came forward, as he always should do, to advocate that which he believed to be for the good of the people.[54]

Eagle was not to be outdone, and at 7 pm addressed 'a very great crowd in front of his committee room', which was on the corner of Clinton Street, and Parliament Street East. He thanked his 358 voters so far:

> and declared his belief that of the 1322 electors who had supported his right honourable rival, at least one thousand were obtained by certain means – ('Ten shillings and a breakfast') – and certainly such a set of ragamuffins did he never behold. Of that number at least 900 came up in a state of beastly intoxication, and they could scarcely repeat the oath; they showed their degradation by coming with their heads down, whereas he could distinguish all his voters by their honest countenances. In the hustings he had been treated with vulgar effrontery, such as he never experienced from Tories, who were open and manly enemies … The refusal to hear [Hobhouse] would prove that the people's confidence was withdrawn from the Whigs.[55]

The polls reopened at 8 am on Friday, 25 July. They closed at 4 pm and the result was announced at 4.15 pm. Hobhouse had polled 1,591 votes, and Eagle just 566, giving

---

[50] *Records of the Borough of Nottingham*, ed. Stevenson *et al.*, viii, 419.

[51] *Records of the Borough of Nottingham*, ed. Stevenson *et al.*, viii, 386.

[52] *Nottingham Review*, 25 July 1834.

[53] Lawrence, *Electing Our Masters*, 31–2.

[54] *Nottingham Review*, 25 July 1834.

[55] *Nottingham Review*, 25 July 1834.

Hobhouse a majority of 1,025. 'The decision', Hobhouse wrote later, 'was announced in silence.[56] It was normal at this stage for the victorious candidate to make a final speech of a non-controversial nature thanking the returning officer, their friends, their supporters, and the voters – much as they still do today. But in this by-election matters seem just to have drifted to a conclusion, somewhat to the surprise of the *Nottingham Review*:

> From the vast majority on one side, and the evident unwillingness of the electors to poll, including the numerous sections consisting of the conservatives and the dissenters generally, the contest may be considered as virtually at an end, and may probably terminate early this day [Friday] … No flags or music have appeared in the streets and in this, as well as many other particulars, the contest differs totally from any previous one.[57]

The contest did not end, in other words, with the traditional celebrations such as the chairing of the candidate, or even the post-election dinner. Hobhouse appeared at the window of his committee room and gave a short speech in which he said he hoped that all animosity would now be at an end. He then went back into the committee room to thank his friends for their support – 'how deeply sensible he was of their kind and valuable assistance at a time when unmerited obloquy had been profusely poured upon him, for having in the hour of danger joined what he considered to be an honest government'. He thanked also his canvassers.[58] But this was a by-election, and possibly because of the speed with which the whole contest had proceeded, only 42% of registered voters cast a vote, by contrast with 64% at the 1832 general election.[59]

Eagle and Boothby also addressed crowds, which then quietly dispersed. According to Hobhouse:

> Eagle had called my supporters ragamuffins, and said that nine-tenths of them were drunk. I believe one-twentieth of them were so; and my impression then was that although the whole constituency was far inferior to that of Westminster, yet there were two or three hundred high spirited, independent men, as intelligent and well- mannered as any to be found in this kingdom.[60]

In the evening, Hobhouse called a meeting of his supporters, and by 8 pm 500 were packed into in the Exchange Hall. Hobhouse, Rancliffe, and Wakefield were all present. Hobhouse told the meeting that having refused to stand for several seats, 'he now found himself in ten days called from private life to take a seat in the Cabinet and was elected member for Nottingham'. The success of the campaign, short though it was, had to be celebrated and the meeting – and the toasts – went on until midnight, when 'the meeting broke up amidst loud cheers'. Hobhouse left before the end, telling his supporters that he would take his seat in the Commons on the coming Monday.[61]

[56]Field, *Date-Book*, 416: July 1834; *Some Account*, iii, 24–5.

[57]*Nottingham Review*, 25 July 1843.

[58]*Nottingham Review*, 25 July 1834.

[59]Salmon, ' "Plumping Contests" ', 43.

[60]*Recollections*, iv, 357.

[61]*Nottingham Review*, 1 Aug. 1834.

Hobhouse left Nottingham on Saturday the 26th 'at an early hour' for London – probably on the 5.30 am London mail, which departed from outside of the *Lion* – but there was still time for him to agree to become an annual subscriber to the General Hospital and the Nottingham Dispensary (5 guineas each per annum).[62]'I left Nottingham the next day', he recorded without comment in his memoir.[63]

Hobhouse was back in London by Monday morning (the 28th) and took his seat in the Commons on the Tuesday morning (the 29th), the same day that the *London Gazette* announced his election victory in Nottingham. A couple of days later he took up the position of first commissioner of the woods and forests and he served in government until Melbourne resigned in November 1834.

What must have galled Hobhouse most of all was that the opposition to him came from Radicals who resented what they saw as the conversion of Nottingham into a 'nomination' borough. In the words of the conservative *Nottingham Journal*: 'is Nottingham for ever to be a close Whig borough?' Hobhouse was viewed as a treasury candidate foisted on the electorate from Downing Street. There was much truth in this, given that he had been shoehorned into the constituency via a writ of acceleration in order to shore up Melbourne's government, although it was clearly frustrating for the Radical element that having found in William Eagle a suitable candidate, Eagle was defeated so decisively at the poll.[64]

Although he was no stranger to electoral controversy, Hobhouse did not enjoy his experience at Nottingham. He described to his old running mate at Westminster, Sir Francis Burdett, the 'most horrible difference' between Westminster and the 'infernal' Nottingham. He added that: 'I am just as ill-used in one place as the other but the electors here are a totally different body of men.' Hobhouse was forced to leave one election meeting with 'characters shrieking', and, in a reference to the flogging issue, throwing 'a mass of cat-o'-nine tails' towards the platform.[65] He was disgusted by the inversion of the social order whereby the candidate had to go out of his way to flatter the voters and their families, and even non-voters, because the distinction was not always clear, while they had the right to interrupt, heckle, and insult him. It is perhaps, therefore, no surprise to find that when Melbourne's ministry fell in November 1834, and a general election was called for January 1835, Hobhouse had himself nominated for his home city of Bristol. However, he was rapidly disabused of the idea that as a native son he would have an electoral advantage: the two tories polled 3,709 and 3,312 to head the poll, and the losing whigs were Baillie with 2,520 and, trailing in a long way fourth, Hobhouse with 1,808.[66] Fortunately for Hobhouse, such were the ways of elections in those days, Nottingham corporation had also nominated him and he was returned for the borough unopposed, which he subsequently represented until 1847.[67]

---

[62] *Nottingham Review*, 25 July 1834; White's *Directory* (1832), 291.

[63] *Recollections*, iv, 357 (Hobhouse does not say if there was a chairing or a dinner: see O'Gorman, 'Campaign Rituals and Ceremonies', 91); *Some Account*, iii, 25.

[64] A.C. Wood, 'Nottingham 1835–1865', *Transactions of the Thoroton Society of Nottinghamshire*, lix (1955), 69–70.

[65] Zegger, *Hobhouse*, 211–12.

[66] *Bristol Gazette*, 15 Jan. 1835, cited in Zegger, *Hobhouse*, 214.

[67] Perhaps surprisingly, to us if not to contemporaries, hardly any mention was made of Byron when Hobhouse came forward for Nottingham, although an editorial in the *Nottingham Review* noted that: 'he [Hobhouse] travelled in 1809 and 1810 into Albania, Romelia, and other provinces of Turkey, along with Lord Byron'. This was, of

© 2020 *The Author. Parliamentary History published by John Wiley & Sons Ltd. on behalf of Parliamentary History Yearbook Trust.*

The 1834 by-election in Nottingham reminds us of a few hard truths about the electoral system. The first is that it was possible to insinuate a candidate into a constituency without too much trouble if everyone else was ready to play the game, in this case Duncannon to be sent to the house of lords, and Hobhouse to rush down to Nottingham in time for the nomination. Of course, it meant that Hobhouse had to endure the rigours of an electoral contest, which he had no doubt hoped to avoid and which he seems to have found particularly troublesome. He was open to accusations that he was a government nominee in a system supposedly reformed just a couple of years earlier with the intention of sweeping away some of the more problematic electoral abuses. Instead, a clause introduced into the legislation in an attempt to provide the king with a means of making sufficient (temporary) peers to ensure that the Reform Act could pass, was used as a way of emptying a seat in order to bring in a government nominee – however radical his credentials.

The *Nottingham Journal*, a predominantly tory paper, was scathing in its denunciation of the system, and how it had functioned. In an account of the contest headed 'Electioneering Anecdotes', it set out the many ways which, in its opinion, the contest demonstrated that very little had changed, despite the 1832 act:

> The late contest has furnished numerous proofs of the ready manner in which the loud-est bawlers for 'purity of election', are ready to barter their 'political independence' for almost as small an equivalent as a mess of pottage. 'Ten shillings, and what you can eat and drink', was the contemptible price which numbers of the electors consented to re-ceive for the exercise of that franchise, for the extension of which, the whole empire was lately thrown into convulsions … These incorruptible ale-house patriots contaminated their fingers with 'base bribes' and forgot all their lofty declamations on 'public virtue' and 'political integrity'. Alas! For the frailty of humanity. Several well authenticated and amusing facts have come to our knowledge, some of which may serve to entertain our readers:- a man 'went to a hatter's to buy him a hat' (as the old tale has it), he threw down half a sovereign, the hatter took up the gold, and was examining its genuineness, when the man candidly observed, 'you need not be afraid of it, I received it from Mester Hobhouse, and it's a good job he's cum, or I should have gone without a new hat a good while longer'. Another man, in a neighbouring village, was asked to go to Not-tingham to give his vote for Sir John; he coldly reminded the applicant that there was a debt of 10s owing on account of a vote given at the last election for Ferguson and Duncannon: this claim was reluctantly allowed. Ten shillings more were demanded for travelling expenses for *four miles* and then 10s 'the regular price' for the vote itself. Thus, by his ingenuity, obtaining 30s for what was only worth 10s at 'marketable prices'. An-other individual who polled for Sir John, congratulated the Baronet on the excellence of his principles, and expressed the pleasure he felt in recording his vote in his favour; but this high-minded elector soon returned to the hustings in a terrible passion, cursing the duplicity and cupidity of the Whigs, and announcing to Sir John the astounding fact, that he had been grossly deceived, for the 'half sovereign' that was to have been placed under a stone in his house, was *not there!* So notorious, indeed, was the practice of paying for votes, that pay-tables were established at public houses for the purpose of

67 (*continued*) course, the great European tour which led to the publication of Byron's first great epic poem, *Childe Harold's Pilgrimage*.

liquidating these 'honest' claims. Other manoeuvres were played off – dead men found representatives at the booths – voters polled twice and thrice by passing through different compartments – and some respectable electors who reside in the country, but who never were at Nottingham during the week, had their names entered on the poll books by some unprincipled rascals, who represented themselves as the individuals on the registry. Such are a few of the impositions played off on the occasion. Assuredly we yet want some Reform, that our Legislators will find difficult to accomplish – what can be said of those who consent to become agents in such proceedings?[68]

The newspaper was right: what had been the point of all the troubles over the Reform Bill, including the firing of the duke of Newcastle's Nottingham castle, if so little had changed and, in particular, bribery remained widespread? It would eventually make a difference but only after disillusionment with the outcome of the legislation had produced the Chartist movement, which was as powerful in Nottingham as anywhere else in the country.

APPENDIX 1: *Events in July 1834*

Wednesday, 16 July	Melbourne becomes prime minister.
Thursday, 17 July	Duncannon elevated to the house of lords.
Friday, 18 July	Hobhouse is nominated for Nottingham and sets out for the town.
Saturday, 19 July	Hobhouse arrives in Nottingham and publishes his manifesto. Canvassing begins.
Sunday, 20 July	Day of rest.
Monday, 21 July	Canvassing: public meeting in the Exchange.
Tuesday, 22 July	Canvassing.
Wednesday, 23 July	Hustings.
Thursday, 24 July	Election – first day.
Friday, 25 July	Election – second day and result: Hobhouse makes speech to supporters and holds a 'party'.
Saturday, 26 July	Hobhouse returns to London.
Tuesday, 29 July	Hobhouse takes his seat in the Commons.
Tuesday, 5 August	Hobhouse makes first speech on return to the Commons.

[68]*Nottingham Review*, 1 Aug. 1834.

Bibliography of the Published Works of Clyve Jones

Compiled by
D. W. HAYTON and
RICHARD A. GAUNT

1972

(With Michael Chapman and Pamela Carr Woods), 'The Characteristics of the Literature Used by Historians', *Journal of Librarianship*, iv, 137–56.

1973

'Two Unpublished Letters of Oliver Cromwell', *Bulletin of the Institute of Historical Research*, xlvi, 216–18.

'The Protestant Wind of 1688: Myth and Reality', *European Studies Review*, iii, 201–22.

'Journal of the Voyage of William of Orange from Holland to Torbay, 1688', *Journal of the Society for Army Historical Research*, li, 15–18.

1976

'Debates in the House of Lords on "the Church in Danger", 1705, and on Dr Sacheverell's Impeachment, 1710', *Historical Journal*, xix, 759–81.

1978

'Seating Problems of the House of Lords in the Early Eighteenth Century: The Evidence of the Manuscript Minutes', *Bulletin of the Institute of Historical Research*, li, 132–45.

1979

(Ed., with David Hayton), *A Register of Parliamentary Lists 1660–1761* (xxvi, 168 pp., University of Leicester History Department, Occasional Publication no. 1: Leicester).

'Godolphin, the Whig Junto and the Scots: A New Lords' Division List from 1709', *Scottish Historical Review*, lviii, 158–74.

1980

(With Eveline Cruickshanks and David Hayton), 'Divisions in the House of Lords on the Transfer of the Crown and Other Issues, 1689–94: Ten New Lists', *Bulletin of the Institute of Historical Research*, liii, 56–87.

1982

(Ed., with David Hayton), *A Register of Parliamentary Lists 1660–1761: A Supplement* (xii, 20 pp., University of Leicester History Department, Occasional Publication no. 3: Leicester).

'The Impeachment of the Earl of Oxford and the Whig Schism of 1717: Four New Lists', *Bulletin of the Institute of Historical Research*, lv, 66–87.

(With John Beckett), 'Financial Improvidence and Political Independence in the Early Eighteenth Century: George Booth, 2nd Earl of Warrington (1675–1758)', *Bulletin of the John Rylands Library*, lxv, 8–35.

(With Geoffrey Holmes), 'Trade, the Scots and the Parliamentary Crisis of 1713', *Parliamentary History*, i, 47–77.

(With Edward Gregg), 'Hanover, Pensions and the "Poor Lords", 1712–13', *Parliamentary History*, i, 173–80.

1983

'James Brydges, Earl of Carnarvon, and the 1717 Hereford By-Election: A Case Study in Aristocratic Electoral Management', *Huntington Library Quarterly*, xlvi, 310–20.

'The Division that Never Was: New Evidence on the Aborted Vote in the Lords on 8 December 1711 on "No Peace without Spain" ', *Parliamentary History*, ii, 191–202.

1984

(Ed.), *Party and Management in Parliament, 1660–1784* (xvi, 205 pp., Leicester: Leicester University Press).

'Introduction', ibid., xiii–xvi.

' "The Scheme Lords, the Neccessitous Lords, and the Scots Lords": The Earl of Oxford's Management and the "Party of the Crown" in the House of Lords, 1711–14', ibid., 123–67.

1985

(Ed., with Geoffrey Holmes), *The London Diaries of William Nicolson, Bishop of Carlisle, 1702–1718* (xxi, 772 pp., Oxford: Clarendon Press).

(With David Hayton), 'A Treasure-House Laid Open' [review article], *Parliamentary History*, iv, 205–8.

1986

(Ed., with David Lewis Jones), *Peers, Politics and Power: The House of Lords, 1603–1911* (xxix, 557 pp., London and Ronceverte, WV: Hambledon Press).

1987

(Ed.), *Britain in the First Age of Party, 1680–1750: Essays Presented to Geoffrey Holmes* (xxii, 292 pp., London and Ronceverte, WV: Hambledon Press).

'The House of Lords and the Growth of Parliamentary Stability', ibid., 85–110.

1989

(Ed.), *A Pillar of the Constitution: The House of Lords in British Politics, 1640–1784* (x, 246 pp., London and Ronceverte, WV: Hambledon Press).

(With John Beckett), 'Introduction: The Peerage and the House of Lords in the Seventeenth and Eighteenth Centuries', ibid., 1–19.

' "Venice Preserv'd; or A Plot Discovered": The Political and Social Context of the Peerage Bill of 1719', ibid., 79–112.

'The Harley Family and the Harley Papers', *British Library Journal*, xv, 123–33.

' "To Dispose in Earnest, of a Place I Got in Jest": Eight New Letters of Sir John Vanbrugh, 1722–1726', *Notes and Queries*, new ser., xxxvi, 461–9.

1990

'Swift, the Earl of Oxford, and the Management of the House of Lords in 1713: Two New Lists', *British Library Journal*, xvi, 117–30.

'The Politics and the Financial Costs of an Episcopal Appointment in the Early Eighteenth Century: The Promotion of William Wake to the Bishopric of Lincoln in 1705', *Huntington Library Quarterly*, liii, 119–29.

(Ed.), 'Parliament and the Peerage and Weaver Navigation Bills: The Correspondence of Lord Newburgh with the Earl of Cholmondeley, 1719–20', *Transactions of the Historic Society of Lancashire and Cheshire*, cxxxix, 31–61.

1991

'Jacobitism and the Historian: The Case of William, 1st Earl Cowper', *Albion*, xxiii, 681–96.

'The London Life of a Peer in the Reign of Anne: A Case Study from Lord Ossulston's Diary', *London Journal*, xvi, 140–55.

'The Parliamentary Organization of the Whig Junto in the Reign of Queen Anne: The Evidence of Lord Ossulston's Diary', *Parliamentary History*, x, 164–82.

1992

'Whigs, Jacobites and Charles Spencer, Third Earl of Sunderland', *English Historical Review*, cix, 52–73.

(With Frances Harris), ' "A Question … Carried by Bishops, Pensioners, Place-Men, Idiots": Sarah, Duchess of Marlborough and the Lords' Division over the Spanish Convention, 1 March 1739', *Parliamentary History*, xi, 254–77.

'A Westminster Anglo-Scottish Dining Group, 1710–12: The Evidence of Lord Ossulston's Diary', *Scottish Historical Review*, lxxi, 110–28.

1993

'1720–23 and All That: A Reply to Eveline Cruickshanks', *Albion*, xxvi, 41–53.

' "Party Rage and Faction" – The View from Fulham, Scotland Yard and the Temple: Parliament in the Letters of Thomas Bateman and John and Ralph Bridges to Sir William Trumbull, 1710–1714', *British Library Journal*, xix, 148–80.

'The New Opposition in the House of Lords, 1720–3', *Historical Journal*, xxxvi, 309–29.

'A London "Directory" of Peers and Bishops for 1708–1709: A Note on the Residential Topography of Politicians in the Reign of Anne', *London Journal*, xviii, 23–30.

1994

'Whigs, Jacobites and Charles Spencer, Third Earl of Sunderland', *English Historical Review*, cix, 52–73.

(Ed.), 'Letters of Lord Balmerino to Harry Maule, 1710–1713, 1721–1722', *Miscellany of the Scottish History Society* (Scottish History Society, 5th ser., vii), 99–168.

1995

(Ed., with G.M. Ditchfield and David Hayton), *British Parliamentary Lists, 1660–1800: A Register* (xxi, 151 pp., London and Rio Grande, OH: Hambledon Press).

'William, First Earl Cowper, Country Whiggery, and the Leadership of the Opposition in the House of Lords, 1720–1723', in *Lords of Parliament: Studies, 1714–1914*, ed. R.W. Davis (Stanford, CA), 29–43.

' "A Fresh Division Lately Grown Up Amongst Us": Party Strife, Aristocratic Investment in the Old and New East India Companies and the Vote in the House of Lords on 23 February 1700', *Historical Research*, lxviii, 302–17.

1996

(Ed.), *The Scots and Parliament* (viii, 147 pp., Edinburgh: Edinburgh University Press; issued as vol. xv, part 1 of *Parliamentary History*).

(With Stephen Taylor), 'Viscount Bolingbroke and the Composition of an Opposition Protest in the House of Lords in 1734 on the Election of the Scottish Representative Peers', *Yale University Library Gazette*, lxxi, 22–31.

1997

'The Parliamentary Organization of the Whig Junto in the Reign of Queen Anne: An Additional Note', *Parliamentary History*, xvi, 205–12.

1998

(Ed., with Stephen Taylor and Richard Connors), *Hanoverian Britain and Empire: Essays in Memory of Philip Lawson* (xxiv, 349 pp., Woodbridge: Boydell Press).

'The House of Lords and the Fall of Walpole', ibid., 102–36.

(Ed., with David Dean), *Parliament and Locality, 1660–1939* (viii, 145 pp., Edinburgh: Edinburgh University Press; issued as vol. xvii, part 1 of *Parliamentary History*).

(Ed., with Stephen Taylor), *Tory and Whig: The Parliamentary Papers of Edward Harley, 3rd Earl of Oxford, and William Hay, M.P. for Seaford 1716–1753* (xciii, 390 pp., Parliamentary History Record Series, i, Woodbridge: Boydell Press),

'Evidence, Interpretation and Definitions in Jacobite Historiography: A Reply to Eveline Cruickshanks', *English Historical Review*, cxiii, 77–90.

1999
'Jacobites under the Beds: Bishop Francis Atterbury, the Earl of Sunderland and the West-minster School Dormitory Case of 1721', *British Library Journal*, xxv, 35–54.

'The Origin of the Leadership of the House of Lords Revisited', *Historical Research*, lxxii, 268–84.

(With David Hayton), 'Peers and Placemen: Lord Keeper Cowper's Notes on the Debate on the Place Clause in the Regency Bill, 31 January 1706', *Parliamentary History*, xviii, 65–79.

2001
'The First Printed "Directory" of British Politicians: A Note on the Residential Topography of the Peers, Bishops and MPs in London in 1729', *London Topographical Record*, xxviii, 55–78.

2002
(Ed., with Sean Kelsey), *Housing Parliament: Dublin, Edinburgh and Westminster* (ix, 206 pp., Edinburgh: Edinburgh University Press; issued as vol. xxi, part 1 of *Parliamentary History*).

2003
'The Bishops and the Extra-Parliamentary Organization of the Whig Junto in the Reign of Queen Anne', *Parliamentary History*, xxii, 183–6.

'The *Squadrone Volante* Deciphered, 1707–1714: The Correspondence of George Baillie of Jerviswood, the Duke of Montrose and the Marquess of Tweeddale, Together with the Keys to the Ciphers Used', *Scottish Archives*, ix, 57–82.

2005
(Ed., with Philip Salmon and Richard W. Davis), *Partisan Politics, Principle and Reform in Parliament and the Constituencies, 1689–1880: Essays in Memory of John A. Phillips* (xxx, 213 pp., Edinburgh: Edinburgh University Press).

(Comp.), 'Bibliography of the Publications of John A. Phillips', ibid., xiii–xvi.

'Lord Oxford's Jury: The Political and Social Context of the Creation of the Twelve Peers, 1711–12', ibid., 9–42.

'Henry Fox's Drafts of Lord Hardwicke's Speech in the Lords' Debate on the Bill on Clan-destine Marriages, 6 June 1753: A Striving for Accuracy', *Electronic British Library Journal*.

'The "Reforming" Sunderland/Stanhope Ministry and the Opening of the 1718–19 Session of Parliament in the House of Lords', *Historical Research*, lxxviii, 58–73.

'Further Evidence of the Splits in the Anti-Walpole Opposition in the House of Lords: A List for the Division of 9 April 1741 on the Subsidy for Austria', *Parliamentary History*, xxiv, 368–75.

'The Postponement of the Peerage Bill in April 1719 Revisited', *Parliamentary History*, xxiv, 226–30.

2006

'The London Topography of the Parliamentary Elite: Addresses for Peers and Bishops for 1706 and 1727–8', *London Topographical Record*, xxix, 43–64.

'The Commons' Address of Thanks in Reply to the King's Speech, 13 November 1755: Rank and Status versus Politics', *Parliamentary History*, xxv, 232–44.

'New Parliamentary Lists, 1660–1800', *Parliamentary History*, xxv, 401–9.

2007

'Robert Harley, Christmas and the House of Lords' Protest on the Attainder of Sir John Fenwick, 23 December 1696: The Mechanism of a Procedure Partly Exposed', *Electronic British Library Journal*.

'The Vote in the House of Lords on the Duke of Ormond's "Restraining Orders", 28 May 1712', *Parliamentary History*, xxvi, 160–83.

2008

'The Parliamentary Organisation of the Whig Junto in the Reign of Queen Anne: A Further Note', *Parliamentary History*, xxvii, 261–4.

'Dissent and Protest in the House of Lords, 1641–1998: An Attempt to Reconstruct the Procedures Involved in Entering a Protest into the Journals of the House of Lords', *Parliamentary History*, xxvii, 309–29.

' "This Waye of Proceeding Would Remoove the Umbrage, and Uneasynesse, of Courte, and Country Heere": The Earl of Abercorn's 1708 Scheme for Reforming the Election of the Scottish Representative Peers', *Scottish Historical Review*, lxxxvi, 27–49.

2009

(Ed.), *British Politics in the Age of Holmes* (x, 208 pp., Oxford: Wiley Blackwell; issued as vol. xxviii, part 1 of *Parliamentary History*).

'Party Affiliation in the House of Lords in 1710: A Contemporary Assessment', ibid., 179–90.

'The Debate in the House of Lords on "No Peace without Spain", 7 December 1711: A New Source', ibid., 191–9.

(Ed.), *A Short History of Parliament: England, Great Britain, the United Kingdom, Ireland and Scotland* (xiii, 386 pp., Woodbridge: Boydell Press).

(With Stephen Farrell), 'The House of Lords, 1707–1800', ibid., 147–69.

'Other Legislatures within the British Isles', ibid., 352–7.

'The Post-Devolution Legislatures', ibid., 358–62.

'Further Proxy Records for the House of Lords, 1660–1720', *Parliamentary History*, xxviii, 429–40.

' "An Affair of Such Vast Importance to the Nation": Parliament and the 1748 Buckingham Assizes Bill', *Southern History*, xxxi, 75–99.

2010

'A Scottish Whig View of the Character of Robert Harley, Earl of Oxford, in 1713', *Electronic British Library Journal*.

'Robert Harley and the Myth of the Golden Thread: Family Piety, Journalism and the History of the Assassination Attempt of 8 March 1711', *Electronic British Library Journal*.

'The Brownlow Estate Bill Select Committee in the House of Lords, 1717: A Glimpse into the Politics and the Workings of the Committee System', *Historical Research*, lxxxiii, 455–64.

'A List of the London Houses of the Nobility of England in 1680', *London Topographical Record*, xxx, 42–50.

'Of Male and Female Heirs; of English and Scottish Peerages: The Fine Tuning of the Peerage Bills of 1719', *Parliamentary History*, xxix, 308–30.

2011

' "Too Wild to Succeed": The Occasional Conformity Bills and the Attempts by the House of Lords to Outlaw the Tack in the Reign of Anne', *Parliamentary History*, xxx, 414–27.

2013

(Ed.), *Institutional Practice and Memory: Parliamentary People, Records and Histories. Essays in Honour of Sir John Sainty* (ix, 291 pp., Oxford: Wiley Blackwell; issued as vol. xxxii, part 1 of *Parliamentary History*).

'The Missing Official Proxy Records of the House of Lords for 1661–2', ibid., 237–52.

'The Duke of Newcastle's Letters on the Fall of Walpole in 1742', *Electronic British Library Journal*.

'Insight into the Work of the Clerks of the House of Lords: Some Case Studies during John Walker Senior's Occupancy of the Office of Clerk Assistant, 1670–1870', *Parliamentary History*, xxxii, 103–27.

'The Extra-Parliamentary Organisation of the Whig Junto in the Reign of William III', *Parliamentary History*, xxxii, 522–30.

2014

(Ed., with James Kelly), *Parliament, Politics and Policy in Britain and Ireland, c. 1680–1832: Essays in Honour of D.W. Hayton* (ix, 275 pp., Oxford: Wiley Blackwell; issued as vol. xxxiii, part 1 of *Parliamentary History*).

(Comp., with Richard A. Gaunt), 'Bibliography of the Published Works of D.W. Hayton', ibid., 8–18.

'The House of Lords and the Excise Crisis: The Storm and the Aftermath, 1733–5', ibid., 160–200.

'Accommodation in the Painted Chamber for Conferences between the Lords and the Commons from 1600 to 1834', *Parliamentary History*, xxxiii, 342–57.

2015

'The Opening of the Impeachment of Robert Harley, Earl of Oxford, June to September 1715: The "Memorandum" of William Wake, Bishop of Lincoln', *Electronic British Library Journal*.

'London Addresses for Eighty-Six Members of Parliament for 1735', *London Topographical Record*, xxxi, 63–78

2019

'Lord Bruce and the Marlborough Election Petition of 1735: An Aristocratic Lobbying of the House of Commons and a Blow against the Ministry of Sir Robert Walpole', *Parliamentary History*, xxxviii, 362–86.

Index

Bourke, Michael, 10th Baron Dunkellin, 107, 115, 120
Bourke, Theobald, 6th Viscount Mayo, 107, 114, 120, 123
Bowen, Huw, historian, 163, 166–7
Boyle, Charles, 4th earl of Orrery, 142
Boyle, Henry, 1st Baron Carleton, 142
Boyle, Richard, 3rd earl of Burlington, 110
Boyle, Richard, 2nd Viscount Shannon, 115, 123
Brabazon, Chambre, 5th earl of Meath, 110
Brabazon, Chaworth, 6th earl of Meath, 108–10, 115, 123
Bradford, 2nd earl of *see* Newport, Richard
Breadalbane, 1st earl of *see* Campbell, John
Brereton, Sir William, 11
Brerewood, Thomas, 98
Bridgeman, Sir Orlando, 38
Bridges, Ralph, 141
Briott, Mrs, 7
Bristol, 200, 217–18
Brodrick, Alan, 1st Baron Brodrick (1st Viscount Midleton), 104, 108–12, 114–15, 117, 123
Brodrick, Thomas, 109
Bromley, William, 136, 138, 141
Brompton Gardens, 91, 94
Brooke, John, historian, 185
Brougham, Henry, 1st Baron Brougham, 202
Broughton, 1st Baron *see* Hobhouse, Sir John Cam
Browne, Peter, bishop, 103, 121, 124
Browning, Reed, historian, 153
Bruce, Thomas, 2nd earl of Ailesbury, 28, 32, 127
Brydges, James, 8th Baron Chandos, 127
Buckden, Hunts., 129
Buckingham, duchess of *see* Villiers, Mary
Buckingham, 1st duke of *see* Sheffield, John
Buckinghamshire, 139
Buckinghamshire, 1st earl of *see* Hobart, John
Bulkeley, Lady Sophia 26
Bunny Park, Notts., 209, 213
Burdett, Sir Francis, 194, 208, 217
Burgoyne, John, 187
Burke, Edmund, 165, 175–6, 184, 189
Burlington, 3rd earl of *see* Boyle, Richard
Burnet, Gilbert, bishop, 51, 129
Bury St Edmunds, 153–4
Butler, Edmund, 6th earl of Mountgarrett, 113–14
Butler, James, 1st duke of Ormond, 19
Butler, James, 2nd duke of Ormond, 100, 102, 104, 107, 138–40
Butler, Theophilus, 1st Baron Newtownbutler, 110, 115, 124
Byng, George, 1st Viscount Torrington, 147
Byron, George Gordon, 6th Baron Byron, 205, 208

Calais, 57
Calcutta, 161
Cam Hobhouse *see* Hobhouse
Cambridge University, 141
Camelford, 1st Baron *see* Pitt, Thomas
Campbell, Archibald, 10th earl (1st duke) of Argyll, 42

Campbell, Archibald, 1st earl of Ilay (3rd duke of Argyll), 142, 144
Campbell, Hugh, 3rd earl of Loudoun, 142
Campbell, John, 2nd duke of Argyll, 77, 132, 144
Campbell, John, 1st earl of Breadalbane, 44, 49–50, 130
Campbell, John, of Cawdor, 157
Campbell, Pryse, 157
Cannon, John, historian, 167
Capel, Henry, 1st Baron Capell, 119
Capell, William, 4th earl of Essex, 151
Carisbrooke Castle, 7, 13–16, 22–3
Carleton, 1st Baron *see* Boyle, Henry
Carlisle, 36, 129
Carlisle, 3rd earl of *see* Howard, Charles
Carmarthen, 1st marquess of *see* Osborne, Thomas
Carnegie, David, 4th earl of Northesk, 130
Carnegy, James, Catholic priest, 66, 69–71, 73, 75–6, 80–2
Caroline, queen consort, 151
Carr, Charles, bishop 115, 125
Carteret, John, 2nd Baron Carteret (2nd Earl Granville), 144, 146, 157
Caryll, John, 53
Caryll, Joseph, 9
Castlecomer, 2nd Viscount *see* Wandesford, Christopher
Caulfeild, William, 2nd Viscount Charlemont, 109, 112, 114, 120, 123
Cavan, 4th earl of *see* Lambart, Richard
Cavendish, Lord John, 178–9
Cavendish, William, 1st duke of Devonshire, 28–9
Cavendish, William, 2nd duke of Devonshire, 29, 132–3, 138
Cavendish, William, 5th duke of Devonshire, 174, 178
Cavendish, William, Lord Cavendish, 4th duke of Devonshire), 149
Cavendish-Bentinck, William, 3rd duke of Portland, 174, 176–9, 181–4, 194, 197
Cecil, John, 6th earl of Exeter, 127
Chaloner, William, 15–17, 23
Chamillart, Miche, 82
Chandos, 8th Baron *see* Brydges, James
Charles I, king, 9–10, 20–2, 35–6
Charles II, king, 19, 20, 22, 24, 28, 36–7, 146, 207
Charles Louis, Elector Palatine, 18
Charles Street, Westminster, 27, 90
Charlett, Arthur, 140
Charlton, Middx., 97
Châtellerault, duchy of, 70, 130
Chatham, 1st earl of *see* Pitt, William
Cheape, Harry, 152
Cheape, James, 152
Cheesley, Sir Robert, 45
Chelsea, 27, 88, 94, 128
Chesterfield, earls of *see* Stanhope
Chetwynd, Mary (née Berkeley), 29
Chetwynd, Walter, 29
Chillingham, Northumberland, 86
Cholmondeley, George, Viscount Malpas (3rd earl of Cholmondeley), 145, 152–3, 155–6

Elcho, Lord *see* Wemyss, David
Elizabeth, princess (da. of. Charles I), 7–8, 10–15, 19–20, 22
Elliot, Sir Gilbert, 183–4
Elliott, Tom, 7
Ellis, Welbore, bishop, 116, 121, 125
Elphinstone, John, 4th Lord Balmerino, 129–30
Ely, bishopric of, 140–1
English Advice to the Freeholders of England (Francis Atterbury, 1714), 140
Erle, Thomas, 142
Erroll, 13th earl of *see* Hay, Charles
Essex, 4th earl of *see* Capell, William
Evans, George, 1st Baron Carbery, 110, 115–16, 123
Evans, John, bishop, 115, 118–19, 125, 129
Evelyn, John, 26
Exeter, 6th earl of *see* Cecil, John
Eye, Suffolk, 97

Fall, James, 43
Falmouth, countess of *see* Berkeley, Elizabeth
Fauconberg, 1st Earl *See* Belasyse, Thomas
Fauconbridge, Thomas, 16
Felton, Sir Thomas, 28, 54
Fenwick, Colonel, 36
Fenwick, Sir John, 57
Ferguson, Sir Robert Craufurd, 206–8
Ferguson, William, historian, 35, 63–4
Ferrard, 1st Baron *see* Tichborne, Henry
Ferrers, 1st Earl *see* Shirley, Robert
Finch, Daniel, 2nd earl of Nottingham, 132–3, 136, 138, 140–1
Finch, Daniel, 8th earl of Winchilsea, 143
Finch, Heneage, 5th earl of Winchilsea, 127
Finch, Henry, 140–1
Fitzgerald, Robert, 19th earl of Kildare, 112, 120, 122
Fitzgerald, William, bishop, 116, 121, 124
Fitzhardinge, 4th Viscount *see* Berkeley, John
Fitzhardinge, Viscountess *see* Berkeley, Barbara
Fitzjames, James, 1st duke of Berwick, 57
Fitzmaurice, Thomas, 21st Baron Kerry, 106, 114, 121, 124
Fitzpatrick, Richard (1748–1813), 185
Fitzpatrick, Richard, 1st Baron Gowran, 110, 116, 123–4
Fitzroy, August Henry, 3rd duke of Grafton, 169
Fitzroy, Charles, 2nd duke of Grafton, 113, 117–18
Fitzroy, Isabella, duchess of Grafton, 26, 29
Fitzwilliam, Richard, 5th Viscount Fitzwilliam, 120, 12
Fitzwilliam *see also* Wentworth-Fitzwilliam
Fitzwilliams, Mr, 16
Fleetwood, Charles, 23
Fleetwood, John, 139
Fleetwood, William, bishop, 129, 141
Fletcher, Andrew, 29
Forbes, George, 4th earl of Granard, 106–7, 109, 112, 115–16, 120, 122
Ford, Charles, 130, 134
Forster, Nicholas, bishop, 111, 115, 125

Fouls, Mr, 38
Fourbin, Claude de, 61
Fowler, Edward, bishop, 128–9
Fox, Charles James, 159–61, 173–7, 179–86, 188, 213
    see also Fox-North coalition
Fox, Henry, 1st Baron Holland, 143, 152, 154
Fox, Stephen, 1st earl of Ilchester, 154, 156–7
Fox *see also* Vassall-Fox
Fox-North coalition, 159, 173–5, 182, 184
Foxite whigs, 182
Franeker University, 52
Frederick Lewis, prince of Wales, 147–8, 151, 156
Freemasonry, 77
Frost, Walter, 16

Gally Knight *see* Knight
Galway, 1st earl of *see* Ruvigny, Henri Massue de
Garth, Sir Samuel, 87
Gastrell, Francis, bishop, 129
Gazetteer and New Daily Advertiser, 187
Geldrup, Mr, 12
General Synod of Ulster, 117
George I, king, 132, 136, 138, 141–2, 146–7
George II, king, 127, 139, 146–8, 151
George III, king, 161, 166, 177, 180, 182–9
Gerard, Philip, 7th Baron Gerard, 150
Germain, Lady Elizabeth, 32
Gill, George, 211–12
Giustinian, Giovanni, 9, 13, 18–20
Gladstone, William Ewart, 199, 202–3
Glamorgan, Treaty of (1645), 20
Glasgow, 78, 83
Glasgow University, 43
Glencoe, massacre at, 44, 49, 54
Gloucester, duke of *see* Henry, prince
Godolphin, Lady Harriet, 30
Godolphin, Mary, 27
Godolphin, Francis, Lord Rialton, 31
Godolphin, Sidney, 1st Earl Godolphin, 26, 28, 30–2, 54, 76, 102
Godwin, Timothy, bishop, 110–11, 115, 118, 125
Golby, John, historian, 193
Gordon, Alexander, 2nd duke of Gordon, 80
Gordon, John, 16th earl of Sutherland, 58–60
Gower, 1st Baron *see* Leveson Gower, John
Gowran, 1st Baron *see* Fitzpatrick, Richard
Grafton, duchess of *see* Fitzroy, Isabella
Grafton, dukes of *see* Fitzroy
Graham, James, 1st duke of Montrose, 130, 132–3, 142, 144
Granard, 4th earl of *see* Forbes, George
Grant, James, 196
Grantham, 1st earl of *see* Auverquerque, Henry de Nassau d'
Granville, 2nd Earl *see* Carteret, John
Granville, George, 1st Baron Lansdown, 95, 141
Granville, John, 1st earl of Bath, 20
Greenhill, William, 9
Greenwich, 138, 141
Gregan Craufurd *see* Craufurd